Essential quantitative methods for business, management and finance

Essential quantitative methods for business, management and finance

Second Edition

Les Oakshott

BSc (Hons), MSc, PGCE
University of the West of England, Bristol

palgrave

First edition 1998
Reprinted five times
Second edition 2001
Published by
PALGRAVE
Houndmills, Basingstoke, Hampshire RG21 6XS and
175 Fifth Avenue, New York, N.Y. 10010
Companies and representatives throughout the world

PALGRAVE is the new global academic imprint of
St. Martin's Press LLC Scholarly and Reference Division and
Palgrave Publishers Ltd (formerly Macmillan Press Ltd).

ISBN 0–333–98576–1   hardback
ISBN 0–333–96335–0   paperback

This book is printed on paper suitable for recycling and made from fully managed and sustained forest sources.

A catalogue record for this book is available from the British Library.

Library of Congress Cataloging-in-Publication Data

Oakshott, Les.
    Essential quantitative methods for business management and finance / Les Oakshott.—2nd ed.
        p. cm.
    Includes bibliographical references and index.
    ISBN 0–333–96335–0 (pbk.)
    1. Business mathematics. 2. Finance—Mathematical models.
    I. Title

HF5691 .O23 2001
650'.01'513—dc21

                                    2001036532

12   11   10   9   8   7
10   09   08   07   06   05

Printed and bound in China

Dedicated to Vicky, Andrew and Kim

Contents

Preface to the second edition

The aim of this second edition is the same as the first; that is, to provide the essential elements of quantitative aspects of business, management and finance in a concise, student-friendly format. This aim is again achieved by providing the subject matter in a clear precise manner and in providing diagrams to illustrate the more complex ideas. The popular in-text activities and end-of-chapter exercises are again included in this new edition. The in-text activities are provided to promote understanding of the principles and are set at frequent intervals throughout each chapter. The solutions to each activity are provided immediately after the activity and add to the student's knowledge, as well as providing an introduction to the next learning point. The end of chapter exercises are made up of:

- *Progress questions*, which help the student remember key points in the chapter
- *Review questions*, which are designed to allow the student to check their comprehension of the subject material
- *Multiple choice questions*, which provide the student with a means of self-assessment of the chapter contents
- *Practice questions*, which are standard problem type questions
- *Assignment*, which is an extended problem and tests a wide range of aspects of the chapter contents

Solutions to the progress questions, the multiple choice questions and some practice questions are provided at the end of the text. Following requests from lecturers, additional questions have been added to each chapter and model answers to practice questions and the assignment will be available on Palgrave's web site, exclusively to lecturers adopting this text. This web site also contains PowerPoint slides and other teaching resources.

Following a thorough review by lecturers a number of additions were suggested. The main request made by all reviewers was the inclusion of spreadsheet exercises. Spreadsheets (namely Excel) are in common use in the teaching of quantitative methods, partly because they remove many tedious calculations, and, perhaps more importantly, because they are in common use throughout the business world. Who, for instance, draws charts by hand these days? Quite detailed Excel instructions have been provided in the text so that students should be able to work on these exercises with minimal help from teaching staff. Although the ability to use a spreadsheet is a vital skill for students, it is also important for students to be able to use a scientific calculator as well. Where relevant, instructions for using a scientific calculator have been provided. Additional topics have also been included in several chapters and the chapter on probability and decision-making has been split into two. The new chapter 'Decision-making under conditions of uncertainty' reflects the increased emphasis in university teaching in this area. The previous chapter on the normal distribution has now been replaced with a chapter called 'Probability distributions'. This chapter includes the binomial and Poisson distributions as well as the normal. Additional topics have been added to the financial mathematics chapter and two-sample hypothesis tests added to the chapter on hypothesis testing. A significance test on the correlation coefficient is now included in the chapter on correlation and regression. There has also been a change in the order of chapters to ensure that the Excel exercises are met earlier on in the text.

I would like to thank the Microsoft Corporation for permission to incorporate screen shots of their Excel® spreadsheet. I would also like to thank the many colleagues at UWE who gave advice and assistance in writing this second edition. In particular, I would like to thank Carol Arnold for help in writing many of the Excel exercises.

Les Oakshott

Notes to the second edition

The Microsoft® Excel2000 spreadsheet has been used throughout this text. As far as the author is aware there is little difference between this version and Excel97, which was more widely used by universities at the time this text was written. In general most of the functions and procedures within Excel have not changed significantly from earlier versions so readers with older versions of Excel should not be at a disadvantage.

Quite detailed Excel instructions have been provided in several chapters. These chapters include: Chapter 3 (Presentation of data), Chapter 4 (Summarising data), Chapter 12 (Correlation and regression), Chapter 13 (Time series analysis), Chapter 14 (Linear programming) and Chapter 17 (Simulation). Students with little experience of Excel should start with the Excel activities in Chapters 3 and 4 before attempting the later ones as these later chapters assume some basic knowledge of Excel.

The use of Excel has also been demonstrated in Chapter 8 (Probability distributions), Chapter 9 (Decision-making under conditions of uncertainty) and Chapter 11 (Testing a hypothesis).

The calculator instructions used in this text is for the Casio fx83WA (the 85WA is an identical solar powered/battery version). The Casio calculator was chosen as it is one of the most popular calculators in use today. Students with a different make or model will need to refer to the instruction book that came with the calculator. The minimum requirement for a scientific calculator to accompany this text is the ability to calculate statistics relating to both univariate and bivariate data. Instructions for using the Casio calculator are given in Chapter 4 (Summarising data) and Chapter 12 (Correlation and regression).

1 Revision mathematics

1.1 Introduction

The aim of this chapter is to provide the basic numeracy skills that will be needed in subsequent chapters. If you have any doubts about your knowledge of particular areas you are recommended to tackle the diagnostic tests that you will find throughout this chapter. If you do not achieve 100% success in any of these tests, try to find out where you went wrong by reading through the remainder of that section. The books listed in the further reading section may also be of help to those of you who need additional practice.

1.2 Number and number operations

Activity 1.1

Write down the answers to the following questions (without a calculator).

1. $4 + (-2)$
2. $4 - (-4)$
3. $5 + (-2) - (-4)$
4. $2 \times (-3)$
5. $-15 \div (-3)$
6. $\dfrac{-10}{2}$
7. $\dfrac{5}{0}$
8. $\dfrac{0}{5}$
9. $3 \times 2 + 8 \div 4$
10. $3 \times (2 + 8) \div 4$

ANSWERS:

1. 2
2. 8
3. 7
4. −6
5. 5
6. −5
7. no solution (∞)
8. 0
9. 8
10. 7.5

Number operations often confuse people, particularly when they involve positive and negative numbers. The easy way to remember the rule is that like signs give a plus while unlike signs give a negative. This is summarised in Table 1.1.

Table 1.1   Number operations

Addition and subtraction	Multiplication	Division
$+(+) = +$	$+ \times + = +$	$+ \div + = +$
$-(-) = +$	$- \times - = +$	$- \div - = +$
$+(-) = -$	$+ \times - = -$	$+ \div - = -$
$-(+) = -$	$- \times + = -$	$- \div + = -$

Another problem is deciding the order in which to carry out a series of calculations. Questions 9 and 10 had the same numbers in the same order but in question 10 a bracket separated some of the figures. There is an order in which mathematical operations are performed. You may have come across the term '*bedmas*', which stands for 'brackets, exponent, division, multiplication, addition and subtraction'. This is not strictly correct as addition and subtraction have equal priority, as do multiplication and division. Where the operations have equal priority the order is taken from left to right. The main point to remember is that if you want a calculation to be done in a particular order you should use brackets to make the order clear. Most scientific calculators should use the bedmas system but it is worth checking with some simple calculations. These calculators will also have the bracket function to allow the order of calculation to be controlled.

1.3 Decimals, fractions and percentages

Activity 1.2

1. Convert the following decimals to fractions in their simplest form.
   (a) 0.2   (b) 0.5   (c) 0.333   (d) 0.125   (e) 0.375

2. Convert the following fractions to decimals.
   (a) $\dfrac{1}{10}$ (b) $\dfrac{1}{5}$ (c) $\dfrac{11}{3}$ (d) $\dfrac{2}{7}$ (e) $\dfrac{3}{8}$

   (f) $\dfrac{7}{3}$ (g) $\dfrac{1}{100}$ (h) $1\frac{3}{4}$

3. Convert the following fractions to percentages.
   (a) $\dfrac{1}{4}$ (b) $\dfrac{1}{2}$ (c) $\dfrac{1}{5}$ (d) $\dfrac{2}{3}$ (e) $\dfrac{3}{4}$

4. Convert the following percentages into fractions in their simplest form.
   (a) 40%   (b) 45%   (c) 60%   (d) 12%   (e) 19%

5. Carry out the following calculations.
   (a) $0.25 + 0.37$ (b) $\dfrac{1}{2} \times 3$ (c) $\dfrac{1}{2}$ of 46%   (d) $\dfrac{4}{5} + \dfrac{2}{3}$ (e) $\dfrac{3}{4} \times \dfrac{3}{2}$

   (f) $\dfrac{3}{4} \div \dfrac{3}{2}$ (g) $0.25 \times \dfrac{1}{5}$ (h) 0.00025×3000

6. Round the following decimals to 3 decimal places.
    (a) 1.5432   (b) 1.5438   (c) 1.5435   (d) 0.000843   (e) 100.2003

7. Write the following numbers to 3 significant figures.
    (a) 1.5432   (b) 1.5438   (c) 1.5435   (d) 0.000843   (e) 100.2003
    (f) 13 256   (g) 1.000561

8. Write down the following numbers in scientific notation.
    (a) 25 438 176 (b) 1 600 000   (c) 0.00001776

ANSWERS:

1. (a) $\frac{1}{5}$ (b) $\frac{1}{2}$ (c) $\frac{1}{3}$ (d) $\frac{1}{8}$ (e) $\frac{3}{8}$

2. (a) 0.1   (b) 0.2   (c) 3.66$\dot{6}$ (d) 0.2857   (e) 0.375
   (f) 2.33$\dot{3}$ (g) 0.01   (h) 1.75

3. (a) 25%   (b) 50%   (c) 20%   (d) 66.66$\dot{6}$% (e) 75%

4. (a) $\frac{2}{5}$ (b) $\frac{9}{20}$ (c) $\frac{3}{5}$ (d) $\frac{3}{25}$ (e) $\frac{19}{100}$

5. (a) 0.62   (b) 1.5   (c) 23%   (d) $1\frac{7}{15}$ (e) $1\frac{1}{8}$
   (f) $\frac{1}{2}$ (g) $\frac{1}{20}$ or 0.05 (h) 0.75

6. (a) 1.543   (b) 1.544   (c) 1.544   (d) 0.001   (e) 100.20

7. (a) 1.543   (b) 1.544   (c) 1.544   (d) 0.000843 (e) 100
   (f) 13 300   (g) 1.00

8. (a) 2.5438176×10^{7} (b) 1.6×10^{6} (c) 1.776×10^{-5}

Fractions, decimals and percentages are used throughout this book and you need to be able to convert a number from one form to another. To convert from a fraction to either a decimal or a percentage all you need to do is to divide the numerator (the number above the line) by the denominator (the number below the line). For a percentage you also need to multiply by 100. To convert a decimal to a fraction you simply have to remember that the first digit after the decimal point is a tenth and the second digit is a hundredth and so on. For example, 0.2 is $\frac{2}{10}$ and this can be simplified by dividing the top and bottom by 2 to give $\frac{1}{5}$. The conversion of a percentage to a fraction is easier as the denominator of the fraction is always 100. So 40% is $\frac{40}{100}$ and this simplifies to $\frac{2}{5}$.

A frequent question asked by students is, how many decimal places should an answer be given to? There is no easy answer to this, although a good rule of thumb to use when analysing data is to give one more place than in the original data. So if your data had one decimal place you should give your answer to two decimal places. Giving more decimal places infers that your answer is accurate to this number of decimals, which is misleading.

However, numbers should only be rounded at the end of a calculation. If you round intermediate values you will introduce rounding errors into your calculations, which can cause major errors in your final figure.

When rounding, remember the rule that numbers below 5 are rounded *down* and numbers of 5 and above are rounded *up*. So 1.5432 is 1.543 to 3 decimal places but 1.5435 is 1.544 to 3 decimal places.

Another form of cutting down the number of digits in an answer is to give a stated number of *significant* figures. In many cases the two systems will give identical results, but the real difference with using significant figures is that zeros are only included when they are significant. Thus 0.01654 becomes 0.017 to three significant figures while 1.01654 would become 1.02. Significant figures can also be used when handling large numbers. For example, 13 256 is 13 000 to 2 significant figures. The zeros have to be added to maintain the place value of the remaining numbers.

If very large or very small numbers are involved it is all too easy to make a mistake and accidentally lose a digit. To avoid this you can use *scientific* notation. Scientific notation is in the form of $a \times 10^b$ where a is a decimal number below 10 and b is the number of places the decimal point needs to be moved to arrive back at the original number. For example, 25 438 176 can be changed to 2.5438176×10^7 as the decimal place has been moved 7 places to the left. Scientific calculators use this method when the number exceeds a set number of digits, except that the base 10 is not displayed – a source of confusion among students!

1.4 Powers and roots

Activity 1.3

Write down the value of the following.

1. 2^3 2. 3^4 3. $\left(\frac{1}{2}\right)^3$ 4. 2^{-3} 5. $\sqrt{81}$ 6. $\sqrt[3]{27}$

ANSWERS:

1. 8   2. 81   3. $\frac{1}{8}$ 4. $\frac{1}{8}$ 5. 9   6. 3

When a number is raised to a power (or exponent) the number is multiplied by itself that number of times. So 2^3 means $2 \times 2 \times 2 = 8$. Powers take precedence in an expression after any brackets. In the calculation of $2 + 6 \times 3^2 - 4$, the order of calculation is as follows.

$$3^2 = 9, \quad 9 \times 6 = 54, \quad 54 + 2 - 4 = 52$$

1.5 Elementary algebra

Activity 1.4

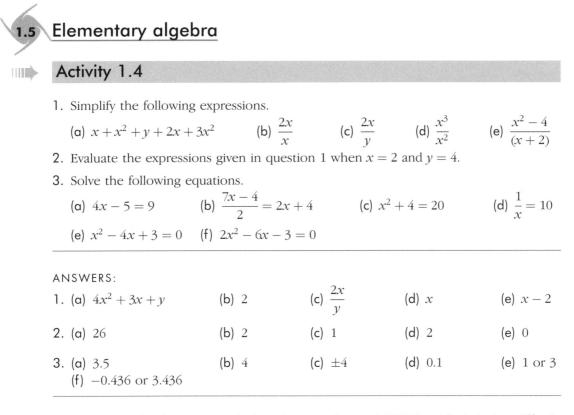

1. Simplify the following expressions.

(a) $x + x^2 + y + 2x + 3x^2$ (b) $\dfrac{2x}{x}$ (c) $\dfrac{2x}{y}$ (d) $\dfrac{x^3}{x^2}$ (e) $\dfrac{x^2 - 4}{(x + 2)}$

2. Evaluate the expressions given in question 1 when $x = 2$ and $y = 4$.

3. Solve the following equations.

(a) $4x - 5 = 9$ (b) $\dfrac{7x - 4}{2} = 2x + 4$ (c) $x^2 + 4 = 20$ (d) $\dfrac{1}{x} = 10$

(e) $x^2 - 4x + 3 = 0$ (f) $2x^2 - 6x - 3 = 0$

ANSWERS:

1. (a) $4x^2 + 3x + y$ (b) 2   (c) $\dfrac{2x}{y}$ (d) x (e) $x - 2$

2. (a) 26   (b) 2   (c) 1   (d) 2   (e) 0

3. (a) 3.5   (b) 4   (c) ± 4 (d) 0.1   (e) 1 or 3
   (f) -0.436 or 3.436

Most students that have not studied mathematics beyond GCSE level find algebra difficult. The idea of replacing numbers by letters is quite abstract and many students do not understand the need for it. Unfortunately some understanding of algebra is essential if you are to successfully complete a quantitative methods course and many chapters in this book assume this understanding.

There are many algebraic techniques but the most important as far as this book is concerned is to be able to solve equations. To achieve this it is necessary to remember that whatever you do to one side of the equation you must do to the other. In solving

$$\frac{7x - 4}{2} = 2x + 4$$

the following steps are carried out:

1. Multiply both sides by 2. The equation then becomes $7x - 4 = 4x + 8$.

2. Subtract $4x$ from both sides to give $3x - 4 = 8$

3. Add 4 to both sides to give $3x = 12$

4. Divide both sides by 3

Giving the answer of $x = 4$.

When the unknown variable is raised to a power the method of solving the equation becomes more complicated and in some cases it is necessary to resort to numerical methods. Quadratic equations are those involving x^2 and the method of solution depends on the equation. For $x^2 + 4 = 20$ the solution follows the method already described. That is, subtract 4 from both sides

$$x^2 = 16$$

and then take the square root of both sides

$$x = \sqrt{16}$$
$$= \pm 4$$

Notice that both $+4$ and -4 are solutions since $(-4)^2 = 16$.

Some quadratic equations can be *factorised*. To factorise an expression we need to find two factors that when multiplied together give the original expression. $x^2 + 2x = 0$ can be factorised by noting that x is a common factor to both terms. If we take out the x we get $x(x + 2) = 0$ and both x and $(x + 2)$ are factors of the original expression. The modified equation is easier to solve than the original as we can see that the equation is true when either $x = 0$ or $(x + 2) = 0$.

That is, $x = 0$ or $x = -2$.

For $x^2 - 4x + 3 = 0$ we need to find two brackets that when multiplied together give these terms. Factorising this type of expression can involve some trial and error but in this case it is fairly easy and will be

$$(x - 3)(x - 1) = 0$$

If you multiply the two brackets you get

$$x^2 - 3x - x + 3 = 0$$

which is the same as the original since $-3x - x = -4x$
The solution to this equation is either

$$x - 3 = 0 \quad \text{or} \quad x - 1 = 0$$

So x is either 1 or 3.

Factorising only works easily for a small number of quadratic expressions, and a more general method is to use a formula. If the expression is in the form $ax^2 + bx + c = 0$, the formula is:

$$x = \frac{-b \pm \sqrt{b^2 - 4ac}}{2a}$$

For example, to solve $2x^2 - 6x - 3 = 0$, we first note that $a = 2$, $b = -6$ and $c = -3$

$$\text{so} \quad x = \frac{-(-6) \pm \sqrt{6^2 - 4 \times 2 \times (-3)}}{2 \times 2}$$

$$= \frac{6 \pm \sqrt{36 + 24}}{4}$$

$$= \frac{6 \pm 7.7460}{4}$$

$$= -0.436 \quad \text{or} \quad 3.436$$

1.6 Indices and logs

Activity 1.5

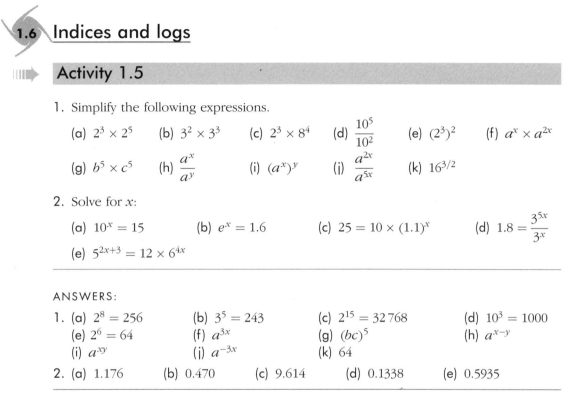

1. Simplify the following expressions.

    (a) $2^3 \times 2^5$ (b) $3^2 \times 3^3$ (c) $2^3 \times 8^4$ (d) $\dfrac{10^5}{10^2}$ (e) $(2^3)^2$ (f) $a^x \times a^{2x}$

    (g) $b^5 \times c^5$ (h) $\dfrac{a^x}{a^y}$ (i) $(a^x)^y$ (j) $\dfrac{a^{2x}}{a^{5x}}$ (k) $16^{3/2}$

2. Solve for x:

    (a) $10^x = 15$ (b) $e^x = 1.6$ (c) $25 = 10 \times (1.1)^x$ (d) $1.8 = \dfrac{3^{5x}}{3^x}$

    (e) $5^{2x+3} = 12 \times 6^{4x}$

ANSWERS:

1. (a) $2^8 = 256$ (b) $3^5 = 243$ (c) $2^{15} = 32\,768$ (d) $10^3 = 1000$
   (e) $2^6 = 64$ (f) a^{3x} (g) $(bc)^5$ (h) a^{x-y}
   (i) a^{xy} (j) a^{-3x} (k) 64

2. (a) 1.176 (b) 0.470 (c) 9.614 (d) 0.1338 (e) 0.5935

In Section 1.4 we saw that if a number is multiplied by itself a number of times then we can simplify the expression by the use of indices – so that $2 \times 2 \times 2 = 2^3$. In general the product of n a's is written as a^n. We say that the *base* (a) is raised to the power of n.

There are 3 important formulae for indices; these are:

$$a^m \times a^n = a^{m+n}$$

$$a^m \div a^n = a^{m-n}$$

$$(a^m)^n = a^{mn}$$

So providing the bases are the same, you can add or subtract the powers.

For example
$$2^3 \times 2^5 = 2^{3+5}$$
$$= 2^8 \cdot$$
$$= 256$$

And
$$\frac{10^5}{10^2} = 10^{5-2}$$
$$= 10^3$$
$$= 1000$$

If m and n have the same value (say x) then $a^x \div a^x = a^0$.

As this expression must also equal 1 then it follows that $a^0 = 1$.

Also $a^1 = a$.

The power can be negative or fractional and $1/a^n$ can also be written as a^{-n} and $a^{1/2}$ is the same as $\sqrt{a}$.

For $16^{3/2}$ we could simplify it as $((16)^{1/2})^3$. Since the square root of 16 is 4, then $4^3 = 64$.

When $Y = a^x$ we can rewrite this as $x = log_a Y$.

The word *log* is short for *logarithm* and this expression is read as x equals log of Y to the base a. There are only two bases you need worry about; these are base 10 and base e. These bases can be found on all scientific calculators; log to base 10 is usually written as *log*, and for base e it is written as *ln*.

There are three important formulae for logs that apply to all bases and these are:

$$\log(uv) = \log u + \log v$$

$$\log(u/v) = \log u - \log v$$

$$\log x^n = n \log x$$

The importance of logs as far as this book is concerned is the ability to use the laws of logs to solve certain types of equations. For example, to solve $5^{2x+3} = 12 \times 6^{4x}$ you would carry out the following steps.

$$\log(5^{2x+3}) = \log(12 \times 6^{4x})$$

$$(2x + 3) \log 5 = \log 12 + \log 6^{4x}$$

$$2x \log 5 + 3 \log 5 = \log 12 + 4x \log 6$$

$$2x \log 5 - 4x \log 6 = \log 12 - 3 \log 5$$

$$2x(\log 5 - 2 \log 6) = \log 12 - 3 \log 5$$

$$2x = \frac{\log 12 - 3 \log 5}{\log 5 - 2 \log 6}$$

$$2x = \frac{1.0792 - 3 \times 0.6990}{0.6990 - 2 \times 0.7782}$$

$$2x = \frac{-1.0178}{-0.8574}$$

$$2x = 1.1871$$

$$x = 0.5935$$

1.7 Mathematical symbols

Activity 1.6

What do the following symbols stand for?

1. $<$ 2. $\leq$ 3. $>$ 4. $\geq$ 5. $\neq$ 6. $\cong$ 7. $\sum$

ANSWERS:

1. less than

2. less than or equal to

3. greater than

4. greater than or equal to

5. not equal to

6. approximately equal to

7. the sum of

We will be using all these symbols in later chapters of the book, particularly the summation sign. If you see the expression $\sum x$ it means add up all the values of x, while $\sum xy$ means multiply the pairs of x and y before summing them. For example, in Table 1.2 there are two columns of numbers which I have called x and y.

Table 1.2 Use of the summation sign

x	y	xy
2	7	14
1	5	5
4	2	8
6	3	18
4	4	16

From this table
$$\sum x = 2 + 1 + 4 + 6 + 4 \quad = 17$$
$$\sum xy = 14 + 5 + 8 + 18 + 16 = 61$$
$$\sum x^2 = 4 + 1 + 16 + 36 + 16 = 73$$

If your calculator has the SD or Statistical Data function many of these calculations can be done automatically for you.

1.8 Graphs and straight lines

Activity 1.7

Which of the following equations represent straight lines?

1. $y = 2x + 5$ 2. $y + 4x = 20$ 3. $y = 8$ 4. $y = x$ 5. $y = x^2$

ANSWER:

All except equation 5.

The equation of a straight line is $y = mx + c$, where m is the gradient and c is the value of y when $x = 0$ (often referred to as the *intercept* on the y-axis). Equation 1 is obviously a straight line with $m = 2$ and $c = 5$. Equation 2 is also a straight line and this may be easier to see if you subtract $4x$ from both sides of the equation.

That is: $y = 20 - 4x$ or $y = -4x + 20$

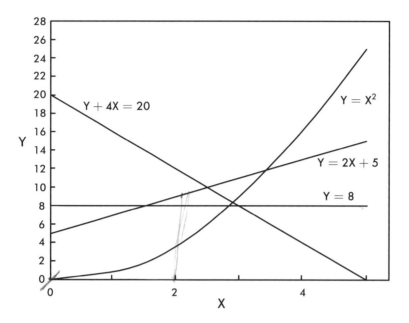

Figure 1.1 Graph for Activity 1.7

This equation is now in the standard form and you should see that $m = -4$ and $c = 20$. Equation 3 is another straight line but this is a special one. This could be written as $y = 0x + 8$ and you will see that $m = 0$; that is, the gradient is zero. This can be therefore be represented as a *horizontal* line. Equation 4 can be written as $y = x + 0$, so this represents a straight line with a gradient of 1 and c of 0. This line passes through the origin of the graph (that is, $x = 0, y = 0$). Equation 5 is *not* a straight line since y increases as the *square* of x. The graphs of these equations are shown in Figure 1.1.

1.9 Solving linear equations graphically

Activity 1.8

Plot the equations $2y + x = 8$ and $y + 2x = 7$ on the same graph and write down the coordinates of the point of intersection.

You should have obtained the graph shown in Figure 1.2. The point of intersection of the two lines is at the point $x = 2, y = 3$. This can be written as (2,3). In this example the coordinates of the point of intersection were both whole numbers, which made it easy to read from your graph. Unfortunately this is not always the case and accurately reading fractional values from a graph is difficult. A better method is the algebraic method of *simultaneous equations*.

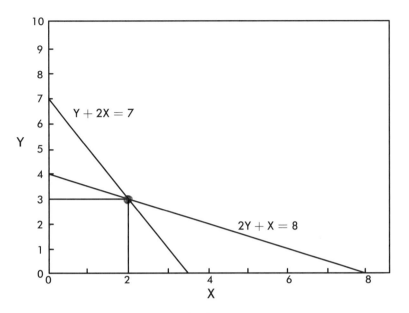

Figure 1.2 Solving equations graphically

1.10 Solving linear equations simultaneously

Activity 1.9

Solve the equations given in Activity 1.8 simultaneously.

Hopefully your answer agreed with the graphical method. The method I prefer is the method of *elimination*. To use this method the two equations are written down as follows:

$$y + 2x = 7 \tag{1}$$

$$2y + x = 8 \tag{2}$$

The coefficients of either x or y must be equal in the two equations and this is achieved by multiplying *both* sides of equation (1) by 2. The equations can now be *subtracted*:

$$2y + 4x = 14$$

$$\underline{2y + x = 8}$$

$$3x = 6 \quad (y \text{ has now been 'eliminated'})$$

That is: $\qquad x = 2$

This value of x can now be substituted back into either equation (1) or (2) to give the value of y. Using equation (2):

$$2y + 2 = 8$$
$$2y = 6$$

Therefore $y = 3$

1.11 Inequations

Activity 1.10

1. What do the following inequations mean?
   (a) $y + 2x \leq 7$ (b) $2y + x \geq 8$

2. How would you represent these two inequations graphically? And what does the term 'intersection' mean in this case?

ANSWERS:

In equation (a) means the sum of the left hand side of the equation must be less than or equal to 7; that is, the sum cannot be greater than 7. Inequation (b) means that the sum of the left hand side of the equation must be at least 8; it cannot be less.

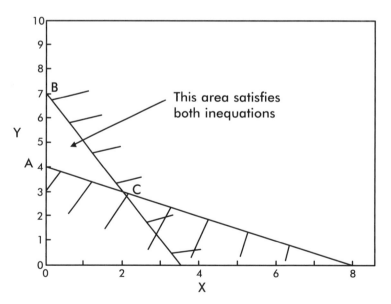

Figure 1.3 Graph for Activity 1.10

Whereas an equation can be represented by a straight line, an inequation is represented by a *region*. The equation $y + 2x = 7$ forms the *boundary* of the region represented by the inequation $y + 2x \leq 7$. Similarly the equation $2y + x = 8$ forms the boundary of the region $2y + x \geq 8$. The region can only be on one side of the boundary and this can be found by inspection; that is, a point is investigated to see if it satisfies the inequation. The easiest point to try is the origin ($x = 0$, $y = 0$), except when the boundary passes through this point. When the region has been found it needs to be identified. This can be done by shading. The normal convention is to shade the *unwanted* region and this is the convention adopted in this book. You can see this in Figure 1.3 opposite.

The intersection of regions is the area on the graph that satisfies *all* inequations. In this example, the area is represented by ABC. Any point within this area (including the boundaries) satisfies both inequations.

1.12 Further reading

Rowe, N. (2000) *Refresher in Basic Maths*, second edition, Continuum International Publication Group, London.

2 Sampling methods

2.1 Introduction

Many decisions made by business and the government are the result of information obtained from sample data, as it is often too costly or impractical to collect data on the whole population. Data may already exist or it may need to be collected. When we have to collect our own data we call it *primary* data, but when it already exists, as in government statistics, we call it *secondary* data. The collection of data can take many forms, but in this chapter we will concentrate on data that is collected from carrying out surveys. Not only do surveys need to be well planned but the recording of the survey information using *questionnaires* also needs careful consideration.

At the end of this chapter you should be able to:

- Understand the difference between a population and a sample
- Understand the difference between probabilistic and non-probabilistic sampling methods
- Choose the correct sampling method for different situations
- Appreciate what constitutes good questionnaire design.

2.2 The basics of sampling

I am sure that you have been a *respondent* in a survey at least once in your life. Have you filled in a *questionnaire* or been stopped in the street and asked some questions? You no doubt know that the purpose of a survey is for some organisation or person to obtain *information* about some issue or product. This information could range from what television programme you watched last night to your views on the government of the day. A survey only collects information about a small subset of the *population*. The population can and often does refer to all the people in Britain or a town, but for statisticians it is also a very general term to refer to all groups or items being surveyed. For instance, it could refer to the viewing habits of all children in a town or, as you will see in a later chapter, it could refer to the weights of jars of coffee produced by a company during a week. The alternative to a survey is to question every member of the population, and when this done it is called a *census*. Unfortunately it is expensive and very difficult to carry out a census, and also unnecessary. A survey of a small subset of the population, called a *sample*, can give surprisingly accurate results if carried out properly. Unfortunately, if not carried out correctly, the results can at best be unreliable and at the worst misleading. Before you carry out a survey you need answers to several questions, such as:

- What is the purpose of this survey?
- What is my *target* population?
- Do I have a list of the population?
- How can I avoid bias in my sample?
- How accurate do I want my survey to be?
- What resources do I have at my disposal?
- How am I going to collect the required data?

It is crucial to be clear about the purpose of the survey. Not only will this dictate your target population but it will also allow you to formulate your questionnaire correctly. For example, if you are interested in consumers' opinion of a new alcoholic drink it would be pointless targeting people under 18 (and unethical). The target population should contain every person that is likely to buy your product or whose views you are particularly interested in.

Once you have selected your target population you need to determine whether there is any list that would allow you to identify every member of the population. This list is called a *sampling frame*, and without this the accuracy of your results can be seriously flawed. However, sometimes a sampling frame is simply not available or difficult to obtain, in which case achieving a *representative* sample will be more difficult, but not necessarily impossible.

Activity 2.1

What would be your target population for a survey on motorway tariffs and would there be a sampling frame available?

If you were only interested in the views of British car drivers then anyone holding a UK driving licence would form your target population. A suitable sampling frame would be records held by the DVLC at Swansea. It will not be 100% accurate as drivers may have changed address and not informed the DVLC, or they may have died.

Once your target population has been chosen and an appropriate sampling frame identified, it is necessary to choose your sample. If the sample is chosen badly your results will be inaccurate due to *bias* in your sample. Bias is caused by choosing a sample that is unrepresentative of the target population. For example, perhaps you wanted to discover people's views on whether a sports field should be sold to a property developer. If your sample contained a large number of people from the local football club then the sample is likely to be biased in favour of one particular group! To avoid bias you need to ensure that your sample is *representative* of the target population. You will see how this can be achieved later.

The purpose of a survey is to obtain information about a population. All other things being equal, the accuracy of the sample results will depend on the sample size; the larger the sample, the more accurate the results. A large sample will clearly cost more than a small one, although the method that is employed to collect the data will also determine the accuracy and cost of the survey. Methods of data collection range from the use of postal questionnaires to 'face-to-face' interviews. Some methods of data collection are expensive but guarantee a good response rate, while others are cheap to administer but are likely to produce quite a poor response. Table 2.1 compares the main methods of collecting data.

Table 2.1   Methods of data collection

	Postal questionnaire	Telephone interviewing	Face-to-face interviewing
Cost	Low	Moderate	High
Response rate	Low	Moderate	High
Speed	Slow	Fast	Fast*
Quantity of information collected	Limited	Moderate	High
Quality of information collected	Depends on how well the questionnaire has been designed	Good	High

*The speed of collecting the data will be high but travelling time by the interviewers may need to be considered.

Activity 2.2

You have been asked to obtain views of the student population at your institution regarding car parking facilities within the campus. What method of data collection would you use?

The best method would probably be face-to-face interviews, but it is unlikely that you would have the resources for this approach. Telephone interviewing is probably not realistic because of the cost and the fact that students' telephone numbers might be difficult to obtain. This leaves you with a postal questionnaire, which should be quite reasonable for this relatively simple type of survey.

There are two types of sampling procedures for obtaining your sample. The first is *probabilistic* sampling, which requires the existence of a sampling frame. The second method is *non-probabilistic* sampling, which does not rely on a sampling frame.

Probabilistic sampling is the most important form of sampling as it allows you to use probability theory to calculate the probability that a particular sample could have occurred by chance.

2.3 Questionnaire design

Questionnaire design is a more of an art than a science and there is no universal design that would be suitable for all situations. The actual design will depend on factors such as:

- The type of respondent (for example, business, consumers, children)
- The method of data collection (postal, telephone or face-to-face)
- The resources available

However, even though no two questionnaires will be identical, it is possible to make a list of some 'dos and don'ts' that should apply to most questionnaires. The most important ones are:

- Do make each question brief and the wording clear and concise with minimal use of jargon. It shouldn't be necessary to explain to the respondent the meaning of a particular question.
- Do keep the length of the questionnaire to a minimum. A maximum of around 20 questions is probably a good guide for most surveys.
- Do make the questions simple to answer.
- Do make the questions specific as possible. A question such as '*Are you a heavy smoker?*' could be interpreted differently by different respondents. It would be much better to give ranges such as '*Do you smoke less than 10 cigarettes a day?*': '*Between 10 and 20?*' and '*Over 20?*'
- Do have a logical sequence to the questions.
- Do start with simple questions such as gender, leaving more complicated questions for later in the questionnaire.
- Don't leave the most important question to last. There is a risk that if a respondent becomes bored with answering a questionnaire he or she may not complete the final section.
- Don't use leading questions. For example, '*What are your views on the level of indirect taxation in the UK?*' is better than '*Do you agree that indirect taxation in the UK is too high?*'
- Do try and avoid asking personal questions. Even information on salary is considered by many people to be personal and most respondents prefer to have salary ranges to select. It is often better to ask this type of question later in the questionnaire. If it is necessary to collect really personal information, a face-to-face interview is essential using experienced interviewers.
- Do use a filtering method if not all questions are applicable to all respondents. For example, '*Did you watch The Bill last night?*' may then be followed by questions relating

to this episode. To avoid asking non-viewers these questions you will need to have an instruction that allows these non-viewers to jump to the next appropriate question.

- Don't ask two questions in one. A question such as *'Is your job interesting and well paid?'* is unlikely to be answered with a simple yes or no.

- Don't ask questions that rely on memory. Asking respondents if they watched *The Bill* last night is acceptable but asking if they watched it last week or last month will not necessarily produce very reliable results.

- Don't ask hypothetical questions. Asking someone what he or she would do under a hypothetical situation (such as winning the National Lottery) is unlikely to lead to reliable results. In some surveys this type of question cannot be avoided, but extra care should be taken in its wording.

- It is generally better to use close-ended questions (see later) rather than allow open answers. However, do allow for the fact that your selection of responses might not be complete by having an 'other' category.

  For example, *'What type of property do you live in?'*
  Terraced house   Semi-detached   Detached   Flat
  This question needs an *'Other'* category since you might find someone who lives on a boat or in a windmill!

- Make the questionnaire attractive and easy to complete. Microsoft Word allows you to create forms for use as questionnaires and you can then distribute these forms as an email attachment if this is appropriate for your sample.

- Do conduct a pilot survey on a small but *representative* sample of the target population. This will test out your design and allow you to fine tune it.

Having looked at some of the more important dos and don'ts of questionnaire design we now need to consider the format of the questions and the most effective method of obtaining reliable responses. Questions are of two forms; *close-ended* questions and *open-ended* questions. Close-ended questions give the respondents a choice of answers and are generally considered much easier to answer and to analyse. However, the limited response range can give misleading results. Open-ended questions, such as *'Why did you buy this product?'*, allow respondents more flexibility in the type of response (you may get answers that you hadn't thought of), but of course this type of question is difficult to analyse. Close-ended questions are the most commonly used type and can take many forms, such as:

- Dichotomous questions. These are questions that have only two answers, such as yes or no.

- Numeric. Some questions ask for a single number, such as the distance travelled to work each day. Where the question is personal (for example, earnings or age) it is best to give a range, such as:
  Less than £10 000   £10 000 to £20 000   Over £20 000

- Multiple choice. Respondents select from three or more choices (the question on salary above is an example of a multiple choice question).

- Likert scale. The question is a statement, such as '*Taxes should be increased to pay for a better health service*', and respondents indicate their amount of agreement using a scale similar to the one below.

Neither agree

Strongly agree   Agree   nor disagree   Disagree   Strongly disagree

- Semantic differential. With this type of question only two ends of the scale are provided and the respondent selects the point between the two ends that represents his views. For example, '*The leisure facilities in my town are*':

Excellent _____ *Poor*

- Rank order. Respondents are asked to rank each option. This type of question is useful if you want to obtain information on relative preferences, but is more difficult to analyse. The number of choices should be kept to a minimum.

2.4 Simple random sampling

With this method every member of the target population has an *equal* chance of being selected. This implies that a sampling frame is required and a method of *randomly* selecting the required sample from this list. The simplest example of this technique is a raffle where the winning ticket is drawn from the 'hat'. For a more formal application a stream of *random numbers* would be used. Random numbers are numbers that show no pattern and each digit is equally likely. A table of random numbers is given in Appendix 2. The method of simple random sampling using random numbers is quite easy to apply, although tedious, as you will see from the following example.

Example 2.1

Table 2.2 is a part of a list of students enrolled on a business studies course at a university.

Say from this 'population' of 25 students you wanted to randomly select a sample of 5 students. How would you do it? You could use the student number (in this case conveniently numbered from 1 to 25) and then try and obtain a match using a stream of two-digit random numbers. For example, suppose you had the following random numbers: 78, 41, 11, 62, 72, 18, 66, 69, 58, 71, 31, 90, 51, 36, 78, 09, 41, 00, 70, 50, 58, 19, 68, 26, 75, 69, and 04. The first two numbers don't exist in our population but 11 does – it is student D. Jeffrey. The next two numbers do not exist but 18 does, and so on. The final sample is numbers 11, 18, 09, 19 and 04, which are students D. Jeffrey, S. Moore, G. Godfrey, F. Muper, and C. Best.

The majority of random numbers were redundant in this case because the population was so small. However, in practice the population would be much larger, but the method remains essentially the same. Most sampling frames are held on computer these days so it is much easier to use the computer to select the sample.

Table 2.2   List of students enrolled on a business studies course

Number	Name	Sex
1	N. Adams	Male
2	C. Atley	Male
3	B. Booth	Female
4	C. Best	Male
5	A. Bently	Male
6	D. Drew	Male
7	K. Fisher	Female
8	P. Frome	Male
9	G. Godfrey	Male
10	J. Holmes	Male
11	D. Jeffrey	Female
12	H. Jones	Male
13	M. Jones	Male
14	N. King	Female
15	K. Lenow	Male
16	A. Loft	Female
17	T. Mate	Female
18	S. Moore	Female
19	F. Muper	Female
20	R. Muster	Female
21	A. Night	Male
22	J. Nott	Male
23	L. Nupper	Male
24	K. Oates	Male
25	O. Patter	Female

Activity 2.3

Randomly select another sample of 5 students from the above list using the random numbers: 09, 55, 42, 30, 27, 05, 24, 93, 78, 10, 69, 09, and 11.

You should have noticed that number 09 occurs twice. What did you do in this case? For practical reasons you should have ignored the second 09 and chosen the next number, 11, instead. Your final sample should have been: G. Godfrey, A. Bently, K. Oates, J. Holmes and D. Jeffrey.

How representative of the target population are these samples? Since the population is so small it is a simple matter to compare each sample with the population. For instance, there are 15 male and 10 female students, which is a proportion of 60% males to 40% females. In the first sample there were 2 males out of 5, a proportion of 40%, and in the second there were 4 males, a proportion of 80%. From this you can see that the first sample was an underestimate of the true number of males, while the second was an overestimate. Another sample could be different again, and you may even get a sample of all the same sex. This variation is called *sampling error* and occurs in all sampling procedures. In Chapter 10 you will be shown how to quantify this error.

It is possible to reduce the sampling error by a slight modification to the simple random sample method. This is applicable when the target population can be categorised into groups or *strata*.

2.5 Stratified sampling

Many populations can be divided into different categories. For example, a population of adults consists of the two sexes; the employed and unemployed, and many other categories. If you think that the responses you will get from your survey are likely to be determined partly by each category, then clearly you want your sample to contain each category in the correct proportions.

Activity 2.4

Using the random numbers 09, 55, 42, 30, 27, 05, 25, 93, 78, 10, 69, 09, 11, 99, 21 and 01, obtain a sample of size 5 that contains the correct proportion of each sex.

Table 2.3   Table ordered by sex

Number	Name	Sex
1	N. Adams	Male
2	C. Atley	Male
3	C. Best	Male
4	A. Bently	Male
5	D. Drew	Male
6	P. Frome	Male
7	G. Godfrey	Male
8	J. Holmes	Male
9	H. Jones	Male
10	M. Jones	Male
11	K. Lenow	Male
12	A. Night	Male
13	J. Nott	Male
14	L. Nupper	Male
15	K. Oates	Male
1	O. Patter	Female
2	B. Booth	Female
3	K. Fisher	Female
4	D. Jeffrey	Female
5	N. King	Female
6	A. Loft	Female
7	T. Mate	Female
8	S. Moore	Female
9	F. Muper	Female
10	R. Muster	Female

You probably realised that your sample should contain 3 males (60% of 5). In order to ensure that you will get exactly 3 males, you should first of all have separated out the two sexes and then obtained two simple random samples, one of size 3 and one of size 2, as shown in Table 2.3.

The two populations have been re-numbered, although this is not essential. The first sample consists of students 9, 5 and 10, that is H. Jones, D. Drew and M. Jones, while the second sample consists of 9 and 1, that is F. Muper and O. Patter.

Stratified sampling is a very reliable method but it does assume that you have a knowledge of the categories of the population. Stratified sampling is often used in conjunction with the next method.

2.6 Multi-stage sampling

If the target population covers a wide geographical area then a simple random sample may have selected respondents in quite different parts of the country. If the method employed to collect the data is of the face-to-face interview type, then clearly a great deal of travelling could be involved. To overcome this problem the area to be surveyed is divided into smaller areas and a number of these smaller areas randomly selected. If desired, the smaller areas chosen could themselves be divided into smaller districts and a random number of these selected. This procedure is continued until the area is small enough for a simple random sample (or a stratified sample) to be selected. The final sample should consist of respondents concentrated into a small number of areas. It is important that the random sample chosen from each area is the same proportion of the population or bias towards certain areas could result. As it is, bias is likely to occur as a result of similarity of responses from people within the same area, but this is the price you pay for reduced travelling time.

Activity 2.5

You have been asked to obtain a sample of television viewers from across Britain using the multi-stage sampling method. How would you select the sample?

The country could be split into counties, or perhaps television regions may be more appropriate in this case. A number of these are chosen at random and these areas divided into district councils. A random sample of districts within each chosen region could now be selected and the selected districts divided into postal areas. Figure 2.1 illustrates the case where HTV West is one of the chosen regions. Within this region, South Gloucestershire and Bristol have been randomly selected, and within South Gloucestershire the postal district of BS12 is one of the selected areas. A simple random sample of all households within BS12 could now be chosen and combined with all the other households chosen in other areas.

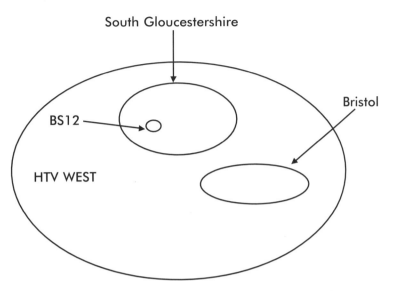

Figure 2.1 Multi-stage sampling

2.7 Cluster sampling

Cluster sampling is similar to multi-stage sampling and is used when a sampling frame is not available. Again a large geographical area is divided into a number of small areas called *clusters*. If necessary these clusters can be further subdivided to obtain clusters which are small enough for *all* members of the cluster to be surveyed. As with multi-stage sampling, a bias will result due to similarities in responses from members of the same cluster. The difference between cluster sampling and multi-stage sampling is that since individual members of a cluster cannot be identified in advance, it is necessary for all members to be surveyed. Random sampling is therefore *not* involved.

Activity 2.6

How would you apply cluster sampling to the population referred to in Activity 2.5?

You would carry out the same procedure to obtain a selected number of postal districts, but these districts may be further subdivided so that individual streets are identified. All households of selected streets would then be surveyed.

2.8 Systematic sampling

This method is normally used with a sampling frame but it can also be used where a sampling frame is not available. However, in this case the size of the population must be known. The idea is that every nth member of a population is selected, where the value of n

is determined by the size of the population and by the required sample size. For instance, if a 5% sample is to be selected from a population of size 1000, then every 50th person will be selected. The start of the sequence is usually chosen at random. For example, if a 20% sample was to be selected from the student population given in Example 2.1, every 5th person would be selected. If you started with, say, the third student, your sample would consist of B. Booth, P. Frome, M. Jones, S. Moore and L. Nupper.

Activity 2.7

You have been asked by a local newspaper to find out what people thought of a particular film that is showing at the local cinema. How would you obtain a sample of 10 people?

Clearly it would be pointless asking people who hadn't seen the film, so your target population would be those people who had recently seen it. The easiest method would be to wait outside the cinema and select people as they left. If there were 300 people watching the film then you would need to stop every 30th person.

Systematic sampling is a very quick and efficient method of obtaining a sample. The sample should be random, provided there is no pattern in the way people are ordered in the population. For example, if a population consists of married couples then it is possible for the sample to consist of all husbands or all wives. To illustrate this point Table 2.4 refers to records taken from a registry office.

Table 2.4 Details taken from a registry office's records

Name	Date of marriage	Nationality
Mr A. Smith	21/3/93	British
Miss N. Taylor	21/3/93	British
Mr F. Barker	22/3/93	British
Miss F. Tooch	22/3/93	Australian
Mr T. Barry	22/3/93	British
Ms K. Larch	22/3/93	Canadian

If you took a systematic sample that took every second person and you started at F. Barker, all your sample would be males.

2.9 Quota sampling

I am sure that you have seen an interviewer in a town centre with a clip board waiting to pounce on some unsuspecting individual! The interviewer is in fact looking for particular groups of individuals that meet the categories that he or she has been asked to interview. Within each group there will be number or *quota* of people required and the survey is complete when the quotas have been reached. Quota sampling is a non-probabilistic version of stratified sampling. The quotas within each group should, like stratified sampling, reflect the proportions within the target population.

Activity 2.8

You want to obtain the views of the local population on the creation of an out-of-town shopping complex. You are told that 30% of the population is aged between 12 and 20, 60% is between 20 and 60, and 10% is over 60. You want a sample of 100 individuals. How would you go about choosing your sample?

Your first decision must be the location and time of the survey. An obvious choice would probably be the town centre on a Saturday when many people are out shopping. To reflect the fact that 30% of the population is aged between 12 and 20 you want a quota of 30 individuals in this age range. Similarly, for the other two age bands you would want 60 and 10 individuals respectively.

Quota sampling is a cheap and quick method of obtaining a sample. It is a particularly popular method for market research surveys and opinion polls. Its main disadvantage is that the sample could be heavily biased in favour of one particular group. For instance, in the case of the shopping centre the group of people who do not shop in the town centre will be omitted.

2.10 Other sampling methods

There are three other non-probabilistic sampling methods that are sometimes used. These are *judgemental*, *purposive* and *snowball* sampling. With judgemental sampling the researcher makes a judgement about what constitute a representative sample. If a government agency was interested in the effects on people's health of car exhaust fumes they would choose areas near cities or motorways to obtain the sample. They would not choose rural areas, except perhaps for a control group.

Purposive sampling is where certain members of the population are purposefully chosen. For example, customers holding store loyalty cards might be asked about planned improvements to the store.

Snowballing is where a sample is chosen using one of the methods mentioned in this chapter and then additional members of the population are generated from this sample. An example could be in the investigation of the miss-selling of pensions that occurred during the late 1980s. A sample of pensioners could be obtained and any person who was persuaded to leave their occupational pension scheme would be asked to name other people that they know were also affected. In this way the sample size could be increased.

Activity 2.9

A market research company is interested in consumers' reaction to a new brand of sun cream. What type of sampling method should they adopt?

Although most of the methods mentioned in this chapter would be suitable, judgemental sampling might be the best method to use in this situation. The researcher's judgement together with sales information could be used to select a few holiday resorts where it is likely that the product is being used. Once a resort has been chosen the researcher could use his or her judgement as to which age range should be sampled and at what time of the day the survey should be conducted.

2.11 Secondary sources of data

In many cases it is unnecessary to carry out a survey as the relevant data has already been collected and published. Much of the data collected by the government is available in the form of statistical publications and can be found in libraries or on the internet. When data has already been collected we say that it is *secondary* data. Secondary data is obviously easier to collect but its one disadvantage is that the quality of it is unknown. This is less of a problem with official sources, although it is still important to ensure that you know how the data was collected and any particular circumstances that might have made the data inaccurate or distorted in some way. This information is usually given in notes at the end of the publication or in footnotes to the relevant table.

One of the most important sources of official statistics is the *Monthly Digest of Statistics*, published by the Government Statistical Service. This monthly publication provides information on a wide range of products and services, such as new car registrations, energy usage, road accidents, industrial output and the retail price index, to name a few. Other official sources include *Annual Abstract of Statistics*, *Economic Trends*, *Regional Trends* and *Social Trends*. The web page <www.statistics.gov.uk> gives comprehensive details of a large selection of government statistical publications. Within this site you can access the online database StatBase®, which is an encyclopaedia of official statistics. The site also allows you to order publications and to download the free newsletter *Horizons*.

Table 2.5   A summary of the sampling methods available

	Sampling frame available (probabilistic sampling)	Sampling frame not available (non-probabilistic sampling)
Population resides in one place	Simple random sampling Systematic sampling	Systematic sampling (if the size of the population is known) Judgemental sampling Purposive sampling
Population geographically scattered	Multi-stage sampling	Cluster sampling Judgemental sampling
Population is defined by categories	Stratified sampling	Quota sampling
Population is small and unknown		Snowballing

2.12 Summary

This chapter has introduced you to various survey methods. It is generally impractical to question every member of a target population, and a sample of this population is selected instead. In order to achieve reliable results a sample should be representative of the target population. Probabilistic sampling methods will give you a representative sample, but these methods require the existence of a sampling frame. Non-probabilistic sampling is generally quicker to carry out but is not as reliable. Table 2.5 summarises the different methods available.

2.13 Further reading

Diamantopoulos, A. and Schlegelmilch, B. (1997) *Taking the fear out of Data Analysis*, The Dryden Press, London (Chapter 2).
Morris, C. (2000) *Quantitative Approaches in Business Studies*, fifth edition, Pitman, London (Chapter 3).

2.14 EXERCISES

The answers to the progress questions, the multiple choice questions and some of the practice questions are given in Appendix 1. Solutions to the remaining questions and the assignment can be found at the web site for this text.

PROGRESS QUESTIONS

These questions have been designed to help you remember the key points in this chapter.
Give the missing word in each case:

1. All the people or things of interest is called a .... population.
2. A subset of the population is called a ....
3. A list of members of the population is called a sampling ....
4. The simplest method of probabilistic sampling is called simple .... sampling.
5. If the sample is not representative of the population you would say that there is .... in the sample.
6. Two or more samples from the same population could give quite different results. This is due to sampling ....
7. .... sampling allows categories within a population to be considered.
8. .... sampling takes every *n*th member of the population.
9. Data collected from a survey is called .... data.

ANSWER *TRUE* OR *FALSE*

10. A census is when all members of the population are surveyed.
11. A postal questionnaire is the fastest method of conducting a survey.
12. Stratified sampling reduces sampling error.
13. Cluster sampling is used in conjunction with a sampling frame.
14. Systematic sampling can be both a probabilistic method and a non-probabilistic method.
15. Dichotomous questions have more than two answers.

REVIEW QUESTIONS

These questions have been designed to help you check your comprehension of the key points in this chapter. You may wish to look further than this chapter in order to answer them fully. You will find the reading list useful in this respect. You can check the essential elements of your answers by referring to the appropriate section.

16. Describe the essential differences between a sample and a population. (Section 2.2)
17. Why does probabilistic sampling require a sampling frame? (Section 2.2)
18. Describe the essential differences between simple random sampling and systematic sampling. (Sections 2.4 and 2.8)
19. When would you use quota sampling? (Section 2.9)
20. Describe the essential features of good questionnaire design. (Section 2.3)

MULTIPLE CHOICE QUESTIONS

21. A sample which is chosen such that every member of the population has an equal chance of being selected is called:

    A... a systematic sample
    B... a simple random sample
    C... a cluster sample

22. A correct statement about *quota* sampling is that:

    A... quota sampling requires random sampling within each quota
    B... quota sampling does not involve any clustering
    C... quota sampling involves some sort of stratification
    D... quota sampling is generally cheaper and more reliable than simple random sampling

23. Raffles are an example of:

    A... simple random sampling
    B... stratified sampling
    C... systematic sampling

24. The most expensive method of collecting data is:

    A... postal questionnaires

    B... telephone interviewing

    C... face-to-face interviewing

25. Multi-stage sampling is used when:

    A... a sampling frame is unavailable

    B... the population is geographically spread out

    C... the population is very large

PRACTICE QUESTIONS

26. Table 2.6 below represents a target population.

    (a) Using the random numbers 2, 9, 4, 3, 6, 7, select a simple random sample of size 3. What is the average age of your sample and what newspapers do they read?

    (b) Stratify your sample by sex and repeat part (a).

    (c) If a systematic sample of size 3 was required and the first person chosen was Steve, who would be the second person chosen?

27. You have been asked to conduct a survey into people's views of the council tax. What would be the target population and what would be a good sampling frame?

28. A football club wants to obtain the views of its supporters on a possible rise in admission charges. It has decided to obtain a simple random sample of members of the supporters' club. Comment on this proposal and suggest alternative target populations and sampling methods.

29. You have been asked to conduct a survey into the attitudes of school leavers to higher education. You intend to carry this out using the face-to-face interview method. How would you obtain your sample?

30. You have been asked to obtain the reaction to the proposal to pedestrianise your local town centre. What survey methods would you use?

Table 2.6 Population for Question 26

Name	Sex	Age	Newspaper read
Alan	M	23	Guardian
Steve	M	36	The Times
Jane	F	47	Mirror
Chris	M	36	Mirror
Julie	F	41	Sun
Stuart	M	37	Mirror
Jill	F	37	Telegraph
John	M	38	Express
Kim	M	48	Sun

31. A clothing company has just been approached by a students' union to stock a range of products suitable for the student market. However, the company wants some evidence that the market would be viable. You have been asked to help design a survey to discover if the students would be prepared to purchase their clothes from this company and what kind of price that they would be prepared to pay.

    (a) You are considering using either stratified or quota sampling to obtain your sample. Explain the differences between the two methods and discuss which method you think would be most suitable. State what categories or 'strata' you might want to consider for this problem, giving reasons why you think that these categories are important.

    (b) Would multi-stage sampling be worth considering for this problem?

    (c) Discuss the types of problems that might arise, both during the design phase and the survey itself. How might you overcome these problems?

32. A company wishes to carry out a survey of its employees to monitor their views on the future of the company. A departmental breakdown of the company's 200 employees is as follows:

Shop-floor/warehouse	80
Service engineers	15
Quality control	20
Marketing and sales	25
Accounts	15
Personnel	10
Administration	25
Catering	10

    A survey of 40 employees is to be conducted. A sampling frame is available, listing the employees by surname in alphabetical order, independent of department.

    (a) Explain how the following sampling methods could be carried out to obtain the sample of 40 employees:

    - simple random sampling
    - systematic sampling
    - stratified sampling
    - quota sampling.

    (b) Discuss the benefits and drawbacks of using quota sampling to obtain the sample of 40 employees.

33. A university is considering introducing a third semester so that students can complete their degrees in 2 years by remaining at the university over the summer vacation. To help the university decide whether this would be acceptable to staff and students, it wants to conduct a survey to establish the views of a cross-section of the university community.

(a) In the context of this problem, describe the terms:

- target population
- sampling frame
- stratified sampling
- multi-stage sampling.

(b) Design 5 questions that you might ask the respondents to the survey. Explain how these questions would help you to satisfy the aims of the survey.

(c) What type of data collection method would you use (postal, telephone or face to face)?

ASSIGNMENT

Conduct a survey on some aspect of the quality of current television programmes. It is important that you do some research into the relevant issues and then conduct a survey using a questionnaire of your own design. Information that you collect from your respondents might include:

- Viewing habits (that is, number of hours spent watching television, favourite programmes, and so on).
- Views on the quality of the programmes watched.
- What improvements they would like to see.
- Demographic information such as age, gender, occupation, and so on.

3 Presentation of data

3.1 Introduction

The human brain finds it difficult to make sense of a large quantity of data. However, once the data is properly organised and presented, a surprising amount of information can be derived from it. This chapter first discusses the type of data that you may come across and then looks at the best ways of displaying it.

At the end of this chapter you should be able to:

- Distinguish between the different types of data
- Tabulate data into an ungrouped or grouped frequency table as appropriate
- Use diagrams to present the data and draw appropriate conclusions from these diagrams
- Distinguish between symmetrical and skewed distributions
- Use a spreadsheet to plot charts

3.2 Data classification

If your idea of data is simply lots of numbers then you may be surprised to learn that there are several different classifications of data. *Continuous* data are data that are measured either on an *interval* scale or a *ratio* scale. For example, temperature is measured on an interval scale, as you can say that 24 °C is 12 degrees hotter than 12 °C, but you cannot say that 24 °C is twice as hot as 12 °C. On the other hand, money is measured on a ratio scale, as £24 is twice as much as £12 as well as being £12 more. The important point to note about continuous data is that they do not have a precise value. The weight of an item can be measured to any degree of accuracy depending on the measuring device used. *Discrete* data are data that take on whole values. The obvious example of discrete data are data obtained by counting. However, there are other examples of discrete data, such as the cost of an item or shoe size. *Ordinal* data are data that are given a numerical value but only for comparison purposes. An example of this type of data are the assessments consumers might give to a product. They might be asked to rate a product using a score from 1 to 5, where 5 is excellent and 1 is poor – although 5 is better than 1, it is not necessarily 5 times better or even 4 points better. *Nominal* data are data that do not have a numerical value and can only be placed in a suitable category. An example of this is hair colour or choice of newspaper. Ordinal and nominal data are usually referred to as *categorical* data.

Activity 3.1

How would you define the following sets of data?

(a) Measurement of the weights of jars of coffee.

(b) Choice of summer holiday.

(c) Weekly earnings by employees at a factory.

(d) Numbers of students following a business studies course.

(e) Market research survey into consumer reaction to a new product.

You should have defined (a) as ratio data since weight will be measured using either the metric or imperial system. (b) is ordinal data since choice will be destination or home/ abroad. (c) will be discrete since employees will earn an *exact* amount, such as £182.55. (d) is also discrete since the number can be found by counting. (e) could be either ordinal or nominal. It would be ordinal if you were asked to give a numerical score and nominal if you were simply asked to say whether you liked or disliked the product.

3.3 Tabulation of data

Example 3.1

A small survey was carried out into the mode of travel to work. The information in Table 3.1 relates to a random sample of 20 employed adults.

Table 3.1 Data for Example 3.1

Person	Mode of travel	Person	Mode of travel
1	car	11	car
2	car	12	bus
3	bus	13	walk
4	car	14	car
5	walk	15	train
6	cycle	16	bus
7	car	17	car
8	cycle	18	cycle
9	bus	19	car
10	train	20	car

||||▶ ## Activity 3.2

How would you classify this data?

This data is categorical (nominal) since mode of travel does not have a numerical value. This information would be better displayed as a frequency table (Table 3.2).

Table 3.2   Frequency table

Mode of travel	Frequency	Relative frequency (%)
Car	9	45
Bus	4	20
Cycle	3	15
Walk	2	0
Train	2	10
Total	20	

$\frac{9}{20} \times 100 = 45\%$

Table 3.3   Data for Example 3.2

Day	No. sold
Monday	10
Tuesday	12
Wednesday	9
Thursday	10
Friday	22
Saturday	14
Monday	11
Tuesday	18
Wednesday	10
Thursday	10
Friday	11
Saturday	9
Monday	13
Tuesday	10
Wednesday	12
Thursday	8
Friday	12
Saturday	12
Monday	11
Tuesday	13
Wednesday	10
Thursday	14
Friday	13
Saturday	12

Frequency is simply the number of times each category appeared. As well as the actual frequency, the *relative frequency* has been calculated. This is simply the frequency expressed as a percentage and is calculated by dividing a frequency by the total frequency and multiplying by 100.

The order in which you write these down is not important, although ordering by descending size of frequency makes comparison clearer.

Example 3.2

The data in Table 3.3 give the number of foreign holidays sold by a travel agent over the past four weeks.

Activity 3.3

How would you classify the data in Table 3.3, and what can you deduce from the figures?

Can the travel agent sell a fraction of a holiday? Assuming that a holiday is a holiday regardless of the duration or the cost, then this is clearly discrete data and would have been obtained by counting. By examining the figures you should see that 10 sales occurs most frequently, although there is a range from 8 to 22 sales. To enable this information to be seen more clearly you could aggregate the data into a table (Table 3.4).

Table 3.4   Frequency table for Example 3.2

Number sold	Frequency
8	1
9	2
10	6
11	3	sold each day
12	5
13	3
14	2
More than 14	2

This table is called an *ungrouped frequency table*, since the numbers sold have not been grouped. This table is a useful way of summarising a small set of discrete data. There are two extreme values or *outliers* of value 18 and 22 sales and these have been included by the use of a 'more than' quantity. From this table you can see that between 10 and 12 holidays are usually sold each day.

Example 3.3

Table 3.5 gives the number of bolts produced by a machine each hour over the past 65 hours, while Table 3.6 gives the length in mm of 80 of these bolts.

Table 3.5   Hourly rate of bolt production

184	250	136	178	231	158	197	159	141	218
223	156	124	177	298	175	231	218	117	149
169	119	174	171	191	202	214	138	127	254
177	181	189	201	198	165	140	100	147	188
296	237	223	267	147	112	238	139	165	125
165	188	230	150	127	251	182	139	159	179
230	183	166	163	194					

Table 3.6   Length   of   bolts   (mm)

49.9	53.8	61.3	45.8	51.2	44.5	55.3	51.4	84.1
55.7	52.7	68.7	52.5	58.8	37.8	44.1	49.9	53.8
64.1	35.9	56.4	55.1	60.6	45.9	54.8	54.0	49.3
46.8	46.5	52.2	33.3	42.9	47.7	56.2	40.5	36.8
47.5	56.3	70.2	35.5	56.7	56.0	56.5	49.5	57.5
52.0	36.8	46.3	42.4	30.2	49.5	36.3	54.6	45.1
30.0	47.0	52.1	53.0	66.1	50.5	56.0	50.9	42.7
42.1	51.2	49.0	49.9	54.4	53.2	43.0	41.3	49.7
42.9	61.1	41.7	35.7	45.0	59.2	60.6	44.7	

Activity 3.4

Look at the data in Table 3.5 and Table 3.6. Can you deduce anything about how many bolts are produced each hour or the length of each bolt? Would it help if ungrouped frequency tables were created as in Activity 3.2?

I expect that you found it quite difficult to draw many conclusions from the data. For Table 3.5 you might have identified the range of production as between 100 and 298 bolts per hour, but what is the 'normal' production rate? Similarly, the smallest bolt is 30.0 mm and the largest is 84.1 mm, but what size are the majority of the bolts? An ungrouped frequency table for either set of data would not be very helpful for two reasons: for both data sets the range of the data is large, which would necessitate a large table, and for Table 3.6 the data is continuous. Continuous data can, by definition, take on any value, so what values would you use in your table? To overcome these problems a *grouped frequency table* is produced. A grouped frequency table is similar to an ungrouped table except that intervals are set up into which the data can be grouped. The number and size of each interval depends on the quantity and range of your data. In general you would have between 8 and 15 intervals and the width of each interval, or the *class interval*, should be a convenient number such as 10, 20, 25 etc. In the case of Table 3.5 the range is $298 - 100 = 198$, and a class interval of 20 would give you 10 intervals, which is about right. The first interval would be 100 to 119; the second 120 to 139, and so on. Once you have decided on the size of each interval you need to allocate each value to one of the intervals. This can be done by using a *tally chart*. A tally chart is simply a foolproof means (or nearly) of ensuring that all items have been allocated. You start with the first value, in this case 184, and find the relevant interval, which is 180 to 199. A '1' is placed in this row. You then do the same with subsequent values, except that when you have four 1s in a row you would draw a line through the group to make the total of 5. This has been done for you in Table 3.7.

Table 3.7 Tally chart

Class interval	Tally
100 to 119	ЈͰͰͳ
120 to 139	ЈͰͰͳ 111
140 to 159	ЈͰͰͳ ЈͰͰͳ
160 to 179	ЈͰͰͳ ЈͰͰͳ 111
180 to 199	ЈͰͰͳ ЈͰͰͳ 1
200 to 219	ЈͰͰͳ
220 to 239	ЈͰͰͳ 111
240 to 259	111
260 to 279	1
280 to 299	11

The next stage is to add up the tally in each interval to give you the frequency. The final grouped frequency table is as follows (Table 3.8):

Table 3.8 Grouped frequency table

Interval	Frequency	Relative frequency (%)
100 to 119	4	6.2
120 to 139	8	12.3
140 to 159	10	15.4
160 to 179	13	20.0
180 to 199	11	16.9
200 to 219	5	7.7
220 to 239	8	12.3
240 to 259	3	4.6
260 to 279	1	1.5
280 to 299	2	3.1
Total	65	100

$\frac{4}{65} \times 100 = 6.15\%$

From this table it appears that the rate of production is quite variable, although the rate is unlikely to be less than 120 or more than 240 bolts per hour.

How would you group the data in Table 3.6? You might decide on a class interval of 5 mm, which would give you 11 intervals. Since the smallest length is 30 mm the first group would start at 30 mm; the second at 35 mm, and so on. But what should the end of each group be? If you used 34 mm you would not be able to allocate a value between 34 and 35 mm. You cannot use the same figure for both the end of one group and the start of the next because this would allow a value to be added to more than one group. It is essential that a value can go into *one, and only one*, interval, so the ranges must be designed to guarantee this. Since the data is continuous the length can be quoted to any degree of accuracy, so the end of each group would be defined as *under* 35 mm and under 40 mm, and so on. In this way a length of 34.9 mm would be in the first group while 35.0 mm would be in the second group.

Activity 3.5

Obtain the grouped frequency table for the data in Table 3.6. What can you deduce about the length of bolts produced?

You should have obtained Table 3.9.

Table 3.9   Grouped frequency table for the length of bolts

Interval	Frequency	Relative frequency (%)
30 to under 35 mm	3	3.75
35 to under 40 mm	7	8.75
40 to under 45 mm	12	15.00
45 to under 50 mm	18	22.50
50 to under 55 mm	18	22.50
55 to under 60 mm	13	16.25
60 to under 65 mm	5	6.25
65 to under 70 mm	2	2.50
70 to under 75 mm	1	1.25
75 to under 80 mm	0	0
80 to under 85 mm	1	1.25

If you look at this table the *distribution* of the lengths are clearer. 76.25% of the values are between 40 mm and 60 mm, with few over 60 mm or less than 40 mm.

In both these examples the class intervals were the same for the whole distribution; that is, 20 in the first case and 5 in the second. However, it is not necessary for the intervals to be equal and you may have two or more different intervals in the same table. In Table 3.9 you might decide to condense the last three intervals into one since the frequencies in these intervals are small. If you do this your last interval will be 70 to under 85 mm, which has a frequency of 2. It is also possible to have an *open* interval at the beginning or end, such as greater than 70 mm or less than 30 mm. However, only use open intervals if you really have to and only if there is a relatively small number of items in this interval.

3.4 Diagrammatic representation of data

Although frequency tables can give you more information than the *raw* data, it can still be difficult to take in all the information that is inherent in the data. Diagrams can help provide this additional information and also display the data in a more visually attractive manner. You do lose some detail but this is a small price to pay for the additional information that diagrams provide. There are several types of diagrams and the choice depends mainly on the type of data, but also on your intended audience.

These days most people will use a spreadsheet when producing diagrams. Spreadsheets can produce high-quality charts which can be easily updated if the data changes. However, some experience of drawing diagrams by hand is still useful.

Example 3.4

The sales by department of a high street store over the past three years are shown in Table 3.10.

Table 3.10   Sales by department and year

	1999	2000	2001
Clothing	£1.7m	£1.4m	£1.4m
Furniture	£3.4m	£4.9m	£5.6m
Electrical goods	£0.2m	£0.4m	£0.5m
Total	£5.3m	£6.7m	£7.5m

An inspection of this data reveals that the total sales have increased over the three years, although clothing has shown a decline. Diagrams should help bring out these and other differences more clearly.

3.4.1 Pie charts

When you want to compare the relative sizes of the frequencies a pie chart is a good choice of diagram. It is normally used for categorical data and each category is represented by a segment of a circle. The size of each segment reflects the frequency of that category and can be represented as an angle. It is rare for people to draw a pie chart by hand as a protractor is required to measure the angles, but if you need to, the angle is calculated by working out the percentage of the category and then multiplying by $360°$. For example, for the sales for 1997 in Example 3.4 the angle would be calculated as follows:

Clothing as a percentage is $\frac{1.4}{7.5} \times 100 = 18.7\%$

The angle is therefore $\frac{18.7}{100} \times 360 = 67°$

The complete pie chart for the sales for 1997 is shown in Figure 3.1. This diagram demonstrates that the furniture department has contributed the bulk of the total sales for this year.

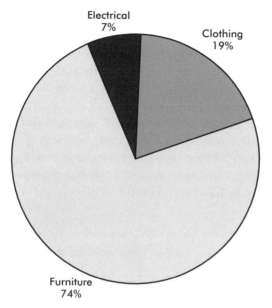

Figure 3.1 Pie chart for sales in 2001

3.4.2 Bar charts

Although pie charts tend to be a popular means of comparing the size of categories it has the disadvantage that they are not suitable for displaying several sets of data simultaneously. You would, for instance, need three separate pie charts to represent the data in Table 3.10. A *simple bar chart* is another useful method of displaying categorical data, or an ungrouped frequency table. For each category a vertical bar is drawn, the height of the bar being proportional to the frequency. The diagram in Figure 3.2 shows the total sales in the form of a simple bar chart.

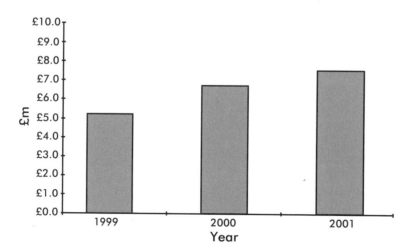

Figure 3.2 A simple bar chart of total sales

When a category is subdivided into several subcategories the simple bar chart is not really adequate as you would need a different bar chart for each subcategory. A *multiple bar chart* is used when you are interested in changes in the components but the totals are of no interest. Figure 3.3 is a multiple bar chart for the data in Table 3.10.

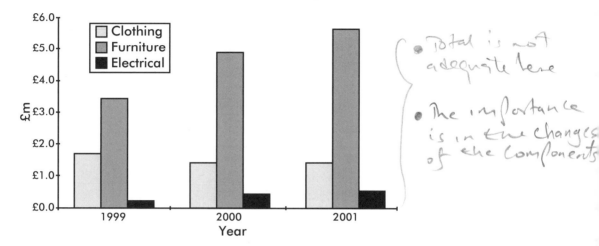

Total is not adequate here

The importance is in the changes of the components

Figure 3.3 A multiple bar chart

If you are interested in comparing totals and seeing how the totals are made up a *component* bar chart is used. Figure 3.4 is a component bar chart for the data in Table 3.10. In this figure you can see the variation in total sales from year to year as well as seeing how each department contributes to total sales. If you are more interested in the proportion of sales in each department a *percentage* bar chart may be of more interest. This is shown in Figure 3.5. This chart is rather like the pie chart with the advantage that several sets of data can be displayed simultaneously.

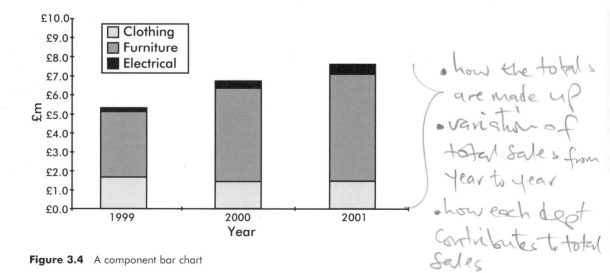

how the totals are made up

variation of total sales from year to year

how each dept contributes to total sales

Figure 3.4 A component bar chart

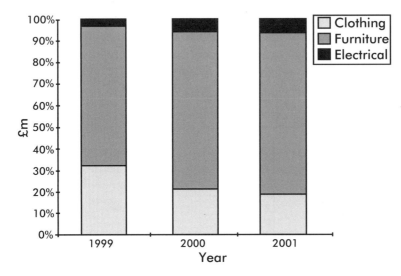

Figure 3.5 A percentage bar chart

3.4.3 Line graphs

When data is in the form of a *time series* a line graph can be a useful means of showing any trends in the data. Figure 3.6 is a line graph for the total sales given in Table 3.10 and clearly shows the rise in sales over the three years. When this type of diagram is shown in company publications you will often find that the scale on the *y*-axis is broken. This will exaggerate the growth in sales or other measure and can be misleading unless you are aware of what is going on. This can be justified if none of the values are near zero, but in this case the break in the scale should be clearly shown. Figure 3.7 shows how this should be done.

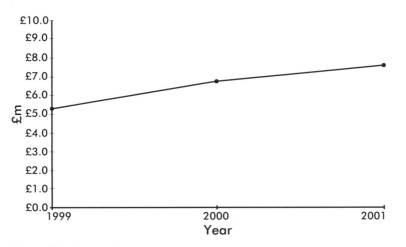

Figure 3.6 Line graph

We will be looking at line graphs in more detail in Chapter 13.

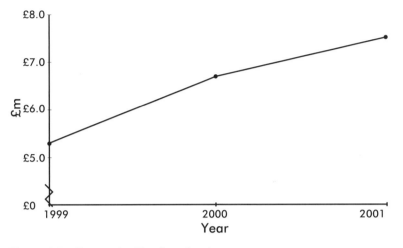

Figure 3.7 Line graph with adjusted scale

Activity 3.6

Use Figures 3.1 to 3.7 to summarise how the sales have varied by department and year.

You should be able to deduce that:

- Total sales have increased over the three years, although the largest increase was between 1999 and 2000
- Most of this increase has been the result of sales of furniture
- Clothing has shown a decrease in sales from 1999 to 2000 but has then remained steady
- The sales of clothing as a proportion of total sales has declined, while the proportion of electrical sales has increased

3.4.4 Histograms

For grouped frequency tables a different type of diagram is normally used. This diagram is called a histogram and although it may look like a bar chart there are some important differences. These are:

- The horizontal axis is a continuous scale, just like a normal graph. This implies that there should not be gaps between bars unless the frequency for that class interval really is zero
- It is the *area* of the bars that is being compared, not the heights. This means that if one class interval is twice the others then the height must be halved, since area = width × height

The histogram shown in Figure 3.8 is for the lengths of bolts given in Example 3.3 and uses an equal class interval of 5 mm.

If the last three intervals were combined, the last class interval would be 15 mm. In this case the frequency of 2 should be *divided* by 3 to give 0.67 and the histogram would have to be redrawn as shown in Figure 3.9. Where there are several different class intervals it is normal practice to divide each frequency by the corresponding class width. The resulting values are called the *frequency density* although it is usually better not to give the vertical axis a label.

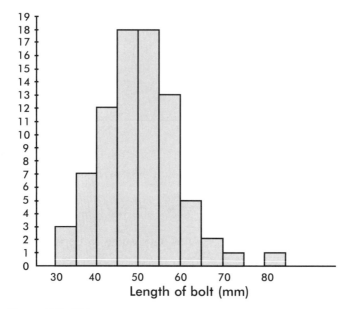

Figure 3.8 Histogram

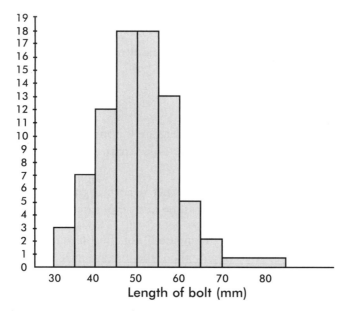

Figure 3.9 Histogram with unequal class intervals

When you draw histograms for discrete data there is a problem in that there is a gap between the end of one interval and the start of the next. You can get round this problem by extending each interval half way to the next or last interval. Thus for the example of the rate of production of bolts, the intervals would become 100.5 to 119.5 and 119.5 to 139.5, and so on.

Activity 3.7

Draw the histogram for the production rate data.

Your diagram should look like the one in Figure 3.10.

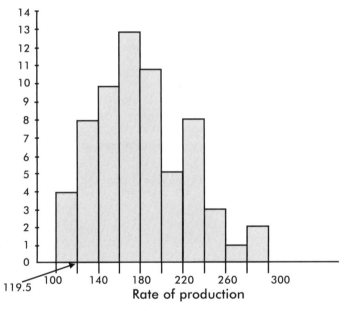

Figure 3.10 Histogram for discrete data

3.4.5 Frequency polygons

To get a better idea about how the data is distributed across the range of possible values of the data, you can join up the mid points of the top of each bar of the histogram. This is shown in Figure 3.11 for the bolt length data.

If the bars are now removed, you are left with a picture of the shape of the underlying distribution of the data. The area under the frequency polygon is the same as the area under the original histogram (Figure 3.12).

This diagram can be quite useful if you want to compare different distributions, as it is possible to plot more than one frequency polygon on the same graph. This is not possible with the other diagrams you have met, as they would look too confusing.

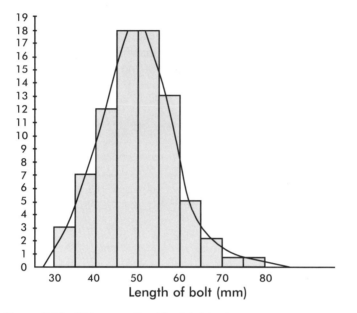

Figure 3.11 Histogram with mid points joined up

Another important use of the frequency polygon is to categorise the shape of the distribution in terms of its degree of symmetry. A distribution that is perfectly balanced is called *symmetrical*, whereas a distribution which has its peak offset to one side is called *skewed*. If the peak is to the left, the distribution is called *right* or *positive* skewed, whereas

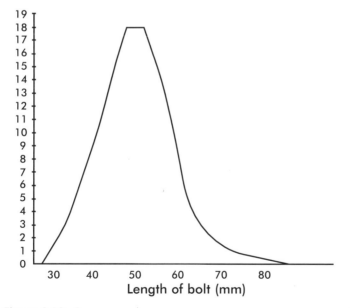

Figure 3.12 Frequency polygon

if the peak is to the right, the distribution is called *left* or *negative* skewed. This may sound illogical but you will discover the reason for this convention in the next chapter. I find it easier to look at the *tail* of the distribution. If the tail is to the right it is right skewed and if the tail is to the left it is left skewed. The diagrams below may help you appreciate the differences (Figure 3.13).

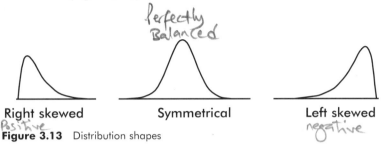

Figure 3.13 Distribution shapes

Activity 3.8

How would you define the shape of the distribution of bolt lengths?

The distribution is approximately symmetrical, although it has a slight right skewness to it.

3.4.6 Ogive

Another diagram can be created by plotting the *cumulative* frequencies. Cumulative frequency is simply a running total of the frequencies. The cumulative frequencies for the bolt length data are shown in Table 3.11.

Table 3.11   Calculation of cumulative frequencies

Interval	Frequency	Cumulative frequency	% cumulative frequency
30 to under 35 mm	3	3	3.75
35 to under 40 mm	7	10	12.50
40 to under 45 mm	12	22	27.50
45 to under 50 mm	18	40	50.00
50 to under 55 mm	18	58	72.50
55 to under 60 mm	13	71	88.75
60 to under 65 mm	5	76	95.00
65 to under 70 mm	2	78	97.50
70 to under 75 mm	1	79	98.75
75 to under 80 mm	0	79	98.75
80 to under 85 mm	1	80	100.00

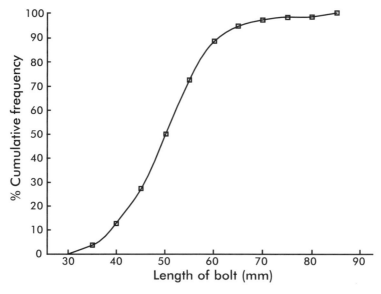

Figure 3.14   Ogive

The percentage cumulative frequencies have also been calculated as you will find that the use of percentages has certain advantages. The cumulative frequency graph or *ogive* can now be drawn. The *upper* boundaries of each class interval are plotted against the (%) cumulative frequencies, as shown in Figure 3.14.

This is a very useful diagram and you will meet this again in the next chapter. For the purposes of this chapter you can treat this graph as a *less than* graph, since the upper-class boundaries were plotted against the cumulative frequencies. So, for example, 12.5% of the lengths are below 40 mm.

 ## Activity 3.9

Determine the proportion of lengths that are:

(a) below 50 mm

(b) below 41 mm

(c) above 63 mm

The answer to (a) can be read directly from the grouped frequency distribution and is 50%. However, for both (b) and (c) you should use the ogive to *interpolate* between two boundaries. To do this you should draw a vertical line up from the *x*-axis at the appropriate value to meet the ogive. You can then draw a horizontal line from this point until it meets the *y*-axis and then it is a matter of reading the cumulative frequency from this axis. This has been done for you in Figure 3.15.

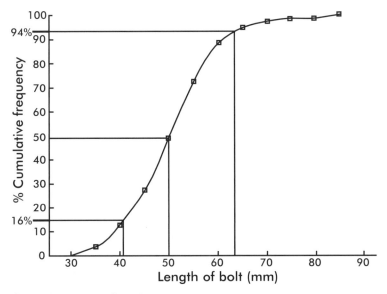

Figure 3.15 Using the ogive

You will see from the diagram that I have drawn lines for all three lengths. The cumulative frequency for (a) is 50% as it should be. The cumulative frequency for (b) is approximately 16%, so 16% of lengths are below 41 mm. The cumulative frequency for (c) is approximately 94% but, as you were asked to find the proportion above 63 mm, you then need to subtract 94 from 100, that is 6%.

3.5 Creating charts with Excel

Very few people draw charts by hand these days, as it is much easier to use a spreadsheet, such as Excel. Charts produced by a spreadsheet also look more professional and they can be immediately updated if the data changes. When drawing charts in Excel you can choose whether to create the chart as an object in the same worksheet as the data or to create the chart in a new sheet. Being able to see the chart next to the data can be useful, but if you want to print out the chart or to copy and paste it in another document it is often easier to create it in a new sheet.

For those of you unfamiliar with spreadsheets, Activity 3.10 will take you through the basics of adding data to a worksheet. More experienced users will probably want to skip this activity.

Activity 3.10

The data below is reproduced from Table 3.10 and shows the sales by department for the 3 years 1999 to 2001.

Table 3.12   High street sales data

Department	1999	2000	2001
Clothing	£1.7m	£1.4m	£1.4m
Furniture	£3.4m	£4.9m	£5.6m
Electrical goods	£0.2m	£0.4m	£0.5m

Enter the above table into Excel.

The instructions below assume that you are a novice in using Excel and take you through the process of entering data in a slow but methodical manner. For those with some experience of Excel you should be able to produce this table of data much faster.

1. STARTING OFF

Type the label 'Clothing' in cell A1 and then press the down arrow key so that the cursor moves to cell A2 and type in the label 'Furniture'. Enter the label 'Electrical goods' in cell A3 and press the <Enter> key.

You will find that the headings are too long for the column in which they are located and will spill over into adjacent cells. Do not worry about this at this stage. Your worksheet should look like the one in Figure 3.16.

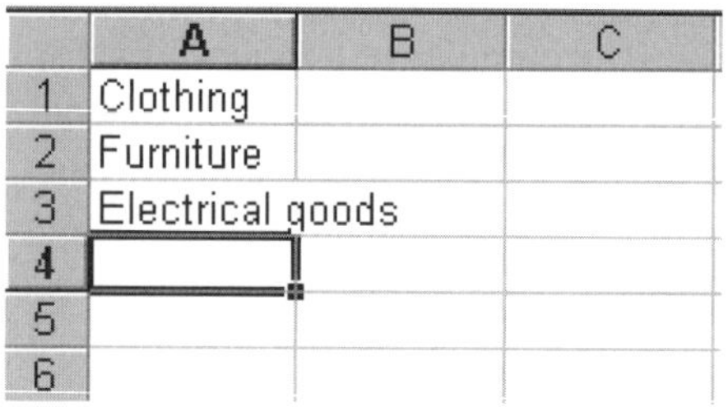

Figure 3.16   Row headings added to the worksheet

2. MOVING CELL CONTENTS

It will be seen that no space has been left on the worksheet for the labels across the top of the table. However, it is very easy to move the content of cells in Excel.

Highlight the three labels you have entered by clicking on the cell containing the words 'Clothing' and, holding down the left mouse button, drag the pointer down the screen so that all three labels are highlighted.

Release the mouse button and the highlight should remain.

Now click on any part of the bottom border of the highlighted box, hold down the mouse button and drag the highlighted box down so that the name 'Clothing' is located in cell A6. Release the mouse button. This operation is called *drag and drop*.

3. ENTERING THE DATA

Type the title 'High street sales (£m)' in cell A2 and press <Enter>. Type 'Year' in B3 and 'Department' in A4, then '1999' in B4, '2000' in C4 and '2001' in D4. Press the <Enter> key after each.

Enter into your worksheet the sales figures as shown Table 3.12, using the arrow keys and mouse pointer to move about the worksheet as appropriate.

Notice that text entries are left-justified – that is the words are located on the left-hand side of the cell – whilst the numbers are right-justified. Some of the row labels are partly hidden.

If you make a mistake entering the data then simply retype the data in the correct cell. The worksheet should now look similar to the one in Figure 3.17.

	A	B	C	D	E
1					
2	High street sales (£m)				
3		Year			
4	Departmer	1999	2000	2001	
5					
6	Clothing	1.7	1.4	1.4	
7	Furniture	3.4	4.9	5.6	
8	Electrical	0.2	0.4	0.5	
9					
10					
11					

Figure 3.17 The worksheet with the data added

4. ADDING THE TOTALS TO THE TABLE

To add the totals for each year you can make use of the Autosum icon Σ in the formatting toolbar as follows. While in cell B10 click on the Σ symbol and it should highlight cells B6 to B9. Press <Enter> if the correct cells are highlighted. You can highlight the correct cells if necessary by holding down the left-hand mouse button. Repeat this for the other two columns. Add the title 'Total' in cell A10.

5. CHANGING COLUMN WIDTHS

Column A may need to be widened. Select it by clicking on the 'A' at the top of the first column. The whole column should be highlighted. Then select *Format, Column, AutoFit Selection*. This will set the column width to accommodate its contents.

6. CENTRING HEADINGS

Click on cell A2 and drag the cursor to D2 then release the mouse button. Select *Format, Cells, Alignment,* then for horizontal text alignment select *Centre across selection* then *OK*. Repeat this routine to centre the text in cell B3. Alternatively, highlight the cells for centring across, then use the *Merge and Centre* button in the formatting toolbar. The worksheet should now look like the one in Figure 3.18

	A	B	C	D	E
1					
2	High street sales (£m)			
3		Year			
4	Department	1999	2000	2001	
5					
6	Clothing	1.7	1.4	1.4	
7	Furniture	3.4	4.9	5.6	
8	Electrical goods	0.2	0.4	0.5	
9					
10	Total	5.3	6.7	7.5	
11					
12					
13					

Figure 3.18   The worksheet with totals and headings centred

7. FORMATTING THE DATA

Since the data is money, you can format it so that Excel will recognise it as such. Highlight the cells B6 to D10 and click on *Format*, *Cells*, *Number*, *Currency* and select one decimal place. Press *OK*.

8. TIDYING UP THE TABLE

To improve the look of the worksheet you can move the table one column along and add a border round the table. The simplest way to move this table is to insert a column by clicking on the 'A' at the top of the column and then right-click on your mouse. Select *Insert* and this will effectively move the whole table right by one column. To insert a border, highlight the whole table and click on the border toolbar ▣ ▾ after first selecting the required one. You could also draw horizontal and vertical lines within the table using the border toolbar. Finally, you might like to bold the headings and increase the font of the main heading to a point size of 12. The final worksheet should look something like the one shown in Figure 3.19.

	A	B	C	D	E	F	G	H	I	J
1										
2		**High street sales (£m)**							
3			Year							
4		**Department**	1999	2000	2001					
5										
6		Clothing	£1.7	£1.4	£1.4					
7		Furniture	£3.4	£4.9	£5.6					
8		Electrical goods	£0.2	£0.4	£0.5					
9										
10		Total	£5.3	£6.7	£7.5					
11										
12										

Figure 3.19   The final Excel worksheet for the high street sales data

9. SAVING YOUR WORK

You should save your work at regular intervals (say every 15 minutes). Select the save icon 💾 and give your *workbook* a name such as 'High street sales'. You can fill in the info box if required.

Activity 3.11

Using the worksheet created in Activity 3.10, create

1. A pie chart for sales in 2001
2. A simple bar chart of total sales for each of the three years
3. A multiple bar chart for sales by year and department
4. A component bar chart
5. A percentage bar chart
6. A line graph for the total sales over the three years

For each chart you need to choose *Insert*, *Chart* or click on the Chart Wizard button in the standard toolbar 📊 .

The charts produced are the same ones that were shown earlier in the chapter and you will be referred back to these charts.

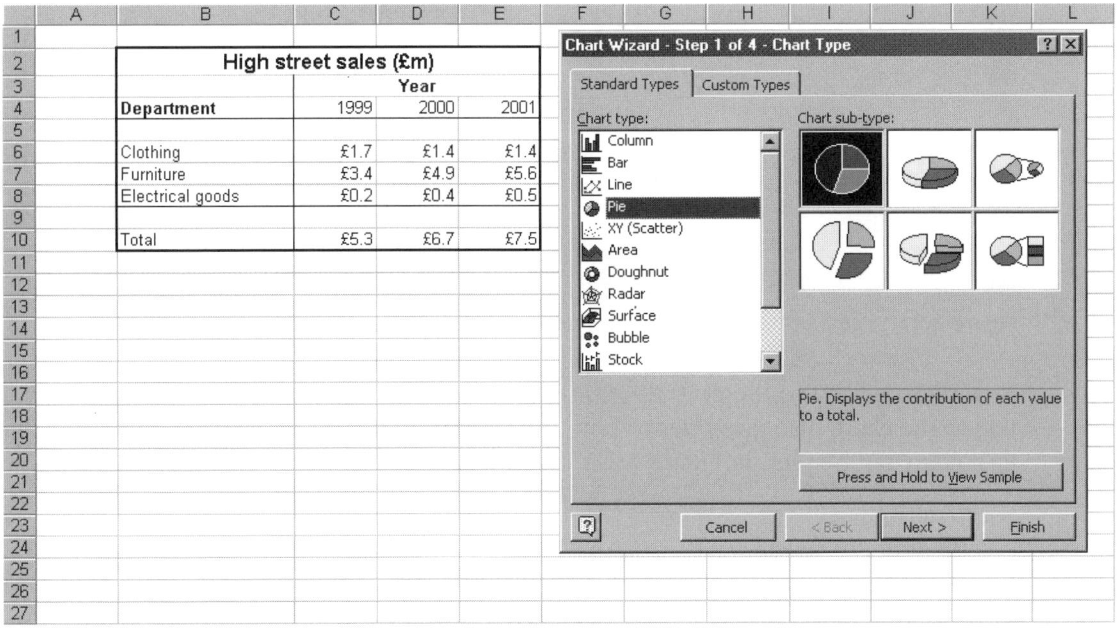

Figure 3.20 Using the Chart Wizard to create a pie chart

1. PIE CHART

Choose 'Pie' as illustrated in Figure 3.20. Click on *Next* and highlight cells B6 to B8 and while holding down the <Ctrl> key on your keyboard highlight cells E6 to E8. Ensure that *Series in Columns* is selected. Click on *Next* and give the chart a title. Click on *As new sheet* and then *Finish*.

The pie chart can be seen in Figure 3.1.

2. A SIMPLE BAR CHART

Vertical bar charts in Excel are called *Column* charts and will be the first one in the list of charts. The first sub-type should be highlighted (*Clustered column*), and you can use this or the second one (*Stacked column*). Click on *Next* and highlight cells C10 to E10. Then click on *Series*, then *Category (X) axis labels*. Highlight cells C4 to E4 and you should see the screen shown in Figure 3.21.

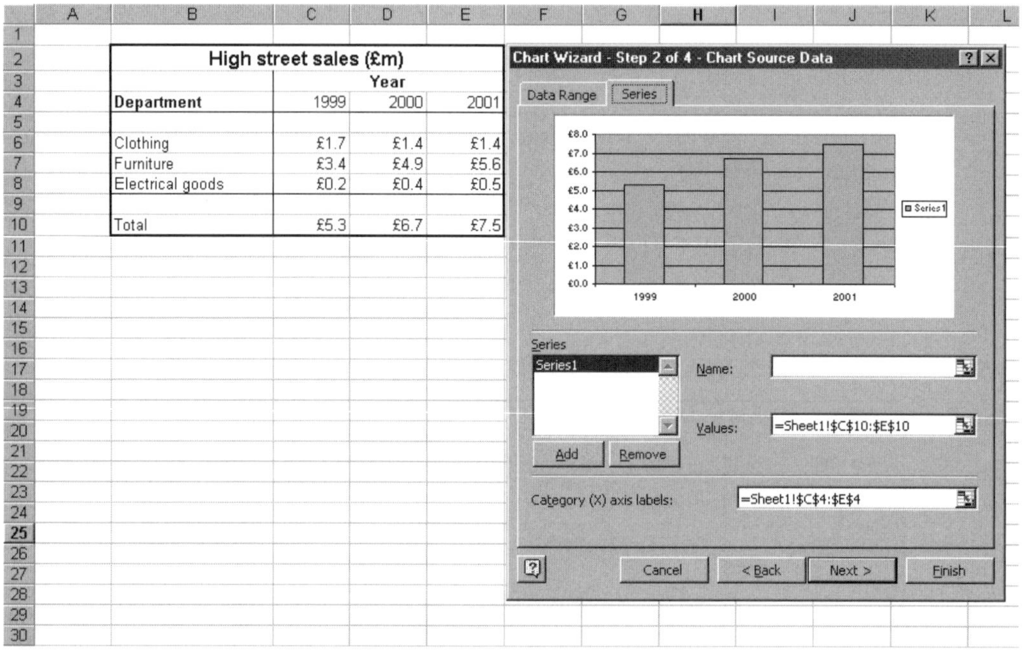

Figure 3.21 Step 2 of the Chart Wizard to create a simple bar chart

Now click on *Next* and remove the tick mark from *Show legend*. Click on Titles and add a title to the chart. Also give titles to both axes. Click on *As new sheet* and then *Finish*. The final chart can be seen in Figure 3.2.

3. A MULTIPLE BAR CHART

Proceed as before, but this time highlight cells B6 to E8. This time you want the legend to show so leave this box ticked but you can choose where the legend should be placed on the chart. Give a main title and titles to both axes as before.

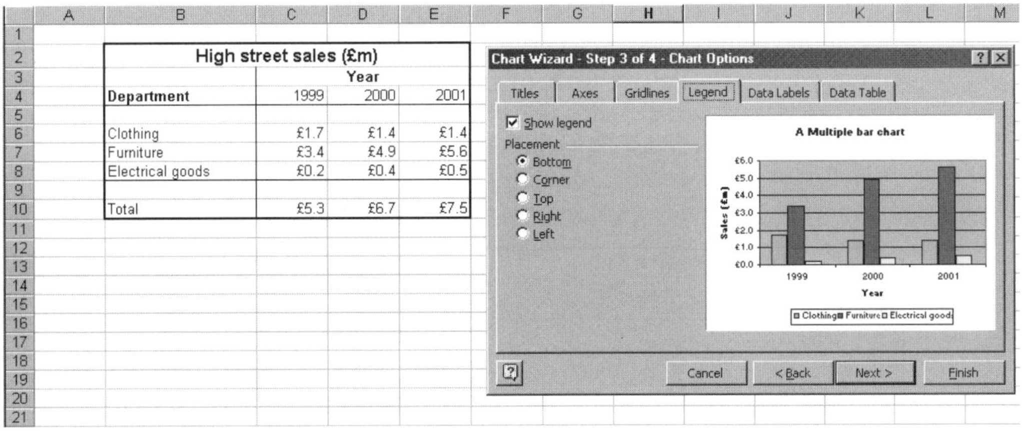

Figure 3.22 Step 3 of the Chart Wizard to create a multiple bar chart

The final chart can be seen in Figure 3.3.

4. COMPONENT BAR CHART

A component bar chart is called a *Stacked column* chart in Excel and is the second sub-type. Proceed exactly as before.

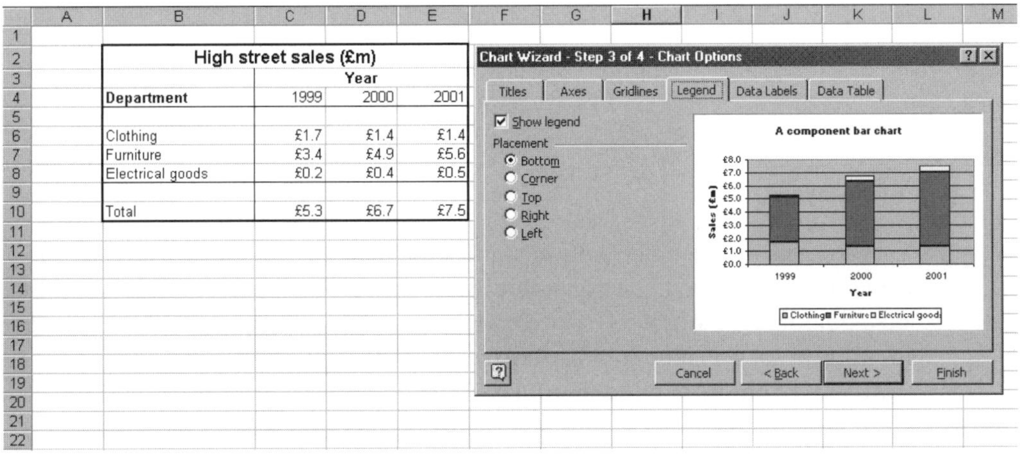

Figure 3.23 Step 3 of the Chart Wizard for creating a component bar chart

The final chart can be seen in Figure 3.4.

5. A PERCENTAGE BAR CHART

This is exactly the same as before except that the third sub-type is chosen (*100% stacked column*). This chart can be seen in Figure 3.5.

6. A LINE GRAPH

For this line graph you should chose sub-type 4 as shown in Figure 3.24. The chart can be seen in Figure 3.6. Note that, as mentioned earlier, the y-axis for this chart need not be started at zero. However, when this is done it is good practice to show a break in the scale. Unfortunately this cannot be achieved automatically in Excel.

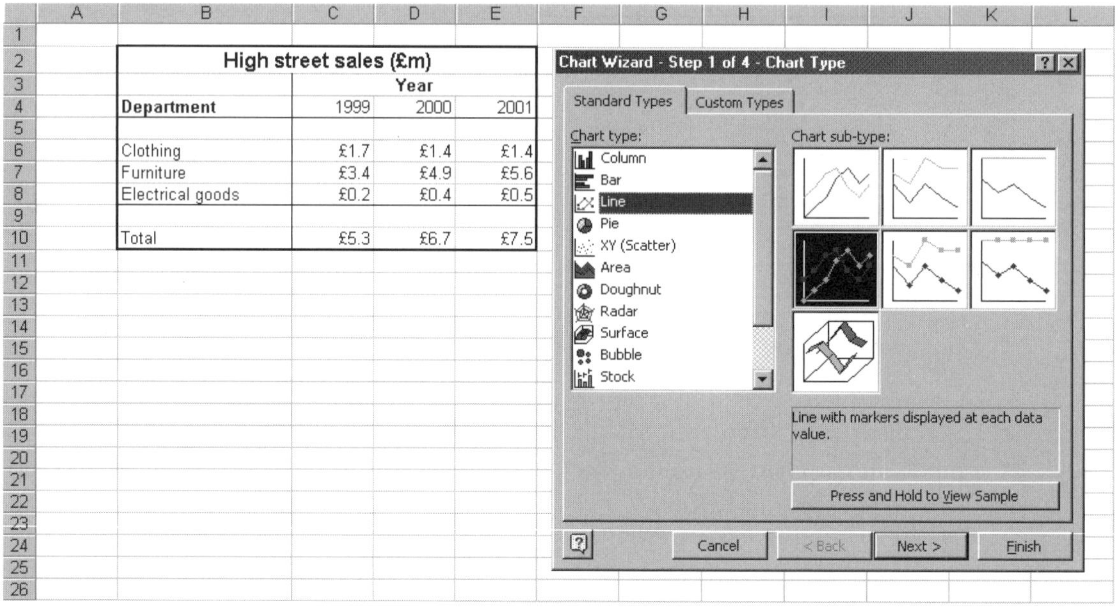

Figure 3.24 Step 1 of the Chart Wizard to creat a line graph

3.6 Summary

This chapter has enabled you to understand the importance of tabulating and presenting data. Data can be continuous, discrete, ordinal or categorical, and the type of data determines the method to use for its presentation. Data is normally aggregated into tables and for continuous and discrete data these tables can be either ungrouped or grouped. For group frequency tables the class interval needs to be decided and a tally chart used to help in the aggregation process. There are several different types of diagram that can be used to display the data more effectively. Pie charts and bar charts can be used for categorical data and for ungrouped discrete data. Line graphs can be used for time series data. Histograms are used for either continuous or discrete data that has been aggregated into a frequency table. A histogram gives you an idea of the shape of the underlying distribution, but a frequency polygon will show this more clearly. If cumulative frequencies are plotted, a cumulative frequency ogive is obtained and this important graph allows you to obtain further information about the distribution.

3.7 Further reading

Burton, G., Carrol, G. and Wall, S. (1999) *Quantitative Methods for Business and Economics*, Longman, New York (Chapter 1).

Morris, C. (2000) *Quantitative Approaches in Business Studies*, fifth edition, Pitman, London (Chapter 5).

3.8 EXERCISES

The answers to the progress questions, the multiple choice questions and some of the practice questions are given in Appendix 1. Solutions to the remaining questions and the assignment can be found at the web site for this text.

PROGRESS QUESTIONS

These questions have been designed to help you remember the key points in this chapter.

Give the missing word in each case:

1. Data that is collected at source is called .... data. *Primary*
2. Data that is obtained by counting is called .... data. *discret*
3. Weight measurements are an example of .... data. *ratio*
4. Data can be aggregated using a .... chart. *Tally*
5. A diagram that is circular in shape is called a .... chart. *Pie*
6. If you want to compare totals a .... bar chart may be applicable. *Component*
7. A histogram is used to display data that has been aggregated into a .... frequency table. *grouple*
8. To show the shape of the distribution a frequency .... can be used. *Polygon*

ANSWER *TRUE* OR *FALSE*

9. A histogram must not have gaps, between bars.
10. A histogram compares heights of each bar.
11. The upper end of each interval should be plotted for a cumulative frequency ogive.
12. A survey into types of heating found in domestic property would form a set of discrete data.
13. Data is aggregated into a grouped frequency table if the quantity of data is very large.
14. Data obtained from a survey into the occupancy of cars could be displayed by a pie chart.

REVIEW QUESTIONS

These questions have been designed to help you check your comprehension of the key points in this chapter. You may wish to look further than this chapter in order to answer them fully. You will find the reading list useful in this respect. You can check the essential elements of your answers by referring to the appropriate section.

15. What is the difference between a grouped and ungrouped frequency distribution? (Section 3.3)
16. Describe the essential differences between a bar chart and a histogram. (Section 3.4)
17. What are the uses of a frequency polygon? (Section 3.4.5)

18. What would the distribution of wages earned by the working population of Britain look like? (Section 3.4.5)

19. What is an ogive? (Section 3.4.6)

MULTIPLE CHOICE QUESTIONS

20. If a researcher is collecting information on the number of company cars owned each year by a company, what type of data are they collecting?

   A... Interval data

   B... Discrete data

   C... Ratio data

   D... Ordinal data

   E... Nominal data

21. Which of the following graphical methods would be most suitable to illustrate the occupations of 50 female adults?

   A... Line graph

   B... Pie chart

   C... Histogram

   D... Component bar chart

22. Which of the following is a true statement when applied to a cumulative frequency curve (ogive)?

   A... Mid points are plotted against cumulative frequencies

   B... Upper class boundaries are plotted against cumulative frequencies

   C... Lower class boundaries are plotted against cumulative frequencies

   D... Mid points are plotted against frequencies

23. The graph of a cumulative frequency distribution is called:

   A... a line graph

   B... a histogram

   C... an ogive

24. The difference between a histogram and a bar chart is:

   A... A histogram represents the frequency, whereas a bar chart represents the number.

   B... With a histogram, areas represent frequencies, whereas with a bar chart, heights represents frequencies.

   C... Histograms are used for comparing categorical data.

25. Nominal data is data that:

   A... Is obtained by measurement.

   B... Is obtained by counting.

   C... Does not have a numerical value.

26. A multiple bar chart is used to compare:

    A... Totals

    B... Changes to components

    C... Grouped data

27. A frequency polygon is used in conjunction with a:

    A... Simple bar chart

    B... Component bar chart

    C... Multiple bar chart

    D... Histogram

28. A frequency distribution that has its peak to the left is called:

    A... Left skewed

    B... Symmetrical

    C... Right skewed

PRACTICE QUESTIONS

29. How would you define the following sets of data?

    (a) The number of hours of sunshine each day at a seaside resort

    (b) The mean daily temperature at a seaside resort

    (c) Daily rainfall (in mm)

    (d) Scoring system for ice dancing

30. A survey was carried out into consumers' preference for different types of coffee. A sample of 20 people gave the following replies:

Person	Preference	Person	Preference
1	instant	11	ground
2	filter	12	instant
3	instant	13	ground
4	filter	14	filter
5	instant	15	instant
6	filter	16	instant
7	ground	17	ground
8	instant	18	filter
9	filter	19	instant
10	filter	20	filter

    (a) Aggregate this data into a suitable table.

    (b) Draw a pie chart of the data.

    (c) Draw a simple bar chart of the data.

31. Table 3.13 represents the sales by department of a high street store. Using Excel or otherwise, draw a component bar chart and a multiple bar chart of the sales. What conclusions can you make about the sales for this store?

Table 3.13   Sales information for Question 31

Department	1999	2000	2001
Menswear	£2.7m	£4.9m	£6.3m
Furniture	£3.4m	£2.3m	£1.5m
Household	£2.5m	£2.4m	£2.5m
Total Sales	£8.6m	£9.6m	£10.3m

32. Table 3.14 shows how the sales of Marla plc were broken down between the company's four sales regions during the years 1997 to 2001.

Table 3.14   Sales information for Question 32

Sales Region	Year (Sales £m)				
	1997	1998	1999	2000	2001
S. West	4.0	2.0	2.2	3.6	3.7
South	6.0	4.9	2.5	3.2	3.7
S. East	7.6	9.1	5.2	4.3	4.2
Wales	1.5	1.4	1.4	1.5	1.6
Totals	19.1	17.4	11.3	12.6	13.2

Using Excel or otherwise,

(a) Draw a simple bar chart to show the total sales for the four-year period.

(b) Draw a component bar chart to show the sales for the years and how they were broken down between the four sales regions.

(c) Draw a multiple bar chart to compare the sales for each region.

(d) Draw a pie chart to show the breakdown of total sales in 2001.

(e) What can you conclude about the sales of Marla plc?

33. The data below relates to the weight (in grams) of an item produced by a machine.

28.8   29.2   30.8   29.2   30.2   30.0   26.8   30.6   29.0   27.8   28.6   30.4

30.8   29.2   30.4   29.6   31.4   30.6   31.0   31.4   31.4   30.0   29.0   29.4

29.0   28.0   26.5   29.6   27.0   23.2   25.2   24.5   28.0   27.0   29.4   27.6

26.2   25.3   26.8   25.8   28.2   28.1   30.0   30.0   27.1   26.1   25.4   23.8

22.8   23.5   25.5   24.0   27.0   28.5   27.2   25.5   25.6   24.5   23.5   22.4

25.2   27.4   27.0   28.2   28.0   28.0   25.8   30.4   26.5   25.2   29.3   27.4

22.1   26.2   23.8   24.8   20.5   20.4   24.6   24.8

(a) Aggregate this data into a suitable frequency table.

(b) Draw a histogram of the data.

(c) Draw a frequency polygon of the data.

(d) Draw a cumulative frequency ogive of the data and demonstrate how it could be used to provide further information about the distribution of weights.

(e) What conclusions can be made about the data from your diagrams?

34. The sickness records of a company have been examined and Table 3.15 shows the number of days taken off work through sickness during the past year.

Table 3.15   Information for Question 34

Days off work	Number of employees
Less than 2 days	45
2 to 5 days	89
6 to 9 days	40
10 to 13 days	25
14 to 21 days	5
22 to 29 days	2

Draw a histogram to represent this distribution and comment on its shape.

35. A survey carried out into 605 small and medium-size companies (SMEs) in the South of England revealed the following information on average sales growth during a period of recession.

Table 3.16   Annual average % sales growth (from previous year) by region

Region	No. of companies	1990	1991	1992
South Western	63	17.3	−1.0	2.5
Southern	143	21.1	3.2	2.4
Eastern	77	11.9	7.6	0.6
South Eastern	48	50.5	25.5	−0.7
Outer London	78	17.3	1.7	2.3
Inner London	191	19.1	17.3	12.6

(a) Using Excel, plot the following charts:

(i) A simple bar chart of the number of companies in each region

(ii) A multiple bar chart with year as the x-axis labels

(iii) A multiple bar chart with region as the x-axis labels

(iv) A line graph of the average change in sales growth from 1990 to 1992

(v) A pie chart of the sales growth for each region during 1992

(b) Write a paragraph summarising your charts.

36. A high street store has gathered the following data about the value in £s of purchases made by a sample of 50 customers.

67.00	55.56	85.21	72.33	63.25	58.00	53.00	53.41	73.33	79.21
65.22	53.25	82.10	46.10	56.00	64.16	55.67	57.00	57.00	58.20
43.20	52.30	98.00	57.21	59.62	52.33	57.77	58.20	58.60	61.22
53.40	67.00	66.32	50.10	60.11	45.00	51.20	53.00	78.54	64.00
41.21	78.61	55.55	48.62	59.99	63.54	76.35	77.00	45.50	55.01

(a) Plot a histogram of the data using suitable class intervals and join up the mid points to form a frequency polygon. Describe the shape of the distribution.

(b) Plot a cumulative frequency ogive and find the following:

(i) The percentage of sales in excess of £70

(ii) The percentage of sales between £52 and £72

(iii) The value of purchases that are exceeded by 10% of sales.

ASSIGNMENT

Find examples (at least three) of diagrams in newspapers, company reports and statistical publications. You should write a paragraph on each diagram discussing the following points.

● The conclusions that you can draw from the diagram

● Whether a different diagram would be more informative

● How the diagram could be misleading (if applicable)

4 Summarising data

4.1 Introduction

Although tables and diagrams allow important features of data to be displayed, these methods of summarising the information are generally qualitative rather than quantitative. In order to provide more quantitative information it is necessary to calculate statistical measures that can be used to represent the entire set of data. Two important measures of the data are the location of the data in terms of a typical or central value and the spread or dispersion of the data around this central value. To complete this chapter successfully you should have worked through Chapter 3 (Presentation of data).

At the end of this chapter you should be able to:

- Calculate the mean, median and mode for small sets of data and also for frequency distributions
- Understand the advantages and disadvantages of each type of average
- Understand the need for measures of spread and to be able to use the cumulative frequency ogive to find the interquartile range
- Calculate the standard deviation for small sets of data and for frequency distributions
- Draw and use box and whisker plots

4.2 Measures of location

I am sure that you have heard of the word 'average'. An average is some kind of representative item within a set of possible items. The word 'location' is used because for numerical data, an average 'locates' a typical value of some distribution. This is not as easy as it may seem as there could be several different values that would serve as this average figure.

Example 4.1

The number of sales made by two salespersons over the past few days has been as follows:

Mike: 3, 2, 1, 32, 2, 1, 1
Janet: 0, 1, 4, 12, 10, 7, 8, 6

Activity 4.1

What would be a good measure of the daily number of sales by each salesperson?

Six out of the seven values for Mike are between 1 and 3 sales per day, while for Janet the values are fairly evenly spread between 0 and 12 sales per day. Do you choose one of the existing values to represent the number of sales per day or do you choose a value that is in between?

   There are in fact three different averages and each can give you different values. The next section defines each one and discusses the advantages and disadvantages of each.

4.2.1   The mean, median and mode

① The mean

The *mean* is defined as the sum of all the values divided by the total number of values. So for Mike the mean number of sales per day is:

$$\frac{3 + 2 + 1 + 32 + 2 + 1 + 1}{7} = 6$$

Notice that the mean is a not one of the values in the set of data. (A mean value can also be a fractional value even if the data values are themselves whole numbers.)

   The mean of a set of numbers is normally referred to as $\bar{x}$ (x bar) and in symbols the formula for the mean is:

Sum of the n values

$$\bar{x} = \frac{\sum x}{n}$$

Number of items

Activity 4.2

Find the mean number of sales per day for Janet.

You should have found that the mean for Janet is also 6. Is 6 sales a good measure of average for both data sets? Certainly for Janet a mean of 6 is quite a good representative value, but for Mike a value between 1 and 3 would be more typical. The problem with the

(2) The Median: Middle value

mean is that it gives equal importance to *all* values, including any extreme values. In Mike's case the value of 32 is clearly influencing the mean. The *median* overcomes this problem by choosing the *middle* value of a set of numbers. In order to find this value the data is first ordered in ascending order as follows:

1, 1, 1, 2, 2, 3, 32

The middle value of this set of 7 numbers is 2, which is a more typical value.

Activity 4.3

Find the median sales for Janet.

You should have found a slight problem here in that there is no single middle number. There are two middle numbers though, which are 6 and 7 and in this case you would take the mean of these two numbers which is 6.5. This is close to the mean value of 6, so in this case either of the two averages are equally suitable.

Which is the better average? This is a difficult question to answer as both have their advantages and disadvantages, as you can see in Table 4.1.

Table 4.1 Comparison of mean and median

	Mean	Median
One of the actual data items?	Not usually	Usually
Equal contribution by all data items?	Yes	No
Influenced by extreme values (outliers)?	Yes	No
Easy to calculate?	Yes	No

The mean and median can both be used for numerical data but not for *categorical* data. The next activity illustrates this point.

Activity 4.4

In Chapter 3 data was provided into a travel to work survey. This data is summarised in Table 4.2.

(3) The mode: Common mode of something

Table 4.2 Results of a travel to work survey

Mode of travel	Frequency
Car	9
Bus	4
Cycle	3
Walk	2
Train	2

Which is the most typical mode of travel?

Clearly the car is the most common mode of travel. The category that occurs the most frequently is called the *mode*. The mode can also be quoted for numerical data.

Activity 4.5

What is the mode for the sales data of Example 4.1?

For Mike, 1 sale occurred most frequently so this is the mode for this group of numbers. However, there is no mode for Janet's sales data since each value occurs once only.

    The mode has limited uses but it can be useful when the most common value or category is required. Can you imagine a shoe shop being interested in the mean or median size of shoe?

4.2.2   The mean, median and mode for a frequency distribution

It is relatively straightforward finding an average of a small set of data, but when large quantities of data are involved, or when the data is supplied in the form of a frequency table, the methods of calculation become more involved.

Example 4.2

The ungrouped frequency table in Table 4.3 gives the daily number of sales made by the sales force of a double glazing company.

Table 4.3   Ungrouped frequency table

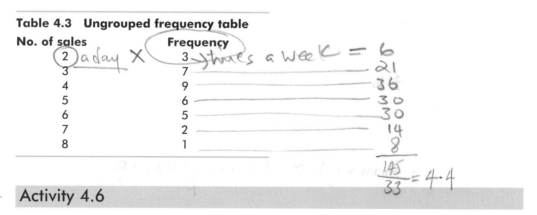

No. of sales	Frequency	
2 (a day) ×	3 (three's a week) =	6
3	7	21
4	9	36
5	6	30
6	5	30
7	2	14
8	1	8
		$\frac{145}{33} = 4.4$

Activity 4.6

What is the mean number of sales made per day by the company's sales force?

The mean could be found by writing the value 2 three times, 3 seven times and so on. You would then add up all the values and divide by the total number of values, which is 33. However, a much easier method is to multiply 2 by 3, 3 by 7 and so on. This will give you the same sum as the longer method. If you let x be the number of sales and f the frequency, the procedure for calculating the mean can be seen in Table 4.4.

Table 4.4 Calculation of the mean

Frequency: how many times the value (number) occurs.

No. of sales x	Frequency f	fx
2	3	6
3	7	21
4	9	36
5	6	30
6	5	30
7	2	14
8	1	8
Total	33	145

The mean is therefore: $\dfrac{145}{33} = 4.4$ sales.

This calculation can be expressed in algebraic notation as follows:

Multiply f by x and sum

$$\bar{x} = \frac{\sum fx}{\sum f}$$

Sum of frequencies

Activity 4.7

What is the median number of sales made per day?

The median for this set of values can be found by remembering that the median is the middle value. Since the data is already in ascending order it is a simple matter of locating the middle value, which will occur at the 17th frequency. If you write down the cumulative frequencies as shown in Table 4.5, you will see that the median must occur when $x = 4$.

Table 4.5 Calculation of the median

x	f	Cumulative f
2	3	3
3	7	10
4	9	19
5	6	25
6	5	30
7	2	32
8	1	33

Modal value

4 most frequent 9

Activity 4.8

What is the modal value of sales?

The modal number of sales is easy to see since 4 sales occurs 9 times, which is the most frequent.

Example 4.3

The group frequency table shown in Table 4.6 refers to the length of 80 bolts produced by a machine.

Table 4.6 Grouped frequency table

Interval	Frequency
30 to under 35 mm	3
35 to under 40 mm	7
40 to under 45 mm	12
45 to under 50 mm	18
50 to under 55 mm	18
55 to under 60 mm	13
60 to under 65 mm	5
65 to under 70 mm	2
70 to under 75 mm	1
75 to under 80 mm	0
80 to under 85 mm	1

highest frequency (modal class)

This is a similar table to that in Example 4.2, except that x does not have a single value. In order to calculate the mean, the *mid value* is used for x. So the mid value for the interval 30 to under 35 would be 32.5 mm. (You can assume that you can get as close as you like to 35 mm.) Although this is an approximation, it is generally a very close one and is normally quite adequate.

Activity 4.9

Calculate the mean for the data in Example 4.3.

Table 4.7 shows how the mean is calculated by making x represent the mid point of the range:

Table 4.7 Calculation of the mean for a frequency distribution

Interval		x	f	fx
30 to under 35 mm	*middle*	32.5	3	97.5
35 to under 40 mm	*value*	37.5	7	262.5
40 to under 45 mm	*of*	42.5	12	510.0
45 to under 50 mm		47.5	18	855.0
50 to under 55 mm	*the*	52.5	18	945.0
55 to under 60 mm		57.5	13	747.5
60 to under 65 mm	*bolts*	62.5	5	312.5
65 to under 70 mm		67.5	2	135.0
70 to under 75 mm		72.5	1	72.5
75 to under 80 mm		77.5	0	0.0
80 to under 85 mm		82.5	1	82.5
	Total		80	4020.0

and the mean is:

$$\frac{4020}{80} = 50.25 \text{ mm}$$

The mean using the raw data is 50.03 mm, so the value obtained using the frequency table is quite a good one. (If you want the check this calculation, the raw data can be found in Example 3.3 of Chapter 3.)

Activity 4.10

What is the median length of a bolt?

The problem with obtaining the median from a grouped frequency table is that the median is likely to lie within an interval. You could locate the required interval and then simply use the mid point as an estimate, but a better approximation is to *interpolate* within the interval. The easiest method is graphical and if a cumulative frequency ogive is drawn the median frequency will be *halfway* up the y-axis. It is often easier to use percentage cumulative frequency, as then the median frequency is 50%. Figure 4.1 is the cumulative frequency ogive for the length of bolts, and you will see that the median is 50 mm, so 50% of bolts are below 50 mm in length and 50% above.

Activity 4.11

What is the modal value of the length of bolts?

It is normal to talk about a *modal class* in a grouped frequency distribution, although it is possible to estimate a single value. The grouped frequency table in Example 4.3 (Table 4.6) suggests that the intervals 45 to under 50 mm and 50 to under 55 mm have the highest

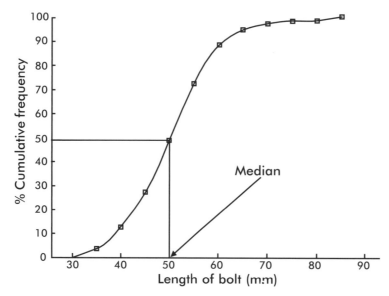

Figure 4.1 Graphical method of obtaining the median

frequency of 18. If these intervals had been separated, the distribution would have said to have been *bimodal*. Since they are together, the modal class is 45 to 55 mm. A single estimate of the modal value could be obtained using the geometric method illustrated in Figure 4.2. You should see that this modal value is approximately 50.5 mm. You might have

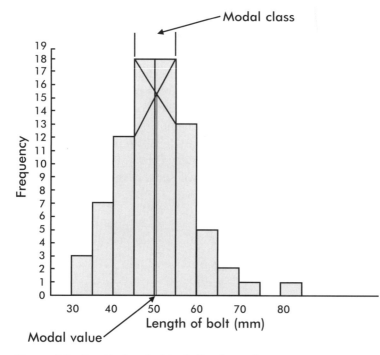

Figure 4.2 Graphical method for finding the mode

noticed that all three averages are very similar. This is because the underlying distribution is approximately *symmetrical*. If the distribution were *right* skewed the mean would be displaced to the *right* of the mode, and if the distribution were *left* skewed the mean would be displaced to the *left* of the mode. The median is between the two but closer to the mean. (Skewness was first discussed in Chapter 3.) Earnings data is a good example of a distribution that is right skewed.

Activity 4.12

The grouped frequency table in Table 4.8 refers to the weight of jars of coffee. What is the average weight of a jar according to this data?

Table 4.8   Grouped frequency table with open classes

Class interval	Frequency
less than 96 g	5
96 to under 98 g	10
98 to under 99 g	15
99 to under 100 g	27
100 to under 102 g	11
more than 102 g	2

The problem with Table 4.8 is the open classes. A mean needs a mid point for each interval, which this data clearly does not have. There is no satisfactory way of calculating the mean for grouped frequency tables with open classes, although some people say you should use the width of the previous or next interval. So the mid point of the first interval

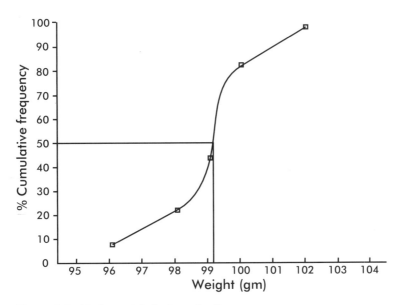

Figure 4.3 Median weight for jars of coffee

would be 95 g and 103 g for the last interval. This approximation *may* be justified if the number of items in the open intervals are small relative to the closed intervals. I think that for open intervals the median is a far better average to use. The median only requires the upper value of each interval and it is not necessary for the ogive to be complete. This is illustrated in Figure 4.3 where you will see that the median is about 99.2 g.

In the calculation of the mean, each value was given an equal weighting. However, there are some circumstances where this is not correct. The next activity illustrates a typical example.

Activity 4.13

The pay rises given to 1000 employees during the year were as follows:

Employee	Pay rise	No. of employees
Manual	1%	700
Clerical	3%	200
Management	8%	100

The company maintains that the average pay rise was 4%. Is this correct?

The company has ignored the fact that the majority of the employees have received 3% or less. To get a better idea of the true average the percentages should be *weighted* by the number of employees in each category, as follows:

$$\frac{1 \times 700 + 3 \times 200 + 8 \times 100}{1000} = 2.1\%$$

This figure is much more representative of the true average pay rise.

4.3 Measures of spread

An average is not always sufficient in describing how a set of data is distributed. The sales data given in Example 4.1 is a typical example. This data has been reproduced below.

Mike:	3, 2, 1, 32, 2, 1, 1
Janet:	0, 1, 4, 12, 10, 7, 8, 6

The mean number of sales per day in both cases was 6, yet the individual figures are quite different. In addition to a measure of location, a measure of *spread* or *dispersion* can also be provided. There are various measures of spread, the simplest is the *range*. The range is the difference between the smallest and largest and for Mike this is $32 - 1 = 31$ sales per day, while for Janet it is $12 - 0 = 12$. So there is a much larger spread in Mike's figures than in Janet's. Unfortunately the range is too easily influenced by extreme values and is not a particularly good measure. Another measure is the *interquartile range* (IQR). To calculate the IQR the data is divided into quarters. If Q_1 is the lower quartile and Q_3 is the upper quartile, then

$$IQR = Q_3 - Q_1$$
(Q_2 is the median)

This method avoids the extremes and thus is more representative than the range. It is normally used with a group frequency table.

Activity 4.14

Calculate the IQR for the data given in Example 4.3.

The easiest method is to draw a cumulative frequency ogive and mark the 25% and 75% limits. This has been done in Figure 4.4 and you will see that the IQR is about $56 - 44 = 12 \, \text{mm}$.

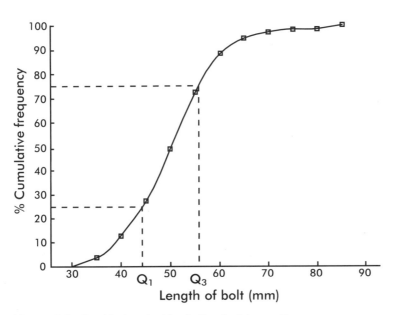

Figure 4.4 Graphical method for finding the interquartile range

Unfortunately this is still not ideal because you are just looking at the middle half of the data and ignoring the rest. A better method is the *standard deviation*.

4.3.1 The standard deviation

A better measure of spread is to calculate the differences between each value and the mean as this will then use all the values. However, you now have as many values as you started with. You could find the average of all these differences, but since some differences

Table 4.9 Calculation of the standard deviation

Sales x	Difference x − 6	Difference squared (x − 6)²
3	−3	9
2	−4	16
1	−5	25
32	26	676
2	−4	16
1	−5	25
1	−5	25
	Total	792

Method ①

will be positive and some negative, you will end up with a mean of zero! You could ignore the negative sign, but a better method (statistically) is to square the differences, as a negative value squared becomes a positive value. If you now average all these squared differences you will end up with an average squared difference. Both the range and IQR were in the same units as the original data, so it would be good if this new measure was also in the same units. This can be arranged by taking the square root of the squared average. This procedure is shown below for Mike's sales data (remember the mean was 6).

$$\text{Mean squared difference} = \frac{792}{7} = 113.1429$$

If we take the square root of this figure we get the standard deviation. That is:

$$\sqrt{113.1429} = 10.6 \text{ sales per day}$$

In algebraic terms the formula for the standard deviation (*s*) is:

sum of the differences squared

Formula ①

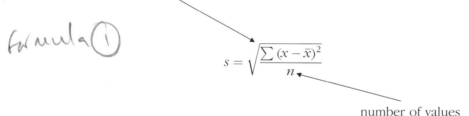

$$s = \sqrt{\frac{\sum (x - \bar{x})^2}{n}}$$

number of values

A slightly simpler formula to use that does not require the mean to be calculated first is:

square the *x*s and sum

Formula ②

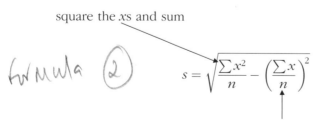

$$s = \sqrt{\frac{\sum x^2}{n} - \left(\frac{\sum x}{n}\right)^2}$$

divide the sum of the *x*s by *n* and then square

Activity 4.15

Calculate the standard deviation for Janet's sales data.

Using the modified formula you should have obtained Table 4.10.

Table 4.10 Calculation of the standard deviation by an alternative formula

x	x^2
0	0
1	1
4	16
12	144
10	100
7	49
8	64
6	36
Totals 48	410

Method ②

$$s = \sqrt{\frac{410}{8} - \left(\frac{48}{8}\right)^2}$$

$$= \sqrt{51.25 - 36}$$

$$= \sqrt{15.25}$$

$$= 3.9 \text{ sales per day}$$

This calculation demonstrates that compared to Mike, Janet has a much smaller variation in her daily number of sales.

Activity 4.16

It has been discovered that a mistake has been made in Janet's sales data given in Example 4.1. Her daily sales are all 3 less than they should be. What should the mean and standard deviation really be?

You should have found the mean to be 9, which is simply 3 more than originally quoted. However, the standard deviation hasn't changed at 3.9. Why is this? This can be explained if you look at Figure 4.5.

The original values have been shifted 3 units to the right. The spread of the new values has not changed so the standard deviation will be the same.

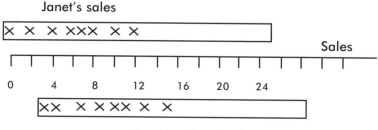

Janet's sales

Janet's sales plus 3

Figure 4.5 Standard deviation remains unchanged

Activity 4.17

If Janet's sales should really be double the figures given in Example 4.1, what would the mean and standard deviation be in this case?

You should have found that both the mean and standard deviation have doubled. By doubling each value the spread has also doubled, as you can see in Figure 4.6.

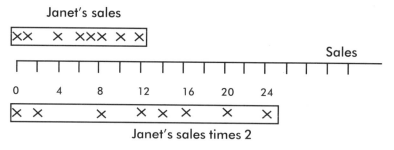

Janet's sales

Janet's sales times 2

Figure 4.6 Standard deviation doubles

4.3.2 The standard deviation for a frequency distribution

A slightly different formula is used for a frequency distribution to reflect the fact that frequencies are involved. The formula normally used is:

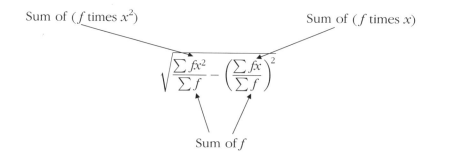

Sum of (f times x^2)   Sum of (f times x)

$$\sqrt{\frac{\sum fx^2}{\sum f} - \left(\frac{\sum fx}{\sum f}\right)^2}$$

Sum of f

Activity 4.18

Calculate the standard deviation of the data in Table 4.6.

The value of x takes the same mid point value as in the calculation of the mean (Activity 4.9). The calculation is shown in Table 4.11.

Table 4.11 Calculation of standard deviation for a frequency distribution

Interval	x	f	fx	x^2	fx^2
30 to under 35 mm	32.5	3	97.5	1056.25	3 168.75
35 to under 40 mm	37.5	7	262.5	1406.25	9 843.75
40 to under 45 mm	42.5	12	510.0	1806.25	21 675.00
45 to under 50 mm	47.5	18	855.0	2256.25	40 612.50
50 to under 55 mm	52.5	18	945.0	2756.25	49 612.50
55 to under 60 mm	57.5	13	747.5	3306.25	42 981.25
60 to under 65 mm	62.5	5	312.5	3906.25	19 531.25
65 to under 70 mm	67.5	2	135.0	4556.25	9 112.50
70 to under 75 mm	72.5	1	72.5	5256.25	5 256.25
75 to under 80 mm	77.5	0	0.0	6006.25	0.00
80 to under 85 mm	82.5	1	82.5	6806.25	6 806.25
Total		80	4020.0		208 600.00

The standard deviation is therefore:

$$\sqrt{\frac{208\,600}{80} - \left(\frac{4020}{80}\right)^2} = \sqrt{2607.5 - 2525.0625}$$

$$= \sqrt{82.4375}$$

$$s = 9.08\,\text{mm}$$

 ## 4.4 Coefficient of variation

If two sets of data have similar means then it is easy to compare the variation by calculating their standard deviations. However, if the means are different then the comparisons of spread will not be so obvious.

 ### Activity 4.19

A hospital is comparing the times patients are waiting for two types of operation. For bypass surgery the mean wait is 17 weeks with a standard deviation of 6 weeks, while for hip replacement the mean is 11 months with a standard deviation of 1 month. Which operation has the highest variability?

The problem here is not only that the means are quite different but also that the units are different (weeks in one case and months in the other). In order to compare the variability the coefficient of variation is calculated. This is defined as:

$$\frac{\text{standard deviation}}{\text{mean}}$$

This is usually expressed as a percentage by multiplying by 100.

For bypass surgery the coefficient of variation is:

$$\frac{6}{17} \times 100 = 35.3\% \quad \text{larger spread/variation}$$

while for hip replacement it is:

$$\frac{1}{11} \times 100 = 9.1\% \quad \text{small spread}$$

Therefore, relative to the mean, the bypass surgery has a larger spread or variation.

4.5 Box and whisker plots

A very useful diagram that summarises information about the location and spread of a set of data is the box and whisker plot. The 'box' represents the middle 50% of the data and the extremities of the box are the quartiles Q_1 and Q_3. The median (Q_2) is marked and will obviously be inside the box. Each 'whisker' represents 25% of the data, and the extremities of the whiskers are the minimum and upper values of the data (or the class intervals).

Activity 4.20

Draw a box and whisker plot for the data given in Table 4.6.

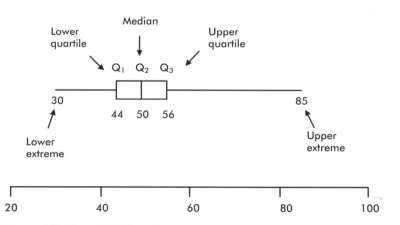

Figure 4.7 Box and whisker plot

The median (Q_2) of this data is 50 mm (see Activity 4.10) and the values of Q_1 and Q_3 are 44 and 56 mm respectively (Activity 4.14). The box and whisker plot is shown in Figure 4.7. Not only does this diagram give you an idea of the average and spread, it also gives tells you about the shape of the distribution of the data. If the box is small compared to the whiskers this indicates a distribution that is bunched in the middle with long tails. A box shifted to one side or the other indicates skewness, as does the position of the median within the box. In the case of the bolt lengths the right hand whisker is slightly longer than the left, suggesting a slight right skewness to the distribution. However, the median is exactly in the middle of the box so this skewness is very small. The box and whisker plot is particularly useful when you have two or more distributions to compare.

4.6 Automatic methods of calculating measures of location and spread

You have probably realised by now that manual methods of calculating statistical measures are tedious and prone to error, particularly when a frequency distribution is involved. An alternative is to use either a scientific calculator or a spreadsheet, such as Excel. However, a word of caution is necessary when you use either of these methods. You will find that your calculator has two standard deviation buttons, which may be labelled $x\sigma_n$ or $x\sigma_{n-1}$ or something similar. In the same way there are two spreadsheet functions that give you the standard deviation. In Excel these area STDEV and STDEVP. The reason for having two standard deviation values is that you may be analysing data that relates to the entire population or you may have sample data. The assumption in this chapter is that we have data relating to a population, in which case you should use the $x\sigma_n$ key or the STDEVP function. In many instances you will be analysing a sample, the purpose of which is to estimate what the population parameters (such as the mean and standard deviation) are likely to be. When we do this the standard deviation will be an underestimate of the true value. This is because the sample is unlikely to contain the full range of values that will be found in the population. To correct for this the denominator in the standard deviation formula is replaced by $n - 1$ and in this case you would use the alternative formula. More about this in Chapter 10.

Activity 4.21

Use the statistical functions on your calculator to find the mean and standard deviation of the data in Example 4.1 (sales figures for Mike and Janet).

Statistical calculators vary both in the way that data is input and the keys that you press to find the required answers. The instructions below refer to the Casio fx83WA and the fx85WA models. These are both popular calculators (the 85WA is a solar/battery powered model) and cost around £10. If you have a different calculator you will need to refer to the instruction book. Whatever the make and model of your calculator, always repeat the calculation as a check that you have input the numbers correctly.

The data values for Mike are 3, 2, 1, 32, 2, 1, 1

Press $\boxed{\text{MODE}}$ $\boxed{2}$ to enter the SD mode.

Press $\boxed{\text{SHIFT}}$ $\boxed{\text{Scl}}$ $\boxed{=}$ to clear the Statistical memory (*Scl* is another function of the red AC button).

Data can now be entered using the data key (*DT*, another function of the *M+* key), in the following way:

3 $\boxed{\text{DT}}$ 2 $\boxed{\text{DT}}$ 1 $\boxed{\text{DT}}$ 32 $\boxed{\text{DT}}$ 2 $\boxed{\text{DT}}$ 1 $\boxed{\text{DT}}$ 1 $\boxed{\text{DT}}$

Press $\boxed{\text{SHIFT}}$ $\boxed{\bar{x}}$ $\boxed{=}$ for the Mean of the data (6)

Press $\boxed{\text{SHIFT}}$ $\boxed{x\sigma_n}$ $\boxed{=}$ for the Standard deviation using n (10.63686313).

Press $\boxed{\text{RCL}}$ $\boxed{\text{C}}$ (NB: this is the 'C' marked in pink, not yellow/blue) for n, the number of values (this is a useful check that you have input all the data).

Now clear the statistical memory and repeat the calculation for Janet's sales figures (0, 1, 4, 12, 10, 7, 8, 6). You should get a mean of 6 sales and a standard deviation of 3.905124838; that is, 3.9 sales.

Activity 4.22

Use the statistical functions on your calculator to find the mean and standard deviation of the data in Table 4.6.

The data in Table 4.6 are a frequency distribution and a calculator is essential for summarising this kind of data. The method used by the Casio fx83WA and fx85WA models is to separate the mid point value and frequency by a semi-colon, which is the same key as the comma. To get the semi-colon you press *SHIFT* and ; as follows:

32.5 $\boxed{\text{SHIFT}}$ $\boxed{;}$ 3 $\boxed{\text{DT}}$

This is repeated for all 11 intervals. (Don't forget to clear the memory first.) The mean and standard deviation is found in the same way as in Activity 4.21. (Mean is 50.25 and standard deviation is 9.079509899; that is, 9.08.)

4.6.1 The use of Excel

A scientific calculator is an essential piece of equipment for calculating the mean and standard deviation of a set of data. However, it is not much help if you want to calculate other statistical measures such as the median and interquartile range. For general statistical manipulation a spreadsheet is highly desirable and is now a fundamental part of a business person's 'toolkit'. Before describing how Excel is used for particular statistical calculations some general details of mathematical operations and statistical functions to be found in this spreadsheet will be described.

FORMULAE

Formulae are a central feature of spreadsheets. They perform operations such as addition, subtraction, multiplication, division, and so on, and comparisons of worksheet values, but they also enable the values in the spreadsheet to be updated simultaneously.

A formula must be identified as such by Excel. To do this you precede the formula expression with an equals sign (=). If the = sign is absent, Excel will assume that the expression is simply text and/or numbers and will display it accordingly.

The *Arithmetic operators* shown in Table 4.12 may be used in your formulae – assume that cell A1 contains the number 6 and B1 contains the number 3.

Table 4.12   Arithmetic operators in Excel

Operator	Formula	Result
+ Addition	=A1+B1	9
− Subtraction	=A1−B1	3
− Negation	= −A1	−6
* Multiplication	=A1*B1	18
/ Division	=A1/B1	2
^ Exponentiation	=A1^B1	216
% Percent	=A1%	.06

In evaluating a formula, Excel will calculate exponents first, then multiplication and division, then addition and subtraction. Where this sequence is not the one you want you should use brackets. The formula =A1+B1*2 would give 12, but =(A1+B1)*2 would give 18.

FUNCTIONS

Functions are special pre-written formulae, which can simplify and shorten formulae in your worksheets, especially those which perform lengthy or complex calculations. For example, instead of typing in the formula =A1+A2+A3+A4, you can use the *SUM* function to build the formula =SUM(A1:A4), where A1:A4 refers to the *range* of cells from A1 to A4. Table 4.13 give a list of some of the more commonly used statistical functions.

Table 4.13   Some statistical functions found in Excel

Syntax	Calculation
=SUM(A1:A6)	Adds the numbers in the cells A1 to A6
=COUNT(A1:A6)	Counts the numbers in cells A1 to A6
=AVERAGE(A1:A6)	Calculates the mean of the numbers in cells A1 to A6
=MEDIAN(A1:A6)	Calculates the median of the numbers in cells A1 to A6
=MODE(A1:A6)	Calculates the mode of the numbers in cells A1 to A6
=QUARTILE(A1:A6,1)	Finds the first quartile of the numbers in cells A1 to A6
=QUARTILE(A1:A6, 3)	Finds the third quartile of the numbers in cells A1 to A6
=MAX(A1:A6)	Finds the maximum of the numbers in cells A1 to A6
=MIN(A1:A6)	Finds the minimum of the numbers in cells A1 to A6
=STDEVP(A1:A6)	Calculates standard deviation using n
=STDEV(A1:A6)	Calculates standard deviation using $n-1$

If you are unsure of the syntax for a function, use the Paste Function button f_x in the standard toolbar. This allows you to select an appropriate function, for which you will then need to supply/confirm cell addresses.

Activity 4.23

The following data sets show the sales made by the 20 staff in the sales department at the head office of Omega Computer Services plc, for the months of August and September 2001. Figures are in £s.

August 01   21 900   12 400   9800   6800   13 050   14 900   15 250   8 900   16 451
13 230   16 450   12 890   13 670   14 700   10 430   11 670   13 200   11 100   19 800
15 700
September 01   12 600   13 500   22 000   34 000   12 500   25 540   21 700   67 800
18 970   16 450   23 220   21 670   17 600   32 420   23 570   14 700   22 400   21 600
26 400   19 700

Use a spreadsheet to summarise both sets of data.

The instructions below assume that you are a novice in the use of Excel and take you through the process of analysing the data in a slow but methodical manner. If you have some experience of Excel you should be able to obtain the answers much faster.

1. USING AUTOSUM
As there are 20 sales staff, enter the numbers 1 to 20 in cells A3 to A22. (The quickest way to do this is to enter the first two numbers and use the autofill facility in Excel.) Enter the data into columns B and C of a new Excel workbook. Label the columns in row 2, and give the worksheet a title in row 1. Save your workbook.

Click on cell B23, below the data in column B. Click on the Autosum button on the standard toolbar. This button is denoted by $\sum$. Excel will enter the formula = *SUM(B3:B22)*. This is a shortcut to the *SUM* function, which could have been typed in.

Click on the tick box in the formula bar, or press the <Enter> key, to enter the formula and perform the calculation. The sum of the sales for August will now appear in cell B23.

2. USING FORMULAE
In cell D3 enter the formula =*(B3+C3)/2*, and press <Enter>. The mean of the sales figures for the first person over the 2 months should be calculated and will appear in cell D3.

3. COPYING FORMULAE
With the cursor still in D3, drag the marker at the bottom right of the cell, down to D22. This will copy the formula to all the rows, to calculate the means for all the salespeople. Select cell D4 and look at the formula. You will notice that it has changed so that it is *relative* to row 3.

Copy the formula from B23, to C23, to obtain the sum of the sales figures for September. Now enter a row heading in cell A23, and a column heading in cell D2 to indicate the meaning of the calculated figures. Highlight cells B3 to D23 then *Format*, *Cells*, *Currency* (with no decimal places) and *OK*. Your worksheet should look like the one in Figure 4.8.

	A	B	C	D	E
1		Sales of Omega			
2	**Sales person**	**Aug-00**	**Sep-00**	**Mean sales**	
3	1	£21,900	£12,600	£17,250	
4	2	£12,400	£13,500	£12,950	
5	3	£9,800	£22,000	£15,900	
6	4	£6,800	£34,000	£20,400	
7	5	£13,050	£12,500	£12,775	
8	6	£14,900	£25,540	£20,220	
9	7	£15,250	£21,700	£18,475	
10	8	£8,900	£67,800	£38,350	
11	9	£16,451	£18,970	£17,711	
12	10	£13,230	£16,450	£14,840	
13	11	£16,450	£23,220	£19,835	
14	12	£12,890	£21,670	£17,280	
15	13	£13,670	£17,600	£15,635	
16	14	£14,700	£32,420	£23,560	
17	15	£10,430	£23,570	£17,000	
18	16	£11,670	£14,700	£13,185	
19	17	£13,200	£22,400	£17,800	
20	18	£11,100	£21,600	£16,350	
21	19	£19,800	£26,400	£23,100	
22	20	£15,700	£19,700	£17,700	
23	**Total sales**	£272,291	£468,340		
24					

Figure 4.8 The data added to the Excel worksheet

4. RELATIVE AND ABSOLUTE CELL ADDRESSES

If you want a particular cell address to remain constant when copied, you need to call it '$A$6', for example, instead of A6. Wherever the formula was copied to, it would still then contain a reference to cell A6.

In cell E2 type the heading 'Commission in August'. In cell E1 type 'Commission rate' and in F1 type '1%'. This is the percentage commission each salesperson gets on his or her monthly sales. In cell E3 enter the formula =B3*F1 using the cursor to point to the cells B3 and F1 instead of typing in the cell references. Cell E3 will display the first person's commission for August.

Copy the formula to E4, and notice that it no longer works because the cell reference F1 is a *relative cell address* and therefore moves as the formula is copied. Edit the formula in cell E3 to make it '$F$1', then copy to the rest of column E. The cell reference '$F$1' is now an *absolute cell address* and therefore will not move as the formula is copied. Pressing the function key *F4* will convert a cell address from relative to absolute and vice versa.

5. MEASURES OF LOCATION

Use the *AVERAGE* function in cell B24, the *MEDIAN* function in cell B25, and the *MODE* function in cell B26, to calculate the mean, median and mode sales values for August. You can drag the cursor across a range of cells to specify the range in a formula.
Label the rows in column A.

Copy the formulae you have just created into cells C24, C25 and C26.

6. FUNCTIONS FOR MEASURES OF DISPERSION

Use the *STDEVP* function to calculate the standard deviation of the August and September sales, in row 27.

Use a formula to calculate the coefficient of variation for the months August and September in row 28.

	A	B	C	D	E	F	G
1		Sales of Omega			Commission rate	1%	
2	Sales person	Aug-00	Sep-00	Mean sales	Commission in August		
3	1	£21,900	£12,600	£17,250	£219		
4	2	£12,400	£13,500	£12,950	£124		
5	3	£9,800	£22,000	£15,900	£98		
6	4	£6,800	£34,000	£20,400	£68		
7	5	£13,050	£12,500	£12,775	£131		
8	6	£14,900	£25,540	£20,220	£149		
9	7	£15,250	£21,700	£18,475	£153		
10	8	£8,900	£67,800	£38,350	£89		
11	9	£16,451	£18,970	£17,711	£165		
12	10	£13,230	£16,450	£14,840	£132		
13	11	£16,450	£23,220	£19,835	£165		
14	12	£12,890	£21,670	£17,280	£129		
15	13	£13,670	£17,600	£15,635	£137		
16	14	£14,700	£32,420	£23,560	£147		
17	15	£10,430	£23,570	£17,000	£104		
18	16	£11,670	£14,700	£13,185	£117		
19	17	£13,200	£22,400	£17,800	£132		
20	18	£11,100	£21,600	£16,350	£111		
21	19	£19,800	£26,400	£23,100	£198		
22	20	£15,700	£19,700	£17,700	£157		
23	Total sales	£272,291	£468,340				
24	Mean sales	£13,615	£23,417				
25	Median sales	£13,215	£21,685				
26	Modal sales	#N/A	#N/A				
27	Standard deviation	£3,457	£11,652				
28	Coefficient of variation	25.4%	49.8%				
29	Lower quartile	£11,528	£17,313				
30	Upper quartile	£15,363	£24,063				
31	IQR	£3,835	£6,750				

Figure 4.9 The completed worksheet

Use the QUARTILE function to calculate the upper and lower quartiles for both sets of data, in rows 29 and 30.

Calculate the Interquartile ranges, in row 31.

The completed worksheet is shown in Figure 4.9.

7. DISPLAYING FORMULAE

Formulae may be displayed in the worksheet by selecting *Tools, Options, View*. Under *Window Options*, tick *Formulae*.

The worksheet will now look like the one in Figure 4.10, and both versions can be printed out if desired.

	A	B	C	D	E
1		Sales of Omega			Commission rate
2	Sales person	36739	36770	Mean sales	Commission in August
3	1	21900	12600	=(B3+C3)/2	=B3*$F$1
4	2	12400	13500	=(B4+C4)/2	=B4*$F$1
5	3	9800	22000	=(B5+C5)/2	=B5*$F$1
6	4	6800	34000	=(B6+C6)/2	=B6*$F$1
7	5	13050	12500	=(B7+C7)/2	=B7*$F$1
8	6	14900	25540	=(B8+C8)/2	=B8*$F$1
9	7	15250	21700	=(B9+C9)/2	=B9*$F$1
10	8	8900	67800	=(B10+C10)/2	=B10*$F$1
11	9	16451	18970	=(B11+C11)/2	=B11*$F$1
12	10	13230	16450	=(B12+C12)/2	=B12*$F$1
13	11	16450	23220	=(B13+C13)/2	=B13*$F$1
14	12	12890	21670	=(B14+C14)/2	=B14*$F$1
15	13	13670	17600	=(B15+C15)/2	=B15*$F$1
16	14	14700	32420	=(B16+C16)/2	=B16*$F$1
17	15	10430	23570	=(B17+C17)/2	=B17*$F$1
18	16	11670	14700	=(B18+C18)/2	=B18*$F$1
19	17	13200	22400	=(B19+C19)/2	=B19*$F$1
20	18	11100	21600	=(B20+C20)/2	=B20*$F$1
21	19	19800	26400	=(B21+C21)/2	=B21*$F$1
22	20	15700	19700	=(B22+C22)/2	=B22*$F$1
23	Total sales	=SUM(B3:B22)	=SUM(C3:C22)		
24	Mean sales	=AVERAGE(B3:B22)	=AVERAGE(C3:C22)		
25	Median sales	=MEDIAN(B3:B22)	=MEDIAN(C3:C22)		
26	Modal sales	=MODE(B3:B22)	=MODE(C3:C22)		
27	Standard deviation	=STDEVP(B3:B22)	=STDEVP(C3:C22)		
28	Coefficient of variation	=B27/B24	=C27/C24		
29	Lower quartile	=QUARTILE(B3:B22,1)	=QUARTILE(C3:C22,1)		
30	Upper quartile	=QUARTILE(B3:B22,3)	=QUARTILE(C3:C22,3)		
31	IQR	=B30-B29	=C30-C29		

Figure 4.10 The Excel worksheet with the formulae shown

Activity 4.24

What does the N/A mean for the mode in the last Activity?

The mode is the value that occurs most frequently. As all the values are different then the data does not have a mode. Excel will give N/A when this occurs.

Activity 4.25

What do the values of the mean and median tell you about the shape of the distribution of data?

If you look at the results you will see that the mean for both months is greater than the median. This means that the distribution is right skewed.

Activity 4.26

Which month has the greatest spread of data?

The standard deviation in September is greater than in August, but then so is the mean. If you look at the coefficient of variation you will see that this statistic is twice as large in September, so this is evidence that there is more variation in this month. The interquartile range is also nearly twice the value in September.

4.7 Summary

In this chapter you have seen the importance of calculating measures of location and spread for sets of data. The mean, median and mode each have their uses in describing the location of data. The mean is easier to calculate than the median but can be distorted by extreme values. The median is the middle value of a set of data that has been ordered in ascending data and is usually one of the data values. The easiest method of finding the median for a frequency distribution is to plot an ogive. The mode is less useful than either the mean or the median, but can be a good measure if you want to know the most common value or interval of a set of data. The mean, median and mode will be equal for a symmetrical distribution, but for a right skewed distribution the mean and median will be greater than the mode, and for a left skewed distribution they will be less than the mode. As well as an average, it is useful to be able to give some indication of the spread or dispersion of a set of data. The range is the simplest measure, but a better measure is the interquartile range. The IQR uses the middle 50% of the data and is therefore less influenced by extreme values. The standard deviation represents the average deviation from the mean and is the universally accepted measure of spread. If you want to compare the spread of two or more distributions it is useful to compare the coefficient of variation, as this takes into account differences in the mean. Finally, this chapter introduced you to a box and whisker plot, which is a very good way of summarising the information on location and spread of a frequency distribution.

4.8 Further reading

Burton, G., Carrol, G. and Wall, S. (1999) *Quantitative Methods for Business and Economics*, Longman, New York (Chapter 2).
Morris, C. (2000) *Quantitative Approaches in Business Studies*, fifth edition, Pitman, London (Chapter 6).

4.9 EXERCISES

The answers to the progress questions, the multiple choice questions and some of the practice questions are given in Appendix 1. Solutions to the remaining questions and the assignment can be found at the web site for this text.

PROGRESS QUESTIONS

These questions have been designed to help you remember the key points in this chapter.

Give the missing word in each case:

1. The mean is the .... of all the values divided by the number of values.
2. The median is the .... value once the values have been arranged in ascending order.
3. The mode is the value that occurs most ....
4. The .... is the simplest measure of spread.
5. The interquartile range represents the middle .... % of the data.
6. The standard deviation represents the mean .... from the mean.
7. The coefficient of variation is the ratio of the .... to the mean.
8. A box and whisker plot allows the .... of the distribution to be observed.

ANSWER *TRUE* OR *FALSE*

9. The mean is usually one of the data values.
10. The mean is easy to calculate.
11. The median divides the data exactly in half.
12. The modal class is the middle of a distribution.
13. A symmetrical distribution always has a mean and median with the same value.
14. To calculate the mean of grouped data it is necessary to 'sum the mid-interval values, multiply by the total of the frequencies and then divide by the total frequency'.

REVIEW QUESTIONS

These questions have been designed to help you check your comprehension of the key points in this chapter. You may wish to look further than this chapter in order to answer them fully. You will find the reading list useful in this respect. You can check the essential elements of your answers by referring to the appropriate section.

15. Compare and contrast the essential differences of the 3 types of average. (Section 4.2)
16. What does the standard deviation tell you about a set of data? (Section 4.3.1)
17. What information does a box and whisker plot give you? (Section 4.5)

MULTIPLE CHOICE QUESTIONS

Questions 18 to 25 refer to the series 3, 1, 4, 2, 3 represented by x.

18. The value of $\sum x^2$ is:

  A... 39   B... 390   C... 1521

19. The value of $(\sum x)^2$ is:

    A... 1521   B... 39   C... 169

20. The MEAN of the series is:

    A... 2.6   B... 3.0   C... 20.6

21. The MEDIAN of the series is:

    A... 2.6   B... 3.0   C... 20.6

22. The RANGE of the series is:

    A... 3   B... 5   C... 8

23. The STANDARD DEVIATION (to 1 decimal place) of the series is:

    A... 3.0   B... 1.0   C... 2.6

24. The COEFFICIENT OF VARIATION (to 1 decimal place) is:

    A... 27.6%   B... 362.4%   C... 39.2%

25. If the number 10 is added to each value of x, the STANDARD DEVIATION of the series is:

    A... 3.0   B... 1.0   C... 2.6   D... 2.0

26. If a distribution has a positive (right) skew, and one mode, then

    A... Mode is greater than the Mean

    B... Mean is less than the Median

    C... Median = Mode

    D... Mean is greater than the Mode

27. What is the approximate value of the interquartile range from the following box plot?

    0   10   20

    A... 8   B... 19   C... 3   D... 5

    The following data are for use in Questions 28 to 30.

    The commission earned by 6 employees in a particular week was as follows:

    £50   £120   £25   £80   £25   £175

28. The mean value of commission to 2 decimal places is:

    A... £65.00   B... £80.00   C... £52.50   D... £25.00   E... £79.17

29. The standard deviation (using n) to 2 decimal places is:

    A... £150.00   B... £125.00   C... £54.12   D... £59.28   E... £6.00

30. The median is:

    A... £65   B... £52.50   C... £80   D... £50

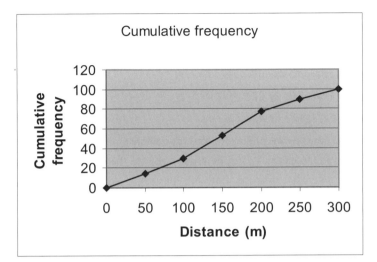

Figure 4.11 Cumulative frequency ogive for Question 31

31. Figure 4.11 represents the distribution of distance travelled to work per week, for 100 workers. Which of the following statements is true?

A... Approximately 40 workers travel 126 miles

B... Approximately 77 workers travel more than 200 miles

C... Approximately 100 workers travel at least 29 miles

D... Approximately 29 workers travel less than 100 miles

The following table refers to Questions 32 and 33. It shows the number of timetabled activities per week for 50 students.

Days timetabled/week	Number of students
1	4
2	8
3	12
4	18
5	8

32. The mean number of days timetabled/week is:

A... 3.36   B... 10   C... 1.16   D... 3

33. The standard deviation (using n) for the number of days timetabled/week is:

A... 3.36   B... 10   C... 1.16   D... 3

PRACTICE QUESTIONS

34. The weekly gross pay of 5 employees was as follows:

£160.24, £183.56, £155.00, £274.50, £174.34

(a) Calculate the mean and median of the data. Which average may be more appropriate, and why?

(b) Calculate the standard deviation of the data.

(c) Recalculate the mean and standard deviation if:

    (i) each value is increased by £20

    (ii) each value is increased by 5%

35. The weighting given to coursework and exam for a quantitative methods course at a university is 40% coursework and 60% exam. If a student gets 74% for the coursework and 56% in the exam, what would be his or her average mark for the unit?

36. The average lifetime for 12 light bulbs is 180.6 hours. Another light bulb gave a lifetime of 200 hours. What would the mean lifetime be if this result was included?

37. The sickness records of a company have been examined and Table 4.14 shows the number of days taken off work through sickness during the past year.

Table 4.14 Data for Question 37

Days off work	Number of employees
Less than 2 days	45
2 to 5 days	89
6 to 9 days	40
10 to 13 days	25
14 to 21 days	5
22 to 29 days	2

(a) What is the mean number of days off work?

(b) What is the median number of days off work?

(c) What is the modal number of days off work?

(d) What is the interquartile range?

(e) What is the standard deviation?

(f) What is the coefficient of variation?

(g) Draw a box and whisker plot and comment on the shape of the distribution.

38. Items are manufactured to the same nominal length on two different machines, A and B. A number of items from each machine are measured and the results are shown in Table 4.15.

Table 4.15 Data for Question 38

Class interval (mm)	Frequency Machine A	Machine B
20 to under 22	5	2
22 to under 24	12	5
24 to under 26	26	20
26 to under 28	11	25
28 to under 30	3	8
30 to under 32	0	2

(a) Find the mean, median and modal values for the two machines.

(b) Find the interquartile range and standard deviation for both machines.

(c) Calculate the coefficient of variation for both machines.

(d) Draw a box and whisker plot for both machines.

(e) Use your results from (a) to (d) to comment on the lengths of items produced by both machines.

39. Table 4.16 shows the wages paid last week to 45 part-time employees of a supermarket chain. Find the mean and the median wage.

Table 4.16   Data for Question 39

Wages (£s)	No. of employees
20 to under 30	2
30 to under 40	4
40 to under 50	6
50 to under 60	12
60 to under 70	11
70 to under 80	9
80 to under 90	1
	45

40. A company is involved in wage negotiations with the trade unions. The current gross weekly wages of the company's employees are summarised in the frequency table (Table 4.17).

Table 4.17   Data for Question 40

Gross weekly wages (£s)	No. of employees
90 to under 110	14
110 to under 140	54
140 to under 160	16
160 to under 200	12
200 to under 240	2
	98

Two proposals are on the table:

Proposal 1: Give the employees an increase in pay equivalent to 10% of the current mean weekly wage.

Proposal 2: Give the employees an increase in pay equivalent to 12.5% of the current median weekly wage.

Compare the costs of the two proposals.

41. A firm purchases four main raw materials. Recently, the prices of these raw materials have increased by the percentages indicated in Table 4.18. This table also shows the estimated amount the company will spend per month on each raw material. The purchasing manager of the company has calculated that the average increase in raw material prices is 15%. Can you find an average that reflects more accurately the increase in costs that the company is likely to incur?

Table 4.18 Data for Question 41

Raw Material	% increase in price	Mean expenditure per month (£)
Lead	10	3000
Copper	4	1000
Zinc	0	650
Adhesives	46	350

42. The production target of a manufacturer is 300 widgets per week. In the first ten weeks production has averaged 284.7 per week. What average must be reached in the final three weeks of the quarter for the original target to be achieved?

43. A salesperson travels 100 miles to Exeter at an average speed of 80 mph. She then returns home at a more leisurely 60 mph. What was the average speed over the 200 miles covered? (No, its not 70 mph!)

44. Miracle Fashions has recorded the sales made during a particular day and these are shown in Table 4.19.

Table 4.19 Data for Question 44

Value of sales (£)	Number of sales in this range
5 to less than 10	50
10 to less than 20	75
20 to less than 30	45
30 to less than 40	38
40 to less than 60	27
60 to less than 100	18

(a) Using your calculator's statistical mode or a spreadsheet, estimate:

   (i) the total sales (in £) during this day
   (ii) the mean value of sales
   (iii) the standard deviation of the value of sales
   (iv) the coefficient of variation of the value of sales

(b) Why are your answers in part (a) only estimates?

(c) A fashion shop across the road has also carried out similar calculations and its coefficient of variation of the value of sales is 40%.

   (i) What can you deduce about the distribution of the value of sales between the two shops?
   (ii) Is this other shop likely to be more or less expensive than Miracle Fashions?

(d) Using the data in the table, draw a percentage cumulative frequency ogive, and from your ogive deduce:

   (i) the median value of sales
   (ii) the interquartile range of the value of sales
   (iii) the percentage of sales that were over £50

ASSIGNMENT

A large bakery regularly takes samples of bread in order to ensure that its product meets quality specifications. Each loaf that is sampled is first weighed, and weight records of 765 'standard' sliced loaves have accumulated over the last few months. The Quality Control Manager would like these records analysed and has aggregated the data into the frequency table shown below (Table 4.20).

Table 4.20 Data for the assignment

Weight range	Number of loaves in this range
780 g to below 790 g	34
790 g to below 795 g	80
795 g to below 800 g	111
800 g to below 805 g	162
805 g to below 810 g	161
810 g to below 815 g	120
815 g to below 820 g	70
820 g to below 830 g	27

Analyse these figures and write a report to the quality control manager. Your analysis should include graphs, diagrams and measures of location and spread of the data.

5 Index numbers

5.1 Introduction

An index is a means of comparing changes in some variable, often price, over time. This is particularly useful when there are many items involved and the prices and quantities are in different units. The most well known index is the retail price index. This index compares the price of a 'basket' of goods from one month to another and is used as a measure of inflation. This chapter looks at the construction and use of different types of indices.

At the end of this chapter you should be able to:

- Calculate a simple one item index
- Calculate the Laspeyres' index
- Calculate the Paasche's index
- Understand how the retail price index is calculated and be able to use it to deflate financial data

5.2 Simple indices

Example 5.1

The price of an item and quantity sold have varied over the past 5 years as follows (Table 5.1):

Table 5.1   Information for Example 5.1

Year	Price	Quantity
1997	£6.00	2500
1998	£6.20	3500
1999	£5.52	3800
2000	£6.95	2000
2001	£8.82	3200

Since 1997 the item has gone up in price by £2.82. But how much has it gone up *relative* to the price in 1997? If 1997 is used as a *base* then it is possible to compare changes in price with this base. The base is given a value of 100 so that a price increase would result in a value above 100 while a price decrease would result in a value less than 100. If £6.00 is equivalent to 100, then £8.82 is equivalent to:

$$\frac{100}{6} \times 8.82 = 147$$

The value 147 is called the *price index* and 1997 is the *base year*. If p_n represents the current year (year n) and p_0 represents the base year, then the price index is:

$$\frac{100}{p_0} \times p_n$$

Or normally it is expressed as:

$$\frac{p_n}{p_0} \times 100$$

Activity 5.1

Using the data in Example 5.1, calculate the price index for each year.

The table you should have obtained is as follows (Table 5.2):

Table 5.2   Price index for Activity 5.1

Year	Price index
1997	100
1998	103
1999	92
2000	116
2001	147

(The figures have been rounded to the nearest whole number)

As well as price, the quantity sold has varied over the year, so a *quantity index* could also be calculated. If q_n represents the current year and q_0 represents the base year, the quantity index is given by:

$$\frac{q_n}{q_0} \times 100$$

So the quantity index for 2001 using 1997 as the base year is:

$$\frac{3200}{2500} \times 100 = 128$$

Activity 5.2

Calculate the quantity index for each year.

You should have obtained the following table (Table 5.3):

Table 5.3 Quantity index for Activity 5.2

Year	Quantity index
1997	100
1998	140
1999	152
2000	80
2001	128

It is rare to calculate an index for just one item; usually you will have several items, as seen in Example 5.2 below.

Example 5.2

The resources used in the manufacture of glass-fibre boats include resin, glass-fibre mat and labour. The price of each of these resources varies and the average price during each of the years 1999 to 2001 is shown in Table 5.4.

Table 5.4 Price data for Example 5.2

Item	1999	2000	2001
Resin	£0.25/l	£0.20/l	£0.18/l
Mat	£0.16/m^2	£0.16/m^2	£0.20/m^2
Labour	£5.50/hour	£5.85/hour	£8.30/hour

Activity 5.3

Calculate the index for each item using 1999 as the base year.

You should have obtained the following table (Table 5.5):

Table 5.5 Price index for Activity 5.3

Item	1999	2000	2001
Resin	100	80	72
Mat	100	100	125
Labour	100	106	151

You can see that the index for resin has shown a decrease while labour has shown the largest increase. But what does this tell you about the cost of production? Is it possible to combine the data in some way so that an aggregate index can be obtained?

Activity 5.4

Could you obtain an aggregate index simply by adding the prices together for each year?

There are two problems with this approach: first, the items are in different units; you have litres, square metres and hours; and second, the importance of each item might be different. If labour is the dominant cost then the aggregate index should reflect this fact. To overcome these problems each item is weighted according to its importance. When this is done you have a *weighted aggregate index.*

5.3 Weighted aggregate indices

In order to weight an index it is necessary to have information on the importance of each item. For the boat example, this could be done by recording the quantities used in its production.

Example 5.3

The quantities required in the production of a boat vary from year to year as production methods change. This can be seen in the Table 5.6.

Table 5.6 Quantity data for Example 5.3

Item	1999	2000	2001
Resin	50l	48l	48l
Mat	200m^2	210m^2	215m^2
Labour	30 hours	27 hours	23 hours

Activity 5.5

How might you use the information in Examples 5.2 and 5.3 to create an aggregate index?

Since price × quantity equals the cost of that item, the aggregate index could be obtained as:

$$\frac{\text{Total cost of production at current prices}}{\text{Total cost of production at base year prices}}$$

There is, however, one problem with this definition. What quantities should we use? Both price and quantities have varied from year to year and for comparison purposes we need to use the same quantities for the numerator and denominator of the index. The choice is to use either the base year quantities or the current year quantities. When you use the former you have a base weighted or *Laspeyres'* index, and when you use the latter you have a current weighted or *Paasche's* index.

5.3.1 Laspeyres' index

The definition of the Laspeyres' index is:

$$\frac{\text{Total cost of base year quantities at current prices}}{\text{Total cost of base year quantities at base year prices}}$$

Using p to represent price and q to represent quantity, this definition can be expressed as:

Sum of current prices times base quantities

$$\text{Laspeyres' index} = \frac{\sum p_n q_0}{\sum p_0 q_0} \times 100$$

Sum of base prices times base quantities

In order to calculate this index for the boat example, you may find it useful to write the data from Examples 5.2 and 5.3 into another table (Table 5.7).

Table 5.7 Price and quantity combined

Item	1999		2000		2001	
	Price	**Qty**	**Price**	**Qty**	**Price**	**Qty**
Resin	£0.25	50	£0.20	48	£0.18	48
Mat	£0.16	200	£0.16	210	£0.20	215
Labour	£5.50	30	£5.85	27	£8.30	23

Activity 5.6

Calculate the Laspeyres' index for 2000 and 2001 using 1999 as the base year.

Each year needs to be calculated separately. These calculations are tabulated in Tables 5.8 and 5.9.

Table 5.8 Calculation of Laspeyres' index for 2000

p_0	q_0	p_n	$p_0 q_0$	$p_n q_0$
0.25	50	0.20	12.5	10
0.16	200	0.16	32	32
5.50	30	5.85	165	175.5
		Sum	209.5	217.5

$$\frac{p_n q_0}{p_0 q_0} \times 100 = \frac{217.5}{209.5} \times 100$$

Table 5.9 Calculation of Laspeyres' index for 2001

p_0	q_0	p_n	p_0q_0	p_nq_0
0.25	50	0.18	12.5	9
0.16	200	0.20	32	40
5.50	30	8.30	165	249
		Sum	209.5	298

So the Laspeyres' index for 2000 $= \dfrac{217.5}{209.5} \times 100 = 103.8$

and for 2001 it is $= \dfrac{298}{209.5} \times 100 = 142.2$

You can see from these calculations that there has been a dramatic increase in the index from 2000 to 2001. This was due to the large increase in labour costs that took place during this period.

5.3.2 Paasche's index

The definition of the Paasche's index is:

$$\frac{\text{Total cost of current year quantities at current prices}}{\text{Total cost of current year quantities at base year prices}}$$

This can again be expressed in algebraic form as:

Sum of current prices times current quantities

$$\text{Paasche's index} = \frac{\sum p_nq_n}{\sum p_0q_n} \times 100$$

Sum of base prices times current quantities

Activity 5.7

Calculate the Paasche's index for the boat building example.

A table can again be used in the calculation. For 2000 the calculations are shown in Table 5.10.

Table 5.10 Calculation of Paasche's index for 2000

p_n	q_n	p_n	p_0q_n	p_nq_n
0.25	48	0.20	12	9.6
0.16	210	0.16	33.6	33.6
5.50	27	5.85	148.5	158.0
		Sum	194.1	201.2

So the Paasche's index for 2000 $= \dfrac{201.2}{194.1} \times 100 = 103.7$

If you repeat these calculations for 2001 you should find that the sum of p_0q_n is 172.9 and the sum of p_nq_n is 242.54. So the Paasche's index for 2001 is:

$$\dfrac{242.54}{172.9} \times 100 = 140.3$$

Both indices give similar results for this data and in general there will not be a great difference between the two unless the weights (quantities) are very different. Table 5.11 summarises the advantages and disadvantages of each index.

Table 5.11 Comparison of the two indices

	Laspeyres' index	Paasche's index
Ease of calculation	Denominator only calculated once	Denominator recalculated each year
Quantities required each year	No, only base quantities required	Yes
Comparability	Direct comparison from year to year	No direct comparison
Accuracy	Weights quickly become out of date	Reflects consumption patterns in current year

In practice the Laspeyres' index is the most commonly used index and the base year is redefined at regular intervals. When the base year is redefined it is a good idea to recalculate the index for previous years. For example, the figures below represent an index for the years 1994 to 2002. The base year was 1994 but it has been decided to change the base year to 1993.

1994	1995	1996	1997	1998	1999	2000	2001	2002
100	105.6	108.9	121.2	142.3	145.1	147.9	148.8	153.1

The index in 1994 becomes

$$\dfrac{100}{153.1} \times 100 = 65.3$$

Activity 5.8

Calculate the index for each subsequent year.

You should have obtained the following figures:

1994	1995	1996	1997	1998	1999	2000	2001	2002
65.3	69.0	71.1	79.2	92.9	94.8	96.6	97.2	100

5.4 Retail price index

Unless you live on a desert island you almost certainly have come across the retail price index or RPI. This measures the change in the price of a 'basket' of goods and is used to measure the level of domestic inflation. This index covers some 600 or so items divided into 14 groups. Each group and each item within a group is given a weight that is designed to reflect the importance of that item. The weights are updated annually by the *Family expenditure survey* and prices of this basket of goods are checked each month.

The RPI can be used to compute the *real* change in earnings or expenditure.

Example 5.4

A company's turnover (in £m) since 1987 has been as follows:

1995	1996	1997	1998	1999	2000
2.3	3.3	4.1	4.2	4.4	4.7

It looks as if turnover has been steadily increasing, but at the same time the RPI has also been increasing. The average value of the RPI since 1995 has been as follows:

1995	1996	1997	1998	1999	2000
149.1	152.7	157.5	162.9	165.4	170.3

(Source: *Monthly Digest of Statistics*)

To calculate the real turnover, the turnover figures are *deflated* as follows:

$$1996: 3.3 \times \frac{149.1}{152.7} = 3.22$$

so a turnover of £3.3m is equivalent to £3.2m at 1995 prices.

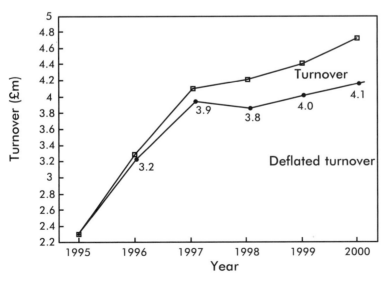

Figure 5.1 Graph for Activity 5.9

Activity 5.9

Calculate the real turnover for the remainder of the years.

You should have obtained the figures shown below:

1995	1996	1997	1998	1999	2000
2.3	3.2	3.9	3.8	4.0	4.1

The picture is now one of increasing turnover until 1997 and then a drop before partially recovering in 2000. This can be seen better in Figure 5.1.

5.5 Summary

This chapter has introduced you to the idea of a index. For a single item or variable a simple index can be used, but if you are monitoring several items then it is necessary to use a weighted aggregate index. There are two main weighted indices: the Laspeyres' index, which is a base weighted index, and the Paasche's index, which is a current weighted index. The Laspeyres' index is easier to use but soon gets out of date, while the Paasche's index reflects consumption patterns in the current year. The retail price index uses consumption patterns as weights and is derived from a family expenditure survey. The RPI is used as a measure of inflation and allows financial data to be deflated.

5.6 Further reading

Burton, G., Carrol, G. and Wall, S. (1999) *Quantitative Methods for Business and Economics*, Longman, New York (Chapter 8).

Morris, C. (2000) *Quantitative Approaches in Business Studies*, fifth edition, Pitman, London (Chapter 7).

5.7 EXERCISES

The answers to the progress questions, the multiple choice questions and some of the practice questions are given in Appendix 1. Solutions to the remaining questions and the assignment can be found at the web site for this text.

PROGRESS QUESTIONS

These questions have been designed to help you remember the key points in this chapter.

Give the missing word in each case:

1. The base year has an index of ...1.0.0.....
2. A simple index is where you have only ..single.. item or variable to monitor.

3. The Laspeyres' index is an example of a ..b.a.s.e. weighted index.
4. The Paasche's index is an example of a Current weighted index.
5. The weights used in the RPI are derived from the .family expenditure survey.
6. The RPI is updated each ..Month

ANSWER *TRUE* OR *FALSE*

7. The Laspeyres' index is easier to calculate. True
8. The Laspeyres' index requires quantities as well as prices to be obtained each year. F
9. You cannot directly compare years with the Paasche's index. F
10. It is not possible to have an index below 100. F

REVIEW QUESTIONS

These questions have been designed to help you check your comprehension of the key points in this chapter. You may wish to look further than this chapter in order to answer them fully. You will find the reading list useful in this respect. You can check the essential elements of your answers by referring to the appropriate section.

11. What are the essential differences between the Laspeyres' index and the Paasche's index? (Section 5.3)
12. What weights are used in the RPI index, and how are they obtained? (Section 5.4)
13. What is meant by the term 'deflated figures', and what is the purpose of it? (Section 5.4)

MULTIPLE CHOICE QUESTIONS

Choose the correct statement in the following multiple choice questions.

14 An index increases from 105 to 110. The change in the index is:

    A. ✓ 5 points   B. . . 4.75 points   C. . . 110 points

15. The Laspeyres' index uses:

    A. . . Base year weights   B. ✓ Current year weights

    C. . . Average expenditure as weights

16. It has been decided to change the base of an index from 1988 to 1993. If the index in 1993 is 148, what would the index in 1988 become after the change?

    A. . . 100   B. . . 32.4   C. . . 67.6   D. . . 148

17. The RPI in 1989 was 115.2 and by 1992 it was 138.5. This represents a rise in the price of goods by:

    A. . . 15%   B. ✓ 20.2%   C. . . 23.3%   D. . . £11.8

18. The turnover by a company in 1987 was £54.5m and in 1989 it was £75m. If the RPI has increased from 101.9 in 1987 to 115.2 by 1989, the real change in the turnover has been:

    A. ✓ £20.5m   B. . . £16m   C. . . £18.1m   D. . . £11.8m

19. If the price index for bananas was 100 in 1993 and that for apples was 110, then the price of a pound of bananas was:

A... Less than for apples   B... More than for apples

C... Impossible to compare with apples

20. A company's turnover for 2 years is given in the following table, along with the RPI for those years.

	1997	1999
Turnover	2.3	3.3
RPI	131	138

The 1999 turnover (to 2 decimal places), deflated to 1997 prices is:

A... 2.42   B... 3.13   C... 3.48   D... 2.18

21. From the following table the Paasche price index for 2000 using 1999 as the base is found by calculating:

	1990		2000	
	Price	Quantity	Price	Quantity
Item 1	10	5	15	6
Item 2	12	2	20	3

$P_n \times q_n$

A... $\dfrac{(15 \times 6) + (20 \times 3)}{(10 \times 5) + (12 \times 2)} \times 100$

B.✓. $\dfrac{(15 \times 6) + (20 \times 3)}{(10 \times 6) + (12 \times 3)} \times 100$

C... $\dfrac{(15 \times 5) + (20 \times 2)}{(10 \times 5) + (12 \times 2)} \times 100$

D... $\dfrac{(15 \times 20) + (6 + 3)}{(10 + 12) + (5 + 2)} \times 100$

$$\frac{(P_n \times q_n) + (P_n \times q_n)}{(P_0 \times q_n) + (P_0 \times q_n)} \times 100$$

PRACTICE QUESTIONS

22. The price and quantity consumed in a normal week of 3 items of food for a family are as follows:

	1990		1994	
	Price	Qty	Price	Qty
Bread	28p/loaf	6 loaves	38p/loaf	6 loaves
Milk	20p/pint	15 pints	29p/pint	12 pints
Tea	96p/packet	1 packet	105p/packet	2 packets

(a) Calculate the Laspeyres' index for 1994 using 1990 as the base year.

(b) Calculate the Paasche's index for 1994 using 1990 as the base year.

23. A person has a portfolio of 4 shares. The price and quantity of shares held between 1987 and 1994 are as follows:

	1987		1994	
Share	Price	No. held	Price	No. held
Company A	160	200	520	500
Company B	350	650	265	250
Company C	105	600	140	400
Company D	53	100	159	200

(a) Calculate the Laspeyres' index for 1994 using 1987 as the base year.

(b) Calculate the Paasche's index for 1994 using 1987 as the base year.

24. The price of a house in a residential district has fallen from £130 000 in 1987 to £95 000 in 1992. What has been the real drop in price if the retail price index has changed from 101.9 in 1987 to 138.5 in 1992?

25. A company's turnover (in £m) since 1987 has been as follows:

1987	1988	1989	1990	1991	1992
15.3	10.3	12.1	15.2	24.4	34.7

What has been the real turnover if the value of the RPI for each of these years has been as follows?:

1987	1988	1989	1990	1991	1992
101.9	106.9	115.2	126.1	133.5	138.5

26. The following table gives the number employed by department and the average salary for that department. Calculate Laspeyres' index and Paasche's index for 2001 using 1993 as the base year.

	1993		2001	
	Number employed	Av. salary (£000s)	Number employed	Av. salary (£000s)
Sales	120	7.5	158	9.0
Admin.	41	10.0	52	12.5
Clerical	25	8.0	30	10.0
Managerial	21	18.0	25	22.4

(Source: Payroll Deptartment)

27. Using the information on the price and quantities used of given materials in 1998 and 2001, calculate for these years:

(i) the Laspeyres' index

(ii) the Paasche's index

| | 1998 | | 2001 | |
Material	Price (£)	Quantity	Price (£)	Quantity
A	3.63	3	4.49	2
B	2.11	4	3.26	6
C	10.03	1	12.05	1
D	4.01	7	5.21	5

28. (a) For the following data on the price of a security over 6 months construct a fixed base index (use August = 100).

Month	Aug.	Sept.	Oct.	Nov.	Dec.	Jan.
Price	155	143	120	139	165	162

  (b) By what percentage has the security price changed between:
  (i) August and January?
  (ii) September and December?

29. The following table gives the average weekly wage and the average retail price index (RPI) for the years 1990–92:

Year	1990	1991	1992
Av. weekly wage (£s)	255.1	271.3	290.7
Av. RPI	126.1	133.5	138.5

  Deflate the wage figures to 1990 values. Comment on the 'real value' of wages over this period of time.

30. The price of a house in a residential district has fallen from £62 000 in 1990 to £57 500 in 1992. What has been the real drop in price? (Use the RPI figures from Question 29.)

31. (a) The RPI figures in Question 29 used January 1987 as the base period (that is, January 1987 = 100). Construct a table of RPIs using the 'average' figures quoted for the years 1990–92 with 1990 as the base period.

  (b) By what percentage has the average RPI changed between:
  (i) 1990 and 1991?
  (ii) 1990 and 1992?
  (iii) 1991 and 1992?

  (c) The average RPI figure for 1997, using January 1987 as the base period, was 157.5.
  (i) Add '1997' to the table constructed in (a).
  (ii) By what percentage has the average RPI changed between 1992 and 1997?
  (iii) What is the average percentage yearly change in the RPI between 1992 and 1997?

ASSIGNMENT

You are to use the library to investigate the composition of the RPI and how it is updated. You should use graphs and diagrams to illustrate its composition and provide examples of how the index is calculated. Discuss how useful this index would be to:

(a) the government as a means of controlling inflation.

(b) a union for wage negotiation purposes.

(c) a pensioner in deciding how well off he or she is likely to be next year.

Finally, comment on the accuracy of the index.

Investment appraisal

6.1 Introduction

Companies are frequently faced with having to decide between a number of investment opportunities. Since capital is frequently limited, a company will want to choose the 'best' project or projects. But what do we mean by 'best' and how can we differentiate between different projects that may look equally attractive? The projects considered in this chapter are those that require an initial capital outlay and then generate income over several years. The life of a project is of paramount importance since a sum of money that will be generated in the future will not be so attractive than money that is available in the present. This chapter looks at several methods that can be used to determine the worth of an investment.

At the end of this chapter you should be able to:

- Understand the reasons for investment appraisal
- Select projects on the basis of their payback periods
- Calculate the accounting rate of return
- Discount a future sum of money
- Select projects on the basis of their net present value
- Calculate the Internal Rate of Return for a project
- Appreciate the limitations of each method
- Use the compound interest formula for different applications

6.2 Measures of investment worth

You may think that it should be easy to judge the worth of an investment. Surely the larger the profit that will be generated, the better? Unfortunately it is not so simple as this as two projects could generate the same total profit but be quite different in the pattern of cash flows. The example below illustrates a typical case.

Example 6.1

BAS Holdings specialises in the development of out-of-town shopping centres. It is currently investigating three possible projects and these are located at Andover (A), Bristol (B) and Carlisle (C). The sites at Andover and Bristol require an investment of £4m each while the site at Carlisle requires an investment of £5m. Income from rents is guaranteed for up to 5 years, after which time BAS Holdings will transfer ownership to the local council. The net cash flows are given in Table 6.1, where year 0 refers to 'now'.

Table 6.1   Cash flows for Example 6.1

Year	Andover (£m)	Bristol (£m)	Carlisle (£m)
0	−4.0	−4.0	−5.0
1	1.0	1.5	0.0
2	1.0	2.5	0.5
3	1.0	0.5	1.5
4	1.0	0.5	2.0
5	1.0	0.0	3.0

In the example above the company has to decide which, if any, of the projects to accept. Even if all projects are profitable the company may not have the resources to proceed with them all. Perhaps it should compare each project in terms of the profit made at the end of the 5 years (4 years in the case of Bristol).

Activity 6.1

What is the total profit for each project?

The profit is simply the sum of the cash flows over the life of each project and is shown in Table 6.2.

Table 6.2   Calculation of total profits

Year	Andover (£m)	Bristol (£m)	Carlisle (£m)
0	−4.0	−4.0	−5.0
1	1.0	1.5	0.0
2	1.0	2.5	0.5
3	1.0	0.5	1.5
4	1.0	0.5	2.0
5	1.0	0.0	3.0
Profit	1.0	1.0	2.0

On the basis of total profit the Carlisle project is best, but this project also has the largest initial investment and income is not generated until year 2. Andover and Bristol give the same profit but notice how differently the earnings are generated; Bristol gives larger cash flows at the start but no earnings are received in year 5, whereas Andover gives a constant flow of earnings for the full 5 years.

You should now appreciate that deciding on the best project is not a simple matter. There are several methods that can be used to compare projects and these fall into two categories. The first category is often termed 'traditional' and involves accounting procedures that do not take into account the time value of money. The second method involves procedures that *discount* future sums of money.

6.3   Traditional methods for comparing projects

There are two main methods in this category. These are the *Payback* method and the *accounting rate of return* (ARR). The payback method simply tells you how long it takes for the original investment to be repaid.

Activity 6.2

What are the payback periods for the three projects given in Example 6.1?

You should have obtained 4 years for Project A, 2 years for Project B and 4 years for Project C. This indicates that the Bristol project is to be preferred since it takes less time for the original investment to be repaid.

The payback method is an easily understood method and favours projects that generate large cash flows early. This is an advantage since early cash flows will help a company's liquidity and also minimise risks of unforeseen problems in the future. However, this method ignores cash flows that are generated after the payback period. For example, with Project C large cash flows are generated in years 4 and 5 and this is not taken into account with the payback method.

The accounting rate of return (sometimes called the return on capital employed) is the ratio of average profits to the capital employed. The capital employed sometimes refers to initial capital and sometimes to average capital. There are also variations concerning what constitutes capital and what constitutes profits. The definition used here refers to initial capital and can be expressed as follows:

$$\text{ARR} = \frac{\text{Average profits}}{\text{Initial capital}} \times 100\%$$

Activity 6.3

Calculate the ARR for all three projects given in the example.

For Project A the average profit is £1m and the initial capital employed is £4m so the ARR is:

$$\text{ARR} = \frac{1}{4} \times 100 = 25\%$$

For Project B the average profit will again be £1m (the total adds up to £5m – the same as Project A). Since the capital employed is £4m, the ARR is again 25%.

For Project C the average profit is:

$$\frac{(0 + 0.5 + 1.5 + 2.0 + 3.0)}{5} = 1.4$$

Since the initial capital is £5m, the ARR is:

$$ARR = \frac{1.4}{5} \times 100 = 28\%$$

On the basis of the ARR, Project C is the better project.

The ARR is easy to calculate but it has many disadvantages, such as not allowing for timing of the cash flows. For example, Project A and Project B are ranked equal even though Project B generates larger cash flows in the first two years.

6.4 Discounted cash flow techniques

The disadvantages of the payback and the ARR methods are that they do not take into account the time value of money. If you were offered £1000 now or £1000 in a year's time, which would you take? I am sure that you would take £1000 now! However, what would be your decision if you were offered £1000 now or £2000 in a year'stime? Unless you were desperate for money, you would probably prefer to wait a year and get the £2000. These two cases are clear cut. But what would be your decision if you were offered £1000 now or £1100 in a year's time? If you could put the money to good use so that after a year you would have more than £1100, then your decision should be to take the £1000 now.

It is clear from this that money in the future is not worth as much as money now, so we need some method of *discounting* future sums of money. In order to understand the idea of discounting, it is first necessary to revise the idea of *simple* and *compound* interest. Simple interest is the expression used when interest on a sum of money is calculated on the principal only. This situation occurs when the interest is withdrawn as it is earned.

Activity 6.4

You decide to invest £8500 in an investment account paying an interest rate of 5% p.a. The interest is paid out to you as it is earned. What interest would you receive at the end of each year?

The answer to this activity is 5% of £8500, which is £425.

Normally the interest is reinvested so that the interest also earns interest. In this case you would use the expression 'compound interest'.

Activity 6.5

You again decide to invest £8500 in an investment account paying an interest rate of 5% p.a. This time, however, all interest is reinvested. How much would the £8500 have grown to at the end of the 10th year?

The principal at the end of the first year is simply the original principal plus the interest earned. That is:

$$8500 + \frac{5}{100} \times 8500 = 8500\left(1 + \frac{5}{100}\right)$$

This is £8500 + £425 = £8925.

The principal at the end of year 2 =
    the principal at the start of year 2 *plus* the amount of interest
    received during the year. That is:

$$8500\left(1 + \frac{5}{100}\right) + 8500\left(1 + \frac{5}{100}\right) \times \frac{5}{100}$$

This can be simplified by noting that the expression $8500\left(1 + \frac{5}{100}\right)$ is common to both terms. The equation can therefore be factorised as follows:

$$8500\left(1 + \frac{5}{100}\right)\left(1 + \frac{5}{100}\right) = 8500\left(1 + \frac{5}{100}\right)^2$$

In general if you invest an initial principal P_0 for n years at an interest rate of r per cent, the principal at the *end* of the nth year is:

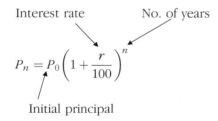

This is called the *compound interest* formula.

So for $P_0 = 8500$, $r = 5$ and $n = 10$, the principal $= 8500\left(1 + \frac{5}{100}\right)^{10} = £13\,846$

Another way of expressing this is that £13 846 in 10 years' time at an interest rate of 5% is equivalent to £8500 now. This is quite a useful idea as it allows you to make a judgement on the value of some future sum of money.

Activity 6.6

You have been promised £10 000 in 5 years' time. What would this amount be worth now, assuming an interest rate of 6%?

To solve this problem the compound interest formula can be used in reverse. That is, P_n is known and you have to calculate P_0. In this case, $n = 5$, $r = 6\%$ and $P_n = 10\,000$, and the equation becomes:

$$10\,000 = P_0 \left(1 + \frac{6}{100}\right)^5$$

$$= 1.3382 \times P_0$$

Therefore $P_0 = \dfrac{10\,000}{1.3382}$

$$= £7473$$

Since this calculation will be repeated many times, you will find it easier to rearrange the compound interest formula to make P_0 the subject of the formula. That is:

$$P_0 = P_n \times \frac{1}{\left(1 + \dfrac{r}{100}\right)^n}$$

The expression $\dfrac{1}{\left(1 + \dfrac{r}{100}\right)^n}$ is called the *discount factor*

For example, for $r = 6\%$ and $n = 5$, the discount factor is $\dfrac{1}{1.3382} = 0.7473$, so $P_0 = 10\,000 \times 0.7473 = £7473$.

Activity 6.7

Discount the sum of £30 000 that is to be received in 4 years' time using an interest rate of (a) 2% and (b) 10%.

You should have found that the discount factors for 2% and 10% are 0.9238 and 0.6830 respectively. Therefore the discounted value of £30 000 is:

$30\,000 \times 0.9238 = £27\,714$ at an interest rate of 2%

$30\,000 \times 0.6830 = £20\,490$ at an interest rate of 10%

6.4.1 Net present value

Activity 6.8

You have been offered either £5000 in 2 years' time or £6000 in 3 years' time. Which would you accept assuming an interest rate of 5.5%?

This is a slightly different problem in that you are asked to compare a sum of money in 2 years' time with a sum of money in 3 years' time. In order to compare the two amounts you need to have a common base. The easiest method is to find the value now of both amounts. The diagram in Figure 6.1 explains this more clearly.

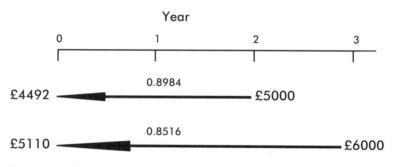

Figure 6.1 Present value of a sum of money

The discount factors are given on top of each arrow and the value at the point of the arrow is the value now of each sum of money. This shows you that £6000 in 3 years' time is the better choice since the *present value* of £6000 is worth more than the present value of £5000 due in 2 years' time. This idea of calculating the present value of a sum of money can be extended to the case where a project generates a series of cash flows and the present value of the sum of these cash flows is required. The interest rate that is used is usually called the *discount rate* and is the *cost of capital* for the company.

Activity 6.9

In the case of BAS Holdings, the company's discount rate is 8%. Calculate the present value for each of the three projects given in Example 6.1.

The calculations are best set out in a table similar to Table 6.3.

From this table you should see that the largest present value is Project C with a total cash flow of £5.13m. However, to achieve this, a capital investment of £5m was required, whereas the other two projects only require an investment of £4m. To obtain the net profit, the investment should be deducted from the present value and, when this is done, the result is called the *net present value* or NPV.

Table 6.3 Calculation of present value

Year	Discount factor	Cash flow (£m)	Andover Present value (£m)	Cash flow (£m)	Bristol Present value (£m)	Cash flow (£m)	Carlisle Present value (£m)
0		−4.0		−4.0		−5.0	
1	0.9259	1.0	0.9259	1.5	1.3889	0.0	0.0
2	0.8573	1.0	0.8573	2.5	2.1435	0.5	0.4287
3	0.7938	1.0	0.7938	0.5	0.3969	1.5	1.1907
4	0.7350	1.0	0.7350	0.5	0.3675	2.0	1.47
5	0.6806	1.0	0.6806	0.0	0.0	3.0	2.0418
			3.9926		4.2968		5.1312

Activity 6.10

What is the NPV for each of the three projects?

The calculations are: £3.9926 − £4 = −£0.0074m for Project A
£4.2968 − £4 = £0.2968m for Project B
£5.1312 − £5 = £0.1312m for Project C

On the basis of the NPV, Project A would result in a loss and is therefore not a profitable investment, while Project B is the most profitable investment.

When you use NPV to select one project out of many you would simply choose the project with the highest figure. You can also use NPV to make a decision about one project. In this case your decision should be as summarised in Table 6.4.

Table 6.4 Decision criterion when using NPV

NPV	Decision
Negative	Reject project
Zero	Indifferent
Positive	Accept project

6.4.2 Internal rate of return

The NPV method is a very useful method as it takes into account the timing of a series of cash flows. However, the decision is dependent on the discount rate used – a larger rate will reduce the NPV and could change the decision from accept to reject. An alternative approach is to calculate the discount rate that will give the NPV of zero. This is called the *Internal Rate of Return* or IRR. If the IRR for a project is greater than or equal to the cost of capital for a company, the project would be acceptable; if not, the project should be rejected. In the case of BAS Holdings, the cost of capital is 8% and any project with an IRR of at least this figure will be acceptable. Calculation of the IRR is not straightforward but an approximate value can be obtained using either a graphical approach or a linear interpolation. For both methods you need to calculate the NPV for two different discount rates. For the greatest accuracy the NPVs should be small, and preferably one should be positive and one negative. For the graphical method these points are plotted on a graph of NPV against discount rate and a line drawn between them. The point where the line crosses the horizontal axis (which represents zero NPV) can then be read from the graph.

Activity 6.11

Find the IRR for Project A.

For Project A, a discount rate of 8% gave an NPV of −£0.0074m. For most practical purposes this is virtually zero, so the IRR is about 8%. However, to get a more accurate answer you could try another discount rate, say 7.5%. The calculations for this discount rate are shown in Table 6.5.

Table 6.5   NPV calculations for a discount rate of 7.5%

Year	Discount factor	Cash flow (£m)	Present value (£m)
0		−4.0	
1	0.9302	1.0	0.9302
2	0.8653	1.0	0.8653
3	0.8050	1.0	0.8050
4	0.7488	1.0	0.7488
5	0.6966	1.0	0.6966
			4.0459

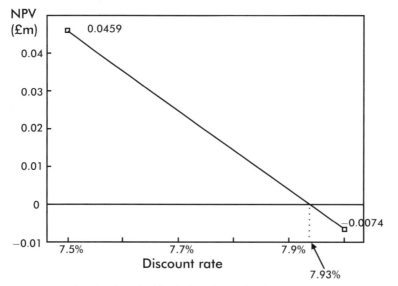

Figure 6.2   Graphical method for finding the IRR for the Andover project

The NPV is $4.0459 - 4 = £0.0459m$. These two values have been plotted in Figure 6.2.

You should find that the line cuts the horizontal axis at 7.93% and this is the value of the IRR for this project. To use the interpolation method the following formula can be used:

$$IRR = \frac{N_1 r_2 - N_2 r_1}{N_1 - N_2}$$

Where an NPV of N_1 was obtained using a discount rate of r_1 and an NPV of N_2 was obtained using a discount rate of r_2.

So for $N_1 = 0.0459$, $r_1 = 7.5\%$, $N_2 = -0.0074$ and $r_2 = 8\%$, the IRR is:

$$IRR = \frac{0.0459 \times 8 - (-0.0074) \times 7.5}{0.0459 - (-0.0074)}$$

$$= \frac{0.42195}{0.0532}$$

$$= 7.93\%$$

Which is the same as the value obtained from the graph.

Activity 6.12

Find the IRR for Project B using the graphical method. (Hint – try discount rates of 11% and 13%.)

These NPV values have been plotted in Figure 6.3 where you will see that the line joining the two points cuts the axis at a discount rate of about 12.1%.

Table 6.6 Calculations for the NPV using discount rates of 11% and 13%

Year	Discount factor @ 11%	Cash flow (£m)	Present value (£m)	Discount factor @ 13%	Present value (£m)
0		−4.0	−4.0		−4.0
1	0.9009	1.5	1.3514	0.8850	1.3275
2	0.8116	2.5	2.0290	0.7831	1.9578
3	0.7311	0.5	0.3656	0.6931	0.3465
4	0.6587	0.5	0.3294	0.6133	0.3067
5	0.5935	0.0	0.0000	0.5428	0.0000
NPV			0.0754		−0.0615

Activity 6.13

Find the IRR for Project C using the formula.

Two rates have been tried: one at 6% which gave an NPV of £0.5304m and one at 8% which gave an NPV of £0.1312m. (You are recommended to do these calculations yourself.)

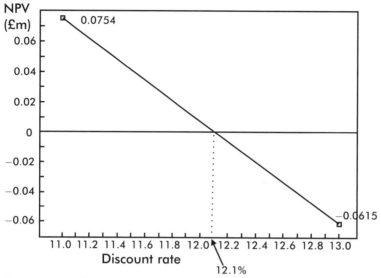

Figure 6.3 IRR for the Bristol project

Substituting these values into the formula gives you:

$$\frac{0.5304 \times 8 - 0.1312 \times 6}{0.5304 - 0.1312}$$

$$= \frac{3.456}{0.3992}$$

$$= 8.66\%$$

The results of the IRR calculations agree with the NPV method; that is, Project A is not profitable while Project B appears to be more profitable than Project C. The advantage of the IRR method is that it allows you to have a benchmark against which projects can be measured, and a rate of return is something that management understand. The disadvantages are that it is more difficult to calculate and does not take into account the absolute value of the cash flows. So, on the basis of IRR, a project giving an NPV of £100 might look better than a project with an NPV of £1m. There is also the problem that in certain circumstances it is possible for the IRR method to give multiple solutions or no solution at all! It is possible to use Goal Seek in Excel to find the IRR. See Chapter 9.3.2 for details on using Goal Seek.

6.5 Other applications of the compound interest formula

6.5.1 Sinking funds

Activity 6.14

A firm wishes to purchase a machine costing £800 in 3 years' time by making 4 equal instalments (the first now, the second at the end of the first year, the third at the end of the second year and the fourth at the end of the third year – that is, when they purchase the machine) in a savings plan paying 5.2% net per annum. How much should each instalment be?

If we assume that the price of the machine will not increase then the investment plan must realise £800 at the end of the third year. If each instalment was for £200 the total amount saved would exceed £800 as a result of the interest received. If you look at Figure 6.4 you will see that the first payment will earn interest for 3 years, the second payment will earn interest for 2 years and the third payment will earn interest for just 1 year. The final payment will be made at the end of the third year and we can assume that the machine will be purchased immediately afterwards. So how would you find the correct amount to save? You could do it by trial and error but a little mathematics would be much more effective! If we call the unknown instalment x, then:

the first instalment will grow to $£x(1.052)^3$ at the end of the plan

the second instalment will grow to $£x(1.052)^2$ at the end of the plan

the third instalment will grow to $£x(1.052)$ at the end of the plan

the fourth instalment will stay at $£x$.

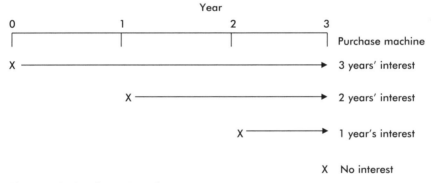

Figure 6.4 Regular savings plan

Total amount accumulated $= x(1.052)^3 + x(1.052)^2 + x(1.052) + x$

This must equal £800. So:

$$x(1.052)^3 + x(1.052)^2 + x(1.052) + x = 800$$

Factorising we get:

$$x((1.052)^3 + (1.052)^2 + 1.052 + 1) = 800$$

$$x[1.1643 + 1.1067 + 1.052 + 1] = 800$$

So $4.323x = 800$

And $x = 800/4.323$

$\qquad = 185.06$

Therefore each instalment should be £185.06.

This type of savings plan is called a *sinking fund*. The method in Activity 6.14 will work for any number of years but it is possible to derive a formula (using the sum of a geometric series) that makes the calculation quicker. The formula is:

$$\frac{x\left[\left(1+\dfrac{r}{100}\right)^{n+1} - 1\right]}{\dfrac{r}{100}}$$

The meaning of the symbols x, r and n is the same as before. (Note: Before using this formula make sure that the timings of the regular payments x correspond to those given in Activity 6.14.)

Activity 6.15

Solve the problem in Activity 6.14 using the sinking fund formula.

We again need to find x, so:

$$\frac{x\left[\left(1+\dfrac{5.2}{100}\right)^{4} - 1\right]}{\dfrac{5.2}{100}} = 800$$

$$x[(1.052)^{4} - 1] = 800 \times 0.052$$

$$0.2248x = 41.6$$

$$x = \frac{41.6}{0.2248}$$

$$= 185.05$$

which is the same as before (apart from the small rounding error).

6.5.2 Constant repayments

This sinking fund formula is a special case of the situation where an amount P_0 is invested followed by regular amounts x. The formula is:

$$P_n = P_0\left(1+\frac{r}{100}\right)^{n} + \frac{x\left[\left(1+\dfrac{r}{100}\right)^{n} - 1\right]}{\dfrac{r}{100}}$$

Activity 6.16

You take out a 25-year repayment mortgage for £50 000 at a fixed interest rate of 6%. Repayments are made at the end of each year and will consist of part interest and part capital. Calculate the amount of the annual repayments.

Since you want the amount owed at the end of the 25-year period to be zero, then $P_{25} = 0$ and $P_0 = -50\,000$ (note P_0 is negative because you owe £50 000)

Substituting these values together with $r = 6$, you get:

$$0 = -50\,000 \times \left(1 + \frac{8}{100}\right)^{25} + \frac{x\left[\left(1 + \frac{8}{100}\right)^{25} - 1\right]}{\frac{8}{100}}$$

$$0 = -50\,000 \times (1.08)^{25} + \frac{x[(1.08)^{25} - 1]}{0.08}$$

$$0 = -50\,000 \times 6.8485 + \frac{x[5.8485]}{0.08}$$

$$0 = -342\,425 + 73.106x$$

$$73.106x = 342\,425$$

$$x = 4684$$

So the annual repayment should be £4684.

If you multiply this amount by 25 you will get £117 100, which is the amount you would pay back over the life of the loan; that is, over double the amount you borrowed!

Activity 6.17

You can only afford to pay back £4500 per year. How long would it take you to pay back the original loan?

This time you know x but not n, so:

$$0 = -50\,000 \times \left(1 + \frac{8}{100}\right)^{n} + \frac{4500\left[\left(1 + \frac{8}{100}\right)^{n} - 1\right]}{\frac{8}{100}}$$

$$0 = -50\,000 \times (1.08)^{n} + \frac{4500[(1.08)^{n} - 1]}{0.08}$$

$$0 = -50\,000 \times (1.08)^{n} + 56\,250 \times (1.08)^{n} - 56\,250$$

$$0 = 6250 \times (1.08)^{n} - 56\,250$$

$$6250 \times (1.08)^{n} = 56\,250$$

$$(1.08)^{n} = \frac{56\,250}{6250}$$

$$= 9$$

To make n the subject of the formula we can take logs of both sides:

$\log(1.08)^n = \log(9)$

Using laws of logs (see Chapter 1.6):

$n \times \log(1.08) = \log(9)$

$n = \dfrac{\log(9)}{\log(1.08)}$

$= \dfrac{0.9542}{0.03342}$

$= 28.55$

So a total of 29 years would be required to pay off the loan for an annual payment of £4500.

6.5.3 Depreciation

Many investments such as consumer items and machinery depreciate so that after a few years the item is worth less than it was when it was first bought. One method of depreciating an item is by the *reducing balance* method. This method assumes that a fixed percentage of the initial capital value of the item is written off each year. This method results in a larger depreciation in the early years, which is what you would normally expect for these types of goods. To solve these problems we can use the compound interest formula, but in this case the interest rate r is the rate of depreciation.

Activity 6.18

An item of machinery is bought for £30 000 and after 10 years its scrap value is £1000. Find (a) the rate of depreciation and (b) its book value after 5 years.

To solve this problem you would use the compound interest formula:

$$P_n = P_0\left(1 + \frac{r}{100}\right)^n$$

For $P_0 = 30\,000$, $P_{10} = 1000$ and $n = 10$ you get:

$1000 = 30\,000 \times \left(1 + \dfrac{r}{100}\right)^{10}$

$\left(1 + \dfrac{r}{100}\right)^{10} = \dfrac{1000}{30\,000}$

$= 0.033$

So $\left(1 + \dfrac{r}{100}\right) = (0.0333)^{\frac{1}{10}}$

$\qquad\qquad\quad = 0.7117$

$\dfrac{r}{100} = 0.7117 - 1$

$\qquad = -0.2883$

$r = -28.83\%$

r is negative since the capital is decreasing in value. So the depreciation rate is 28.83%.

The book value is the value of the asset at a particular point in time. To calculate the book value after 5 years we simply use the calculated value of r in the formula, that is:

$P_5 = 30\,000 \times \left(1 - \dfrac{28.83}{100}\right)^5$

$\quad\; = 30\,000 \times 0.1826$

$\quad\; = £5478$

6.5.4 Compound interest with continuous compounding

IIII▶ **Activity 6.19**

The sum of £5000 is invested at 6% per annum compound interest. Find the value of the investment at the end of 5 years if interest is compounded (a) annually, (b) monthly, and (c) daily.

For the annual case you would use the compound interest formula with $r = 6\%$. That is:

$P_5 = 5000 \times \left(1 + \dfrac{6}{100}\right)^5$

$\quad\; = 5000 \times 1.3382$

$\quad\; = £6691$

If compounded monthly, the interest rate would be 0.5% per month (6/12) and the time period would be 60 (5 × 12 months). So the value of the investment at the end of 5 years would be:

$P_5 = 5000 \times \left(1 + \dfrac{0.5}{100}\right)^{60}$

$\quad\; = 5000 \times 1.3489$

$\quad\; = £6744.50$

If compounded daily, the interest rate would now be 0.01644% per day (6/365) and the time period would be 1825 (5 × 365).

$$P_5 = 5000 \times \left(1 + \frac{0.01644}{100}\right)^{1825}$$

$$= 5000 \times 1.3498$$

$$= \pounds 6749$$

As you can see the amounts are gradually increasing as the time period gets less. In the limit (that is, when the interest is continuously compounded), the value of an investment after n years is given by:

$$P_n = P_0 e^{\frac{r \times n}{100}}$$

Where r is the annual interest rate and e is the exponential function (and can be found on all scientific calculators).

$$P_n = 5000 e^{\frac{6 \times 5}{100}}$$

So: $= 5000 \times 1.3499$

$= \pounds 6749.50$

6.6 Summary

The main emphasis of this chapter has been methods for appraising investments. Two classes of methods were looked at. The first uses traditional accounting procedures such as the payback method and the accounting rate of return while the second category uses discounted cash flow techniques. Each method has its advantages and disadvantages, but common sense should tell you that methods that take into account the timing of investments should be better than one that doesn't. To conclude this session it would be useful to summarise the decisions that would be made for choosing the 'best' of the three projects using the four methods described (and a discount rate of 8%).

Table 6.7 Summary of the different methods of investment appraisal

Method	A	B	C	Decision
Payback	4 years	2 years	4 years	B
ARR	25%	25%	28%	C
NPV	−£0.0074m	£0.2968m	£0.1312m	B
IRR	7.93%	12.1%	8.66%	B

6.7 Further reading

Burton, G., Carrol, G. and Wall, S. (1999) *Quantitative Methods for Business and Economics*, Longman, New York (Chapter 9).

Morris, C. (2000) *Quantitative Approaches in Business Studies*, fifth edition, Pitman, London (Chapter 16).

6.8 EXERCISES

The answers to the progress questions, the multiple choice questions and some of the practice questions are given in Appendix 1. Solutions to the remaining questions and the assignment can be found at the web site for this text.

PROGRESS QUESTIONS

These questions have been designed to help you remember the key points in this chapter.

Give the missing word in each case:

1. Payback period is the number of years that an investment will take to be ....
2. ARR stands for accounting rate of ....
3. Simple interest is where the interest is .... as it is earned.
4. Compound interest is where the interest is ....
5. NPV stands for net .... value.

ANSWER *TRUE* OR *FALSE*

6. The smaller the ARR the better.
7. A future amount of money is worth less than it would today.
8. The NPV of a project depends on the discount rate used.
9. A project is acceptable if the NPV is less than zero.
10. A project is acceptable if the IRR is less than the company's cost of capital.

REVIEW QUESTIONS

These questions have been designed to help you check your comprehension of the key points in this chapter. You may wish to look further than this chapter in order to answer them fully. You will find the reading list useful in this respect. You can check the essential elements of your answers by referring to the appropriate section.

11. What are the advantages and disadvantages of the payback method? (Section 6.3)
12. What is the difference between simple and compound interest? (Section 6.4)
13. What are the essential differences between the NPV and IRR methods? (Sections 6.4.1 and 6.4.2)
14. What are the problems with using the IRR method? (Section 6.4.2)

MULTIPLE CHOICE QUESTIONS

15. If the average profits over the life of a project was £50 000 and the initial investment was £300 000, the ARR is:

    A... 50%   B... 16.67%   C... 0.1667   D... 30%

16. An investment of £10 000 is made at an interest rate of 5%. If all interest is reinvested the principal at the end of 10 years (to the nearest £) is:

    A... £16 289   B... £162 890   C... £15 000

17. The discount factor for a period of 5 years at a discount rate of 6.5% is:

    A... 0.7299   B... −0.7299   C... 0.7282   D... 1.7299

Questions 18 and 19 refer to a construction project that involves an outlay of £100 000 now. The future net cash flows at the end of each year for this project are summarised in the table below. The discount factors for each year for a discount rate of 9% are also provided.

Year	Discount factor	Cash flow
1	0.9174	50 000
2	0.8417	50 000
3	0.7722	10 000
4	0.7084	10 000

18. The payback period for the project is:

    A... 1 year   B... 2 years   C... 3 years   D... 4 years

19. The net present value (NPV) for the project is found by

    A... Adding up the cash flow figures for all 4 years and subtracting £100 000
    B... Adding up the discount factors for all 4 years and multiplying by the sum of the cash flows and subtracting £100 000
    C... Calculating the present value of each cash flow, adding up these present values for all 4 years and subtracting £100 000
    D... Finding the average profit, and then dividing by the initial capital

20. Internal rate of return (IRR) refers to:

    A... The discount rate that makes two NPVs the same
    B... The discount rate that makes the NPV zero
    C... The discount rate that makes the NPV negative
    D... The largest NPV from a choice of projects

Questions 21 to 24 refer to the two projects 'X' and 'Y' given below.

Year	Project X Cash flow (£000's)	Project Y Cash flow (£000's)
0	−100	−110
1	40	0
2	60	30
3	20	100

21. The payback period for Project X is:

    A... 1 year   B... 2 years   C... 4 years

22. On the basis of ARR the most profitable project is:

    A... Project X   B... Project Y   C... No difference

23. The NPV for Project Y at a discount rate of 9% is:

    A... £20 000   B... −£7531   C... £10 000

24. On the basis of IRR the most profitable project is:

    A... Project X   B... Project Y   C... No difference

25. A sinking fund allows you to calculate:

    A... The present value of a series of future sums of money

    B... The future sum of a series of cash flows

    C... The annual instalment necessary to create a sum of money in the future

    D... The constant payment that will pay off a loan taken out now

26. The payments to pay off a mortgage is an example of

    A... Depreciation of an asset

    B... A sinking fund

    C... Constant repayments

    D... Continuous compounding

27. An investment account paying 6% p.a. interest, compounded continuously, is opened with £1000. The amount in the account at the end of the year is nearest to:

    A... £1060   B... £1061   C... £1062   D... £1063

PRACTICE QUESTIONS

28. £50 000 is invested at 5.5% for 6 years. If all interest is reinvested

    (a) What would be the amount accumulated at the end of the 6 years?

    (b) How much interest would have been received during the 6 years?

29. A car is purchased for a £3000 deposit and 5 annual payments of £1000. What is the cost of the car at today's prices if a discount rate of 8% is assumed?

30. A project involves an investment of £2m and is guaranteed to produce an income of £0.5m each year for the next 5 years. Compare and contrast different methods for evaluating the

worth of this project. Assume that the income occurs at the end of each year and that the discount rate is 7%.

31. A project costs £5m to set up, and a return of £2m p.a. for the next 3 years is guaranteed. A project will only be accepted if the internal rate of return is greater than 14%. Should the project be accepted?

32. On 1 January 1995 you invested £1000 in a building society's 5-year fixed rate account paying 5.4% net per annum. How much will be in the account on 1 January 2000 if no funds or interest are withdrawn throughout the period of the investment?

33. A car is purchased for a £4500 deposit and 5 annual payments of £1000. What is the cost of the car at today's prices if a discount rate of 7.5% is assumed?

34. A firm is considering the purchase of one of two machines. The first (machine A), costing £4000, is expected to bring in revenues of £2000, £2500 and £1500 respectively in the 3 years for which it will be operative, while the second (machine B), which costs £3900, produces revenues of £1500, £2500 and £2000, and has the same lifetime. Neither machine will have any appreciable scrap value at the end of its life. Assuming a discount rate of 8%, compare and contrast different methods for evaluating which machine should be purchased. (Hint to calculating IRRs: a discount rate of 25% gave NPVs of −£32 and −£76 for machines A and B respectively.)

35. A company has the choice of two investments, both costing an initial £15 000. The first will yield cash flows of £6000 per year for 3 years (the first payment receivable 1 year after investment), while the second will yield a lump sum of £19 000 at the end of the 3 year period. Assuming a discount rate of 5% which investment should be chosen? (Hint to calculating IRRs: a discount rate of 10% gave NPVs of −£79.2 and −£725.3 for investments 1 and 2 respectively.)

36. A machine which currently costs £800 will increase in price by 4% per year as a result of inflation.

    (a) What will the machine cost in 3 years' time?

    (b) If a firm wishes to purchase this machine in 3 years' time by making 3 equal instalments (the first now, the second in one year's time and the third in two years – that is, one year before the purchase), in a savings plan paying 5.2% net p.a., how much should each investment be?

37. A machine is purchased for £3750 and generates a revenue of £1310 per year for 5 years. After this time, it ceases to be productive and has no scrap value.

    (a) Assuming a discount rate of 11.2 %, calculate its net present value.

    (b) Find a discount rate at which the net present value becomes negative, and use it to estimate the internal rate of return.

38. A firm wishes to provide a sinking fund in order to replace equipment that has a life span of 10 years. If the cost of the equipment will be £1m in 10 years' time, what annual amount do they need to put aside in an account paying 7% p.a.?

39. You decide to take out a 20-year mortgage for £65 000 at an annual interest rate of 7.5%.

    (a) What would be the annual repayment?

(b) If you could increase the annual amount paid to £7000, how much money would you save over the life of the mortgage?

40. You have just bought a car for £12 000 from a garage that promises to buy the car back from you for £5000 in 3 years' time.
    (a) What is the rate of depreciation?
    (b) Given this rate of depreciation, what will the car be worth at the end of the first year?

41. Which is better; a savings account paying 7% p.a. where interest is compounded annually, or an account which pays an annual rate of 5% but where the interested is compounded continuously?

ASSIGNMENT

MOS plc is a computer software company and its main business is the development of payroll systems. Recently it has also developed a number of specialised machine control systems and the company is keen to expand into this area. However, the risks in developing these types of systems are much greater than for payroll systems. This is partly to do with the fact that there is a risk that the software will not work, but also to do with the fact that it takes much longer for the project to be completed. A payroll system can be developed in under a year, while for control systems the development time can be 2 to 3 years. The policy of the company is to lease the software for a fixed period of time and during this period the client pays an annual rental that diminishes with time.

Table 6.8 Information for the assignment

Year	Project A (£000s)	Project B (£000s)	Project C (£000s)
0	−60	−80	−500
1	30	40	0.0
2	30	20	0.0
3	20	20	0.0
4	10	20	500
5	10	5	300
6			200
7			100

When MOS receives a request for a piece of software, a valuation exercise takes place. This valuation exercise looks at the financial implications as well as any technical problems. For payroll systems the market is very competitive and there is very little room for manoeuvre. However, for control systems there is much more flexibility in pricing. As with any small company, MOS has a limited amount of capital available, which currently amounts to £500 000 obtained through bank loans. MOS currently pays interest at a rate of 8.5% p.a.

MOS has options on three projects. Project A and Project B are payroll systems and both involve an expenditure of less than £100 000, while Project C is a specialised control system that involves an expenditure of £500 000. Details of the expenditure and leasing rental are shown in Table 6.8. Use investment appraisal techniques to decide which (if any) of the projects should be accepted. Write a note to the Project Manager of MOS plc explaining your results and recommendations.

7 Introduction to probability

7.1 Introduction

It is difficult to go very far in solving business problems without a basic understanding of probability. The 'laws of chance' underpin many decisions that are made in real life. For example, when we carry out a survey we need to know how the sample data relate to the target population. Our insurance premiums are determined by the chance of some mishap occurring and quality control systems are built around these laws. This chapter contains all the basic rules and methods of probability that will be required in subsequent chapters. At the end of this chapter you should be able to:

- Calculate simple probabilities
- Calculate probabilities of compound events using the rules of addition and multiplication
- Use probability trees to solve problems
- Use Bayes' theorem to modify probabilities when new information is received

7.2 Basic ideas

The value of a probability can be given either as a fraction, as a decimal or as a percentage. An event with a probability of zero is termed impossible, while an event with a probability of 1 or 100% is termed certain. Figure 7.1 below may help you to picture the idea of the probability measure.

Probabilities can be obtained in a number of ways. The simplest is the *subjective* method where you estimate what you think the probability of a particular event will be. For example, a sales manager may estimate that the probability of high sales for a particular product is 60%. This figure may be based on market research or experience of a similar product, but it is unlikely to involve any calculations.

Another method is the *empirical* approach. This method uses measurement to estimate probabilities. For example, you may wish to determine the probability of a defective

Probability scale

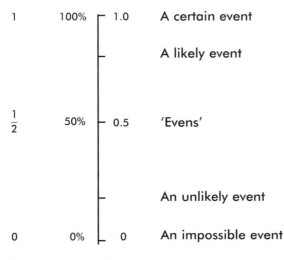

Figure 7.1 Probability scale

electrical component being produced by a particular process. If you test 100 components and find 5 defective, then you would say that the probability of a defective component being produced is $\frac{5}{100}$ or 0.05. That is, probability =

$$\frac{\text{number of times a particular event occurred}}{\text{total number of trials or 'experiments'}}$$

The particular event here is finding a defective component and the 'experiment' is picking, testing and classifying a component as either good or defective.

Activity 7.1

Toss a coin 10 times and use the above formula to calculate the probability of a head.

Did you get a probability of 0.5? This, as you will see shortly, is the 'correct' answer, but 10 tosses is a very small number of experiments. If you tossed the coin a further 10 times you would quite likely get a different answer. This is the basis of *sampling error*, which we shall come back to in a later chapter (Chapter 10). You will also see that the sampling error in this case could be reduced by tossing the coin a larger number of times; that is, the larger the number of tosses, the nearer you will get to a probability of 0.5.

However, to obtain the theoretical probability of a head you would use a different method, called the *a priori* approach. This is similar to the empirical approach, except that you can work out *in advance* how many times a particular event should occur. In the coin tossing activity you know that there is only one head, so that the probability of a head is $\frac{1}{2}$ or 0.5. If you picked a card from a pack, the probability of an Ace is $\frac{4}{52}$ or 0.0769, since there are 4 Aces in a pack. The definition can be written as:

$$\frac{\text{number of ways in which a particular event can occur}}{\text{total number of outcomes}}$$

This definition assumes that all outcomes are equally likely; that is, there is no bias associated with a particular outcome. This definition would not apply to, say, a race involving 10 horses, since the probability that any horse will win is unlikely to be 0.1. The *odds* would reflect such factors as form, jockey, trainer, etc.

Activity 7.2

You pick a card from a pack. What is the probability that it is a picture card?

To answer this question you would have listed the picture cards in a suit. These are Jack, Queen, King and Ace. Since there are 4 suits you should have decided that there will be $4 \times 4 = 16$ ways in which a particular outcome can occur. The probability of a picture card is therefore $\frac{16}{52} = 0.3077$.

7.3 The probability of compound events

It is frequently required to find the probability of two or more events happening at the same time. For example, an aircraft has many of its controls duplicated so that if one fails the other would still function. But what is the probability that both systems will fail? The way that probabilities are combined depend on whether the events are *independent* or whether they are *mutually exclusive*. Two (or more) events are said to be independent if the occurrence of one does not affect the occurrence of the other. The two aircraft systems will be independent if the failure of one system does not change the probability of failure of the other system. Two (or more) events are mutually exclusive if either event can occur, but not both. One card drawn from a pack cannot be a Jack and an Ace. However, a Jack and a Diamond are not mutually exclusive since the selected card could be both. When the set of all possible outcomes are known, they are said to be *mutually exhaustive*, and the sum of the probabilities of a set of outcomes that are mutually exclusive *and* mutually exhaustive must equal 1. For example, there are four suits in a pack of cards and the probability of selecting a card from either suit is $\frac{13}{52}$ or 0.25. The sum of these probabilities is 1, since a card must come from one (and only one) of the suits. This idea will allow you to calculate a probability if the other or others are known. If, say, the probability of a defective component is 5%, then the probability that it is not defective is 95%.

A – a Jack   B – an Ace

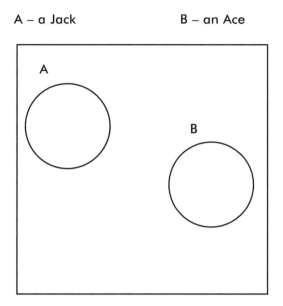

Figure 7.2 Venn diagram for mutually exclusive events

Compound events can be more easily solved if a diagram is drawn. One useful diagram is the *Venn* diagram. A Venn diagram is made up of a square, the inside of which encloses all possible outcomes. The events of interest are represented by circles. The Venn diagram in Figure 7.2 represents two events, A and B. Event A is being dealt a Jack, which has a probability of $\frac{4}{52}$ or 0.0769, and Event B is being dealt an Ace, which also has a probability of $\frac{4}{52}$. The probability of being dealt either a Jack *or* an Ace is:

$$P(\text{Jack or Ace}) = P(\text{Jack}) + P(\text{Ace})$$
$$= 0.0769 + 0.0769$$
$$= 0.1538$$

However, if Event B is being dealt a Diamond then the two events overlap, as shown in Figure 7.3. If the two probabilities are now added, the intersection of the two events (shown shaded) will have been added twice. This intersection, which represents the case of being dealt a Jack of Diamonds (with a probability of $\frac{1}{52}$ or 0.0192), must be subtracted from the sum of the two probabilities. That is:

$$P(\text{Jack or Diamond}) = P(\text{Jack}) + P(\text{Diamond}) - P(\text{Jack of Diamonds})$$
$$= 0.0769 + 0.25 - 0.0192$$
$$= 0.3077$$

A – a Jack   B – a Diamond

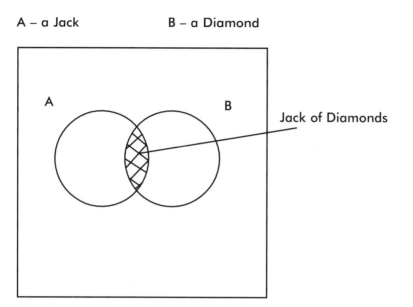

Figure 7.3 Venn diagram for events that are not mutually exclusive

In general if P(A) means the probability of Event A and P(B) the probability of Event B then:

   P(A or B) = P(A) + P(B) − P(A and B)

This is known as the *addition rule*.

NOTE: If the two events are mutually exclusive, as in the first example, then there is no intersection and P(A and B) is zero.

 ## Activity 7.3

The police regularly carry out spot checks on heavy goods vehicles. During one particular month the results are as shown in Table 7.1.

Table 7.1   Results from checks on heavy goods vehicles

	Overweight	Not overweight	Total
Driving time exceeded	15	25	40
Driving time not exceeded	20	40	60
Total	35	65	100

Assuming that these results are typical of all heavy goods vehicles on the road, what is the probability that if a vehicle was stopped at random it would either be overweight or the driver would have exceeded the allowed driving time?

The key to this question is the word *or*. And since it is possible both for the vehicle to be overweight and for the driver to have exceeded the permitted driving time, the events are not mutually exclusive. Using the addition law you should have obtained the following result:

$$P(\text{time exceeded}) = \frac{40}{100} \text{ or } 0.4$$

$$P(\text{overweight}) = \frac{35}{100} \text{ or } 0.35$$

$$P(\text{time exceeded and overweight}) = \frac{15}{100} \text{ or } 0.15$$

$$\text{So the } P(\text{time exceeded or overweight}) = 0.4 + 0.35 - 0.15$$

$$= 0.6$$

That is, there is a 60% chance that either the lorry would be overweight or the driver would have exceeded the driving time.

7.4 Conditional probability

If the probability of Event B occurring is dependent on whether Event A has occurred, you would say that Event B is conditional on Event A, and is written $P(B|A)$, which means probability of B given A has occurred.

When Event A and Event B are independent, $P(B|A) = P(B)$. Sampling without replacement is a good example of conditional probability. If two students are to be chosen randomly from a group of 5 girls and 4 boys, then the probability that the first person chosen is a girl is $\frac{5}{9}$ or 0.5556, and the probability that it is a boy is $1 - 0.5556 = 0.4444$.

The probability that the second person is a girl depends on the outcome of the first choice.

First choice	Probability of second choice being a girl
boy	$\frac{5}{8}$ or 0.625
girl	$\frac{4}{8}$ or 0.5

In the first case the number of girls remains at 5, but in the second case there are only 4 girls to choose from. Note that in both cases the total number of students left is 8, since one has already been chosen.

If you want to know the probability of the first student being a girl *and* the second student being a girl, you will need to use the *multiplication rule*. If the events are dependent, as in this example, the rule is:

$P(A \text{ and } B) = P(A) \times P(B|A)$

So $P(\text{girl and a girl}) = 0.5556 \times 0.5 = 0.2778$.

If two (or more) events are independent the rule simplifies to:

$P(A \text{ and } B) = P(A) \times P(B)$

For example, if an aircraft has a main and a back-up computer and the probability of failure of either computer is 1%, then the probability of both failing is $0.01 \times 0.01 = 0.0001$ or 0.01%.

Activity 7.4

A light bulb manufacturer produces bulbs in batches of 50, and it is known from past experience that 5 of each batch will be defective.

If two bulbs are selected without replacement from a batch, what is the probability that both will be defective?

The probability that the first bulb is defective is $\dfrac{5}{50} = 0.1$, but the probability that the second is defective is $\dfrac{4}{49} = 0.0816$, since the total number of bulbs has been reduced by one and there must be one less defective bulb. The probability that both bulbs are defective is therefore:

$0.1 \times 0.0816 = 0.00816$

This probability is very small, so if you did in fact get two defective bulbs you should be suspicious concerning the claimed defective rate. (This idea forms the basis of some quality control schemes.)

7.5 Tree diagrams

A very useful diagram to use when solving compound events, particularly when conditional probability is involved, is the tree diagram. This diagram represents different outcomes of an experiment by means of branches. For example, in the student example the two 'experiments' of choosing an individual can be represented by the tree diagram in Figure 7.4. The first experiment is represented by a small circle or node, and the two possible outcomes are represented by branches radiating out from the node. The event and probability are written alongside the branch. The second experiment is again represented by a node and you will notice that this node appears twice, once for each outcome of the first experiment. Branches again radiate out from each node, but notice that the probability is different depending on what happened in the first experiment.

You will see that the compound events have been written at the end of each route in Figure 7.4. If you add up these probabilities you will see that they sum to 1. This is because the routes are mutually exclusive and *mutually exhaustive*. They are mutually exclusive because one and only one of the routes can be followed, and they are mutually exhaustive

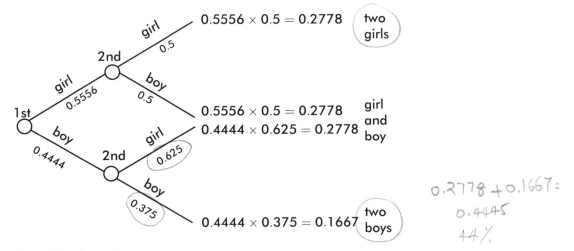

Figure 7.4 A tree diagram

because all possible routes have been shown. From this diagram various probabilities could be evaluated using the law of addition. For example, the probability of getting two students of the same sex is $0.2778 + 0.1667 = 0.4445$.

It is unlikely that you would use a tree diagram to solve a simple problem like this, but consider the following problem.

Example 7.1

The demand for gas is dependent on the weather and much research has been undertaken to forecast the demand accurately. This is important since it is quite difficult (and expensive) to increase the supply at short notice. If, on any particular day, the air temperature is below normal, the probability that the demand will be high is 0.6. However, at normal temperatures the probability of a high demand occurring is only 0.2, and if the temperature is above normal the probability of a high demand drops to 0.05. What is the probability of a high demand occurring if, over a period of time, the temperature is below normal on 20% of occasions and above normal on 30% of occasions?

The tree diagram is shown in Figure 7.5. Since the demand *depends* on temperature, the first node refers to temperature and there are three branches: below normal, normal and above normal. The probability of the temperature being normal is $1 - (0.2 + 0.3) = 0.5$. The compound probability for each route has been written at the end of the route, so that the probability of there being a high demand given that the temperature is below normal is $0.2 \times 0.6 = 0.12$. Since there are three routes where the demand could be high, the law of addition is used and the probability is:

$$0.12 + 0.10 + 0.015 = 0.235$$

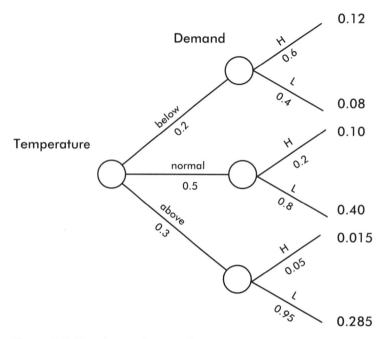

Figure 7.5 Tree diagram for Example 7.1

Activity 7.5

A company purchases electronic components in batches of 100 and the supplier guarantees that there will be no more than 5 defective components in each batch. Before acceptance of a particular batch the company has a policy of selecting without replacement two components for testing. If both components are satisfactory the batch is accepted and if both are defective the batch is rejected. However, if only one is defective another component is selected and if this is satisfactory the batch is accepted, while if it is defective, the batch is rejected. If the probability that a component is defective is 5%, what is the probability that the batch will be accepted?

You could answer this question without a tree diagram, but it is strongly recommended that diagrams are used whenever possible. The diagram is shown in Figure 7.6 where it will be seen that each node has two outcomes: either OK or defective. At the start of the process the probability that the first selection will give a defective component is $\frac{5}{100}$ or 0.05, and the probability that it will be OK is 0.95. If the first component was defective, then the probability that the second is also defective is reduced to $\frac{4}{99}$ or 0.04040, since there is one less defective component *and* one less component in total. The remaining probabilities have been found using a similar reasoning.

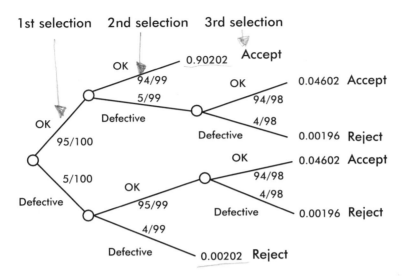

1st selection   2nd selection   3rd selection

Figure 7.6 Tree diagram for Activity 7.5

The compound probabilities have been written at the end of each route together with the decision; that is, accept or reject. There are three routes where the decision is to accept, and the addition law can be used to give the probability that the batch will be accepted. That is:

$$0.90202 + 0.04602 + 0.0462 = 0.99406$$

The probability that the batch will be rejected is $1 - 0.99406 = 0.00594$. This can be confirmed by adding the probabilities separately.

As in Activity 7.4, it is unlikely that a batch would be rejected. However, if it was, you would have grounds to question the supplier about the true number of defective items in a batch. This type of problem comes under the category of quality control.

7.6 Bayes' theorem

This theorem is based on the idea that in many situations we begin an analysis with some *prior* or initial probability estimate for the event we are interested in. This probability can come from historical data, previous experience, a pilot survey, and so on.

Then, we receive additional information from a survey, test, report, and so on, so that we are able to update our prior probability and calculate, using Bayes' theorem, what is known as our *posterior probability*.

Example 7.2

You are a manager of a company that manufactures 'set top' boxes for digital TV. There is a large demand for these boxes and retailers are urgently asking for delivery. To speed up delivery you could cut out the time-consuming testing of each box, but you are worried that defective boxes would then be returned, which would tarnish the company's reputation. From past experience you know that about 5% of boxes would be expected to be faulty.

You now select a box. What is the chance that it is faulty? Clearly it is 5% or 0.05. This is our *prior* probability. Perhaps it is possible to do a 'quick and dirty' test on the box, but you know that this test is not very reliable. It is believed that the test will indicate that the box is defective 20% of the time when it is in fact perfectly OK. If the box is defective the test should get it right 90% of the time; that is, the test is better at getting it right when the box is defective. This means that the test is *biased*.

If you do this quick test on a box and it fails, how do you revise your prior probability in the light of this result?

Activity 7.6

Draw a probability tree showing the different outcomes when the test is applied to both a good and a defective box.

For each branch of the tree there are two outcomes of the test; either pass or fail. The probability tree with the probabilities added is shown in Figure 7.7.

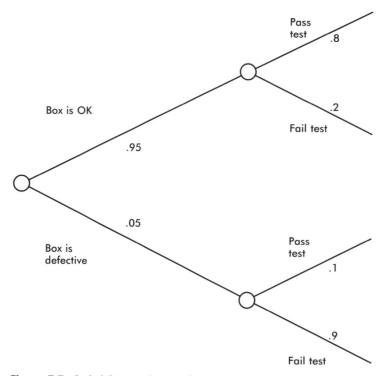

Figure 7.7 Probability tree diagram for Example 7.2

Activity 7.7

Imagine that you have 1000 boxes to test. How many boxes would you have along the different branches?

As there are 1000 boxes, then 950 of these will be good boxes and 50 will be defective. Of the 950 good ones, there will $950 \times 0.8 = 760$ that pass the test while the remaining 190 will fail. Of the 50 that are defective, there will be $50 \times 0.1 = 5$ that pass the test while the remaining 45 will correctly fail it. This information has been added to the probability tree and you can see this in Figure 7.8.

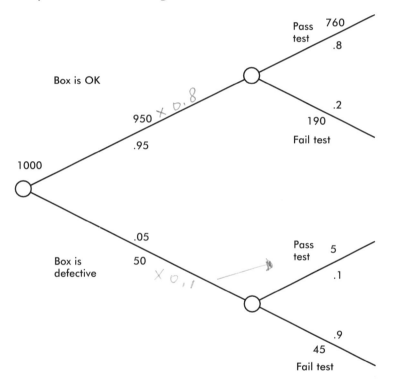

Figure 7.8 The tree with 1000 boxes split between the different branches

Activity 7.8

What is the probability that if you picked one of the 1000 boxes at random it would fail the test?

190 good boxes failed the test and 45 defective boxes failed the test. The total number that failed is therefore $190 + 45 = 235$, and the probability that a box would fail the test is

$$\frac{235}{1000} = 0.235$$

Activity 7.9

What is the probability that a box is defective given that it failed the test?

Out of the 235 boxes that failed the test, 45 came from boxes that were defective, so the probability that the chosen box is defective is $\frac{45}{235} = 0.1914$. So this new information has allowed us to revise our probability of a defective box from 5% to 19%.

Activity 7.10

Repeat the last three activities using 100 boxes.

You should have found that you still get the same probabilities even though you are dealing with fractions of a box when the boxes are defective. In fact it is not necessary to even consider the number of boxes at all as all you are really doing is multiplying probabilities together. Figure 7.9 is the formal probability tree diagram for the problem using Bayes'

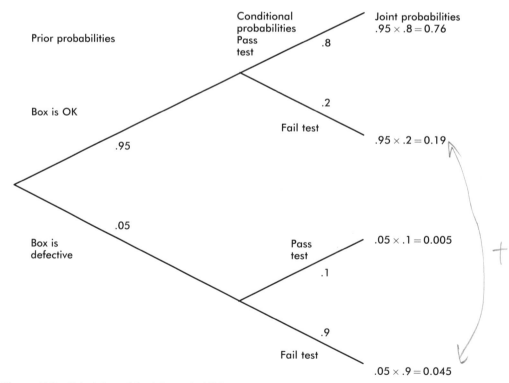

Figure 7.9 Calculation of the joint probabilities

theorem. The probability of the test being correct or not is the *conditional* probability as it is conditional on the first branch of the tree. The probabilities at the end of the tree are the *joint* probabilities as they are obtained by multiplying the prior and conditional probabilities together. The probability that a box would fail the test is the sum of the relevant joint probabilities; that is, $0.19 + 0.045 = 0.235$, and this is the same value as we obtained before. The probability that the a box is defective given that it failed the test is called the *posterior* probability, and for our problem it is

$$\frac{0.045}{0.235} = 0.1914$$

To summarise this procedure we

- Construct a tree with branches representing all the prior probabilities
- Extend the tree adding the new information obtained. Write the conditional probabilities on these branches
- Calculate the joint probabilities
- To obtain the posterior probabilities, divide the appropriate joint probability by the sum of the corresponding joint probabilities.

As a formula this is:

$$P(B\,|\,A) = \frac{P(B\ AND\ A)}{P(A)}$$

Where B is the event 'box is defective' and A is the event 'it failed the test'.

Bayes' theorem is a very powerful technique in solving probability problems and we will come back to an important application of this theorem when we look at decision trees in Chapter 9.

 ## 7.7 Permutations and combinations

Problems frequently exist where selections are made from groups of items. In these cases it is useful to be able to calculate the number of selections that are possible. The method used depends on whether the order of the selection is important or not. If it is, you should use *permutations*. The number of permutations, where r items are to be selected from a group of size n, is given by the formula:

$$^{n}P_{r} = \frac{n!}{(n-r)!}$$

Where $n!$ is read as *factorial n* and means $(n-1) \times (n-2) \times (n-3) \times ,\ldots$. For example, $5! = 5 \times 4 \times 3 \times 2 \times 1 = 120$ (Note: $1! = 1$ and by definition $0! = 1$.) If you have a scientific calculator you should find that it has a $^{n}P_{r}$ button, which is much easier than using the formula.

IIII➡ ## Activity 7.11

Bank cheque cards usually have a 4-digit 'pin' number so that they can be used in a cash dispenser. What is the probability that a thief, finding your card, could hit on the correct combination at the first attempt?

The order is important here because, for example, 1234 is a different number from 4321. There are 10 possible digits (0 to 9) so the number of ways of selecting 4 from 10 is:

$$^nP_r = {}^{10}P_4$$

$$= \frac{10!}{(10-4)!} = \frac{10!}{6!}$$

$$= \frac{10 \times 9 \times 8 \times 7 \times 6 \times 5 \times 4 \times 3 \times 2 \times 1}{6 \times 5 \times 4 \times 3 \times 2 \times 1}$$

$$= 5040$$

So there is only a 1 in 5040 chance of the thief finding the correct permutation. As a probability this is:

$$\frac{1}{5040} = 0.000198$$

Where the order is *not* important, you would use *combinations*. The formula for this is as follows:

$$^nC_r = \frac{n!}{r!(n-r)!}$$

Again, most scientific calculators should contain this function.

IIII➡ ## Activity 7.12

What is the probability of getting 4 heads from 10 tosses of a coin?

Order here is not important, since 4 heads followed by 6 tails is no different to 6 tails followed by 4 heads. The combination formula will therefore give you the number of ways of obtaining 4 heads from 10 tosses of a coin. That is:

$$^nC_r = {}^{10}C_4$$

$$= \frac{10!}{4! \times (10-4)!}$$

$$= \frac{10 \times 9 \times 9 \times 7 \times 6!}{4 \times 3 \times 2 \times 1 \times 6!}$$

$$= 210$$

Since the probability of a head is 0.5 and each toss of the coin is independent, the probability of getting any combination of heads and tails must be $(0.5)^{10} = 0.0009765$. If you now try and picture the problem as a tree diagram you should realise that this is simply the compound probability of one route of the tree. Since 210 routes contain 4 heads, the probability of getting 4 heads in 10 tosses is:

$$210 \times 0.0009765 = 0.2051$$

7.8 Expected value

If you toss a coin 100 times, you would *expect* 50 heads and 50 tails. That is, the expected number of heads is $0.5 \times 100 = 50$. In general it is a long-run average, which means it is the value you would get if you repeated the experiment long enough. It is calculated by multiplying a value of a particular variable by the probability of its occurrence and repeating this for all possible values. In symbols this can be represented as:

$$\text{Expected value} = \sum px$$

Where $\sum$ means the 'sum of'.

Activity 7.13

Over a long period of time a salesperson recorded the number of sales she achieved per day. From an analysis of her records it was found that she made no sales 20% of the time, one sale 50% of the time and 2 sales 30% of the time. What is her expected number of sales?

The x in this case takes on values of 0, 1, and 2 and

$$\text{expected value is} = 0.2 \times 0 + 0.5 \times 1 + 0.3 \times 2$$
$$= 0 + 0.5 + 0.6$$
$$= 1.1 \text{ sales}$$

This is just like working out the mean value of a group of numbers, where the probabilities are the frequencies or 'weights'. And, just like the mean, the expected value will not necessarily be a whole number.

Expected values are frequently used to calculate expected monetary values, or EMV. This is illustrated in the next activity.

Activity 7.14

An investor buys £1000 of shares with the object of making a capital gain after 1 year. She believes that there is a 5% chance that the shares will double in value, a 25% chance that they will be worth £1500, a 30% chance that they will only be worth £500 and a 40% chance that they will not change in value. What is the expected monetary value of this investment, ignoring dealing costs?

The EMV is found in a similar manner to the expected number of sales in Activity 7.1, that is:

$$0.05 \times 2000 + 0.25 \times 1500 + 0.3 \times 500 + 0.40 \times 1000$$

$$= 100 + 375 + 150 + 400$$

$$= £1025$$

So the EMV is £1025, an expected profit of £25.

7.9 Summary

This chapter has introduced you to some of the basic rules of probability. Probability is an essential prerequisite for studying many topics later in this text including probability distributions and decision analysis. Perhaps the most difficult part of probability is when we are dealing with compound events, particularly when one event is conditional on another event occurring. Whenever compound events occur it is often possible to represent the events by a tree diagram. Tree diagrams can simplify what at first sight appears to be a very difficult problem. This is especially true when we are using Bayes' theorem.

7.10 Further reading

Burton, G., Carrol, G. and Wall, S. (1999) *Quantitative Methods for Business and Economics*, Longman, New York (Chapter 5).
Morris, C. (2000) *Quantitative Approaches in Business Studies*, fifth edition, Pitman, London (Chapter 8).

7.11 EXERCISES

The answers to the progress questions, the multiple choice questions and some of the practice questions are given in Appendix 1. Solutions to the remaining questions and the assignment can be found at the web site for this text.

PROGRESS QUESTIONS
These questions have been designed to help you remember the key points in this chapter.

Give the missing word in each case.

1. Probability is measured on a scale from 0 to ....
2. Probabilities that are obtained by measurement are called .... probabilities.

3. Probabilities that are obtained by guesses are called .... probabilities.

4. The sum of the probabilities of a series of mutually exclusive and mutually exhaustive events is ....

5. The .... law is used when you want to find the probability of Event A occurring or Event B.

6. The .... law is applicable when you want to find the probability that both Events A and Event B will occur.

7. Bayes' theorem allows us to update our .... probabilities.

8. The probabilities resulting from the application of Bayes' theorem are called the .... probabilities.

ANSWER *TRUE* OR *FALSE*

9. Probability cannot exceed 1 or 100%.

10. If you got 9 consecutive heads in 9 tosses of a coin, then the next toss will almost certainly be a tail.

11. Two tosses of the same coin is an example of independent events.

12. The correct name for a combination lock is a permutation lock.

13. Expected value is a long-run average.

14. A posterior probability follows the updating of a prior probability.

REVIEW QUESTIONS

These questions have been designed to help you check your comprehension of the key points in this chapter. You may wish to look further than this chapter in order to answer them fully. You will find the reading list useful in this respect. You can check the essential elements of your answers by referring to the appropriate section.

15. Compare and contrast the different methods of obtaining probabilities. (Section 7.2)

16. Under what circumstances would the addition law of probability be used? (Section 7.3)

17. Under what circumstances would the multiplication law of probability be used? (Section 7.3)

18. Under what circumstances would you use Bayes' theorem? (Section 7.6)

19. What are the essential differences between permutations and combinations? (Section 7.7)

MULTIPLE CHOICE QUESTIONS

20. $P(B \mid A)$ means:

    A... The probability of B divided by the probability of A

    B... The probability of B given that A has occurred

    C... The probability of A given that B has occurred

    D... The probability of A times B

21. If $P(A) = P(A \mid B)$, the events A and B are

    A... Mutually exclusive   B... Mutually exhaustive   C... Statistically independent

22. If three coins are tossed, the probability of exactly one head occurring is:

    A... 3/8   B... 2/3   C... 1/8   D... 1/4

23. If two events, A and B, are *statistically independent*, the occurrence of A implies that the probability of B occurring will be:

    A... 0   B... unchanged   C... 1   D... unknown

24. If a fair coin is tossed 9 times and a head is obtained on each toss, the probability that the next toss of the coin will produce a tail is:

    A... 0   B... 0.5   C... 1.0   D... less than 0.5   E... more than 0.5

25. The probability that the 1600 train from Bristol Parkway station to Paddington is late is 0.6. The probability that the train will be late on at least one of the next two days is:

    A... 0.36   B... 1.20   C... 0.84   D... 0.6

26. Below are the results of a survey of 100 companies.

	Turnover increased	Turnover didn't increase
Company has a web page	30	30
Company doesn't have a web page	10	30

    What is the probability that a company showed an increase in turnover given that they have a web page?

    A... $\dfrac{30}{100}$ B... $\dfrac{30}{40}$ C... $\dfrac{40}{60}$ D... $\dfrac{30}{60}$

27. Out of a group of 20 students there are 3 who play a musical instrument. Two students are picked at random. The probability that both students play a musical instrument is:

    A... $\dfrac{6}{380}$ B... $\dfrac{6}{400}$ C... $\dfrac{9}{400}$ D... $\dfrac{9}{380}$

28. If the prior probability is 0.4 and the corresponding conditional probability is 0.3, then the joint probability is:

    A... 0.4   B... 0.3   C... 0.7   D... 0.12

PRACTICE QUESTIONS

29. A bag contains 5 red discs, 3 yellow discs, and 2 green discs.

    (a) A disc is picked from the bag. What is the probability that the disc will be:

        (i) red?   (ii) yellow?   (iii) not yellow?

    (b) Two discs are picked from the bag *with* replacement. What is the probability that the discs will be:

        (i) both red?   (ii) 1 red and 1 yellow?

    (c) Repeat part (b) if the discs are picked *without* replacement.

30. What is the probability that if you pick a card from a pack it will be:

    (a) an Ace?   (b) a red card?   (c) an Ace or a red card?

31. A box contains 50 light bulbs, of which 4 are defective. You purchase two bulbs from this box. What is the probability that both will be defective?

32. The probability that a double glazing salesperson will make a sale on a particular day is 0.05. What is the probability that over a three-day period the salesperson will make:

    (a) 3 sales?   (b) exactly 1 sale?   (c) at least 1 sale?

33. A mail order firm knows that it will receive a 20% response rate to any literature it circulates. In a new geographic location 8 circulars are mailed as a market test. Assuming that the response rate is still applicable to this new location, calculate the probability of the following events:

    (i)   All 8 people respond
    (ii) No one responds
    (iii) Exactly 2 people respond

34. How might you try to assess the following probabilities?:

    (a) the probability that the FT index will rise in value tomorrow
    (b) the probability that a jar of coffee, filled by an automatic process, will weigh less than the stated weight
    (c) the probability that you might win the top prize in the National Lottery
    (d) the probability that the ageing process will eventually be reversed

35. Three machines – A, B and C – operate independently in a factory. Machine A is out of action for 10% of the time, while B is out of action 5% of the time and C is out of action for 20% of the time. A rush order has to be commenced at midday tomorrow. What is the probability that at this time:

    (a) All three of the machines will be out of action?
    (b) None of the machines will be out of action?

36. A company is engaged in a civil engineering project. The probability that the project will be delayed by bad weather is 0.3, while the probability that it will be delayed by geological problems is 0.2. What is the probability that the project will be delayed by both bad weather and geological problems?

37. A box contains 20 spark plugs, of which 6 are substandard. If two plugs are selected from the box without replacement, what is the probability that both will be substandard?

38. The probability of the FT 30 index rising on a particular day is 0.6. If it does rise then the probability that the value of shares in a publishing company will rise is 0.8. If the index does not rise then the publishing company shares only have a 0.3 probability of rising. What is the probability that tomorrow the publishing company's shares will rise in value?

39. (a) A light bulb is to be selected at random from a box of 100 bulbs, details of which are given below.

Type of bulb	Defective	Satisfactory
60 watts	20	40
100 watts	10	30

Find: (i) P(bulb is defective)

(ii) P(bulb is defective|selected bulb is 60 watts)

(b) Suppose that the company receiving the bulbs has a policy of selecting, without replacement, two bulbs from each box when it is delivered. It then applies the following decision rules:

If both bulbs are satisfactory then the box will be accepted.

If both bulbs are defective, the box is returned to the supplier.

If one bulb is defective, a third bulb is selected and the box is only accepted if this bulb is satisfactory.

What is the probability that a box, referred to above, will be accepted?

40. Marla plc is trying to decide whether it markets its new car immobiliser nationwide. The sales of the product will depend to some extent on the demand for car immobilisers, and the marketing department has suggested that the probability of high demand is 0.2 and medium to low demand is 0.8. However, it is possible to modify these probabilities by a market research exercise, but the probability that the research will be correct is only 0.6. What is the probability that the demand is really high given that the market research indicates that it will be high?

ASSIGNMENT

Car insurance companies are interested in the probabilities of different coloured cars getting involved in accidents. For example, red cars have historically been involved in a disproportionate number of accidents. Conduct a survey to find the proportion of the different coloured cars on a stretch of road near you. Convert these proportions into probabilities. These will be your prior probabilities.

You are now given access to recent accident records for that stretch of road and discover that the probability that a red car will be involved in an accident is 0.03; a blue car 0.015; and all others 0.023. Given that there is an accident, what is the probability that the car involved is red?

8 Probability distributions

8.1 Introduction

This chapter examines some very important probability distributions. The *binomial* distribution is a discrete distribution and is used when there are only two possible outcomes. The *Poisson* distribution is another discrete distribution and is used for modelling events that occur at random. The final distribution you will meet is the *normal* distribution and this (continuous) distribution has applications in almost all aspects of daily life, such as deciding whether the weight of a loaf of bread is outside acceptable limits or whether a child's height or weight is abnormal in some way.

To complete this chapter successfully you should have already worked through Chapter 3 (Presentation of data), Chapter 4 (Summarising data) and Chapter 7 (Introduction to probability).

On completing this chapter you should:

- Understand the difference between continuous and discrete probability distributions
- Be able to calculate binomial probabilities
- Be able to calculate Poisson probabilities
- Be able to use the Poisson distribution as an approximation to the binomial distribution
- Understand how the shape of the normal distribution is affected by the mean and standard deviation of the data
- Be able to use the normal distribution table
- Be able to use the normal distribution as an approximation to both the binomial and Poisson distributions

8.2 Discrete and continuous probability distributions

The differences between discrete and continuous data were discussed in Chapter 3, but essentially discrete data is obtained by *counting*, whereas continuous data is obtained by *measurement*. So counting the number of loaves of bread baked over a period of time would give you data that only contained whole numbers (assuming that the bread is only sold as complete loaves), while recording the weight of each loaf of bread baked would give you data that could take on any value.

Example 8.1

Data on the number and weight of a 'standard' loaf of bread were collected over a period of time and aggregated into Table 8.1.

Table 8.1   Frequency table for the data on the number and weight of loaves of bread

Number of loaves baked		Weight of each loaf	
Number	Frequency	Weight range	Frequency
20	8	770 g to below 775 g	3
21	12	775 g to below 780 g	17
22	24	780 g to below 785 g	44
23	26	785 g to below 790 g	100
24	35	790 g to below 795 g	141
25	35	795 g to below 800 g	192
26	30	800 g to below 805 g	191
27	28	805 g to below 810 g	150
28	21	810 g to below 815 g	90
		815 g to below 820 g	42
		820 g to below 825 g	14
		825 g to below 830 g	9

In order to compare the two data sets in more detail, diagrams could be used. A *bar chart* would be appropriate for the number of loaves baked, while a *histogram* is necessary for the weight data (see Chapter 3). These diagrams are shown in Figures 8.1 and 8.2.

The histogram gives you an idea of the underlying distribution of the data; that is, it shows you how the data is *distributed* across the range of possible values. This kind of distribution is called an *empirical* distribution because it is obtained by measurement or

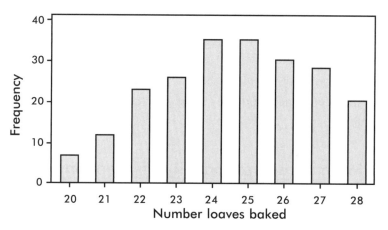

Figure 8.1   Bar chart for the number of loaves baked

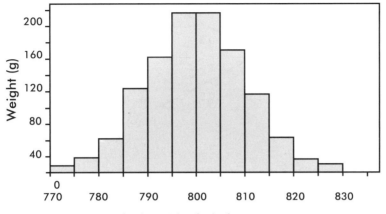

Figure 8.2 Histogram for the weight of a loaf

observation. There are also distributions that can be derived mathematically. The three most common distributions are the binomial distribution, the Poisson distribution and the normal distribution.

8.3 The binomial distribution

This is a discrete probability distribution and arises when

- a variable can only be in one of two states (an either|or situation)
- the probability of the two outcomes are known and constant from trial to trial
- the number of trials is known and constant
- successive events are independent

The obvious example to use here is a coin since it can be in one of two states, either a head (H) or a tail (T). However, the binomial distribution can be used in many applications, such as quality control where an item can be either defective or not defective.

If a coin is tossed once, there are only two outcomes with equal probability, but if you toss a coin twice (or toss two coins once), the outcome could be one of the following:

2 heads, or
2 tails, or a
head and a tail

There are two ways of getting a head and a tail, since either coin could be head or a tail. The best way of illustrating the outcomes is by mean of a tree diagram. Figure 8.3 shows that there are 4 'routes' to the tree. At the end of each route the number of heads has been indicated, together with the probability of that route. The number of ways of getting 2, 1, and 0 heads is 1, 2, and 1 respectively, and the probability of any route is $0.5 \times 0.5 = 0.25$ (or $(0.5)^2$). Therefore the probability of getting 1 head is $2 \times 0.25 = 0.5$.

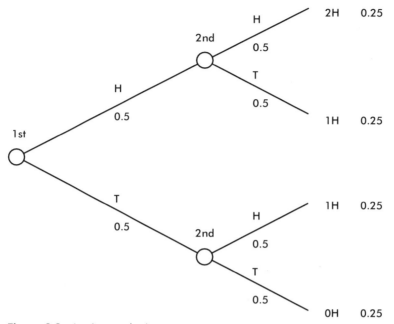

Figure 8.3 A coin tossed twice

Activity 8.1

Draw the tree for the case where a coin is tossed three times. What is the probability of

(i) one head, and

(ii) two heads?

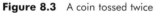

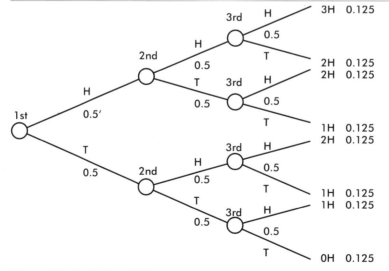

Figure 8.4 A coin tossed 3 times

The tree has become a little more complicated and is shown in Figure 8.4. The number of ways of getting 3, 2, 1, or 0 heads is 1, 3, 3, and 1 respectively and the probability of following any route is now $(0.5)^3 = 0.125$. The probability of getting 1 head is therefore $3 \times 0.125 = 0.375$ and the probability of getting 2 heads is also 0.375.

If you repeat this for 4 heads you should find that the number of ways of getting 4, 3, 2, 1, 0 heads is 1, 4, 6, 4, and 1 respectively, and the probability of following any route is $(0.5)^4 = 0.0625$. If you now write the number of ways of getting various combinations of heads in a table similar to the one below, you should see how easy it is to carry on the sequence.

1 toss				1		1		
2 tosses			1		2		1	
3 tosses		1		3		3		1
4 tosses	1		4		6		4		1

Activity 8.2

Continue the sequence for 5 tosses of the coin.

For 5 tosses the sequence will be 1, 5, 10, 5, 10, 5, 1 since $1+4=5$ and $4+6=10$. This known as *Pascal's triangle* and it gives you the number of ways an event will occur. Although it is quite feasible to do this for a small number of tosses of the coin, what would happen if you tossed the coin 10, 20 or even 50 times? Fortunately, this series is the same as finding the number of ways of choosing r items from n (see Chapter 7.7) and is given by:

$$^nC_r = \frac{n!}{r!(n-r)!}$$

Activity 8.3

How many ways are there of getting 4 heads from 10 tosses of a coin?

Using the formula we get:

$$^{10}C_4 = \frac{10!}{4! \times (10-4)!}$$
$$= 210$$

This is fine for a coin where the probability of each event is 0.5, but what about more general problems? Where an item can be in one of two states and the probability of both states is known and constant, the ideas just discussed can be used. For example, about 5% of people are in blood type AB, so the probability that any one person has this blood type is 0.05. What is the probability that in a group of 10 people, 4 will have this blood type? This is a binomial problem because a person either does or does not have this blood type. The probability that a person doesn't is 0.95 $(1-0.05)$. If 4 people have this blood type then it follows that 6 do not, so the probability of a route of the probability tree giving this combination is:

$$(0.05)^4 \times (0.95)^6 = 0.00000459$$

Since there are 210 ways of getting this combination (see earlier in this Activity), the probability of 4 people out of 10 with blood type AB is:

$$210 \times 0.00000459 = 0.00096$$

If general if p is the probability of a 'success', where success is defined as a person or item being in a particular state, then the binomial distribution can be defined as follows:

$$P(r) = {}^nC_r P^r (1-P)^{n-r}$$

where n is the number of trials and r the number of successes. To use this formula you simply need to know the values of P, n and r. For example, suppose that you wanted to find the probability that 2 or more people in the group of 10 had blood of type AB. You could find the probability of 2, 3, 4, and so on, and then add the probabilities together. However, there is an easier way – this is to use the fact that the probabilities must sum to 1, so $P(r \geq 2) = 1 - (P(0) + P(1))$. This reduces the number of calculations from 9 to 2. (With larger values of n, the saving is even more pronounced.)

Activity 8.4

Calculate the probability of $P(r \geq 2)$ for the example above.

The calculation of $P(0)$ is easy since there is only one route in this case and ${}^{10}C_0 = 1$. So:

$$P(0) = (0.5)^0 \times (0.95)^{10} = 0.59874$$

(note: anything raised to the power of 0 is 1)

For the calculation of $P(1)$, ${}^{10}C_1 = 10$, so:

$$P(1) = 10 \times (0.05)^1 \times (0.95)^9 = 0.31512$$

and $P(r \geq 2) = 1 - (0.59874 + 0.31512)$

$$= 0.08614, \text{ or about } 8.6\%$$

An easier method is to use the cumulative binomial function in Excel. The function name is BINOMDIST(number_s,trials,probability_s,Cumulative)

Where:
Number_s is the number of successes in trials [that is, r]
Trials is the number of independent trials [that is, n]

Probability_s is the probability of success on each trial [that is, p]
Cumulative is a logical value that determines the form of the function. If cumulative is
TRUE, then BINOMDIST returns the cumulative distribution function, which is the
probability that there are at most number_s successes; if FALSE, it returns the probability
mass function, which is the probability that there are number_s successes.
(*Taken from the Help facility in Excel.*)

By setting *cumulative* as *true* we get the cumulative probability of r successes or less in n
trials. So, in the above example, to find the probability that 2 or more had blood group AB
you would first need to use the BINOMDIST function to find the probability of 1 or less.
The function would therefore be:

BINOMDIST(1,10,0.05,true)

Excel returns a probability of 0.9139, so if we subtract this from 1 we get 0.0861, which is
the same as we got above. To avoid using Excel repeatedly, a table for selected values of n,
r and p is provided in Appendix 2. This table gives you the probability of r successes or
less, so to find the probability for $n = 10$ and $r = 1$ you would need to subtract the
probability from 1 as before. Part of the binomial table is shown in Table 8.2 where the
probability of 0.9139 has been highlighted.

**Table 8.2 Part of the binomial table to be found in
Appendix 2**

n	r	0.01	*p* 0.05	0.1
10	0	0.9044	0.5987	0.3487
10	1	0.9957	**0.9139**	0.7361
10	2	0.9999	0.9885	0.9298

Activity 8.5

Use Excel to find the probability of $P(0)$, $P(1)$, $P(2)$, $P(3)$, $P(4)$ and $P(5)$ when $n = 5$ and
$p = 0.2$. Plot these values in the form of a bar chart. How would you describe the shape of
the distribution?

We would now set cumulative as false, and the results using Excel are:

BINOMIST(0,5,0.2.false) = 0.32768
BINOMIST(1,5,0.2.false) = 0.40960
BINOMIST(2,5,0.2.false) = 0.20480
BINOMIST(3,5,0.2.false) = 0.05120
BINOMIST(4,5,0.2.false) = 0.00640
BINOMIST(5,5,0.2.false) = 0.00032

The chart in Figure 8.5 shows that the distribution is *right skewed*.

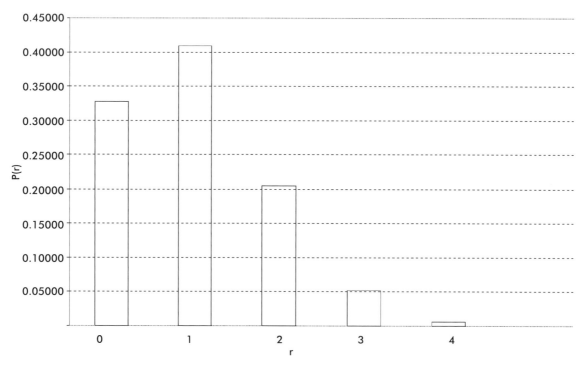

Figure 8.5 Bar chart for Activity 8.5

Activity 8.6

Repeat Activity 8.5 for $n = 20$ and $p = 0.2$ (stop when $P(r)$ is zero to 4 decimal places).

You should have obtained the chart similar to the one in Figure 8.6. Notice that the distribution is now much less skewed. (We shall return to the shape of the binomial distribution later.)

8.3.1 The mean and standard deviation of the binomial distribution

The mean of a binomial distribution is np.
    The standard deviation is given by the formula:

$$\sigma = \sqrt{np(1-p)}$$

Activity 8.7

What is the mean and standard deviation of the binomial distribution with $n = 5$ and $p = 0.2$? (that is, for Activity 8.5)

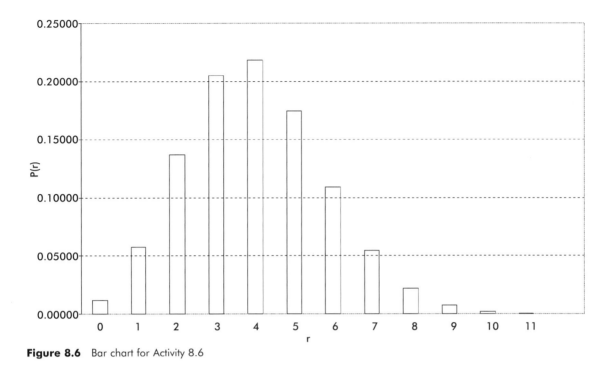

Figure 8.6 Bar chart for Activity 8.6

The mean is $10 \times 0.2 = 2.0$.

The standard deviation is $\sqrt{10 \times 0.2 \times 0.8} = 1.265$

As the standard deviation is a measure of spread it would be interesting to see how many standard deviations would be needed to cover the distribution. One standard deviation would give a range of $2.0 \pm 1.265 = 0.735$ to 3.265. Looking at Figure 8.5 we can see that this includes $r = 1$ to $r = 3$ inclusive. Adding the probabilities for these we get

$$0.4096 + 0.2048 + 0.0512 = 0.6656$$

So about 67% of the distribution is covered by one standard deviation.

Activity 8.8

What proportion of the distribution is covered by two standard deviations?

In this case we have $2.0 \pm 2 \times 1.265 = -0.53$ to 4.53

This covers the first 4 values of r and the probabilities add to 0.9997. So about 99.7% is covered by two standard deviations, which is virtually the whole distribution.

||||➡ ## Activity 8.9

Repeat Activity 8.8 for the case where $n = 20$ and $r = 0.2$ (that is, Activity 8.6).

The mean is $20 \times 0.2 = 4$

The standard deviation is $\sqrt{20 \times 0.2 \times 0.8} = 1.789$

For two standard deviations we get a range of $4 \pm 2 \times 1.789 = 0.422$ to 7.589

This covers the distribution from $r = 1$ to $r = 7$ and adding the probabilities for these values of r we get 0.9563, which is almost 96%.

   You will find that most observation rarely fall outside the range of the mean plus or minus two standard deviations. You will meet this idea again when we look at the normal distribution.

8.4 The Poisson distribution

The Poisson distribution is another example of a discrete probability distribution. Like the binomial distribution the Poisson distribution again models the either|or situation but in this case the chance of a particular event occurring is very small. That is, the event is 'rare'. Also, we are normally only given the mean occurrence of the event instead of the probability. The Poisson distribution is often used in situations where the event is unlikely (accidents, machine failures) or where the event occurs at random (arrivals of calls at a switchboard, for example).

   The formula for the Poisson is less complicated than the binomial, and the probability of r events in a given unit (of time or length, and so on) is as follows:

$$P(r) = \frac{e^{-m}m^r}{r!}$$

Where m is the mean number of events in the same unit and e is the constant $2.7182818\ldots$ and can be found on many scientific calculators (usually in the form e^x).

   A typical example of the Poisson distribution is as follows:

The number of calls to a switchboard is random, with a mean of 1.5 per minute. What is the probability that there are no calls in any one minute?

All we need to do is to substitute $r = 0$ and $m = 1.5$ into the equation. That is:

$$P(0) = \frac{e^{-1.5}(1.5)^0}{0!}$$

$$= 0.2231$$

(Since $e^{-1.5} = 0.2331$, $1.5^0 = 1$ and $0! = 1$)

Activity 8.10

What is the probability that:

(i) There are more than 2 calls in any one minute?

(ii) There are less than 6 calls in a 5-minute period?

It is not possible to calculate the answer to (i) directly since the maximum number of calls that could be received is not specified (in fact there is no maximum). However, as in the binomial distribution the probability can be found by noting that the sum of the probabilities must equal 1.

So, $P(r > 2) = 1 - (P(0) + P(1) + P(2))$

That is, $P(r > 2) = 1 - (0.2231 + 0.3347 + 0.2510)$

$$= 0.1912$$

Question (ii) is a little more difficult since the time period has been changed from a minute to 5 minutes. However, all that needs to be done is to work out the average rate over 5 minutes, which is 7.5 (5×1.5) and then continue as before. That is:

$P(r < 6) = P(0) + P(1) + P(2) + P(3) + P(4) + P(5)$

To make this calculation easier we could use Excel. The function for the Poisson distribution is:

POISSON(x,mean,cumulative)

Where:

x is the number of events [that is, r]

Mean is the expected numeric value [that is, m]

Cumulative is a logical value that determines the form of the probability distribution returned. If cumulative is TRUE, POISSON returns the cumulative Poisson probability that the number of random events occurring will be between zero and x inclusive; if FALSE, it returns the Poisson probability mass function that the number of events occurring will be exactly x.

(*Taken from the Help facility in Excel.*)

Using Excel we get:

POISSON(5,7.5,true) $= 0.2414$

So $P(r < 6) = 0.2414$

An alternative to using Excel is to use the cumulative Poisson probability table in Appendix 2. This table gives you the probability of r or less events. Part of the Poisson table is shown in Table 8.3 where the probability of 0.2414 has been highlighted.

Table 8.3 Part of the Poisson table to be found in Appendix 2

		r
mean	5	6
0.1	1.0000	1.0000
7.2	0.2759	0.4204
7.3	0.2640	0.4060
7.4	0.2526	0.3920
7.5	**0.2414**	0.3782
7.6	0.2307	0.3646

8.4.1 The use of the Poisson distribution as an approximation to the binomial distribution

As you will probably have noticed it is a little easier to calculate probabilities using the Poisson distribution than it is using the binomial distribution. In some circumstances it is possible to use the Poisson distribution instead of the binomial distribution. The error you will get as a result will be quite small providing the following conditions are met:

- The number of trials, n, is large (greater than 30)
- The probability of a success, p, is small (less than 0.1)
- The mean number of successes, $n \times p$, is less than 5

Activity 8.11

A batch contains 1% defective items and a sample of size 40 is chosen. What is the probability that there are exactly 2 defective items? Are the conditions for using the Poisson distribution instead of the binomial met for this problem?

This is a binomial problem and the answer using the binomial distribution is:

$$P(2) = 40C_2 \times (0.01)^2 \times (1 - 0.01)^{38}$$

$$= 780 \times 0.0000682$$

$$= 0.0532$$

However, we can also use the Poisson to solve this problem because n is large, p is small and the mean number of defects is 0.4 (40×0.01) which is less than 5.

Using the Poisson distribution for r = 2, we get:

$$P(2) = \frac{e^{-0.4} \times (0.4)^2}{2!}$$

$$= 0.0536$$

which is an error of less than 1%.

8.4.2 The mean and standard deviation of the Poisson distribution

The *variance* of the Poisson distribution is equal to the mean. So the standard deviation, which is the square root of the variance is equal to the square root of the mean. In symbols this becomes:

$$\sigma = \sqrt{m}$$

For example, if the mean is 1.5 then the standard deviation will be $\sqrt{1.5} = 1.225$.

8.5 The normal distribution

Many observations that are obtained from measurements follow the normal distribution. For example, the heights of people and the weights of loaves of bread are approximately normally distributed. The normal distribution is completely symmetrical or bell shaped. The mean, mode and median of this distribution all lie at the centre of the bell, as you can see in Figure 8.7.

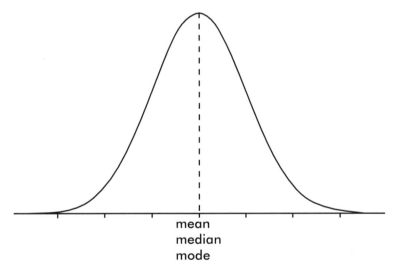

mean
median
mode

Figure 8.7 The normal distribution

The normal curve has the following properties:

1. The curve is symmetrical about the mean.

2. The total area under the curve is equal to 1 or 100%. This means that probability can be equated to area.

3. The horizontal axis represents a continuous variable such as weight.

4. The area under the curve between two points on the horizontal axis represents the probability that the value of the variable lies between these two points.

5. As the distance between two points gets less, the area between the two points must get less. Taking this to its logical conclusion, the probability of a specific value is zero. It is therefore only meaningful to talk about ranges, such as 800 g to 810 g.

6. The position and shape of the curve depends on the mean and standard deviation of the distribution. As the standard deviation gets larger, the curve will get flatter and extend further on either side of the mean.

Activity 8.12

The average weight of a 'standard' loaf of bread is 800 g and the weights are normally distributed. If a loaf is selected at random, what is the probability that it will weigh less than 800 g?

Property 1 above says that the normal curve is symmetrical about the mean, so that 50% of the loaves will be below the mean weight of 800 g and 50% will be above. Hence the probability will be 0.5 or 50%.

Activity 8.13

What proportion of loaves weigh more than 815 g?

This problem has been illustrated diagrammatically in Figure 8.8, where the area representing all loaves with a weight exceeding 815 g has been shaded.

This shaded area is clearly a small proportion of the total area, but it would be difficult to estimate the actual figure from the diagram alone. Tables are used to obtain this area but, before you can do this, you need to understand the properties of the *standard normal distribution*.

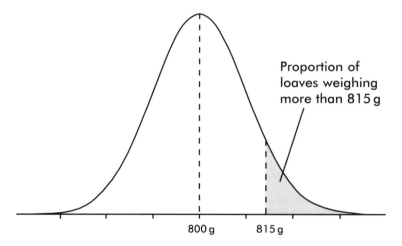

Proportion of loaves weighing more than 815 g

800 g   815 g

Figure 8.8 Distribution of the weight of a loaf of bread

8.5.1 The standard normal distribution

The standard normal distribution has a mean of zero and a standard deviation of 1. This is illustrated in Figure 8.9. The figures along the horizontal axis are number of standard deviations and are called the Z values. You will see from the diagram that the majority of the distribution is covered within 3 standard deviations either side of the mean.

To demonstrate the use of the normal table you should now refer to the table provided in Appendix 2. The table provided in this book gives you the area in the *right hand tail* of the distribution, but other tables may give the area in a different way. (Once you have used one table you should find it a simple matter to use a different type.)

The first column gives the Z value to one decimal place and the first row gives the second place of decimals. For example, for a Z value of 0.55, you would look down the first

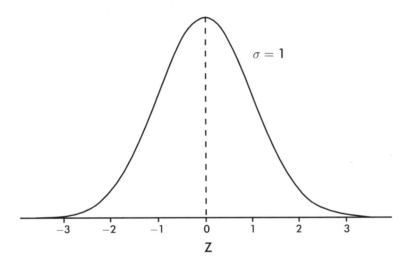

Figure 8.9 The standard normal distribution

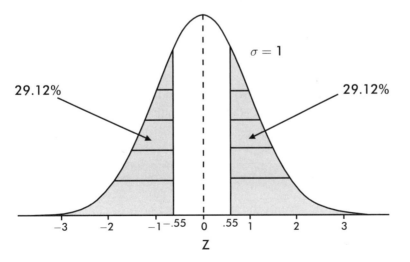

Figure 8.10 Areas under the normal distribution

column until you found 0.5 and then across until you were directly under 0.05. The area is 0.2912, or 29.12%. This is the area in the tail for Z being greater than 0.55. Since the distribution is symmetrical, the area being less than $Z = -0.55$ is also 29.12%. You will see these areas shaded in Figure 8.10.

Activity 8.14

What is the area between a Z value of 1 and -1?

The area of the curve for Z greater than 1 is 0.1587 or 15.87%. To find the area from the mean to any Z value you need to use the fact that half the distribution has an area of 0.5. So to find the area from the mean to $Z = 1$ you would subtract this from 0.5. That is, $0.5 - 0.1587 = 0.3413$. Since the distribution is symmetrical, the area from 0.0 to -1.0 is also 0.3413. The area from -1 to $+1$ is therefore 0.6826. In other words, 68.26% of the normal curve is covered by ±1 standard deviations. This area can be seen in Figure 8.11 below.

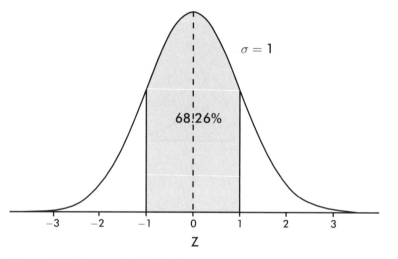

Figure 8.11 Diagram for Activity 8.14

If you repeat this for $Z = 2$ and $Z = 3$, you should find that just over 95% (95.44%) of the normal distribution is covered by ±2 standard deviations, and almost 100% (99.73%) is covered by ±3 standard deviations.

Activity 8.15

What is the value of Z if the area of the upper tail is 5%?

This problem is illustrated in Figure 8.12. To solve this problem the normal table is used in reverse. That is, the table is inspected to find the area of 0.05. This figure does not exist,

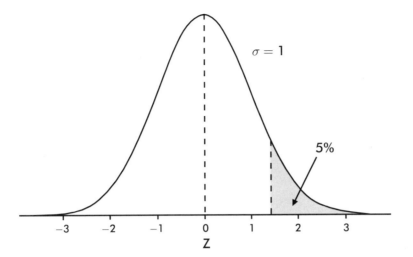

Figure 8.12 Diagram for Activity 8.15

but you should find that a Z value of 1.64 gives an area of 0.0505, while a Z value of 1.65 gives an area of 0.0495. The most accurate value of Z would be the average of these two values, which is 1.645.

8.5.2 Standardising normal distributions

Unfortunately, most normal distribution problems do not have a mean of zero or a standard deviation of 1, so the normal table cannot be used directly to solve general problems. However, all you have to do is to calculate the number of standard deviations from the mean, and this can be done quiet easily, as follows: subtract the mean value from the particular value (x) that you are interested in and then divide this value by the standard deviation. For example, if the mean is 5 and the standard deviation is 2, then a value of 9 is two standard deviations from the mean. This calculation is called the *Z transformation* and is given by:

$$Z = \frac{x\text{-mean}}{\text{standard deviation}}$$

If x is less than the mean, the value of Z will be negative. This negative value simply indicates that x is to the left of the mean. Since the distribution is symmetrical about the mean, you can ignore the sign when using the table.

Activity 8.16

A batch of loaves is baked. The weight of the loaves is normally distributed with a mean of 800 g and a standard deviation of 10 g. What proportion of loaves will weigh more than 815 g?

This is the same problem that you met in Activity 8.13 (see Figure 8.8), but you now should be able to solve this using the normal table. However, you first have to transform the problem using the Z formula. You should first note that:

$$Z = \frac{815 - 800}{10} = 1.5$$

That is, 815 g is 1.5 standard deviations away from the mean.

It is now a simple matter of looking up $Z = 1.5$ in the normal table. If you do this you should get an area of 0.0668 or 6.68%, which means that 6.68% of all loaves weigh more than 815 g. This is represented in Figure 8.13.

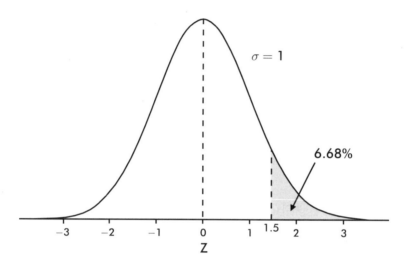

Figure 8.13 Diagram for Activity 8.16

The problem can become slightly more difficult, as illustrated in the next activity.

Activity 8.17

A loaf is chosen at random. What is the probability that the weight will lie between 810 g and 812 g?

To find the probability it is necessary to find the area shown shaded in Figure 8.14. This area cannot be found directly, but it can be found by *subtracting* the area greater than 812 from the area greater than 810. To do this it is necessary to calculate two Z values as follows:

$$\frac{810 - 800}{10} = 1.0 \quad \text{and} \quad \frac{812 - 800}{12} = 1.2$$

The areas from the normal table are 0.1587 and 0.1157 and the required area is:

$$0.1587 - 0.1151 = 0.0436$$

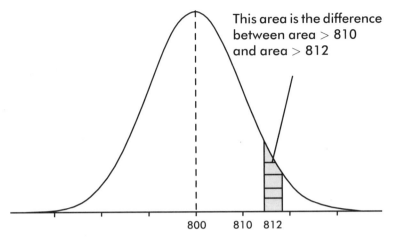

Figure 8.14 Diagram for Activity 8.17

The probability that the weight will be between 810 g and 812 g is therefore 0.0436 or 4.36%. Alternatively you could say that 4.36% of all loaves weigh between 810 g and 812 g.z

Activity 8.18

What proportion of loaves weigh between 790 g and 805.5 g?

To solve this problem you should note that the required area is the *sum* of the two areas A and B (see Figure 8.15). To calculate area A it is necessary to find the area greater than 805.5 and then subtract this from 0.5. (Don't forget the tables used in this book give the area in the *right hand* tail of the distribution.) The calculation is as follows:

$$Z = \frac{805.5 - 800}{10} = 0.55$$

This gives an area of 0.2912 and area A is therefore $0.5 - 0.2912 = 0.2088$.
    Area B is found in a similar manner.

$$Z = \frac{790 - 800}{10} = -1.0$$

The negative sign indicates that the area is to the left of the mean and can be ignored for the purposes of obtaining the area from the normal table. Area B is therefore $0.5 - 0.1587 = 0.3413$.
    The combined area is $0.2088 + 0.3413 = 0.5501$ or 55.01%, which is the proportion of loaves with weights between 790 g and 805.5 g.
    In addition to calculating the probability or proportion of a variable having a value between specified limits, it is possible to carry out the reverse process. This is illustrated in the next activity.

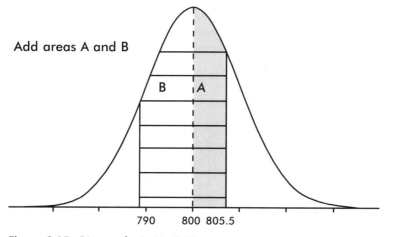

Figure 8.15 Diagram for Activity 8.18

Activity 8.19

The baker wishes to ensure that no more than 5% of loaves are less than a certain weight. What is this weight?

The diagram for this problem can be seen in Figure 8.16. It is necessary to calculate the value x, but first the Z value corresponding to an area of 5% must be found. Although this area is in the lower tail, the method is identical to that used when the area in the upper tail has been given. (Don't forget the distribution is symmetrical about the mean.) The value of Z for an area of 5% is 1.645, but because it is to the left of the mean, the value is negative; that is, -1.645. Substituting this value into the formula gives:

$$-1.645 = \frac{x - 800}{10}$$

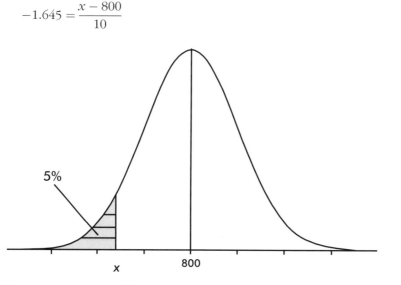

Figure 8.16 Diagram for Activity 8.19

Multiplying both sides by 10 gives:

$$-16.45 = x - 800$$

Then adding 800 to both sides:

$$x = 800 - 16.45$$

$$= 783.6\,\text{g}$$

So no more than 5% of the batch should weigh less than 783.6 g.

Although the preceding activities cover the most common applications, it is possible to use the Z formula to calculate either the mean or the standard deviation. This is demonstrated next.

Activity 8.20

A large number of loaves were weighed and it was found that 8% weighed less than 783.6 g. Assuming that the standard deviation hasn't changed, what has happened?

This problem is illustrated in Figure 8.17. If the standard deviation hasn't changed, then the only conclusion is that the mean has changed or it is not what it was thought to be. Again, it is necessary to work backwards. The Z value corresponding to a proportion of 8% is 1.405, which will again be negative. The value of x is 783.6 and it is required to find the value of the mean.

$$-1.405 = \frac{783.6 - \text{mean}}{10}$$

Multiplying both sides by 10 gives:

$$-14.05 = 783.6 - \text{mean}$$

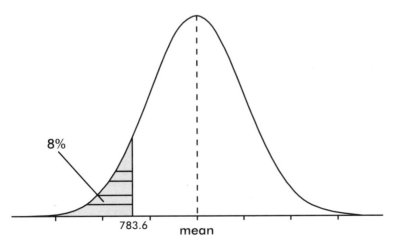

Figure 8.17 Diagram for Activity 8.20

then adding 14.05 to both sides:

$$0 = 797.7 - \text{mean}$$

that is: mean $= 797.7\,\text{g}$

8.5.3 The normal distribution as an approximation to the binomial distribution

If a particular binomial distribution is symmetrical it is possible to use the normal distribution to solve binomial problems. The conditions that make the binomial distribution symmetrical are that both $n \times p$ and $n \times (1 - p)$ are greater than 5. This means that p needs to be near to 0.5 and n should be large.

Activity 8.21

Use Excel to plot the binomial distribution for $n = 30$ and $p = 0.3$.

You should have obtained Figure 8.18 and you should notice that the distribution is approximately symmetrical.

The next activity will show you how to use the normal distribution as an approximation to the binomial.

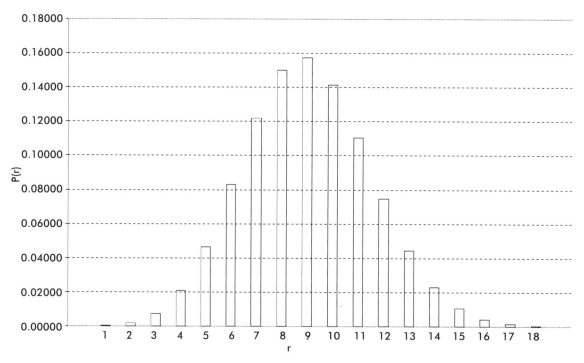

Figure 8.18   Binomial distribution with $n = 30$ and $p = 0.3$

Activity 8.22

The probability of a defective item is 0.3. If a sample of 30 were taken, what is the probability that at least 5 were defective?

Using the binomial table in Appendix 2 we would find the probability of 4 or less defectives, which is 0.0302.

The probability of at least 5 defectives is then:

$$P(r \geq 5) = 1 - 0.0302$$
$$= 0.9698$$

To solve this problem by the normal distribution it is first necessary to calculate the mean and standard deviation. The mean is $n \times p = 30 \times 0.3 = 9.0$ and the standard deviation is:

$$\sqrt{30 \times 0.3 \times 0.7} = 2.51$$

It is then necessary to make a *continuity correction*. This is because the binomial distribution is a discrete probability distribution whereas the normal distribution is a continuous one. To get around this problem it is assumed that the discrete value 5 is a continuous variable in the range 4.5 to 5.5. To find the probability greater than 4, the value 4.5 is used, as you can see in Figure 8.19.

This problem now becomes one of finding $P(r > 4.5)$, which is $1 - P(r < 4.5)$ and

$$Z = \frac{4.5 - 9}{2.51}$$
$$= -1.79$$

$$P(Z < -1.79) = P(Z > 1.79)$$

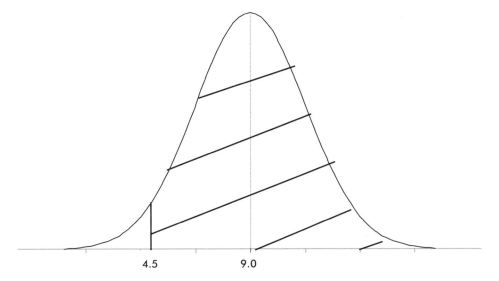

Figure 8.19 Normal approximation to the binomial for Activity 8.22

and from the normal table the probability is 0.0367, so the required probability is: $1 - 0.0367 = 0.9633$, which compares well with the correct value of 0.9698.

8.5.4 The normal distribution as an approximation to the Poisson distribution

The normal distribution can also be used to solve Poisson problems. This is valid provided the mean is greater than about 10.

Activity 8.23

The number of calls to a switchboard is random, with a mean of 1.5 per minute. What is the probability that there are less than 6 calls in a 5-minute period?

We looked this problem in Activity 8.10 where we calculated the probability to be 0.2414 To solve this problem using the normal distribution you would note that the mean is 7.5 calls in a 5-minute period. (The mean of 7.5 is less than the recommended level, so it will be interesting to see how good the approximation will be in this case.)

To use the normal distribution, the continuity correction again needs to be applied. In this case the probability of less than 5.5 calls needs to be found. The standard deviation is the square root of the mean (7.5), which equals 2.739.

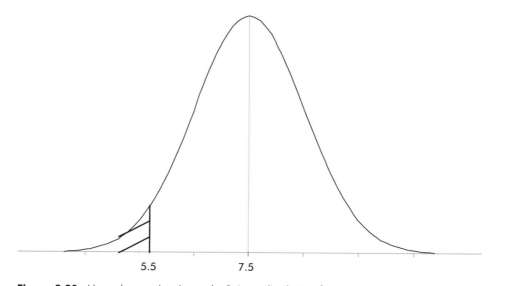

Figure 8.20 Normal approximation to the Poisson distribution for Activity 8.23

The calculation is straightforward using the normal distribution:

$$Z = \frac{5.5 - 7.5}{2.739}$$
$$= -0.7302$$

$$P(r < 5.5) = P(Z < -0.7302)$$
$$= P(Z > 0.7302)$$
$$= 0.2327 \text{ (from the normal table)}$$

This represents an error of just under 4%.

8.6 Summary

In this chapter you have examined three very important distributions. The binomial distribution is a discrete probability distribution and is used where there are just two possible outcomes to a process or experiment. The second distribution was the Poisson distribution and models situations that occur at random. The third distribution is the normal distribution, which is a continuous probability distribution and the most important probability distribution in statistics. For the normal distribution you saw how to use tables to obtain the area within the standard normal distribution and to obtain the Z value given the area. You have also seen how to transform a general normal distribution problem into the standard normal so that the problem can be solved.

8.7 Further reading

Burton, G., Carrol, G. and Wall, S. (1999) *Quantitative Methods for Business and Economics*, Longman, New York (Chapter 6).
Morris, C. (2000) *Quantitative Approaches in Business Studies*, fifth edition, Pitman, London (Chapter 9).

8.8 EXERCISES

The answers to the progress questions, the multiple choice questions and some of the practice questions are given in Appendix 1. Solutions to the remaining questions and the assignment can be found on the web site for this text.

PROGRESS QUESTIONS
These questions have been designed to help you remember the key points in this chapter.
Give the missing word in each case:

1. The binomial is an example of a .... distribution.
2. The Poisson distribution is used when events occur at ....
3. The normal curve is .... about the mean.
4. The total area under the normal curve is ....
5. The position and shape of the normal curve is determined by the .... and ....
6. As the standard deviation gets larger the spread of the curve ....
7. The normal distribution is an example of a .... distribution.

ANSWER *TRUE* OR *FALSE*

8. Gender is an example of a binomial process.

9. The shape of the binomial distribution with $n = 10$ and $p = 0.01$ will be symmetrical.

10. Arrivals of cars at a petrol station is an example of a Poisson process.

11. A Z value is a probability.

12. The normal distribution is a 'bell' shape.

13. If the area in the right-hand tail of the normal distribution is 5%, then the area to the left of this tail is 95%.

14. If the area in each tail of the normal distribution is 5% then the area in the centre of the distribution is 95%.

REVIEW QUESTIONS

These questions have been designed to help you check your comprehension of the key points in this chapter. You may wish to look further than this chapter in order to answer them fully. You will find the reading list useful in this respect. You can check the essential elements of your answers by referring to the appropriate section.

15. What are the conditions that make the use of the binomial distribution valid? (Section 8.3) What are the conditions that allow you to use the Poisson distribution as an approximation to the binomial distribution? (Section 8.4.1)

16. What are the properties of the normal distribution? (Section 8.5)

17. Why is it necessary to have a standard normal distribution and what is it? (Section 8.5.2)

18. Give examples of data that may conform to the normal distribution. (Section 8.5)

MULTIPLE CHOICE QUESTIONS

19. The mean of a binomial process with number of trials of 20 and the probability of success of 0.05 is

    A... 0.05

    B... 20

    C... 1.0

20. A binomial distribution with a p value of 0.4 and n of 20

    A... can be approximated by the Poisson distribution

    B... can be approximated by the normal distribution

    C... cannot be approximated by either distribution

21. A Poisson distribution with a mean of 16 has standard deviation of

    A... 4

    B... 16

    C... 256

22. The standard normal distribution has a mean of

    A... 0

    B... 1

    C... 1.5

23. The normal distribution is applicable to

    A... discrete data

    B... continuous data

    C... ordinal data

24. The weights of packets of biscuits is normal with a mean of 400 g and a standard deviation of 10 g. A packet was selected at random and found to weigh 420 g. How many standard deviations away from the mean does this weight represent?

    A... 10

    B... 1

    C... 2

    D... 20

25. What proportion (approximately) of a normal distribution is covered by ± 2 standard deviations?

    A... 50%

    B... 95%

    C... 99%

Questions 26 and 27 refer to the distribution of the weight of packets of biscuits. The weights follow a normal distribution with mean of 400 g and standard deviation of 10 g

26. The probability that a packet chosen at random would weigh more than 425 g is:

    A... 0.0668

    B... 0.1587

    C... 0.9938

    D... 0.0062

27. 2.5% of packets weigh less than a certain amount. This weight is:

    A... 419.6 g

    B... 402.5 g

    C... 380.4 g

    D... 350.0 g

PRACTICE QUESTIONS

28. If a coin is tossed 5 times, how many ways are there of getting 3 heads?

29. What is the probability of getting 3 heads if a coin is tossed 5 times?

30. The sex ratio of newborn infants is about 105 males to 100 females. If 4 infants are chosen at random, what is the probability that:

    (a) All four are males?

    (b) Exactly three are male?

    (c) Two are male and two are female?

31. The quality control manager of a company is concerned at the level of defective items being produced. Out of a batch of 20 items, 2 were found to be defective. Should the quality control manager be concerned given that in the past the defective rate has been 3%?

32. A shopkeeper finds that 20% of the cartons containing 6 eggs he receives are damaged. A carton is picked at random, checked and returned to the consignment. The procedure is repeated a further 3 times. What is the probability that out of the 4 cartons inspected

    (a) none were undamaged?

    (b) at least 3 were undamaged?

33. Calls arrive at a switchboard according to the Poisson distribution. If the average number of calls received in a 5-minute period is 6.7, find the probability that:

    (a) There are less than 4 calls received in a 5-minute period.

    (b) There are more than 7 calls received during a 5-minute period.

    (c) There are no calls received in a 1-minute period.

34. Several lengths of plastic tubing are examined for the number of flaws in intervals of given length. If 1500 flaws are found in 1000 intervals each of 1 mm, find the probability, assuming a Poisson distribution of

    (a) at least 2 flaws in an interval of 1 mm

    (b) an interval between two consecutive flaws being greater than 5 mm.

35. What is the area in the tail of the distribution for a Z value of 1.25?

36. What is area between the Z values of 1.45 and 2.45?

37. What is the area between Z values of −0.67 and 1.05?

38. A particular normal distribution has a mean of 5 and a standard deviation of 1.5. What is the area corresponding to a value:

    (a) greater than 6?

    (b) less than 4?

    (c) between 4 and 6?

    (d) between 6.5 and 7.5?

39. The daily demand for petrol at a garage is normally distributed with a mean of 20 000 litres and a standard deviation of 7200 litres. What is the probability that the demand in any one day is:

    (a) greater than 25 000 litres?

    (b) greater than 17 000 litres?

    (c) between 20 000 and 25 000 litres?

    (d) between 30 000 and 35 000 litres?

40. The length of a special type of bolt is normally distributed with a mean diameter of 5.5 mm and a standard deviation of 0.4 mm. Bolts are only acceptable if their diameter is between 4.5 and 6 mm. What proportion of bolts will be accepted?

41. The specification for the length of an engine part is a minimum of 50 mm and a maximum of 55 mm. A batch of parts is produced that is normally distributed with a mean of 54 mm and a standard deviation of 2 mm. Parts cost £10 to make. Those that are too short have to be scrapped; those too long are shortened at a further cost of £8.

    (a) Find the percentage of parts that are

        (i) undersize;
        (ii) oversize.

    (b) Find the expected cost of producing 1000 usable parts.

42. As an incentive for customers to spend more money on its credit card a bank has decided to award high spending customers with a free gift. However, it doesn't want to give gifts to more than 5% of customers. If the mean spend per customer is £135 with a standard deviation of £55, what balance should the company specify? However, at the end of the first month it was found that 8% of customers qualified for the free gift. What has happened? Assuming that the standard deviation hasn't changed, calculate the new mean spend per customer.

43. Crumbly Biscuits produces golden cream biscuits which are sold in notional 300 g packets. The weights of these packets are normally distributed with a mean of 320 g and a standard deviation of 10.4 g.

    (a) What is the probability that if you select a packet at random it will weigh:

    (i) less than 300 g?
    (ii) more than 325 g?
    (iii) between 318 and 325 g?

    (b) Out of a batch of 500 packets, how many would weigh less than 300 g?

    It has been decided to reduce the mean weight to 310 g. What would the standard deviation need to be if no more than 3% of packets must weigh less than 300 g?

44. A company that is considering the launch of a new product estimates that the possible demand for the product, in its first year, will be approximately normally distributed with a mean of 2000 units and a standard deviation of 500 units. What is the probability that the first-year demand will be:

    (a) over 2500 units?
    (b) over 2800 units?
    (c) less than 1600 units?

45. A large departmental store has analysed the monthly amount spent by its credit card customers and found that it is normally distributed with a mean of £100 and a standard deviation of £15. What percentage of people will spend:

(a) over £130?

(b) over £120?

(c) below £70?

(d) between £100 and £130?

(e) between £115 and £130?

What is the minimum amount spent of:

(f) the top 10%?

(g) the top 3% of customers?

46. If IQ scores for a certain test are approximately normally distributed with a mean of 100 and a standard deviation of 15, find the probability of a randomly selected individual scoring:

(a) 115 or more

(b) 130 or more

(c) between 115 and 130

47. The weekly demand for a liquid oil-based product that is marketed by a company is normally distributed with a mean of 2000 gallons and a standard deviation of 500 gallons. How many gallons of the product must the company have in stock at the start of the week to have only a 0.06 probability of running out of stock, assuming that no further supplies of the product are available during the week?

48. The weights of articles produced by a machine are normally distributed with a mean of 16 g and a standard deviation of 0.5 g. Only articles that have weights in the range 15.75 g to 16.75 g are acceptable and the remainder must be scrapped.

(a) What percentage of output will be scrapped?

(b) If an average of 10 000 units are produced per week and each scrapped unit costs £7, what will be the average weekly cost of scrapped units?

(c) A new machine can be hired at a cost of £10 000 per week. This would also produce articles with a mean of 16 g, but the standard deviation of the weights would be only 0.2 g. Is it worth hiring the new machine? (Assume that the old machine would have no scrap value.)

49. A company has to decide which of two possible new products, A or B, it should launch. A computer risk analysis package suggests that the profit that will result if A is developed is normally distributed with a mean of £15 million and a standard deviation of £9 million. The profit that would be generated by developing product B is also normally distributed, with a mean of £10 million and a standard deviation of £5 million. Which product should the company launch to minimise its chances of incurring a loss?

ASSIGNMENT

Goodtaste Ltd, a coffee manufacturer, has recently been prosecuted for selling an underweight 100 g jar of coffee. You have been asked to give assistance to the quality control manager who is investigating the problem.

Jars are filled automatically and the filling machine can be preset to any desired weight. For the 100 g jars of coffee a weight of 101 g is set. There is no subsequent checking of the weight of individual jars, although samples are occasionally taken to check for quality. The standard deviation will depend to a certain extent on the mean weight, but for weights between 90 g and 110 g it is virtually constant at 1.5 g.

You have been asked to apply your knowledge of the normal distribution to the problem. In particular you have been told that prosecution only occurs when the product is underweight by more than 2%, so you need to find the probability that such a weight could happen by chance.

(a) Assuming that the mean weight is 101 g, what proportion of jars are:

  (i)   under 100 g in weight?
  (ii) under 98 g in weight?
  (iii) under 97 g in weight?
  (iv) over 100 g?
  (v)   within 2 g of the marked weight?

(b) What should the mean weight be set to in order that the probability of a jar weighing less than 98 g is less than 0.1%?

(c) Write a short note to the quality control manager summarising your results.

Decision-making under conditions of uncertainty

9.1 Introduction

All companies have to make decisions and almost always these decisions are made under conditions of uncertainty. This is simply because decision-making requires the ability to forecast future events, which is of course notoriously difficult, particularly when the future we wish to forecast is a long way off. Because of the uncertainty associated with future events a number of techniques have been developed that incorporate probability into the calculations. This means that it is not necessary to be precise about the future. Other techniques allow the decision-maker's attitude to risk to be taken into account, which is important as some decision-makers are prepared to risk making a loss if there is a chance of making big profits.

To complete this chapter successfully you should have worked through Chapter 7 (Introduction to probability).

At the end of this chapter you should be able to:

- Understand how to make decisions using payoff tables
- Calculate expected monetary values
- Solve decisions using decision trees
- Use Bayes' theorem in decision-making
- Use a spreadsheet to carry out sensitivity analysis on a decision tree
- Calculate expected value of perfect and imperfect information
- Understand the idea of utility

9.2 Payoff tables

A payoff table is simply a table that gives the outcome (for example, profits) of a decision under different conditions or *states of nature*. These states of nature may relate to possible demand for a product or they could be related to the national or global economy. The following are the most commonly used decision criteria.

- Maximax rule
- Maximin rule
- Minimax regret rule
- Hurwicz criterion
- Expected monetary value
- Expected opportunity loss

The *maximax* rule chooses the 'best of the best' and is a rule favoured by decision-makers who are *risk-seekers*. The *maximin* rule chooses the 'the best of the worst' and is a rule favoured by decision-makers who are *risk-averse*. The *minimax regret* rule minimises the maximum *opportunity loss*. The opportunity loss is the loss that occurs through not taking the best option. To work out the opportunity loss you have to subtract each payoff for a particular state of nature from the best that could be achieved given that state. The *Hurwicz* criterion, like the minimax regret rule, attempts to give a compromise between the cautious maximin rule and the optimistic maximax rule. However, unlike the minimax regret rule, weights are assigned to the best and worst payoff for each decision option and the option with the highest weighted payoff is chosen.

The weighted payoff is calculated as:

$$\alpha \times \text{worst payoff} + (1 - \alpha) \times \text{best payoff}$$

The value of α (alpha) depends on the decision-maker's attitude to risk. The smaller the value, the bigger risk he is prepared to take; when $\alpha = 0$ the decision will be the same as for the maximax rule.

Expected monetary value or EMV is an expected value (see Chapter 7.8) in monetary terms. In this context it is a long-run average and is found by multiplying each payoff by the probability that this payoff will occur and adding. The option that maximises the EMV is chosen.

Expected opportunity loss or EOL is essentially the same technique as the EMV method except that the probabilities are applied to the opportunity loss table and the option that *minimises* the EOL is chosen.

Example 9.1

A car accessory company, Marla plc, has developed a new car immobiliser and has to decide whether to market the product nationwide, to sell by mail order or to sell the patent to a large chain of motor accessory shops. The cost of distributing nationwide is very high but the potential profits could also be large. There is less risk with selling by mail order but the potential profits would also be less. The safe option is to sell the patent, but in this case the chance of making large profits would be lost. How does Marla make its decision given that it has limited knowledge of the likely demand for the product? The estimated profits for each decision depend on the state of the market, which has been defined as high, medium and low. The probability that the state of the market will be high, medium or low has been estimated as 0.25, 0.3 and 0.45, respectively. The expected profits (in £000s) are given in the Table 9.1.

Table 9.1   Profits (£000s) for Marla plc

	State of the market		
Decision	**High (p = 0.25)**	**Medium (p = 0.3)**	**Low (p = 0.45)**
Nationwide	95	52	−26
Mail order	48	24	19
Sell patent	25	25	25

Activity 9.1

What are the best decisions using the maximax and maximin rules?

The largest payoff is 95 (£000s) for the 'sell nationwide' decision when the market is high. This is the decision that would be made using the maximax rule. The worst payoff for each decision is −26, 19, 25, and the highest of these is 25 so the decision under the maximin rule is to sell the patent.

Activity 9.2

What is the best decision using the minimax regret rule?

This rule requires you to create an opportunity loss table as described earlier. The largest payoff when the market is high is 95, so if the mail order option was taken instead this would mean that a 'loss' of 95 − 48 = 47 (£000s) would be made through not taking the best option. The complete opportunity loss table is shown in Table 9.2.

The largest loss for each decision is 51, 47 and 70. The smallest of these is 47, so the best decision under this rule is to sell by mail order.

Activity 9.3

What is the best decision using the Hurwicz criterion with an alpha of 0.6?

Table 9.2 Opportunity loss table (in £000s) for Example 9.1

| Decision | State of the market | | |
	High	Medium	Low
Nationwide	0	0	51
Mail order	47	28	6
Sell patent	70	27	0

The weighted payoff is calculated from

$$\alpha \times \text{worst payoff} + (1 - \alpha) \times \text{best payoff}$$

So for the decision to sell nationwide the worst payoff is -26 and the best is 95 so the weighted payoff is therefore

$$0.6 \times (-26) + 0.4 \times 95 = 22.4$$

Repeating this for the decisions to sell by mail order and to sell the patent we get:

Mail order: $0.6 \times 19 + 0.4 \times 48 = 30.6$

Sell patent: $0.6 \times 25 + 0.4 \times 25 = 25$

So under this criterion and using $\alpha = 0.6$, the decision is to go for the mail order option.

Activity 9.4

What is the best decision using the expected monetary value criteria?

Nationwide: $0.25 \times 95 + 0.3 \times 52 + 0.45 \times (-26) = 27.65$

Mail order: $0.25 \times 48 + 0.3 \times 24 + 0.45 \times 19 = 27.75$

Sell patent: $0.25 \times 25 + 0.3 \times 25 + 0.45 \times 25 = 25$

This suggests that, on average, choosing the 'mail order' option would give you a slightly higher payoff at £27 750.

Activity 9.5

What is the best decision using the expected opportunity loss criterion?

The probabilities are applied to Table 9.2, and the result is:

Nationwide: $0.25 \times 0 + 0.3 \times 0 + 0.45 \times 51 = 22.95$

Mail order: $0.25 \times 47 + 0.3 \times 28 + 0.45 \times 6 = 22.85$

Sell patent: $0.25 \times 70 + 0.3 \times 27 + 0.45 \times 0 = 25.6$

The decision that would minimise the EOL is again the mail order option. (The EMV and EOL decision rules should always agree.)

9.2.1 The value of perfect information

Imagine that a market research company could forecast the demand for the new car immobiliser (Example 9.1) perfectly. How much would it be worth paying for this market research? If the market research company reported that demand would be low, the best option would be to sell the patent, whereas if it said that demand would be high, the option to sell nationwide would be chosen. Of course, high demand only occurs 25% of the time, medium demand 30% of the time and low demand 45% of the time. Therefore it is possible to work out the *expected* payoff if you had this perfect information. This is called the expected value *with* perfect information. The expected value *of* perfect information (EVPI) is simply the difference between the expected value with perfect information and the best EMV.

Activity 9.6

What would be the expected value of perfect information for the payoff table given in Table 9.1?

The expected value with perfect information will be:

$$0.25 \times 95 + 0.3 \times 52 + 0.45 \times 25 = 50.6$$

The EVPI is therefore:

$$50.6 - 27.75 = 22.85, \text{ or } \pounds 22\,850$$

This is the maximum amount that a decision-maker would be prepared to pay for this information. (You should note that this is the same figure as the expected opportunity loss calculated in Activity 9.5.)

9.3 Decision trees

Payoff tables are useful when there is only one decision to make, but often a sequence of decisions are necessary. This is called *multiple-stage* decision-making and for these cases decision-makers generally prefer to use *decision trees*. Decision trees are similar to probability trees (see Chapter 7.5) except that as well as probabilistic (or chance) branches there are also decision branches. Decision branches allow the decision-maker to compare alternative options, while the chance branches handle the probabilistic nature of an outcome. The skeleton of a single-stage decision tree is shown in Figure 9.1.

The square node represents the point where the decision is made, while the round nodes represent the point at which chance takes over. The decision tree is drawn from left

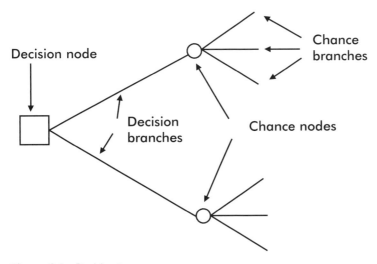

Figure 9.1 Decision tree

to right, but to evaluate the tree you work from right to left. This is called the *roll back* method. You first evaluate the EMV at each chance node and then at the decision node you select the 'best' EMV (don't forget, 'best' can be lowest cost as well as largest profit).

Although a decision tree is not normally used for single-stage decision problems the next activity continues to use Example 9.1 since we know what the answer is using the EMV criterion.

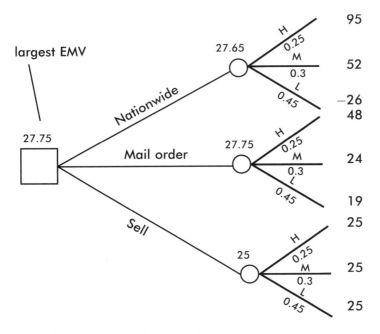

Figure 9.2 Decision tree for Marla plc

Activity 9.7

Use the decision tree approach to solve Example 9.1.

The decision tree for this problem has been drawn in Figure 9.2, and you will see that the outcomes for each decision and state of the market have been written at the end of each probabilistic branch. As before, the best decision is to sell by mail order.

The next problem illustrates a multi-stage decision problem.

Example 9.2

The Delma Oil company has obtained government approval to drill for oil in the Bristol Channel. This area is known to contain oil deposits and industry sources believe that there is a 50% chance that oil will be found in a commercially viable quantity. The cost of the drilling programme is believed to be £30m but this could be more than offset by the potential revenue, which is put at £100m at today's prices.

The company could carry out test drillings at different sites, which would only cost £5m. From historical data, tests are likely to indicate a viable field 65% of the time. However, these tests are not completely reliable and the probability that they are correct is only 0.7. That is, if the tests are positive there is a 70% chance that a viable quantity of oil will be found, and if negative there is only a 30% (100 – 70) chance that oil will be found in a viable quantity.

The company could sell its rights to drill in the area, but the revenue obtained will depend on the outcome of the tests (if carried out) and are as follows:

Tests indicate oil	£35m
Tests don't indicate oil	£3m
No tests carried out	£10m

Activity 9.8

What decisions should the company make given this information?

This problem involves two decisions. The first decision is whether to test drill and the second decision is whether to start its drilling programme. In order to solve this decision problem you would carry out the following three steps:

STEP 1
Draw the decision tree. This is shown in Figure 9.3. You will see that the decision nodes have been numbered 1, 2 and 3 while the chance nodes have been labelled as a, b, c and d. The values at the end of each branch of the tree represent the *net* outcome. For instance,

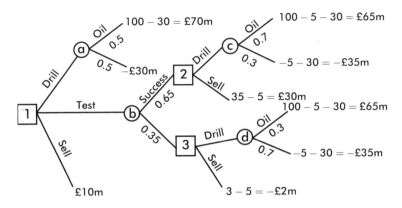

Figure 9.3 Decision tree for the Delma Oil company

if drilling is carried out without any tests and oil is found, the net outcome is a profit of £100m − £30m = £70m, whereas if no oil is found a loss of £30m is made.

STEP 2
Working from the right, the EMV at the chance nodes a, c and d are calculated as follows:

Node	EMV
a	$0.5 \times 70 + 0.5 \times (-30) = \£20m$
c	$0.7 \times 65 + 0.3 \times (-35) = \£35m$
d	$0.3 \times 65 + 0.7 \times (-35) = -\£5m$

(The EMV at node b cannot be calculated until Step 3.)

STEP 3
The roll back technique is now employed. At decision node 2, the decision is to either drill or sell. Sell will give you £30m, whereas drilling will give you £35m. The option that gives the largest EMV is to drill, and so this is the option that would be taken. The value 35 is put above node 2 and the sell option is crossed out. If you repeat this for node 3 you should find that the best option here is to sell. The EMV at chance node b can now be calculated and you should find that this is £22.05m ($0.65 \times 35 + 0.35 \times (-2)$). You can now go to decision node 1 and compare the three decisions. You should find the following:

Drill:	£20m
Test:	£22.05m
Sell:	£10m

The best decision is to test first. If the test gives successful results, only then should drilling start; *otherwise* the rights should be sold for £3m. You will see this analysis summarised in Figure 9.4.

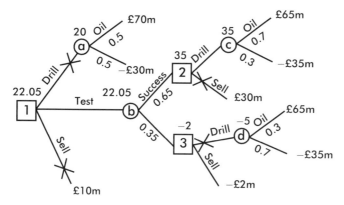

Figure 9.4 Completed decision tree for Delma Oil company

9.3.1 Decision trees and Bayes' theorem

In Example 9.2 you were given all the relevant probabilities, but in general you are more likely to be given just the *prior* probabilities and the *conditional* probabilities. You would then need to work out the relevant *posterior* probabilities using Bayes' theorem. You met Bayes' theorem in Chapter 7.6 where you used it to modify a prior probability given some new information. The next example requires you to use the same technique before you are able to solve the decision problem.

Example 9.3

A small motor component company, CleanFuel, is trying to decide whether to market a fuel additive which it claims will improve fuel consumption. Unfortunately there are a number of competitors in the market who are also working on the same product and CleanFuel knows that if it decides to market the product it will face stiff competition from other companies.

Instead of marketing the product itself, it could sell the rights to it for £2m. However, if it goes ahead and markets the product itself, it estimates that the probability that sales will be high is only 0.2. The profit resulting from these high sales is put at £10m, but if the sales are low (with a probability of 0.8) they will end up making a loss of £1m. An alternative is to commission a market research survey to see if motorists would purchase the product. This market research would indicate either high or low sales. From past experience CleanFuel knows that this particular market research company are better at predicting high rather than low sales. When sales have turned out to be high the company has been correct 75% of the time, but when sales have been low the company has only managed a 65% success rate.

The market research is confidential, so even if the results of the research indicate low sales it will still be possible to sell the rights for £2m. Of course, CleanFuel could also decide to market the product whatever the results of the survey.

Activity 9.9

Draw a decision tree for this problem.

The tree you should have obtained is shown in Figure 9.5.

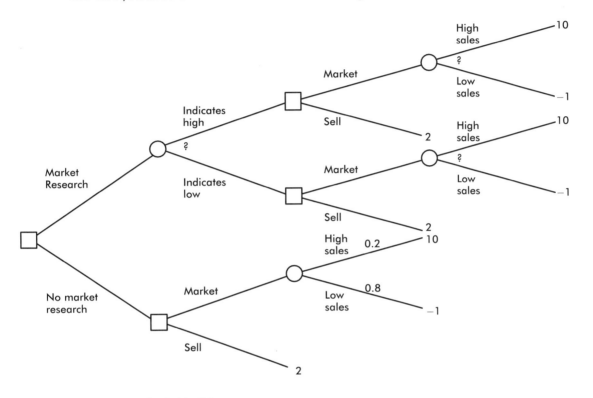

Figure 9.5 Decision tree for Activity 9.9

Notice that there are some probabilities that we don't appear to know. These are the probability of the market research giving a high and low forecast and the probability of high and low demand given the different outcomes of the market research. These probabilities can be obtained by the use of Bayes' theorem. The prior probabilities are 0.2 for high sales and 0.8 for low sales.

Activity 9.10

Draw a probability tree diagram and calculate, using Bayes' theorem the following probabilities:

   p(market research indicates high sales)
   p(market research indicates low sales)
   p(high sales|market research indicates high sales)
   p(low sales|market research indicates high sales)

p(high sales|market research indicates low sales)
p(low sales|market research indicates low sales)

Figure 9.6 gives the probability tree diagram, where you will see that the joint probabilities have been added to the end of each branch.

p(market research indicates high sales) $= 0.15 + 0.28$

$$= 0.43$$

p(market research indicates low sales) $= 1 - 0.43$

$$= 0.57$$

p(high sales|market research indicates high sales) $= \dfrac{0.15}{0.43}$

$$= 0.349$$

p(low sales|market research indicates high sales) $= 1 - 0.349$

$$= 0.651$$

p(high sales|market research indicates low sales) $= \dfrac{0.05}{0.57}$

$$= 0.088$$

p(low sales|market research indicates low sales) $= 1 - 0.088$

$$= 0.912$$

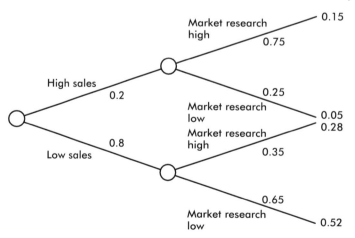

Figure 9.6 Probability tree diagram for Activity 9.10

These probabilities can now be added to the decision tree and the tree rolled back to show that the best decision is to commission the market research and only to market the product if the research suggests that the sales will be high, otherwise sell the rights. You can see the final tree in Figure 9.7.

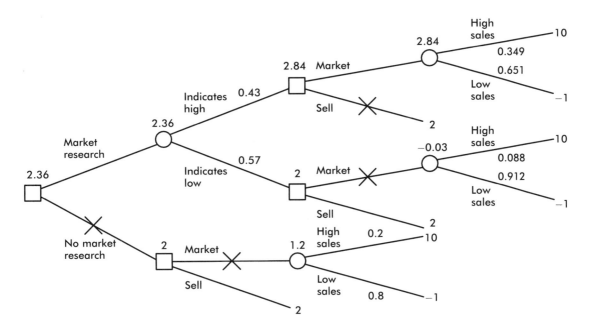

Figure 9.7 The completeed decision tree for Example 9.3

The preceding calculations did not make any reference to the cost of market research. It would be important for CleanFuel to know whether the cost of the market research is reasonable. An upper limit to how much to spend on market research is relatively easy to work out as it is the difference between the 'market research' and 'no market research branches' in Figure 9.7. The 'no market research' branch implies that the rights to the product will be sold for £2m.

|||⊳ ## Activity 9.11

What is the maximum amount of money it would be worth CleanFuel paying for the market research?

The difference between the two branches is £0.36m (2.36 − 2). This is called the *expected value of imperfect information* (EVII) as it takes account of the fact that the market research is not completely reliable. CleanFuel should therefore not pay more than £0.36m for the market research.

9.3.2 Sensitivity analysis

The major difficulty with decision analysis is estimating the probabilities and the expected returns. In many cases the probabilities are simply best guesses. In decision analysis, the sensitivity of the recommended decision to changes in any of the estimated values should be investigated. The most effective way to look at how sensitive the final decision is to changes in the probabilities is to see how big a change in one of the probabilities is necessary for you to change your decision. If only a small change in probability is required then you would say that the decision is sensitive to the value of the probability. If it would take a large change in probability then you could say that the decision is insensitive to changes in the probability or the decision is *robust*. To investigate the sensitivity of the decision it is normal to find the probability that makes you *indifferent* between two decisions.

Activity 9.12

How much can the probability of a successful test in the Delma Oil company problem (Example 9.2) be allowed to vary before the decision changes from 'test first' to 'drill without test'?

You might have tried to solve this activity by trial and error, but this is not recommended as it can be tedious and there are better methods available. As the probability of success falls the EMV at node b will also fall. When this EMV becomes £20m we will be indifferent to 'test first' and 'drill without test'. To find this point of indifference we could calculate the EMV at node b using a different value of the probability of success. The original value

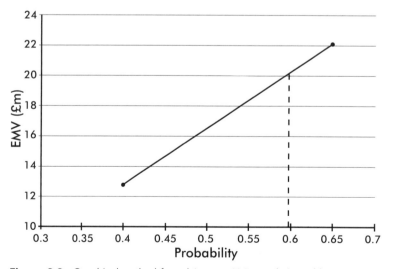

Figure 9.8 Graphical method for solving sensitivity analysis problems

and the new EMV could then be plotted and the point of indifference found graphically. To illustrate this method let us calculate the EMV using a probability of success of 0.4. The EMV at node b will then be:

$$0.4 \times 35 + 0.6 \times (-2) = £12.8m$$

This and the original value are plotted on the graph shown in Figure 9.8. The line between the two points intersects the £20m gridline at a probability of just under 0.6. From this we can deduce that the decision will change once the probability falls below this figure. Since the original probability was 0.65 this is a relatively small change in probability. We can therefore say that the decision whether to test drill or not is quite sensitive to the probability of a viable oil field.

An alternative algebraic method is to call the probability p and the EMV at node b then becomes:

$$35 \times p + (-2) \times (1 - p) = 35p - 2 + 2p$$
$$= 37p - 2$$

The decision will change when the value of this expression is less than £20m. That is:

$$37p - 2 < 20$$

that is, $37p < 22$

therefore, $p < 0.595$

which agrees with the answer found from the graphical method.

Activity 9.13

Investigate the sensitivity of the decision on whether to carry out market research or not for the CleanFuel problem (Example 9.3) to changes in the probability of the market research company successfully predicting high sales.

When sales were high the success rate of the market research company was given as 75%; that is, the probability of success when sales were high was 0.75. To investigate changes in this probability we would need to determine what this probability would have to become for the decision to change from 'conduct market research' to 'don't conduct market research'. This problem is much more difficult to solve than for Activity 9.12 as any change in this probability makes many changes within the decision tree itself. The most effective method of carrying out sensitivity analysis on complex decision problems is to use the *goal seeking* routine in Excel. In fact, it is a good idea to use a spreadsheet for all decision tree problems as you can then see the effects of changing any of the inputs, such as the probabilities or outcomes immediately. To do this it is advisable to use the *drawing* toolbar in Excel to draw the tree diagram and enter the inputs as parameters at the top of the sheet. You can then enter formulae at appropriate points in the diagram. Figure 9.9 is a screen shot of the worksheet for the CleanFuel problem.

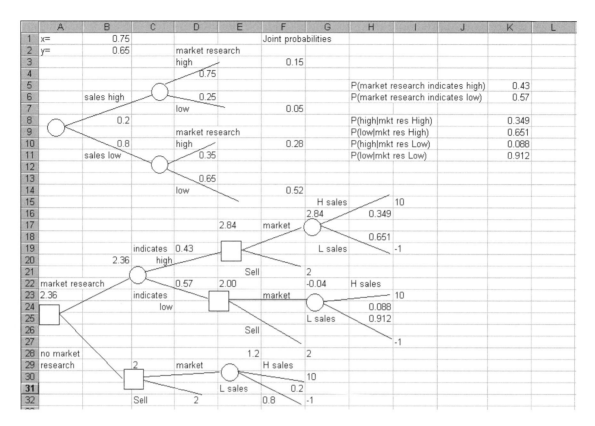

Figure 9.9 The decision tree for Example 9.3 added to an Excel spreadsheet

The probabilities of the market research company making accurate forecasts when sales are high and low respectively can be seen in cells B1 and B2 and have been labelled as 'x' and 'y'. The value we are interested in is contained within cell B1. The goal seek routine can be found under *Tools*, *Goal Seek*. The *Set cell* is the cell that currently contains the value of 2.36, which we want to change to the value 2 (the EMV without market research). The *By changing cell* is cell B1, which currently contains the value 0.75. The dialog box for the Goal Seek routine can be seen in Figure 9.10.

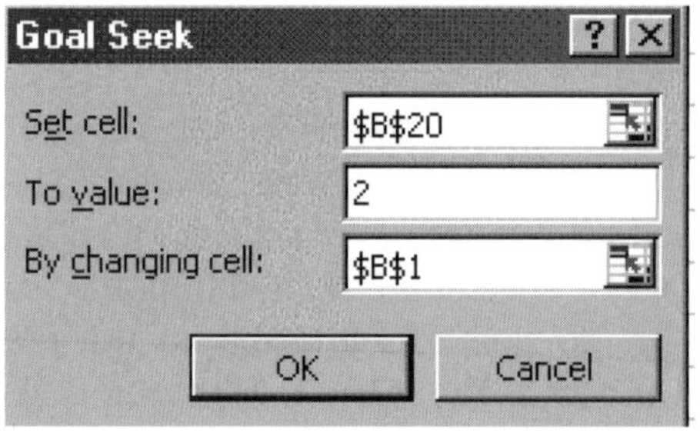

Figure 9.10 The Goal Seek dialog box

The result of using Excel's Goal Seek can be seen in Figure 9.11, where you will see that the probability 'x' which is necessary to make you indifferent between market research and no market research is 0.525. This means that if the probability of successfully predicting high sales fell from 0.75 to below 0.525 the decision would change from 'carry out market research' to 'don't carry out market research'. This is quite a large difference so we could say that the decision is fairly insensitive to changes in this probability.

	A	B	C	D	E	F	G	H	I	J	K	L	M	N
1	x=	0.525				Joint probabilities								
2	y=	0.65		market research										
3				high		0.105								
4				0.525										
5								P(market research indicates high)			0.385			
6		sales high		0.475				P(market research indicates low)			0.615			
7				low		0.095								
8		0.2						P(high|mkt res High)			0.273			
9				market research				P(low|mkt res High)			0.727			
10				high		0.28		P(high|mkt res Low)			0.154			
11		sales low		0.35				P(low|mkt res Low)			0.846			
12		0.8												
13				0.65										
14				low		0.52								
15							H sales		10					
16							2.00	0.273						
17					2.00	market								
18								0.727						
19			indicates	0.385			L sales		-1					
20		2	high											
21						Sell	2							
22	market research		0.615	2.00		market	0.70	H sales						
23	2		indicates					10						
24			low					0.154						
25						Sell	L sales	0.846						
26														
27								-1						
28	no market					1.2	2							
29	research		2	market			H sales							
30								10						
31						L sales	0.2							
32		Sell		2			0.8	-1						
33														

Goal Seek Status

Goal Seeking with Cell B20 found a solution.

Target value: 2
Current value: 2

OK Cancel Step Pause

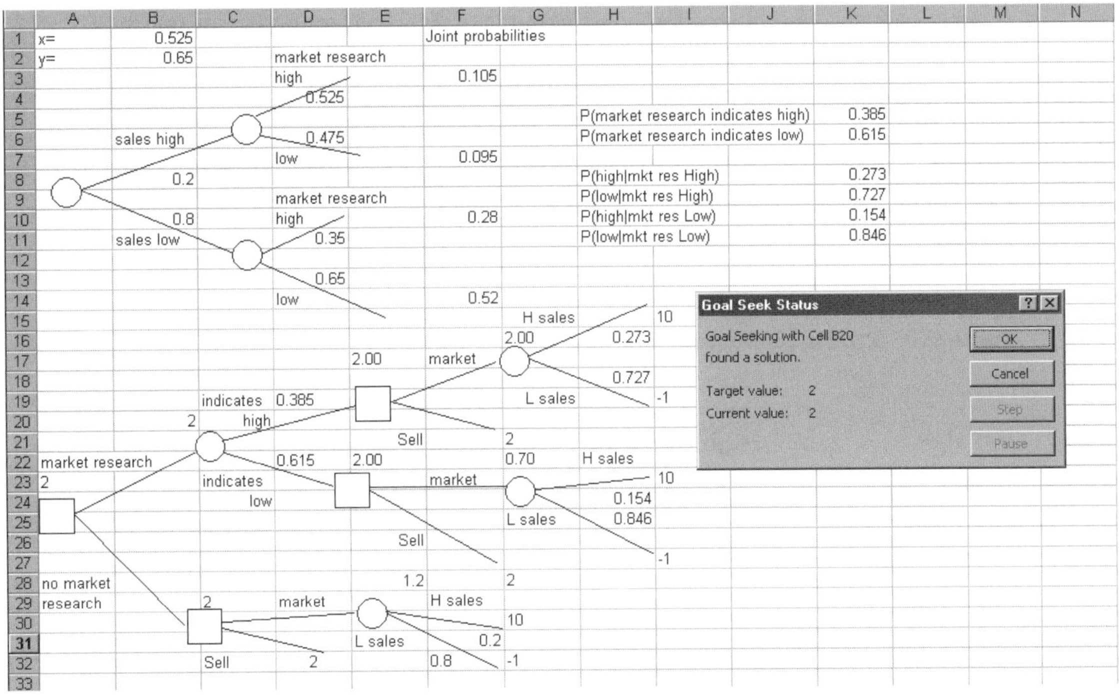

Figure 9.11 Result of using Goal Seek in Excel

Activity 9.14

Investigate the sensitivity of the decision on whether to carry out market research or not for the CleanFuel problem (Example 9.3) to changes in the probability of the market research company successfully predicting low sales.

You should have found that the probability 'y' has now become 0.5, which is not such a large fall as in the probability of successfully predicting high sales. The decision is therefore more sensitive to changes in this probability.

9.4 Utility

The EMV criterion is a very useful and popular method for choosing between a number of alternatives. However, its main drawback is that it takes no account of the decision-maker's attitude to risk. Some decision-makers are *risk-seekers* in that they are prepared to take the risk of making a loss if there is also a chance (even if this chance is small) of making large gains. Other decision-maker's are *risk-averse* in that they would always choose the safe option to avoid the risk of making a loss. One method of taking a decision-maker's attitude to risk into account is to evaluate their *utility* function. The idea is to convert monetary values into a scale between 0 and 1 in such a way that the change in the utility reflects changes in the decision-maker's preference for different amounts of money. In order to obtain this information a decision-maker is asked a number of questions.

Example 9.4

The owner of Marla plc (Example 9.1) has called in a firm of consultants to help her decide on the best decision for her company. Table 9.3 is a repeat of the data already provided earlier in this chapter.

Table 9.3 Profits (£000s) for Marla plc

	State of the market		
Decision	High (p = 0.25)	Medium (p = 0.3)	Low (p = 0.45)
Nationwide	95	52	−26
Mail order	48	24	19
Sell patent	25	25	25

In order to determine the owner's attitude to risk, the consultants asked her the following question.

'*Would you prefer to accept a sum of £52 000 or to enter a lottery where the chance of winning £95 000 is 60% and the chance of losing £26 000 is 40%?*'

The owner thought for a few seconds and decided that she would rather take the £52 000. The interviewer then kept raising the probability of winning the lottery until he reached the point where the owner could not make up her mind which option she would prefer; that is, she was indifferent between taking the £52 000 or entering the lottery. This occurred at a probability of 0.9. This procedure was repeated for the sum of £25 000 and £19 000, and the probability at which she was indifferent between the certain sum of money (£25 000 or £19 000) and entering the lottery was 0.7 and 0.65 respectively.

The approach to finding a decision-maker's utility function by the method described in Example 9.4 is called the *probability-equivalence* approach. The largest of all the possible payoffs in the decision is given the utility of 1 and the smallest the utility of 0. In Table 9.3 we have the following values (in £000s) to consider: 95, 52, 48, 25, 24, 19, −26. The largest value, 95, is given the utility of 1 and the smallest value, −26, is given the utility of 0. From the answers to the owner's questions we are now able to work out her utility(u) for values of £52 000, £25 000 and £19 000 as follows.

$$u(52) = 0.9u(95) + 0.1u(-26)$$
$$= 0.9 \times 1 + 0.1 \times 0$$
$$= 0.9$$

So once the point of indifference has been established the utility for a particular monetary value is simply the probability of the best outcome of the lottery.

Activity 9.15

Find the utility of the remaining monetary values.

$$u(25) = 0.7$$
$$u(19) = 0.65$$

Unfortunately we do not have the utilities of either £48 000 or £24 000 (although as £24 000 is so close to £25 000 we could assume it is about 0.69). To find £48 000 we could draw a graph of utility against monetary value as shown in Figure 9.12. Interpolating this graph we can estimate the utility of £48 000 as about 0.87.

The final step is to substitute the monetary values in Table 9.3 with the calculated utility values and find the decision that maximises the expected utility.

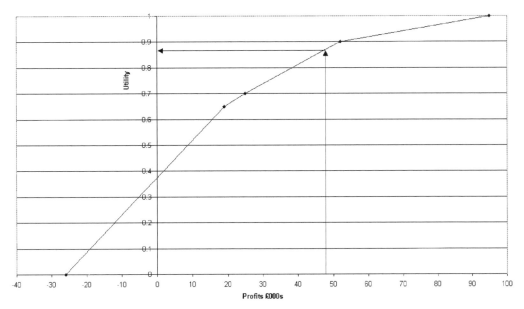

Figure 9.12 Graph showing the utility function for Example 9.4

Activity 9.16

Calculate the expected utilities for each decision and decide on the best option using this criterion.

Table 9.4 gives the utility values for each alternative and state of nature.

Table 9.4 Profits (£000s) for Marla plc

Decision	State of the market		
	High ($p=0.25$)	Medium ($p=0.3$)	Low ($p=0.45$)
Nationwide	1	0.9	0
Mail order	0.87	0.69	0.65
Sell patent	0.7	0.7	0.7

The expected utilities are:

   Nationwide: $0.25 \times 0.1 + 1 \times 0.9 + 0.45 \times 0 = 0.52$

   Mail order: $0.25 \times 0.87 + 0.3 \times 0.69 + 0.45 \times 0.65 = 0.72$

   Sell patent: $0.25 \times 0.7 + 0.3 \times 0.7 + 0.45 \times 0.7 = 0.7$

The decision has not changed – it is still 'sell by mail order' but there is now very little to choose between this and the risk free option 'sell patent'. Notice too that there is now a

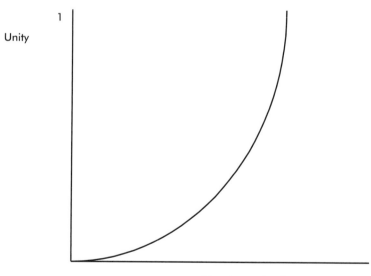

Figure 9.13 A curve of the utility function for a decision-maker who is risk-seeking

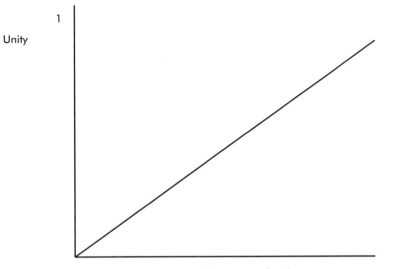

Figure 9.14 A curve of the utility function for a decision-maker who is risk-neutral

bigger difference between 'sell nationwide' and the other two options. This reflects the fact that the owner is risk-averse – she doesn't want to risk the possible loss of £26 000.

Figure 9.12 that we drew previously is a graph of the owner's utility function. You will notice that this is a concave shape. For a decision-maker who is a risk-seeker you would get a curve that is convex and for someone who is risk-neutral you would get a straight

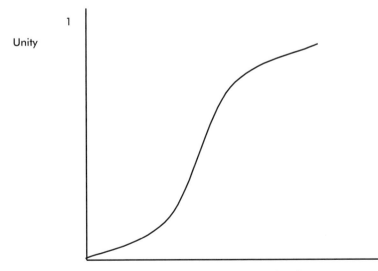

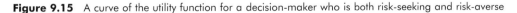

Figure 9.15 A curve of the utility function for a decision-maker who is both risk-seeking and risk-averse

line. Figures 9.13 and 9.14 illustrate these different utility functions. Figure 9.15 is the utility function for someone who is risk-seeking at lower monetary levels but risk-averse at higher monetary levels.

9.5 Summary

This chapter has introduced you to some important techniques used in decision-making. Most decisions are made under conditions of uncertainty and many techniques use ideas from probability theory. In particular, Bayes' theorem can be useful in analysing decision trees when additional information is available that allows prior information to be improved. New information has a value and it is important to see how much new information would be worth to a decision-maker. Ways of obtaining this information were explored in the chapter. Probabilities are, of course, often only subjective estimates and it is important to see the effect on a decision for changes in these probabilities. This is called sensitivity analysis and a spreadsheet is able to carry out this analysis much faster than by hand.

9.6 Further reading

Goodwin and Wright (1998) *Decision Analysis for Management Judgement*, second edition, Wiley, London (Chapter 5).

9.7 EXERCISES

The answers to the progress questions, the multiple choice questions and some of the practice questions are given in Appendix 1. Solutions to the remaining questions and the assignment can be found on the web site for this text.

PROGRESS QUESTIONS
These question have been designed to help you remember the key points in this chapter.
Give the missing word in each case.

1. The maximax rule chooses the .... of the ....
2. The minimax regret rule minimises the maximum .... loss.
3. EMV stands for .... monetary value.
4. Decision trees are suitable for .... stage decision problems.
5. EVPI stands for expected value of .... information.
6. Decision .... are a diagrammatic way of solving decision problems.
7. Bayes' theorem can be used to update .... information.
8. Utility reflects the decision-maker's attitude to ....

ANSWER *TRUE* OR *FALSE*

9. The maximin rule chooses the 'best of the worst'.

10. The maximax rule is the rule for decision-makers who are risk-averse.

11. Expected value is a long-run average.

12. In a decision tree decision nodes are represented by circles.

13. If it takes a large change in a probability to make the decision change we say that the decision is sensitive to changes in this probability.

14. A decision-maker who has a utility function that is convex in shape is said to be a risk-seeker.

REVIEW QUESTIONS

These questions have been designed to help you check your comprehension of the key points in this chapter. You may wish to look further than this chapter in order to answer them fully. You will find the reading list useful in this respect. You can check the essential elements of your answers by referring to the appropriate section.

15. What are the essential differences between the maximax, maximin and minimax regret rules? (Section 9.2)

16. What are the essential features of a decision tree and how does it differ from a probability tree? (Section 9.3)

17. Why is sensitivity analysis important in decision-making? (Section 9.3.2)

18. What are the essential differences between EVPI and EVII? (Sections 9.2.1 and 9.3)

19. What is the main drawback with the EMV criterion and how does utility overcome this drawback? (Section 9.4)

MULTIPLE CHOICE QUESTIONS

Table 9.5 Payoff table (in £m) for Questions 20 to 29

	Level of demand		
Decision	**High ($p = 0.4$)**	**Medium ($p = 0.1$)**	**Low ($p = 0.5$)**
A	2.3	0.1	−1.5
B	3.4	0.5	1.8
C	1.5	1.2	1.0
D	6.3	−1.2	−2.4

20. The maximax decision is .... (either A, B, C or D).

21. The maximin decision is .... (either A, B, C or D).

22. The minimax regret decision is .... (either A, B, C or D).

23. The decision using the Hurwicz criterion using an alpha of 0.7 is .... (either A, B, C or D).

24. The decision using the EMV criterion is .... (either A, B, C or D).
25. The decision using the EOL criterion is .... (either A, B, C or D).
26. The value of perfect information (EVPI) is

    A... 3.54 B... 2.31 C... 1.23 D... 0.18

27. A decision-maker who is risk-averse would choose option .... (either A, B, C or D).
28. A decision-maker who is a risk-seeker would choose option .... (either A, B, C or D).
29. A decision-maker who is risk-neutral would choose option .... (either A, B, C or D).

PRACTICE QUESTIONS

30. A company intends to market a new product, and it estimates that there is a 20% chance that it will be first in the market and this will give it £2m revenue in the first year. However, if it is not first in the market the expected revenue will only be £0.5m. What is the EMV?
31. Please refer to Figure 9.16 for this question and note that the objective is to maximise EMV.

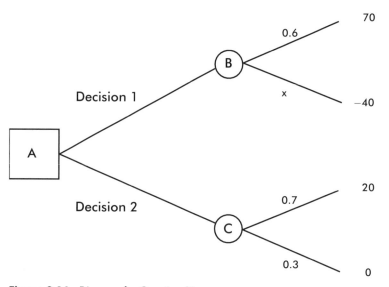

Figure 9.16 Diagram for Question 31

   (i)   What is the value of x?
   (ii) What is the EMV at probabilistic node B?
  (iii) What is the EMV at probabilistic node C?
  (iv) What should the decision be at decision node A?

      A... Decision 1   B... Decision 2

   (v) What should the value of x be in order that you will be indifferent to choosing between decision 1 and 2?

32. An inventor develops a new product. Having made the product he has three choices of what to do with it:

1. Manufacture the product himself
2. Allow someone else to make it and be paid on a royalty basis
3. Sell the rights for a lump sum

The profit which can be expected depends on the level of sales and is shown in Table 9.6 (in £000s).

Table 9.6   Payoff table for Question 32

	High sales	Medium sales	Low sales
Manufacture	80	40	−20
Royalties	50	30	10
Sell	20	20	20

The probabilities associated with the level of sales are 0.2, 0.5 and 0.3 for high, medium and low sales respectively.

(a) Write down the best decision using:

   (i)   the maximax rule
   (ii) the maximin rule
   (iii) the minimax regret rule

(b) Calculate the best decision using the expected monetary value.

(c) A survey might help to determine the likely level of sales. What is the maximum amount that the inventor should be prepared to pay for this survey?

33. An owner of a campsite is trying to decide whether to build a swimming pool, a tennis court or an indoor bar area. She can only afford to build one of these and she needs help in deciding which one to choose. The profitability of each will, to some extent depend on the weather. If the weather if hot, campers would prefer the swimming pool, but if the summer is cool, an indoor bar will be more profitable. The owner has estimated the annual profitability (in £000s) of each option for three states of nature (the weather) as shown in Table 9.7.

Table 9.7   Payoff table for Question 33

	Weather		
	Hot	Average	Cool
Swimming pool	100	50	30
Tennis courts	70	90	40
Bar	50	100	170

(a) Write down the best decision using:

    (i) the maximax rule

    (ii) the maximin rule

    (iii) the minimax regret rule

(b) If the probability of a hot summer is 0.2 and a cool summer is 0.35, calculate the best decision using the expected monetary value.

34. An investment trust manager wishes to buy a portfolio of shares and he has sufficient funds to buy either portfolio A, portfolio B or portfolio C. The potential gains from the portfolio will depend upon the economy over the next 5 years and the following estimates (in £m) have been made.

Table 9.8 Payoff table for Question 34

	Growth	Stable	Recession
A	5	2	−2
B	4	7	−4
C	4	4	4

(a) Write down the best decision using:

    (i) the maximax rule

    (ii) the maximin rule

    (iii) the minimax regret rule

(b) The manager estimates that the probability that the economy will grow over the next 5 years is 0.5, while the probability of a recession is put at 0.2. Calculate the best decision using the expected monetary value criterion.

(c) A leading economist is prepared to give more accurate estimates of these probabilities for a fee of £50 000. Would it be worthwhile employing the economist?

35. You are considering the purchase of some new computerised machinery for your factory, and have to decide between buying it immediately or waiting for a few months, since the price of the equipment has been falling steadily over the past year. You have been advised that, if you wait for six months, there is a 60% chance that the price will fall to £12 000; otherwise it will remain steady at £16 000.

    If you buy now, the £16 000 cost can be reduced by the £2000 saving which you expect will result from the increased efficiency due to the new machine being operative over the 6-month period.

(a) Assuming that your objective is to minimise expected costs, what course of action should you take?

(b) The estimate that there is a 60% chance that the price will fall is only very rough. By how much must this probability decrease before you would be indifferent between buying the equipment now and delaying the purchase?

36. A department store has to decide whether to expand on its existing site in the town centre or to move to a new site on the outskirts. There is a possibility that a rival store may open a branch in the town centre in the near future. If it does so, the first store's total profits over the next 5 years will be £10m if it does not move, as against £16m if it does.

    If the rival store does not open, total profits for the town centre site are estimated at £40m, and for the new site at £32m. The probability of the rival store opening is estimated to be about 70%. Which decision would maximise expected profit? (For simplicity, you should ignore factors like the time value of money.)

37. Cast Iron Construction plc (CIC) is a company specialising in high-rise office blocks. They have recently decided to consider building in third world countries and they have a choice of 2 sites. One is in the earthquake prone island of Tutamolia and the other is in the politically unstable country of Flesomnial.

    The building cost of £5m is the same for both countries and it is estimated that that the return over 10 years for each country will also be the same at £20m. However, in Tutamolia, CIC have a choice of strengthening the building at a further cost of £5m. If they do this the probability that the building will collapse if an earthquake occurs is only 0.01 whereas if no strengthening work is done the probability that the building would collapse is 0.7.

    The probability that an earthquake will occur in the next 10 years is put at 0.1. If an earthquake does occur anytime during the 10 years and the building collapses the company will forfeit the return of £20m, and in addition they will have to pay compensation to the government of £10m.

    If CIC decides to build in Flesomnial there is a 20% chance that the country will be taken over by a dictator and the company will not receive any return on its investment.

    (a) Draw a decision tree for this problem and use this decision tree to determine the decision that will maximise CIC'c expected return.

    (b) The probability that an earthquake will occur is really only a guess. What should this probability become before the decision found in part (a) changes.

38. At its latest meeting, an investment club is trying to decide which investment out of 3 possible ones to buy this month.

Table 9.9 Payoff table for Question 38

	Stock market movement (in £00)		
Investment	Rising	Stable	Falling
A	150	25	−100
B	90	50	0
C	−10	10	50

A member has estimated the potential returns on these investments over the next 6 months given 3 different scenarios relating to the movement of the stock market (Table 9.9).

(a) Write down the best decision if:

    (i) the club was risk-seeking

    (ii) the club was risk-averse

(b) Write down the opportunity loss table and obtain the best decision using the minimax regret criterion.

(c) If the probability of the stock market rising is 0.2 and 0.6 for a fall, calculate the best decision using the EMV criterion.

(d) What is the expected value of perfect information (EVPI)?

(e) To decide the club's attitude to risk, each member took part in an exercise designed to evaluate their utility function. The result of one member's answers are as follows:

'I am indifferent between investing in a share that would give me a return of £9000 for certain or entering a lottery that will give me a 0.5 probability of a £15000 return and a 0.5 probability of a −£10000 return.'

'I am indifferent between investing in a share that would give me a return of £2500 for certain or entering a lottery that will give me a 0.3 probability of a £15000 return and a 0.7 probability of a −£10000 return.'

    (i) Sketch the member's utility function and comment on what it shows.

    (ii) From your sketch estimate the utilities for returns of £5000, £1000, £0 and −£1000. What is the best decision for the club that would maximise the expected utility?

39. Pizza Classic is a family-run pizza delivery company that have been in the Bristol area for over 20 years. In their current 3-year business plan they have estimated the probability of high and low demand for their pizzas as 0.55 and 0.45 respectively. They have also estimated that the net present value (using a discount rate of 10%) of income will be £750 000 if the demand is high and £375 000 if the demand is low. (They assumed that the demand will either be high or low for all 3 years.)

The company are now considering setting up an internet site where customers could order their pizzas. The start-up costs of this venture would be £20 000 (payable now). It is believed that an internet site would increase the amount spent per customer and therefore net income from both high and low demand would increase as shown in the following table.

Year (end)	1	2	3
High demand	£300 000	£400 000	£400 000
Low demand	£150 000	£250 000	£200 000

If the company decides to go ahead with the plan it could employ consultants to conduct a marketing campaign. The consultants would charge £30 000 and they believe that there is an 80% chance that their campaign will be a success and customers will approve the plan. If the campaign is a success it is believed the probability of high demand would increase to 0.65. If the consultants conclude that customers are not likely to use the site, the company will abandon the idea of an internet site.

(a) Using a discount rate of 10% calculate the net present value for both high and low demand over the next 3 years (assume that income occurs at end of each year and that the discount factors for years 1 to 3 are 0.9090, 0.8264 and 0.7513, respectively).

(b) Draw a decision tree for the problem.

(c) Determine the optimal decision for the company.

(d) What is the maximum amount that you would be prepared to pay the consultants?

(e) The probabilities used by Pizza Classic are really only guesses. How might you test the sensitivity of the outcome to changes in these probabilities?

40. Jayes Pharmaceutical has a number of high earning products, including the new A1 asthma spray. Preliminary sales of this product suggest that profits per unit sold amounts to £10.

However, a recent report in an American journal suggests that it can cause an allergic reaction in up to 1% of people using the spray. The company now has a dilemma: should it continue selling the spray, knowing that there is this risk, or should it abandon it and re-market an older, less effective spray?

If it continues to sell this product and allergies develop, the company will have to compensate the buyer and the loss in profits will cost the company £20 per unit.

If the company decides to abandon the product and sell the older version it would expect to earn a profit of £1.50 per unit.

An alternative is to supply a free allergy testing kit worth £1 with each product sold. If the test is positive, the customer will get a full refund. This test is not perfectly reliable, however, and the probability that the test will correctly indicate that someone will be allergic is only 0.9 and the probability that it will give a false positive reading is 0.3. The company would not be able to recover the costs of supplying this kit, so the company would effectively make a loss of £11.

(a) Draw a probability tree diagram showing the prior and conditional probabilities.

(b) Calculate the probability that the test will be positive.

(c) Calculate the following posterior probabilities:

(i) probability that a person is allergic if the test is positive.

(ii) probability that a person is allergic if the test is negative.

(d) Draw a decision tree to determine the best course of action.

(e) If the company expected to sell 500 000 of these units per year, write down the annual profits from all three courses of action.

ASSIGNMENT

Chix laboratory have recently come up with a method of producing joints of 'chicken' from non-animal products. The process is quite revolutionary and the taste and texture of the 'meat' is believed to be indistinguishable from the real thing. The product should also have an advantage in terms of price and shelf life (the product need not be stored in a refrigerator and will stay in good condition for up to two weeks).

However, the cost of setting up production is very high at £1m and it is not at all certain that consumers will accept the product. The marketing department have assessed the risk and believe that there is only a 30% chance that consumers will approve of the product. If consumers do approve then sales are estimated to be around £2.5m p.a., but if the reaction is negative then sales will amount to no more than £0.7m p.a. (the catering market is virtually guaranteed to want the product).

The risk could be reduced by carrying out a survey to gauge public reaction to the product. From past experience this kind of survey produces accurate results 85% of the time. (That is, if the survey indicates a favourable response, the probability that a favourable response occurs is 0.85 and similarly, if the survey suggests a negative response, the probability that a negative response occurs is 0.85.) The cost of this survey will be £100 000.

The product manager assigned to this new product line is Graham Green and he has requested your help in deciding whether to commission a survey or to proceed immediately with full production. You explain that the decision is perhaps more complicated than he thinks and the following options are available to him:

1. Proceed with full production.
2. Commission a survey. Whatever the results of the survey there are two further options; that is, proceed with full production or abandon the project.
3. Abandon the project.

Following discussions with the marketing department, you decide that carrying out the marketing survey before going into full production will not affect the expected sales revenue. You have also assumed that the probability that the survey will indicate a favourable response is 0.3.

(a) Draw a decision tree for the problem and decide what the correct decisions should be.
(b) Investigate the sensitivity of your answer changes to the probability of a favourable response.

10 Analysis and interpretation of sample data

10.1 Introduction

You were introduced to the idea of sampling in Chapter 2. In that chapter the problems of recording information about the whole 'population' were discussed and the need for sampling became apparent. Information from a sample is subject to error and the purpose of this chapter is to be able to quantify this error. This is achieved by stating the margin of error round the sample estimate of some population parameter. This is called a confidence interval.

To complete this chapter successfully you should already have worked through Chapter 2 (Sampling methods) and Chapter 8 (Probability distributions).

On completing this chapter you should be able to:

- Obtain best estimates of the mean and standard deviation of a population
- Calculate confidence intervals for a population mean
- Calculate confidence intervals for a population percentage

10.2 Samples and sampling

Sampling is an extensive and in many cases controversial technique. Whenever there is a general election in this country the question of sampling accuracy is raised and this was most evident in the 1992 election where the polls incorrectly forecast a Labour majority. However, sampling people's views and intentions is notoriously difficult and even the best sampling plan can fail in these circumstances. Fortunately, when sampling is done by measurement, the results tend to be much more reliable. Sampling in industry and business tends to be of the measurement kind, and it will be this aspect of sampling that will be emphasised here.

Activity 10.1

Why is it necessary to take samples?

The alternative to taking samples is to measure or test every member of the population. (The word 'population' in this context doesn't necessarily mean people; it is used to define all the items or things that are of interest, such as all television sets produced by a company in a day.) It is impractical to measure or test every member of the population for the following reasons:

● *It would take too long.* Measuring or testing can be time consuming and it is simply not always feasible to find the necessary time.

● *It is too expensive.* Testing costs money as inspectors need to be employed and goods that are to be tested take up space and cannot be sold until the testing is complete.

● *Some tests are destructive.* Sometimes goods have to be tested to destruction, and if all the goods were tested there would be nothing left to sell!

● *The total population is unknown.* There are occasions when the size of the population is so large as to be considered infinite (without limit). In other cases the size of the population is simply unknown.

Activity 10.2

You work for a company that manufactures plastic containers. The raw material is supplied in granular form and is delivered in 100 kg bags. The granules have to be tested for fire resistance and you are given the job of selecting the material for testing. How would you go about this task?

Since this is likely to be destructive testing, the only option available to you is to test a sample from each consignment. It is important that more than one bag is tested, since one particular bag may not be typical of the rest of the batch. Perhaps this bag happens to be old stock, or is different in some way. Whenever you take samples you must ensure that the samples are selected at *random*; that is, every member of the population has an equal chance of being selected. (See Chapter 2.) In this case you would need to randomly select a number of bags and then test a small quantity from each of the bags selected. The number of bags chosen and the amount of material tested from each bag would depend on the specific requirements of the test.

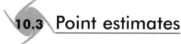

10.3 Point estimates

The whole purpose of obtaining a sample from a population is to obtain estimates of various population *parameters*, such as the mean, the standard deviation or percentage.

These parameters can also be obtained for the sample, and it is the purpose of this section to show how the population parameters and the sample *statistics* are related. However, before continuing, it is necessary to define the symbols that are to be used throughout this (and the next) chapter.

The convention is to use Greek letters for the population parameters and normal letters for the sample statistics. The various symbols used are given below.

Parameter	Population	Sample
Mean	μ	$\bar{x}$
Standard deviation	σ	s
Percentage	π	P

The one exception to this rule is that the size of the population is usually referred to as N and the sample size as n.

Example 10.1

10 samples of plastic granules were tested for fire resistance and the combustion temperature (in °C) are as follows:

Sample No.	1	2	3	4	5	6	7	8	9	10
Temperature	510	535	498	450	491	505	487	500	501	469

Activity 10.3

What is the mean and standard deviation of these figures in Example 10.1, and what can you conclude about the whole batch?

You should have found the mean to be 494.6 °C with a standard deviation of 21.85 °C. (See Chapter 4 if you are not sure about these calculations.) You will probably not be surprised to learn that the 'best' (or *unbiased*) estimate of the population mean is $\bar{x}$. Therefore the best estimate of the mean of the batch is 494.6 °C. But what is the best estimate of the population standard deviation? It is not s; the sample standard deviation as s is an underestimate of the true figure. To understand this, imagine that the population of temperatures follows some probability distribution. This distribution has a few extreme values but most of them are clustered around the mean. The population standard deviation is a measure of spread, and all values, including the extreme ones, contribute to this value. However, if a sample is chosen at random the sample is most unlikely to include any of the extreme values, and therefore the spread and hence the standard deviation of the sample will be *less* than the population. You should also realise that as the sample gets larger, the standard deviation will get closer and closer to the population value (σ) since the chance of selecting an extreme value increases.

So how is σ calculated? Fortunately there is quite a simple formula relating s and σ:

$$\sigma = s\sqrt{\frac{n}{n-1}}$$

This is known as *Bessel's correction factor*.

You will see that as n gets larger, the factor under the square root gets closer to 1, which ties in with the discussion above. For 'large' samples, which are generally considered to be anything above 30, this correction is usually ignored. You will also find that if you are using a calculator to calculate σ you do not need to worry about the correction factor, as there are normally two buttons for standard deviation. This has already been mentioned in Chapter 4, but perhaps now is the time to explain the two different formulae. The formula derived for the standard deviation in Chapter 4 was:

$$s = \sqrt{\frac{\sum (x-\bar{x})^2}{n}}$$

If we now substitute this value of s into Bessel's correction factor, we get:

$$\sigma = \sqrt{\frac{\sum (x-\bar{x})^2}{n}} \times \sqrt{\frac{n}{n-1}}$$

$$= \sqrt{\frac{\sum (x-\bar{x})^2 n}{n \times (n-1)}}$$

$$= \sqrt{\frac{\sum (x-\bar{x})^2}{n-1}}$$

This explains why some calculators have a σ_{n-1} button as well as a σ_n button. The σ_{n-1} button will give you the population estimate without having to apply the correction factor.

If you apply either the correction factor or use the direct method, you should find that the estimate of the population standard deviation for the data in Example 10.1 is 23.03 °C.

10.4 Sampling distribution of the mean

Imagine that you took lots and lots of samples and calculated the mean of each. Each mean is an estimate of the population value, and therefore the 'mean of the means' should be an even better estimate. If you then plotted the distribution of the means, what shape would you expect the distribution to be? The answer is that the shape would tend towards the *normal* curve. The degree of agreement with the normal curve depends on two factors:

● The distribution of the population values
● The sample size

If the population values are normally distributed, the 'sampling distribution of the means' would also be normal. If the population is not normally distributed, the agreement with the normal distribution depends on the sample size; the larger the sample size, the closer the agreement. This very important result is known as the *central limit theorem*.

In addition, the spread of this sampling distribution depends on the sample size; the larger the sample size, the smaller the spread (that is, the standard deviation). The standard deviation of the sampling distribution is called the *standard error*, as it measures the error that could arise in your estimate due to the spread of the sampling distribution. To avoid confusion with the standard error of the sampling distribution of a percentage, which will be discussed later, the standard error of the sampling distribution of the means will be referred to as STEM (the STandard Error of the Mean). Is it necessary to collect many samples in order to calculate the value of STEM? Fortunately not, as there is a relationship between σ and STEM. This relationship is as follows:

$$\text{STEM} = \frac{\sigma}{\sqrt{n}}$$

So the larger the sample size (n), the smaller the value of STEM, which makes sense.

These ideas are illustrated in Figure 10.1. Two sampling distributions are shown: one for a sample size of 4, and one for a sample size of 16. The population distribution (assumed normal in this case) has been superimposed on to the diagram.

You will see that the mean of each sampling distribution is the same and equal to the population value. You would normally only take one sample, and from Figure 10.1 you can see that the mean of a sample can lie anywhere within the relevant sampling distribution, although it is more likely to be near the centre than in the tails. This variation depends on the value of STEM, so the smaller this figure, the more reliable your estimate of the population mean will be.

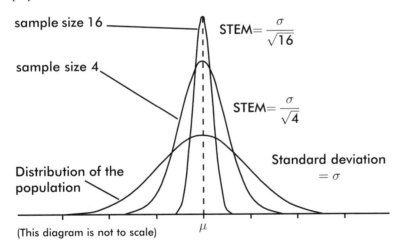

(This diagram is not to scale)

Figure 10.1 Sampling distribution of the means

Activity 10.4

The standard deviation of the population of combustion temperatures for the plastic granules is known to be 23.75 °C. What is the value of STEM for a sample of size 10 and for a sample of size 40?

The value of STEM when $n = 10$ is:

$$\text{STEM} = \frac{23.75}{\sqrt{10}}$$

$$= \frac{23.75}{3.1623}$$

$$= 7.510$$

That is, 7.510 °C. When $n = 40$, STEM becomes:

$$\text{STEM} = \frac{23.75}{\sqrt{40}}$$

$$= \frac{23.75}{6.3246}$$

$$= 3.755$$

That is, 3.755 °C. Notice that to halve the value of STEM, the sample size was increased fourfold. Calculation of the sample size necessary to give a prescribed level of accuracy will be discussed later.

10.5 Confidence intervals for a population mean for large samples

Rather than simply quote the value of STEM, a much better idea of the reliability of your estimate is to specify some limits within which the true mean is expected to lie. These limits are called confidence limits or intervals.

When calculating confidence intervals it is necessary to decide what level of confidence you wish to use. The most common level is 95%, which means that you are 95% confident that the true mean lies within the calculated limits. Or, put another way, there is a 5% chance that the true mean doesn't lie within these limits. Other limits are frequently used, such as 90%, 99% and 99.9%; but remember that as the confidence level gets closer to 100%, the interval gets larger and larger (at 100% it would be infinitely large).

The *normal distribution* (see Chapter 8, p. 163) can be used to calculate these limits when the sample size is large as, according to the central limit theorem, the sampling distribution of the sample mean will be approximately normal. A large sample is generally considered to be 30 or over.

Figure 10.2 illustrates the Z values that enclose 95% of the standard normal distribution. The values ±1.96 have been found from the normal table (Appendix 2) by noting that the area (or probability) in either tail is 0.025 $\left(\frac{0.05}{2} \right)$.

From your knowledge of the normal distribution, you will know that any normal distribution can be transformed into the standard normal distribution using the formula:

$$Z = \frac{x - \mu}{\sigma}$$

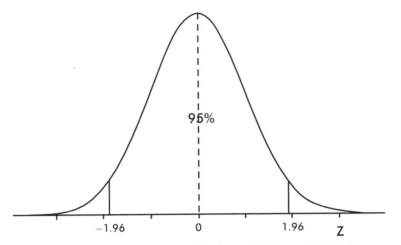

95%

−1.96   0   1.96   Z

Figure 10.2 95% confidence interval for the standard normal distribution

However, this formula is for individual x values. For a sampling distribution of the means, the x needs to be replaced by $\bar{x}$ and σ needs to be replaced by STEM. The formula then becomes:

$$Z = \frac{\bar{x} - \mu}{\text{STEM}}$$

If you rearrange this formula to make μ the subject, you will get:

$$\mu = \bar{x} \pm Z \times \text{STEM}$$

This is the equation you would use to calculate confidence intervals using the normal distribution. For 95% confidence intervals, the Z value is 1.96 and the formula becomes:

$$\mu = \bar{x} \pm 1.96 \times \text{STEM}$$

How would you use this formula? The next example should help you.

Example 10.2

Imagine that you work for the quality control unit of a sugar producer. One of your tasks is to weigh samples of 1 kg bags of sugar, and from a sample of 36 bags you obtain a mean weight of 0.985 kg and a standard deviation of 0.056 kg.

Activity 10.5

What is the 95% confidence interval for the true mean weight of bags of sugar?

From the discussion on point estimates, you know that the best estimate of the true mean is 0.985 kg. That is:

$$\mu = 0.985 \, \text{kg}$$

As we have a large sample the population standard deviation can be approximated by the sample standard deviation, and so the value of STEM is:

$$\frac{\sigma}{\sqrt{n}} = \frac{0.056}{\sqrt{36}}$$
$$= 0.00933$$

Therefore the 95% confidence interval for the true mean is:

$$0.985 \pm 1.96 \times 0.00933$$
$$= 0.985 \pm 0.018$$
$$= 0.985 - 0.018 \quad \text{and} \quad 0.985 + 0.018$$
$$= 0.967 \quad \text{and} \quad 1.003 \, \text{kg}$$

The 0.967 kg is the *lower* limit and 1.003 kg is the *upper* limit. The ± 0.018 is often called the *half width* of the confidence interval. It is usual to write this confidence interval as:

0.967, 1.003 kg (or 0.967 to 1.003 kg)

If you took another 36 bags you would get a slightly different sample mean and therefore the confidence interval will be different. Hopefully both these confidence intervals would contain the true mean, but if you took 20 different samples you would expect that one of these intervals would not contain the true mean. That is, there is a 1 in 20 or 5% chance that your confidence interval would not contain the true mean. This is illustrated in Figure 10.3 where confidence intervals for 5 sample means have been drawn, two of which do not contain the true mean.

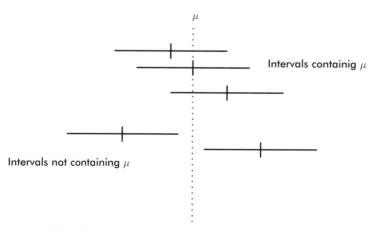

Figure 10.3 Diagram to illustrate confidence intervals

If you wanted to reduce the chance of the interval not containing the true mean you could calculate 99% confidence intervals. From the normal table, the value of Z for 0.005 (1% divided by 2) is 2.58, so the 99% confidence interval is:

$$0.985 \pm 2.58 \times 0.00933$$

$$= 0.985 \pm 0.024$$

$$= 0.961, 1.009 \, \text{kg}$$

The interval is wider, which was expected. Now there is only a 1% chance that the true mean will be outside these limits. If these limits are too wide, the only way to reduce them (for the same confidence level) is to increase the sample size.

10.6 Confidence intervals for a population mean for small samples

For large samples we were able to make use of the central limit theorem in our assumption that the sampling distribution of the sample mean will be normal no matter what the shape of the distribution of the population. We were also justified in using the sample standard deviation in place of the population standard deviation in the calculation of STEM. However, for small samples neither of these assumptions holds, so even if we assume that the population is normal we have a problem with the standard deviation. The reason for this is that the uncertainty generated by estimating σ decreases the reliability of the confidence interval. To overcome this problem a different distribution is used, called the '*t-distribution*'. This distribution is symmetrical like the normal, but it is flatter. This 'flatness' increases the percentage of the distribution in the 'tails' and this means that the confidence interval, for the same confidence level, is wider. The amount of 'flatness' decreases with increase in n, the sample size. When n is 50 there is virtually no difference between the two distributions, and even for a sample size of 30 the difference is quite small.

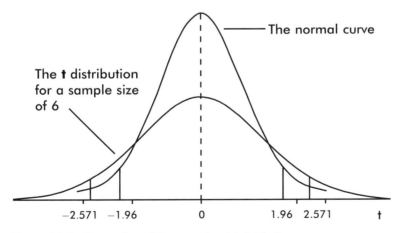

Figure 10.4 Comparison of the normal and *t*-distributions

Figure 10.4 shows the *t*-distribution for a sample size of 6, together with the normal distribution for comparison.

The *t*-table is given in Appendix 2. If you compare this table with the normal table, you will see two important differences. First, the numbers within the table are *t*-values and not probabilities; second, the numbers in the first column are different. These numbers are the *degrees of freedom* (df) of the sample. Degrees of freedom can be thought of as the 'freedom' that you have in choosing the values of the sample. If you were given the mean of the sample of 6 values, you would be free to choose 5 of the 6 but not the sixth one. Therefore there are 5 degrees of freedom. The number of degrees of freedom for a single sample of size n is $n - 1$. For a very large sample (shown as ∞ in the table) the t and Z distributions are exactly the same. Since the *t*-distribution is a little easier to use, you might prefer to use this table when you want the Z value of one of the 'standard' probabilities. In the table supplied in this book these 'standard' probabilities are 0.2, 0.1, 0.05, 0.025, 0.01, 0.005, 0.001 and 0.0001.

To use this table you would first decide on the probability level. For a 95% confidence interval you would choose the 0.025 level, since this represents 2.5% in each tail. For a sample size of 6, the degrees of freedom is 5, so the *t*-value for 5 degrees of freedom at 95% confidence level is 2.571. This value has been shown in Figure 10.4. (Remember that the *t*-distribution is symmetrical about the mean of zero, so the equivalent value in the left hand side of the distribution is -2.571.)

The formula for calculating confidence intervals using this distribution is the same as when the normal distribution was used, except that Z is replaced by t and is therefore:

$$\mu = \bar{x} \pm t \times \text{STEM}$$

Activity 10.6

In Activity 10.3 you calculated the mean and standard deviation of the combustion temperatures of a sample of size 10 to be 494.6 °C and 21.85 °C respectively. Calculate the 95% confidence intervals for true mean combustion temperature of the entire batch.

The best estimate of σ was 23.03 °C, so the value of STEM is:

$$\frac{23.03}{\sqrt{10}} = 7.283$$

To find the 95% confidence interval for the true mean, you would use the *t*-table in Appendix 2 to find the appropriate value of t. The value of t for 9 degrees of freedom, with a probability of 0.025, is 2.262. Substituting this value into the equation for μ gives you:

$494.6 \pm 2.262 \times 7.283$

$= 494.6 \pm 16.5$

$= 478.1, 511.1\,°C$

So the true mean combustion temperature of the whole consignment lies between 478.1 °C and 511.1 °C at the 95% level of confidence.

10.7 Confidence interval of a percentage

Percentages occur quite frequently in the analysis of survey results; for example, the percentage of people who like a particular product, or the percentage of students over the age of 25. Provided n is large and the percentage is not too small or too large, the sampling distribution of a percentage can be approximated by the normal distribution.

The standard error of the sampling distribution of percentages (STEP) is:

$$\text{STEP} = \sqrt{\frac{P(100 - P)}{n}}$$

Where P is the sample percentage.

The calculation of a confidence interval for a percentage is similar to that of the mean, that is:

$$\pi = P \pm Z \times \text{STEP}$$

Activity 10.7

A survey among 250 students revealed that 147 were female. What is the 95% confidence interval for the true percentage of female students?

The value of P is $\frac{147}{250} \times 100 = 58.8\%$ That is, the survey suggested that 58.8% of the student population is female. The value of STEP for this problem is:

$$\sqrt{\frac{58.8 \times (100 - 58.8)}{250}}$$

$$= 3.113$$

The value of Z for 95% confidence is 1.96, so the confidence interval becomes:

$$58.8 \pm 1.96 \times 3.113$$

$$= 58.8 \pm 6.1$$

$$= 52.7, 64.9$$

That is, the true percentage lies somewhere between 52.7% and 64.9%.

10.8 Calculation of sample size

Since the value of both STEM and STEP depend on the sample size, the width of the confidence interval for the same confidence level can be reduced by increasing the value of n. For the sugar example (Activity 10.5) the half width of the interval – that is, the difference between the lower or upper limit and the sample mean – is 0.018 kg for a confidence level of 95%. This was obtained by multiplying STEM by 1.96; that is:

Half width of confidence interval $= 1.96 \times$ STEM

$$= 1.96 \times \frac{\sigma}{\sqrt{n}}$$

If you wanted to reduce this half width to, say, 0.015 kg, then you need to calculate the value of n required to achieve this reduction. That is:

$$1.96 \times \frac{0.056}{\sqrt{n}} = 0.015$$

Since $\sigma = 0.056$ (see Example 10.2)

Rearranging this equation gives:

$$\sqrt{n} = \frac{1.96 \times 0.056}{0.015}$$

$$= 7.3173$$

So $n = 53.5$

So a sample size of about 24 would be required to achieve an accuracy of ± 0.015 kg.

Activity 10.8

What sample size would be required to reduce the half width for the percentage of female students from 6.1% to 1%?

The calculation is similar to that for the mean. That is:

$$1.96 \times \text{STEP} = 1.0$$

The value of P is 58.8%, so:

$$1.96 \times \sqrt{\frac{58.8 \times (100 - 58.8)}{n}} = 1.0$$

Dividing both sides by 1.96 and squaring gives:

$$\frac{58.8 \times 41.2}{n} = 0.2603$$

Therefore:

$$n = \frac{58.8 \times 41.2}{0.2603}$$

$$= 9306.8$$

That is, a sample of about 9000 students would need to be selected to ensure this level of accuracy!

 ## 10.9 Finite populations

The assumption that has implicitly been made in this chapter is that the population is infinitely large, or at least much larger than the sample. The reason for this is that all sampling is done *without* replacement. That is, you would not measure or test the same person or item twice. This has no effect when the population is large, but for small populations, the probability that an item will be selected will change as soon as one item has been selected. (See Chapter 7.) To overcome this problem, the standard error (either STEM or STEP) is modified. This is achieved by multiplying the value by the *Finite Population Correction Factor*, which is:

$$\sqrt{\frac{(N - n)}{(N - 1)}}$$

Where N is the size of the population.

Activity 10.9

In the sugar example (Example 10.2) STEM was 0.00933. What is the value of STEM if the size of the population is 100?

The value of STEM is multiplied by the correction factor, that is:

$$0.00933 \times \sqrt{\frac{(100 - 6)}{(100 - 1)}}$$

$$= 0.00933 \times 0.9744$$

$$= 0.00909$$

Which is a *reduction*. (Since STEM is reduced, confidence intervals will also be reduced.)

As N gets larger relative to n, the correction factor approaches 1 and can therefore be ignored. For example, if you try $N = 10\,000$ and $n = 10$, you should get a value of 0.9995.

10.10 Summary

In this chapter you were shown how to quantify the error that arises as a result of sampling. This is only possible because of the central limit theorem, which states that the sampling distribution of the means is approximately normal. Using the properties of the normal distribution, we are able to determine the interval within which some population parameter, such as the mean or percentage, is expected to lie. This interval is called a confidence interval, as you are able to specify the level of confidence you have with the calculated interval.

10.11 Further reading

McClave, J. and Sincich, T. (2000) *Statistics*, eighth edition, Prentice Hall, New Jersey (Chapter 7).
Morris, C. (2000) *Quantitative Approaches in Business Studies*, fifth edition, Pitman, London (Chapter 10).

10.12 EXERCISES

The answers to the progress questions, the multiple choice questions and some of the practice questions are given in Appendix 1. Solutions to the remaining questions and the assignment can be found at the web site for this text.

PROGRESS QUESTIONS

These questions have been designed to help you remember the key points in this chapter.

Give the missing word in each case.

1. All items of interest is called a ....
2. A subset of all items of interest is called a ....
3. A single estimate of some variable of interest is called a .... estimate.
4. The best estimate of the true mean is the .... mean.
5. The standard deviation of a sample is .... than the true figure.
6. An interval estimate is also known as a .... interval.

ANSWER *TRUE* OR *FALSE*

7. The Z table is used when the sample size is large.
8. The *t*-distribution approaches the normal distribution as the sample size increases.
9. It is necessary to be given the standard deviation of the population for the *t*-distribution to be used.
10. As the sample size increases, the error in your estimate decreases.
11. For small samples the *t*-distribution should be used.

12. The use of the normal distribution to calculate confidence intervals for a percentage is only an approximation.
13. If the sample size doubles, the half width of the confidence interval reduces by a half.
14. A 95% confidence interval means that 95% of samples will have a mean or percentage within this interval.

REVIEW QUESTIONS

These questions have been designed to help you check your comprehension of the key points in this chapter. You may wish to look further than this chapter in order to answer them fully. You will find the reading list useful in this respect. You can check the essential elements of your answers by referring to the appropriate section.

15. Why is it necessary to take samples? (Section 10.2)
16. Explain the importance of the central limit theorem to statistics. (Section 10.4)
17. Describe the essential differences between the normal and the *t*-distributions. (Sections 10.5 and 10.6)
18. What effect does sample size have on a confidence interval? (Section 10.8)
19. What effect does a small population have on a confidence interval? (Section 10.9)

MULTIPLE CHOICE QUESTIONS

Questions 20 to 23 refer to the sample 34.5, 25.7, 20.1, 38.9, 33.0, 33.2, 22.8 and 30.5, denoted by *x*. This sample was taken from a large population denoted by *P*.

20. The mean of *x* (to 2 decimal places) is:

    A... 25.26   B... 29.84   C... 39.55

21. The standard deviation of *x* (to 2 decimal places) is:

    A... 5.99   B... 6.40   C... 25.26

22. The best estimate of the standard deviation of *P* is:

    A... 5.99   B... 6.40   C... 25.26

23. The value of STEM is:

    A... 2.26   B... 2.12   C... 5.99

24. The sampling distribution of the means follows:

    A... a uniform distribution   B... a normal distribution
    C... an empirical distribution   D... a *t*-distribution

25. The standard deviation of the sampling distribution of the means is called:

    A... STEM   B... STEP   C... σ D... μ

26. The standard deviation of the sampling distribution of a percentage is called:

    A... STEM   B... STEP   C... σ D... μ

Questions 27 and 28 refer to a sample of 50 credit card holders who were questioned about how much they owed on all credit cards held. The average amount owed by all 50 people was £1300 with a standard deviation of £460. It can be assumed that this is representative of all credit card holders.

27. The 95% confidence interval is given by:

    A... $1300 \pm 1.96 \times 65.05$

    B... $1300 \pm 1.96 \times 460$

    C... $1300 \pm 1.96 \times 9.2$

    D... $1300 \pm 1.96 \times 50$

28. 20% of the 50 people questioned had more than 3 credit cards. The 95% confidence interval of the percentage of all credit card holders who had more than 3 credit cards can be found from:

    A... $20 \pm 1.96 \times 4.47$

    B... $20 \pm 1.96 \times 7.07$

    C... $20 \pm 1.96 \times 3$

    D... $20 \pm 1.96 \times 5.66$

29. To reduce the width of a confidence interval (that is, the difference between the upper and lower bounds) you would:

    A... Increase the size of the sample

    B... Decrease the size of the sample

    C... Use a larger confidence level instead

    D... Not possible

30. As part of a quality control system, a simple random sample of 100 units was taken from a large batch of production and tested. Ten units were found to be faulty. Therefore the 95% confidence limits for the overall percentage of faulty items in the batch will be closest to 10% plus or minus:

    A... 1%   B... 2%   C... 3%   D... 6%

PRACTICE QUESTIONS

31. A university contains 16 000 students and it is required to find out how many students have part-time jobs. 50 students are selected at random and of these, 20 admitted to working during term time. What is the value of:

    (a) the size of the population?

    (b) the sample size?

    (c) the sample percentage?

    (d) the estimate of the true percentage?

    (e) the 95% confidence interval of the true percentage?

32. A sample of six packets of tea is selected from a production line. The contents of these packets are 9.4, 9.1, 10.2, 8.9, 10.9 and 9.2 g respectively. Obtain the 95% confidence interval estimate of the mean net weight of a packet, if the weights are normally distributed.

33. A random sample of 100 adult females from the population of a large town has a mean height of 169.5 cm with a standard deviation of 2.6 cm. Construct a 95% confidence interval for the mean height of all adult females in the town.

34. A sample of 60 people was asked if they thought that if children watched video 'nasties' they were more likely to commit a crime. Out of the sample, 45 thought that they would. Calculate the 95% confidence interval for the true percentage.

35. The weight of each of 10 specimens of carbon paper was found to be (in grams):

    7.4, 8.3, 10.9, 6.9, 7.9, 8.2, 8.6, 9.1, 9.9, 10.0

    Given that the weights are normally distributed, construct (a) 95% and (b) 99% confidence intervals for the true mean of the population weights.

36. A credit card company wants to determine the mean income of its card holders. A random sample of 225 card holders was drawn and the sample average income was £16 450 with a standard deviation of £3675.

    (i) Construct a 99% confidence interval for the true mean income.

    (ii) Management decided that the confidence interval in (i) was too large to be useful. In particular, the management wanted to estimate the mean income to within £200, with a confidence level of 99%. How large a sample should be selected?

37. From a population of 200, a sample of 40 people were asked for their views on capital punishment. 12 people thought that hanging should be imposed for certain crimes. Estimate the 95% confidence interval for the true percentage.

38. A company involved in a market research survey takes a random sample of 800 orders which were delivered in a given month. Of these orders, 320 went to customers aged under 21. Estimate the percentage of all the company's orders which went to this age group during the month in question, with 95% confidence.

39. In a sample of 200 of a company's business customers, 160 say that they are likely to make a further purchase within the next 12 months. Estimate the percentage of all the company's customers who will make a further purchase within the next year with 95% confidence.

40. An insurance company is concerned about the size of claims being made by its policy holders. A random sample of 400 claims had a mean value of £230 and a standard deviation of £42. Estimate the mean size of all claims received by the company:

    (i) with 95% confidence   (ii) with 99% confidence

41. A quality control inspector wishes to estimate the mean weight of bags of cement leaving a production line on a particular day to within 2 g at the 95% level of confidence. It is known that the standard deviation of the weights remains fairly constant at 60 g. How large a sample should the inspector take?

42. A company wants to estimate, with 95% confidence, the percentage of people in a town who have seen its press advertisements. The company would like its estimate to have a margin of error of ±4%. How large a sample of people will they need to take if:

    (a) a preliminary estimate suggests that the true percentage is about 10%?

    (b) no preliminary estimate is available?

ASSIGNMENT

The latest internal accounts for an off-licence chain showed that the annual sales of wines and spirits had fallen by more than 30%. This fall has been blamed on the relaxation of the limits of duty free goods that can be brought into Britain from EU countries from 1993.

In order to test this theory it was decided to ask a random sample of shoppers if they intend to travel to France this year. Of the 75 shoppers questioned, 27 were certain to go to France at least once. It was also decided to ask a random sample of 60 returning holiday makers how much they had spent on duty free alcohol. Of these 60, 8 refused to answer, and for the remaining 52 people the average spend was found to be £37.26, with a standard deviation of £35.97.

(i)   What is the percentage of shoppers who said they were definitely making at least one trip to France this year?

(ii) Calculate the 95% confidence interval for the true percentage of shoppers who intend to travel to France this year. Interpret this interval.

(iii) Calculate the 95% confidence interval for the true mean amount spent on duty free alcohol for all holiday makers returning from France.

(iv) Calculate the number of shoppers to be questioned so that the half width of the confidence interval for the percentage of shoppers who intend to travel to France is no more than 3%.

(v)   The half width of the confidence interval for the average spend on duty free alcohol wants to be reduced to £5. How many holiday makers need to be sampled?

(vi) What reservations (if any) do you have about this kind of survey?

11 Testing a hypothesis

11.1 Introduction

In Chapter 10 you saw how to analyse a sample so that estimates of some population parameters, such as the mean or percentage, could be obtained. In this chapter the emphasis is slightly different in that you are told the value of the population parameter and then use the sample to confirm or disprove this figure. For example, you may want to determine the effect on fuel consumption of a particular make of car by modification to the carburation system, or you may want to determine if a trade union can be sure that if a ballot was called, the majority of the membership would vote for strike action. In both these examples a *hypothesis* would be made concerning the population and this hypothesis tested using the sample data.

To complete this chapter successfully you should have read through Chapter 10 (Analysis and interpretation of sample data).

On completing this chapter you should be able to:

- Understand the ideas behind hypothesis testing
- Perform tests of hypothesis on a mean of a population
- Perform tests of hypothesis on a percentage
- Carry out a 'goodness of fit' test
- Apply the chi-square test to categorical data
- Use Excel in hypothesis testing

11.2 The purpose of hypothesis testing

Activity 11.1

The light bulbs manufactured by Bright Lights are designed to last for 1000 hours on average. How can the company be sure that the average lifetime of a large batch of bulbs really is 1000 hours?

The mean lifetime could be found by testing a sample of bulbs and constructing a confidence interval within which the true mean is likely to lie. If the interval does contain 1000 hours, then you could assume that the true mean really is 1000 hours.

Alternatively, you could construct a confidence interval for the supposed true mean of 1000 hours and see if the sample mean was contained within this interval.

However, there is a third approach. This approach makes the *hypothesis* that any departure from the supposedly true mean by the sample mean is simply due to chance effects. It is then a matter of calculating the probability that this sample result could have occurred by chance. This is the general idea of hypothesis testing – it assumes that the hypothesis is true and then tries to disprove it. This hypothesis is known as the *null* hypothesis. If the null hypothesis is rejected, an *alternative* hypothesis is accepted. The null hypothesis is called H_0 and the alternative hypothesis H_1.

The null hypothesis is tested at a particular *significance level*.
This level relates to the area (or probability) in the tail of the distribution being used for the test. This area is called the *critical region*, and if the *test statistic* lies in the critical region, you would infer that the result is unlikely to have occurred by chance. You would then reject the null hypothesis. For example, if the 5% level of significance was used and the null hypothesis was rejected, you would say that H_0 had been rejected at the 5% (or the 0.05) significance level, and the result was *significant*.

These ideas apply to all types of hypothesis tests. The precise form of each hypothesis and the calculations necessary to test H_0 depend on the test being carried out. There are very many tests that can be applied to samples. The most important group are *parametric* tests. These tests compare sample statistics with the population parameters and make assumptions about the form of the sampling distribution. *Non-parametric* (or distribution-free) tests are more general and do not insist on such stringent conditions. They can also be used where the data can only be ordered (ordinal data) rather than measured. However, non-parametric tests are less discriminating; that is, the results tend to be less reliable.

Whatever the test, the steps for checking the hypothesis are the same. This is:

Step 1. Set up the null and alternative hypotheses and determine (usually from tables) the boundaries of the critical region. These boundaries are called the *critical values*.
Step 2. Calculate the test statistic.
Step 3. Decide whether to accept or reject H_0.

11.3 Large sample test for a population mean

The normal distribution can be used to solve problems involving means if the population is normal *and* the standard deviation of the population (σ) is known. If normality cannot be assumed then a large sample size will ensure that the sampling distribution of the means is approximately normal.

However, as in the calculation of confidence intervals (see Chapter 10) σ may be unknown and has to be estimated from the sample. In these cases the normal distribution can be used as an approximation, provided the sample size is large.

The formula for Z is also the same as that used in the derivation of the formula for confidence intervals. That is:

$$Z = \frac{\bar{x} - \mu}{\text{STEM}}$$

Where $\bar{x}$ is the mean of the sample, μ is the mean of the population, and STEM is the standard error of the sampling distribution of the means, and is given by:

$$\text{STEM} = \frac{\sigma}{\sqrt{n}}$$

where n is the sample size.

Activity 11.2

The distribution of the lifetime of all bulbs made by Bright Lights is normal, and the standard deviation of the population is known to be 120 hours. A sample of 30 bulbs were tested and the mean lifetime was found to be 1100 hours. Is this consistent, at the 5% level of significance, with the supposed true mean of 1000 hours?

STEP 1

Set up H_0 and H_1 and decide on the critical values.

The null hypothesis in this case is that the true mean lifetime is 1000 hours. The alternative hypothesis can be one of three statements. These are:

> The true mean is *not* equal to 1000 hours

or   The true mean is greater than 1000 hours

or   The true mean is less than 1000 hours

Using symbols, the null and alternative hypotheses become:

$H_0: \mu = 1000$ hours $H_1: \mu \neq 1000$ hours

or $H_1: \mu > 1000$ hours

or $H_1: \mu < 1000$ hours

(The ':' is the mathematical shorthand for 'such that')

The first form of the alternative hypothesis is used for a *two tailed* (or a two sided) test and the other two forms are used for *one tailed* tests. The two tailed test is used when you have no reason to suppose that the true mean could be either greater than or less than the value given by the null hypothesis. The one tailed test is used when you are more interested in one side of the supposed mean than the other. The golden rule when carrying out hypothesis tests is that H_0 and H_1 are set up *before* the test is carried out (and preferably before the data is collected). You may find the diagrams in Figure 11.1 and Figure 11.2 helpful in clarifying the situation.

In Figure 11.1 the critical values of ± 1.96 mark the boundaries of the two critical regions at the 5% significance level. These values are found from the normal table in Appendix 2.

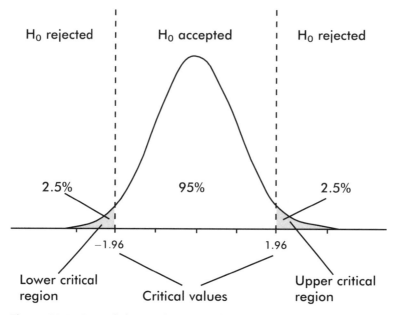

Figure 11.1 Two tailed test at the 5% significance level

If the test statistic (Z) is either greater than the right hand critical value or less than the left hand value, then H_0 is rejected. If Z lies in between the two critical values then H_0 is accepted – *or you should really say that you do not have sufficient information to reject H_0.*

The left hand diagram of Figure 11.2 illustrates the case where the alternative hypothesis is of the 'less than' kind. There is only one critical region in this case and you would reject H_0 if Z was *less* than the critical value of -1.645. The reason that the critical value is different than for the two tailed case is that the area in the one tail is now the full amount (5% in this example) and not half as it was before. The right hand diagram is for the 'greater than' case, and the same reasoning applies here as in the left hand diagram. That is, H_0 would be rejected if Z was *greater* than 1.645.

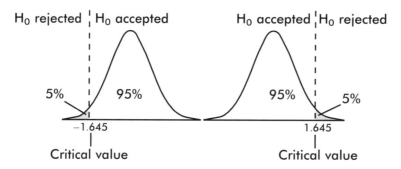

Figure 11.2 One tailed test at the 5% significance level

The light bulb example would be a two tailed test because there is nothing in the wording of the problem that suggests that you are more interested in one side of the mean. So the null and alternative hypotheses for this example are:

$$H_0 : \mu = 1000 \, \text{hours} \qquad H_1 : \mu \neq 1000 \, \text{hours}$$

and the critical values are ± 1.96.

STEP 2

Calculate the test statistic.

In this problem, $n = 30$, $\mu = 1000$, $\sigma = 120$, and $\bar{x} = 1100$. Therefore STEM $=$

$$\frac{\sigma}{\sqrt{n}} = \frac{120}{\sqrt{30}}$$

$$= 21.9089$$

And:

$$Z = \frac{\bar{x} - \mu}{\sqrt{n}}$$

$$= \frac{1100 - 1000}{21.9089}$$

$$= \frac{100}{21.9089}$$

$$= 4.56$$

This is your test statistic.

STEP 3

Decide whether to accept or reject H_0.

It is now necessary to decide if this value of Z could have happened by chance, or if it is indicative of a change in the population mean.

Since Z (4.56) is greater than 1.96 and is therefore in the critical region, you can reject H_0 at the 5% level of significance. This is shown clearly in Figure 11.3, below, where the 0.1% significance level ($Z = 3.3$) has also been added. The result is significant, and you would conclude that there has almost certainly been a change in the mean lifetime of light bulbs.

The following activity illustrates the use of one tailed tests.

Activity 11.3

The mean fuel consumption for a particular make of car is known to be 33 mpg with a standard deviation of 5.7 mpg. A modification to this car has been made that should reduce fuel consumption. 35 cars are fitted with this device and their fuel consumption is recorded

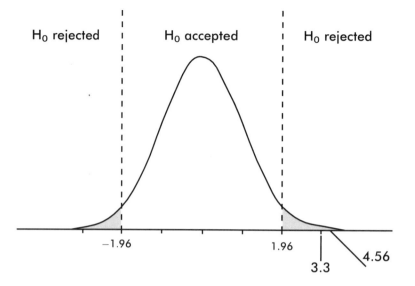

Figure 11.3 Diagram for Activity 11.2

over 12 months. At the end of this period the mean fuel consumption of the 35 cars is found to be 34.8 mpg. Is there any evidence, at the 5% level of significance, that the fuel consumption has been improved?

This is a one tailed test since it is hoped that the modification will improve the fuel consumption – there is nothing to suggest that fuel consumption will be made worse. The Z-test can be used without assuming normality because the sample is 'large' (over 30).
   The null and alternative hypotheses for this problem are:

$H_0 : \mu = 33\,\text{mpg}$ $H_1 : \mu > 33\,\text{mpg}$

And the critical value of Z at the 5% significance level is 1.645.

$\sigma = 5.7\,\text{mpg},$ $\bar{x} = 34.8$ and $n = 35$

Therefore: $\text{STEM} = \dfrac{5.7}{\sqrt{35}}$

$= 0.9635$

and the test statistic is: $Z = \dfrac{34.8 - 33.0}{0.9635}$

$= 1.868$

Since 1.868 is greater than the critical value of 1.645, you would reject the null hypothesis. That is, there is a *significant* difference between the mean fuel consumption before and after the modification has been fitted. You would conclude that the modification appears to have improved the fuel consumption of this particular make of car.

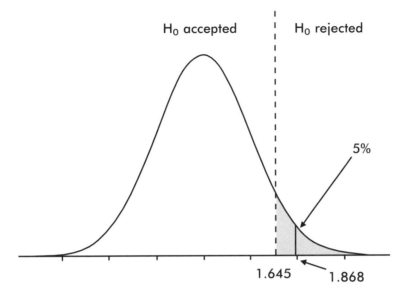

Figure 11.4 Diagram for Activity 11.3

It is important to draw a diagram when carrying out hypothesis tests. The diagram for this problem is shown in Figure 11.4.

This diagram clearly shows that the test statistic is in the critical region, and H_0 should therefore be rejected. You may have noticed that H_0 would *not* have been rejected if the test had been two tailed. (Compare this diagram with Figure 11.1.) This is why it is so important to ensure that you are justified in using a one tailed test, as the chance of rejecting H_0 is greater in the one tailed case.

11.4 Small sample test for a population mean

As in the case of confidence intervals, it is necessary to assume that the population is normal and to use the *t*-distribution instead of the normal distribution. The formula for the *t*-statistic is:

$$t = \frac{\bar{x} - \mu}{\text{STEM}}$$

Which is identical to the expression for Z. The formula for STEM is also the same, except that the standard deviation used is the estimate obtained from the sample. That is:

$$\text{STEM} = \frac{\sigma}{\sqrt{n}}$$

The same considerations apply concerning the critical region, except that the critical value is obtained from the *t*-distribution on $n - 1$ degrees of freedom (Appendix 2). For example, the critical value on 7 degrees of freedom at the 5% significance level is ± 2.365 for a two tailed test, and ± 1.895 for a one tailed test.

The following activity may help you understand the differences between the Z and *t*-tests.

Activity 11.4

A tomato grower has developed a new variety of tomato. This variety is supposed to give good crops without the need for a greenhouse. One of the supposed attributes of this tomato is that the average yield per plant is at least 4 kg of fruit. A gardening magazine decides to test this claim and grows 8 plants in controlled conditions. The yield from each plant is carefully recorded and is as follows:

Plant:	1	2	3	4	5	6	7	8
Yield	3.6	4.2	3.3	2.5	4.8	2.75	4.2	4.6

Do these data support the grower's claim at the 5% level of significance? (It can be assumed that the yield per plant is normally distributed.)

This is a one tailed test, since the claim is that the yield should be *at least* 4 kg. The null and alternative hypotheses are therefore:

$$H_0 : \mu = 4 \, \text{kg} \qquad H_1 : \mu < 4 \, \text{kg}$$

(The alternative hypothesis is less than 4 kg because the gardening magazine is attempting to disprove the claim.)

The critical value on 7 degrees of freedom at a significance level of 5% for a one tailed test is -1.895. (This figure was obtained from the t-table in Appendix 2).

Estimates of the mean and standard deviation of the yield from this sample are:

$$\bar{x} = 3.74 \qquad \sigma = 0.8466$$

$$\text{and} \qquad \text{STEM} = \frac{0.8466}{\sqrt{8}}$$

$$= 0.2993$$

The test statistic is therefore:

$$t = \frac{3.74 - 4}{0.2993}$$

$$= -0.869$$

Since -0.869 is *greater* than -1.895, you cannot reject H_0. (You may find it easier to ignore the negative signs and just compare 0.869 with 1.895, in which case 0.869 is *less* than 1.895.) Alternatively, you could draw a diagram as shown in Figure 11.5.

This diagram confirms that the test statistic is not in the critical region, and therefore it is not possible to reject H_0. That is, it hasn't been possible to disprove the grower's claim.

NOTE: In practice the *experimental design* for this example would be a little more involved than has been suggested here.

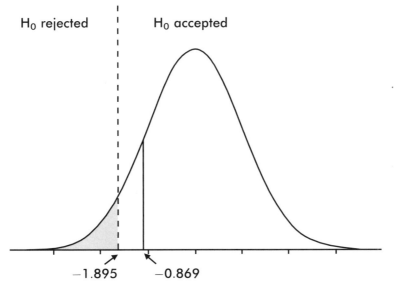

Figure 11.5 Diagram for Activity 11.4

11.5 The Z-test for a population percentage

Testing a sample percentage against some expected or hypothesised value (π) is another important test. The test given here is based on the assumption that n is large and π is not too large or too small.

The standard error of the sampling distribution of a percentage (STEP) was given in Chapter 10 as:

$$\sqrt{\frac{P(100 - P)}{n}}$$

Where P is the sample percentage.

However, for hypothesis testing it is the population parameter, π, that must be used. With this substitution, the equation for STEP becomes:

$$\text{STEP} = \sqrt{\frac{\pi(100 - \pi)}{n}}$$

The Z statistic is similar to that used for the test on a mean and is:

$$Z = \frac{P - \pi}{\text{STEP}}$$

The following activity illustrates how the test would be carried out.

 ## Activity 11.5

A trade union is considering strike action and intends to ballot its large membership on the issue. In order to gauge the likely result of the ballot, a survey was conducted among a random sample of members. Of the 60 people surveyed, 36 were in favour of a strike. Would the ballot give the required simple majority for a strike?

For a strike to be called, at least 50% of the membership must agree. Anything less would not be good enough. The null and alternative hypotheses should therefore be:

$H_0 : \pi = 50\%$ $H_1 : \pi > 50\%$

The cut-off point for the decision is 50% and the test will determine whether the sample percentage (P) of $\dfrac{36}{60} \times 100 = 60\%$ is significantly *greater* than 50%.

The critical value for a one tailed test at the 5% level is 1.645.

So: $$\text{STEP} = \sqrt{\dfrac{50 \times (100 - 50)}{60}}$$

$$= 6.455$$

and the test statistic is: $$Z = \dfrac{60 - 50}{6.455}$$

$$= 1.549$$

Since 1.549 is less than 1.645, H_0 cannot be rejected. That is, it appears that there may not be a majority for strike action. However, the critical value and test statistic are quite close, and therefore the result is hardly conclusive. (Don't forget that the survey result is only a 'snapshot' of people's opinion at one instant in time. Some people may not have been entirely honest with their answers and others may change their opinion before the ballot.)

Figure 11.6 below confirms that the test statistic is just in the acceptance region.

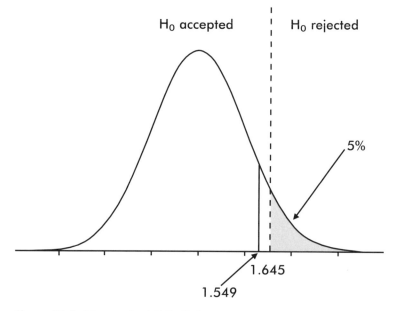

Figure 11.6 Diagram for Activity 11.5

11.6 Hypothesis tests involving two population means

The tests we have looked at so far are for a single sample. In many situations we may have collected two samples and we want to test to see if the two population means are the same. As in the single sample case we have different tests for large and small samples. We also have another factor to consider: are the samples independent of each other or not? Samples that are independent mean that the measurements of one sample are not influenced by the second sample. In some situations, once we have chosen (randomly) the members of the first sample the members of the second sample will not be independent. For example, you might want to compare the reading ability of children before and after following a reading programme. The reading scores of a group of children represent the first sample and the second sample is represented by the reading scores of the *same* children at the end of the reading programme. The second sample is therefore related to the first sample by the identity of the child. There are good reasons why you should use this *paired* approach but it requires a test that doesn't demand independence. The mathematics involved in applying all these tests are more complicated than for the single sample case and the use of statistical software such as MINITAB™ or SPSS™ is recommended. However, it is also possible to use a spreadsheet to carry out some of the tests and the use of Excel will be demonstrated where appropriate.

11.6.1 Large sample tests for two independent population means

We normally wish to set up the null hypothesis that the difference in the means of the two populations will be zero; that is:

H_0: $\mu_1 - \mu_2 = 0$

The alternative hypothesis can be either one or two tailed. That is:

H_1: $\mu_1 - \mu_2 \neq 0$ for a two sided test, and

H_1: $\mu_1 > \mu_2$ or $\mu_1 < \mu_2$ for a one sided test.

For a large sample we can assume that the difference between the means of the two sampling distributions is normally distributed with a mean equal to the difference of the population means and a standard error of:

$$\sigma_{(\bar{x}_1 - \bar{x}_2)} = \sqrt{\left(\frac{\sigma_1^2}{n_1} + \frac{\sigma_2^2}{n_2} \right)}$$

As in the single sample case, the population standard deviations are required, but provided that each sample size (n_1 and n_2) is at least 30 we can use the estimate given by the samples as an approximation.

The test statistic will be

$$Z = \frac{(\bar{x}_1 - \bar{x}_2) - (\mu_1 - \mu_2)}{\sigma_{(\bar{x}_1 - \bar{x}_2)}}$$

Activity 11.6

A high street store was interested to discover if credit card customers spent more or less than cash customers. A random sample of 50 credit card customers were found to have spent £55.30 on average with a standard deviation of £18.45, while a random sample of 40 cash customers were found to have spent £52.75 on average with a standard deviation of £17.22. Is there any evidence at the 5% significance level that there is any difference between the mean amounts spent by the two types of customers?

This is a two tailed test and the null and alternative hypotheses will be:

$$H_0: \mu_1 - \mu_2 = 0 \qquad H_1: \mu_1 - \mu_2 \neq 0$$

The standard error will be $\sqrt{\left(\dfrac{18.45^2}{50} + \dfrac{17.22^2}{40}\right)} = 3.7711$

And the test statistic will be $\dfrac{(55.30 - 52.75) - 0}{3.7711} = 0.676$

Since this is less than 1.96 we cannot reject H_0 and must conclude that there is no evidence to suggest that credit card customers spend more or less than cash customers.

11.6.2 Small sample tests for two independent population means

Just as in the single sample case we need to use the t-distribution instead of the normal. Both populations from which the samples have been taken should be approximately normally distributed with equal variances (variance is the square of the standard deviation). If the conditions of normality cannot be met it is possible to use *non-parametric* tests; details of which can be found in McClave and Sincich (2000). A modified test is available if the equality of variance cannot be assumed. The standard error for the small sample case is slightly different than for large samples. It is:

$$\sigma_{(x_1-x_2)} = \hat{\sigma}\sqrt{\left(\frac{1}{n_1} + \frac{1}{n_2}\right)}$$

where $\hat{\sigma}$ is the estimate of the *pooled* standard deviation of the populations and is given by:

$$\hat{\sigma} = \sqrt{\frac{(n_1 - 1)s_1^2 + (n_2 - 1)s_2^2}{n_1 + n_2 - 2}}$$

The test statistic is given by:

$$t = \frac{(\bar{x}_1 - \bar{x}_2) - (\mu_1 - \mu_2)}{\sigma_{(\bar{x}_1-\bar{x}_2)}}$$

The critical value at a particular significance level and $(n_1 + n_2 - 2)$ degrees of freedom can be found from tables (see Appendix 2).

Activity 11.7

A health magazine has decided to test the claim of the makers of a new slimming pill that has just come on the market. The company claims that the pill will allow people to lose weight if taken daily. The health magazine obtained a sample of 14 people who agreed to take the pill for a month. This group was split into two, a sample of 8 who would be given the slimming pill and a control group of 6 who would (unknown to them) be given a placebo (a fake slimming pill). The weight change at the end of the month is given in Table 11.1 where a minus indicates a loss of weight and a positive figure indicates a gain in weight.

Table 11.1 Weight change (in lbs) data for Activity 11.7

Sample 1	Sample 2 (control group)
−2	−2
−6	0
3	−5
−10	8
0	4
2	0
−4	
−9	

It would of course be possible to apply the single sample test on the sample of 8 people to see if the mean weight change is different to zero. However, the use of a control group is quite common in medical research as it allows unknown factors such as people's 'belief' in a product to be taken into account.

If we assume that the health magazine is not biased in its opinion of the pill, this is a two tailed test and the null and alternative hypotheses will be:

$$H_0: \mu_1 - \mu_2 = 0 \qquad H_1: \mu_1 - \mu_2 \neq 0$$

The mean and standard deviation (using $n-1$) for sample 1 are −3.25 and 4.862, respectively. The equivalent figures for the control group are 0.833 and 4.579, respectively. The pooled standard deviation is therefore:

$$\hat{\sigma} = \sqrt{\frac{(8-1)4.862^2 + (6-1)4.579^2}{8+6-2}}$$

$$= 4.746$$

The test statistic is:

$$t = \frac{(-3.25 - 0.833) - 0}{4.746}$$

$$= -0.860$$

The critical value on 12 degrees of freedom at 5% significance level is -2.179. As the test statistic is greater than this value we cannot reject H_0 and conclude that there is no evidence that the slimming pill has any affect on weight change.

This test could be performed using Excel. To do this the two samples of data are put into two columns (say A2 to A9 and B2 to B7). The easiest way to find the correct function for the two-sample t-test is to use the function wizard f_x. The appropriate function to use is TTEST and Figure 11.7 is a screen shot of the worksheet containing the dialog box for this function. Notice that *Type* in the wizard dialog box allows you to choose between different forms of the two-sample t-test. As we are assuming equal variances the appropriate value is 2. The value given by the TTEST function is 0.137 and this is the probability of obtaining a test statistic at least as extreme as the one obtained. It is the area in the tail(s) of the distribution for this value of the test statistic. This probability is often called *the observed significance level* or *p-value*. If we were testing at the 5% (0.05) level then a p-value less than this figure will be significant and we would reject the null hypothesis. However, in our case 13.7% is greater than 5% so we cannot reject H_0. This is the same conclusion that we came to by comparing the test statistic with the critical value. Statisticians usually prefer the p-value approach as it gives more information about the result of the test.

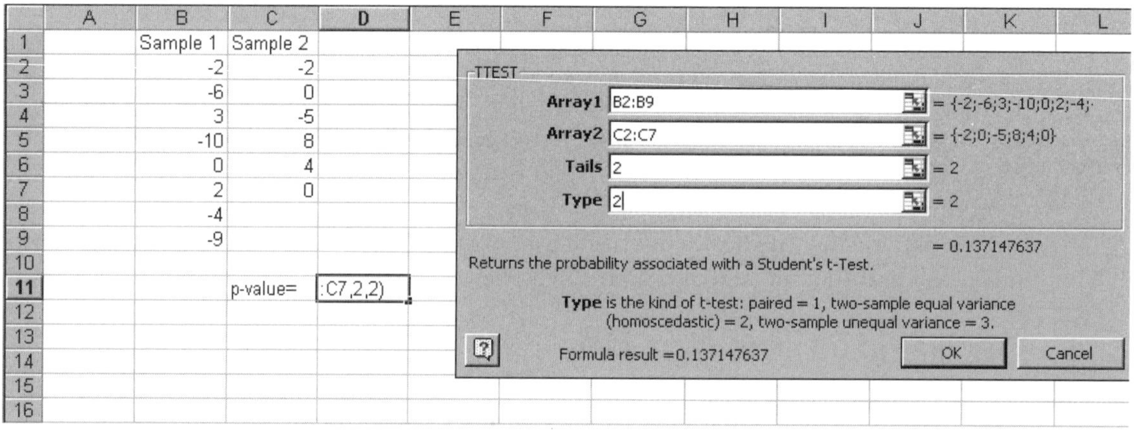

Figure 11.7   Use of the function wizard for solving Activity 11.7

11.6.3   Paired samples

We have already mentioned that the two-sample t-test is only valid when the two samples are independent. In many cases this assumption is not valid as the data is *paired*; that is, each observation of one sample is paired with an observation in the other sample. This can occur if identical conditions apply to pairs of observations. The null hypothesis is that the *difference* of the population means, μ_d, is zero and the alternative hypothesis can be either one or two tailed, depending on whether we believe the difference could be positive, negative or not equal to zero. The test statistic for this test is:

$$t = \frac{\bar{x}_d - \mu_d}{\sigma_{\bar{d}}}$$

Where $\bar{x}_d$ is the sample mean of the n differences and μ_d is the population mean difference if the null hypothesis is correct (usually zero), $\sigma_{\bar{d}}$ is the standard error of the differences and is given by:

$$\sigma_{\bar{d}} = \frac{s_d}{\sqrt{n}}$$

Where s_d is the standard deviation of the differences.

Activity 11.8

A publishing company has developed a new reading scheme that is supposed to improve the reading ability of children. In order to be able to justify its claim, 12 children were first given a standardised reading test before taking part in the programme. At the end of the programme they were tested again. The test scores before and after the programme can be found in Table 11.2.

Table 11.2   Test scores for Activity 11.8

Child	Before	After	Difference
A	110	108	−2
B	121	122	1
C	95	98	3
D	80	90	10
E	130	132	2
F	100	105	5
G	105	105	0
H	85	90	5
I	95	96	1
J	100	98	−2
K	82	85	3
L	135	132	−3

Do these data support the company's claim?

The data are not independent because each member of the 'before' sample is related to a member of the 'after' sample by the attributes of the child. The advantage of this design is that it only looks at the differences between each child; it ignores the variation between children, which could be large. If the reading programme had had no effect you would expect the true average difference in test scores to be zero. The null hypothesis is therefore:

H_0: $\mu_d = 0$

The alternative hypothesis is one tailed because we are testing to see if the programme improves reading ability (it is unlikely to make it worse), so:

H_1: $\mu_d > 0$

The differences (after–before) can be found in Table 11.2, and the mean of the differences is 1.92 with a standard deviation of 3.655. The standard error of the differences is:

$$\sigma_{\bar{d}} = \frac{3.655}{\sqrt{12}}$$

$$= 1.055$$

And the test statistic is:

$$t = \frac{1.92 - 0}{1.055}$$

$$= 1.820$$

The critical value of t at the 5% significance level and on 11 $(12 - 1)$ degrees of freedom is 1.796. We can therefore reject H_0 at the 5% significance level and conclude that there is some evidence that the new reading programme does increase reading ability as represented by the testing method. Of course, a child's reading ability may well have increased without following the programme, so in practice a control group would be involved in the *experimental design*.

This test could have again been conducted using the same TTEST function as we used in Activity 11.7. Figure 11.8 is a screen shot of the Excel worksheet using the function wizard. You will notice that the *p*-value is 0.048 or 4.8%, which is just below 5% and therefore we reject H_0.

11.7 Hypothesis tests involving two population percentages

As well as conducting tests between two means it is possible to conduct tests between two percentages. Provided the sample sizes are large, the difference between the two percentages $(\pi_1 - \pi_2)$ will be normally distributed. The null hypothesis will be:

H_0: $\pi_1 - \pi_2 = 0$

And H_1 can be either one or two sided.

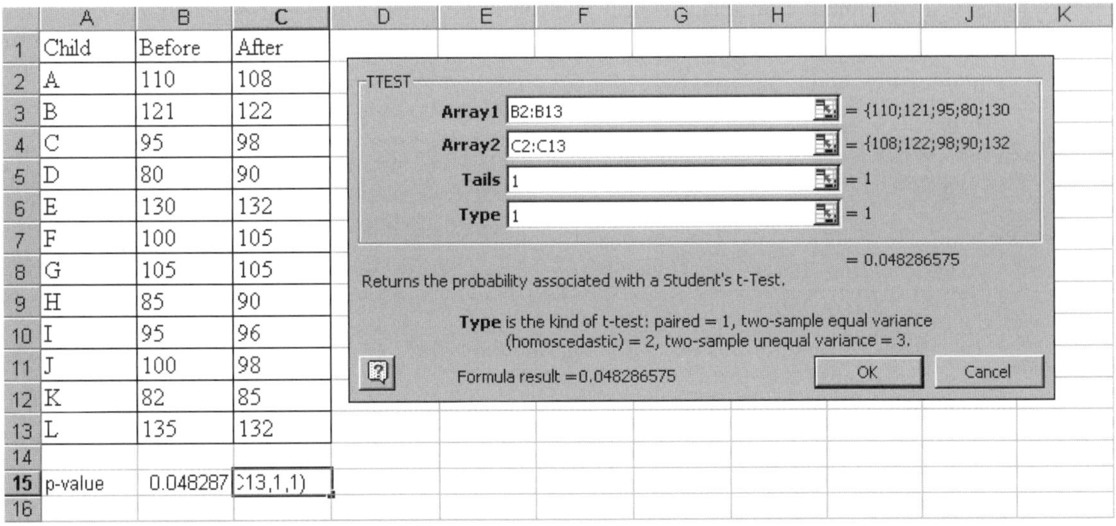

	A	B	C	D	E	F	G	H	I	J	K
1	Child	Before	After								
2	A	110	108								
3	B	121	122								
4	C	95	98								
5	D	80	90								
6	E	130	132								
7	F	100	105								
8	G	105	105								
9	H	85	90								
10	I	95	96								
11	J	100	98								
12	K	82	85								
13	L	135	132								
14											
15	p-value	0.048287	13,1,1)								
16											

TTEST

Array1	B2:B13	= {110;121;95;80;130
Array2	C2:C13	= {108;122;98;90;132
Tails	1	= 1
Type	1	= 1

= 0.048286575

Returns the probability associated with a Student's t-Test.

Type is the kind of t-test: paired = 1, two-sample equal variance (homoscedastic) = 2, two-sample unequal variance = 3.

Formula result = 0.048286575

OK   Cancel

Figure 11.8 Screen shot of the function wizard for solving Activity 11.8

The standard error of the differences between the two percentages is:

$$\sigma_{(P_1-P_2)} = \sqrt{\hat{P}(100-\hat{P})\left(\frac{1}{n_1}+\frac{1}{n_2}\right)}$$

Where $\hat{P}$ is the estimate of the population proportion and is given by:

$$\hat{P} = \frac{n_1 P_1 + n_2 P_2}{n_1 + n_2}$$

P_1 and P_2 refer to the two sample proportions.

The test statistic is:

$$Z = \frac{(P_1 - P_2) - (\pi_1 - \pi_2)}{\sigma_{(P_1-P_2)}}$$

Activity 11.9

A top hairdresser has just opened two hairdressing salons in a large town and he is interested in whether there are any differences in the type of customers that use these two salons. During one month a random sample of customers at both salons were asked to complete a questionnaire. From the analysis of the questionnaire it was discovered that out of 200 customers at Top Cuts, 56 were under the age of 25. At Smart Cuts, 54 out of 150 were in this age bracket. Is there any difference in the percentage of under 25s at the two salons?

This is a two tailed test and the null and alternative hypotheses are:

$$H_0: \pi_1 - \pi_2 = 0 \qquad H_1: \pi_1 - \pi_2 \neq 0$$

$$P_1 = \frac{56}{200} \times 100 \qquad P_2 = \frac{54}{150} \times 100$$

$$= 28\% \qquad\qquad = 36\%$$

So:

$$\hat{P} = \frac{200 \times 28 + 150 \times 36}{200 + 150}$$

$$= 31.4\%$$

The standard error of the differences is:

$$\sigma_{(P_1-P_2)} = \sqrt{31.4(100 - 31.4)\left(\frac{1}{200} + \frac{1}{150}\right)}$$

$$= 5.013$$

The test statistic is:

$$Z = \frac{(28 - 36) - 0}{5.013}$$

$$= -1.596$$

As this is greater than -1.96 we cannot reject H_0 and therefore conclude that there is no evidence to suggest that the percentage of customers in the under 25 age group is different in the two salons.

11.8 The chi-square hypothesis test

All the tests discussed so far in this chapter are called *parametric* tests in that they are testing a parameter (either the mean or proportion). However, there are also *non-parametric* tests and the text by McClave and Sincich (2000) contains many tests in this category. Perhaps the most useful non-parametric test is the chi-square test and there are two forms of this test. The first form, called the *'goodness of fit test'*, tests to see if the data fits some distribution. The second form of the test is called the *test of association* and tests to see if there is any association between categories in a two-way table. For both forms of the tests you have to count the number of data items that are observed to be in a particular category. The test statistic is calculated using the following formula:

$$\sum \frac{(O - E)^2}{E}$$

Where O represents the observed count and E represents the expected count. The formula simply says: 'Find the difference between the observed and expected frequency of one category, square this value to remove any negative signs and then divide by the expected frequency for that category. Repeat this for all categories and sum the individual answers.'

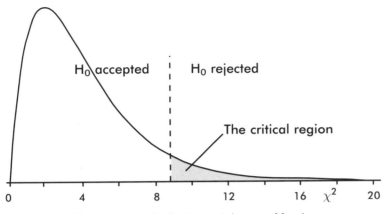

Figure 11.9 The chi-square distribution on 4 degrees of freedom

This test statistic follows the χ^2 distribution (pronounced *chi-square*). The shape of this distribution depends on the degrees of freedom of the data. For example, for 4 degrees of freedom you would get the shape shown in Figure 11.9.

The area under the curve is again 1, but only one tail is used for the critical region – the upper tail. The area representing 5% has been indicated, and H_0 would be rejected if the test statistic was in this region.

The critical value of χ^2 is found from the χ^2 table that you will find in Appendix 2. For example, the critical value on 4 degrees of freedom at the 5% (0.05) significance level is 9.488.

11.8.1 The 'goodness of fit' test

Suppose you threw a six-sided die 36 times. You would *expect* the faces numbered 1 to 6 to appear the same number of times; that is, 6. However, you might *observe* a rather different frequency.

⫸ Activity 11.10

Try this experiment for yourself and record the number of times each face appeared.

Suppose you got the following:

Face	1	2	3	4	5	6
Frequency	4	6	9	5	4	8

Is your observed frequency due to chance effects or does it indicate that the die is biased in any way? (in this example, face 3 occurs most). The null hypothesis is that the die is fair and the alternate hypothesis is that it is biased; that is:

H_0 : die is fair H_1 : die is biased

Since the sum of the frequencies is fixed, you are 'free' to choose 5 of them; therefore the degrees of freedom is 5. From the χ^2 table, the critical value on 5 degrees of freedom and at the 5% significance level is 11.070. If the test statistic is greater than this value, H_0 will be rejected.

To calculate the χ^2 statistic you need to subtract the observed values from 6, square the result and then divide by 6. This calculation is shown in Table 11.3.

Table 11.3 Chi-square calculation for Activity 11.10

O	E	(O – E)	(O – E)²	$\frac{(O - E)^2}{E}$
4	6	−2	4	0.667
6	6	0	0	0.000
9	6	3	9	1.500
5	6	−1	1	0.167
4	6	−2	4	0.667
8	6	2	4	0.667
				3.668

The sum of these values is 3.668 and this is compared with the critical value of 11.070. H_0 cannot be rejected and you would have to assume that the die was fair. The diagram in Figure 11.10 demonstrates that the test statistic is not in the critical region.

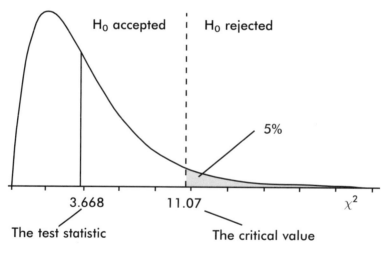

Figure 11.10 Diagram for Activity 11.10

This is quite a simple application of the 'goodness of fit' test, since the expected values follow a uniform distribution (that is, each 'category' has the same expected value). However, the test can be applied to any situation where it is possible to calculate the expected values. The normal distribution (see Chapter 8) is one example where these expected values could be calculated. In this example you might want to discover whether a set of data follows this distribution. The degrees of freedom are found from the formula:

$$v = n - 1 - k$$

Where n is the number of pairs of observed and expected frequencies, and k is the number of population parameters estimated from the sample. For the normal distribution both the mean and the standard deviation have to be estimated, so k is 2 in this case.

11.8.2 The test of association

Example 11.1

The Personnel Manager of a company believes that monthly paid staff take more time off work through sickness than those staff who are paid weekly (and do not belong to the company sickness scheme). To test this theory, the sickness records for 531 randomly selected employees who have been in continuous employment for the past year were analysed. Table 11.4 was produced, which placed employees into 3 categories according to how many days they were off work through sickness during the past year. For example, 95 monthly paid employees were off sick for less than 5 days.

Table 11.4 Number of days off sick by type of employee

Type of employee	Number of days off sick		
	Less than 5 days	5 to 10 days	More than 10 days
Monthly paid	95	47	18
Weekly paid	143	146	112

Activity 11.11

Is there any association between type of employee and numbers of days off sick?

Table 11.4 is known as a *contingency* table. The null and alternative hypotheses are:

H_0: There is no *association* between type of employee and number of days off sick.
H_1: There is an association between type of employee and number of days off sick.

In order to calculate the χ^2 test statistic it is necessary to determine the expected values for each category. To do this you first have to work out the row and column totals, as shown in Table 11.5.

Table 11.5 Table for Activity 11.11

Type of employee	Number of days off sick			Total
	Less than 5 days	5 to 10 days	More than 10 days	
Monthly paid	95	47	18	160
Weekly paid	143	146	112	401
Total	238	193	130	561

You now need to apply some basic ideas of probability (see Chapter 7) to the problem. If an employee was chosen at random, the probability that he or she was monthly paid would be $\frac{160}{561}$ and the probability that he or she would have been off sick for less than 5 days is $\frac{238}{561}$. Therefore, using the multiplication rule for two probabilities, the probability that the person is both monthly paid *and* in the 'less than 5 days' category is $\frac{160}{561} \times \frac{238}{561}$.

Since there are 561 employees in total, the *expected* number of employees with both these attributes is

$$\frac{160}{561} \times \frac{238}{561} \times 561$$
$$= \frac{160 \times 238}{561}$$
$$= 67.9$$

This could be written as:

$$\text{Expected value} = \frac{\text{Row Total} \times \text{Column Total}}{\text{Grand Total}}$$

and is applicable for all cells of a contingency table. The rest of the expected values can now be worked out and a table (Table 11.6) set up similar to the one used for the 'goodness of fit' test.

Table 11.6 Calculation of the chi-square test statistics

O	E	(O − E)	(O − E)²	$\frac{(O - E)^2}{E}$
95	67.9	27.1	734.41	10.816
47	55.0	−8.00	64.0	1.164
18	37.1	−19.1	364.81	9.833
143	170.1	−27.1	734.41	4.318
146	138.0	8.00	64.00	0.464
112	92.9	19.10	364.81	3.927
				30.522

The sum of the χ^2 values is 30.522, and this is the test statistic for this problem. The critical value depends on the degrees of freedom of this table. As you know, degrees of freedom relates to the number of values that you are free to choose. If, for example, you chose the value for the top left hand cell in Table 11.5, the bottom left hand cell is determined since the two cells must add to 238. Likewise, you could choose the next cell along, but then all other cells are determined for you. So, for this problem, there are 2 degrees of freedom. Fortunately, there is a formula for calculating the degrees of freedom which is:

(number of columns − 1) × (number of rows − 1)

In Table 11.5, there are 3 columns (excluding the total column) and 2 rows, so the degrees of freedom are:

$$(3 - 1) \times (2 - 1) = 2$$

The critical value for 2 degrees of freedom at the 5% significance level is 5.991, and at the 0.1% significance level it is 13.816. Therefore, since the test statistic is greater than 13.816, H_0 can be rejected at the 0.1% significance level, and you could conclude that there does seem to be an association between staff category and the number of days off sick.

It is possible to be more specific about this association by looking at the individual χ^2 values and also the (O − E) column. The two largest χ^2 values are 10.816 and 9.883. These both relate to the monthly paid staff and it suggests that this group of employees has a higher frequency in the 'less than 5 days category' than expected, but a lower frequency in the 'more than 10 days' category.

The χ^2 test for association is a very important and useful test in the area of statistics in particular, and decision-making in general. However, there are a few problems that you need to be aware of.

LOW EXPECTED VALUES

The test statistic follows the χ^2 distribution provided the expected values are not too small. The guideline that is normally adopted is that the expected value for any cell should be greater than 5. If an expected value less than 5 occurs it is possible to combine categories until this value is achieved. Of course, there must be at least 3 rows or 3 columns to be able to do this.

TWO BY TWO TABLES

The χ^2 distribution is a continuous distribution, whereas the sample data is discrete. Normally the sample size is sufficient to avoid making a continuity correction, but this will be needed for 2×2 tables. The correction required is to *subtract* 0.5 from the *absolute* value of the difference between the observed and expected values. For example, if the difference was −2.7, the corrected value would be −2.2 (not −3.2).

TABLES OF PERCENTAGES

The χ^2 test is applied to tables of frequencies, *not* percentages. If you are given a table of percentages you will need to convert it to frequencies by multiplying each percentage by the total frequency. If you are not given the total frequency then it is not possible to use this test.

11.9 Summary

This chapter has introduced you to a few important tests that can be carried out on sample data. These tests are called hypothesis tests because some hypothesis is made concerning a population parameter or parameters. For large samples (over 30) we can use the Z-test but when the sample is small we should use the *t*-test. The *t*-test compensates for the uncertainty in the value of the sample standard deviation. We can also conduct tests on two samples, and the form of the test depends not only on the size of the sample but also on whether the two populations can be considered independent of each other. We also looked at the chi-square test. There are two forms of the chi-square test; one is the 'goodness of fit' test and the other is the test of association. Figure 11.11 summarises the different tests applicable to means and proportions.

Figure 11.11 Summary of tests applicable to means and proportions

11.10 Further reading

McClave, J. and Sincich, T. (2000) *Statistics*, Prentice Hall, New Jersey (Chapters 8 and 9).
Morris, C. (2000) *Quantitative Approaches in Business Studies*, fifth edition, Pitman, London (Chapter 11).

11.11 EXERCISES

The answers to the progress questions, the multiple choice questions and some of the practice questions are given in Appendix 1. Solutions to the remaining questions and the assignment can be found at the web site for this text.

PROGRESS QUESTIONS
These questions have been designed to help you remember the key points in this chapter.

Give the missing word in each case.

1. H_0 is called the .... hypothesis.
2. H_1 is called the .... hypothesis.
3. The boundaries of the critical region are called .... values.
4. The test using the normal distribution is called the .... test.
5. For a two tailed test at 5% confidence interval, the area in each tail is ....
6. The chi-test is applied to .... data.

ANSWER *TRUE* OR *FALSE*

7. If the critical value is 1.96 and the test statistic is 2.34, the null hypothesis should be rejected.
8. In order to decide whether to use a one or two tailed test, you would inspect the data.
9. You would use the *t*-test if the population cannot be assumed to be normal.
10. Only one tail of the distribution is used in the chi-square test.
11. The chi-square distribution is symmetrical about the mean.
12. The chi-square test cannot be applied to a table of percentages.
13. The sample percentage P *is used to calculate STEP when carrying out a hypothesis test of a percentage.*

REVIEW QUESTIONS
These questions have been designed to help you check your comprehension of the key points in this chapter. You may wish to look further than this chapter in order to answer them fully. You will find the reading list useful in this respect. You can check the essential elements of your answers by referring to the appropriate section.

14. Under what circumstances would you use a one tailed test rather than a two tailed one? (Section 11.3)

15. Why is it preferable to use large samples for hypothesis tests? (Sections 11.4 and 11.5)

16. What is the difference between a two-sample *t*-test and a paired *t*-test? (Section 11.6)

17. What problems might you come across in carrying out the chi-square test, and how would you overcome them? (Section 11.8)

MULTIPLE CHOICE QUESTIONS

18. The alternative hypothesis for a one tailed test can be of the form:

    A... $\mu =$ B... $\mu \neq$

    C... $\mu <$ or $\mu >$

19. The degrees of freedom for a *t*-test of a mean if the sample size is 10 is:

    A... 10   B... 9   C... 11

20. The degrees of freedom for a contingency table of size 2×5 is:

    A... 10   B... 7   C... 4   D... 3

21. Expected values in a contingency table should be:

    A... greater than 5   B... less than 5

    C... greater than 30

22. The critical region is in:

    A... The tails of a distribution

    B... The middle of a distribution

    C... Either the middle or the tails of a distribution

23. The chi-square distribution is:

    A... Symmetrical about a mean value

    B... Right skewed

    C... Left skewed

24. If a significance level of 1% is used rather than 5%, the null hypothesis is:

    A... More likely to be rejected

    B... Less likely to be rejected

    C... Just as likely to be rejected

25. You want to find out if there are likely to be more car accidents on certain days of the week. You record the number of accidents on a given stretch of road over a long period of time and summarise the results by total number of accidents for each day of the week. What statistical test would you use to answer your question?

    A... Z-test of a mean

    B... Z-test of a proportion

    C... Paired *t*-test

    D... Chi-square 'goodness of fit' test

    E... Chi-square test of association

Questions 26 to 28 refer to a manufacturer of fruit juices. Rumour has reached the Trading Standards officer that the manufacturer is deliberately underfilling his cartons of orange juice and it is decided to take a sample to check this claim. The stated contents on the carton are 100 ml.

26. The null hypothesis is:

   A... The mean is 100 ml
   B... The mean is greater than 100 ml
   C... The mean is less than 100 ml
   D... The mean is not 100 ml

27. The alternative hypothesis is:

   A... The mean is 100 ml
   B... The mean is greater than 100 ml
   C... The mean is less than 100 ml
   D... The mean is not 100 ml

28. A sample of 36 cartons is measured and they are found to have a mean of 99 ml and a standard deviation of 6 ml. The test statistic is found from:

   A... $Z = \dfrac{100 - 99}{1.0}$

   B... $Z = \dfrac{99 - 100}{1.0}$

   C... $Z = \dfrac{100 - 99}{6}$

   D... $Z = \dfrac{99 - 100}{6}$

29. Which of the following statements is true concerning the chi-square test of association?

   A... The table must contain percentages
   B... The expected values must all be the same
   C... All the expected values must be at least 5
   D... The expected values must be whole numbers

30. Under what conditions would you use the paired t-test?

   A... When there is a single sample of data
   B... When the two samples of data are independent
   C... When the two samples of data are not independent
   D... When there are two proportions

31. As part of a quality control system, a simple random sample of 10 units was taken from a large batch of production and tested to see if the mean weight had changed from the expected 10 g. The test you would use under these circumstances would be the:

A... Z-test of a proportion

B... *t*-test of a mean

C... Paired *t*-test

D... Chi-square 'goodness of fit' test

E... Chi-square test of association

32. Data has been obtained on the amount of alcohol consumed in a week for people of different ages. Consumption has been categorised as low, moderate or high. The test you would use to discover if there was any association between age and consumption is the:

A... Z-test of a mean

B... Z-test of a proportion

C... Paired *t*-test

D... Chi-square 'goodness of fit' test

E... Chi-square test of association

PRACTICE QUESTIONS

33. What is the critical value for a two sided Z-test at 5% significance?

34. What is the one sided critical *t*-value at 1% significance for a sample size of 12?

35. What is the critical chi-square value for a contingency table of size 4×3 at 5% significance?

36. A company has analysed the time its customers take to pay an invoice over the past few years and has found that the distribution is normal, with mean of 5.8 weeks and a standard deviation of 2.3 weeks. In order to speed up payment the company threatened to charge interest if bills were not paid within 3 weeks. A sample of 10 customers was then analysed and the mean time to pay had been reduced to 4.9 weeks. Is there any evidence that the mean time for all its customers had actually been reduced?

37. A motorcycle is claimed to have a fuel consumption which is normally distributed with mean 54 mpg and a standard deviation of 5 mpg. 12 motorcycles are tested and the mean value of their fuel consumption was found to be 50.5 mpg. Taking a 5% level of significance, test the hypothesis that the mean fuel consumption is 54 mpg.

38. The lifetime of electric light bulbs produced by a given process is normally distributed and is claimed to have a mean lifetime of 1500 hours. A batch of 50 was taken, which showed a mean lifetime of 1410 hours. The standard deviation of the sample is
90 hours. Test the hypothesis that the mean lifetime of the electric light bulbs has not changed.

39. A company has been accused of selling underweight products. This product is supposed to weigh 500 g; a sample of 6 was weighed and the results were:

   495, 512, 480, 505, 490, 502

Is there any evidence that the mean weight is less than 500 g? (the weight of the product is known to be normally distributed.)

40. The Speedwell Building Society has claimed that there has been a significant increase in the percentage of its customers taking out fixed-rate mortgages. In the past, 30% of customers had

this type of mortgage, but during the past week 60 out of 150 new mortgages have been at a fixed rate. Is the claim by the building society correct?

41. The number of accidents occurring at a large construction site during the past week has been as follows:

Mon	Tue	Wed	Thurs	Fri
6	5	6	8	12

Is there any evidence that accidents are more likely on certain days of the week?

42. In Britain a survey was carried out of 171 radio listeners who were asked what radio station they listened to most during an average week. A summary of their replies is given in Table 11.7, together with their age range.

Table 11.7 Data for Question 42

	Age range		
	Less than 20	**20 to 30**	**Over 30**
BBC	22	16	50
Local radio	6	11	16
Commercial	35	3	12

(a) Is there any evidence that there is an association between age and radio station?

(b) By considering the contribution to the value of your test statistic from each cell and the relative sizes of the observed and expected frequencies in each cell, indicate the main source of the association, if any exists.

43. A component produced for the electricity industry is supposed to have a mean outside diameter of 10 inches. The mean diameter of a sample of 36 components taken from today's output is 9.94 inches with a standard deviation of 0.018 inches. Does this suggest that the production process is not meeting the specifications?

44. Before a special promotion, the percentage of customers who bought your product at a certain supermarket was 36%. After the promotion a random sample of 200 shoppers at the supermarket revealed that 80 of them had bought the product. Is there evidence of a significant change?

45. In the week before Christmas it was hoped that the mean takings of a shop's branches would be £40 000. However, 40 randomly sampled branches has mean takings of only £37 000 with a standard deviation of £6000. Does this suggest that the mean takings of all the branches was significantly different from the target figure?

46. A bank claims that 60% of people who apply for a personal loan will be granted it. However, a random sample of 500 loan applications contains only 250 which were successful. Does this suggest that the success rate is significantly different from 60%?

47. You are approached one day by a sales manager who has used a computer package to calculate the mean size of order placed by all the company's customers last year. His calculations show that the mean size of order placed was £36.90 with a standard deviation of £4.20.

The manager wants advice on how to carry out a hypothesis test to see if the mean size of order placed last year was significantly different from the previous year's figure (this was £30.58). What would your advice be?

48. An inspection by the Environmental Health Department has recently taken place at a company that processes and packs cooked food. The inspectors expressed concern at the amount of dust that was detected in the air within the Cooked Meat department. Although the quantity of dust does not exceed the legal limit, the inspectors recommended that the extractor fans be replaced as soon as possible.

    The company looked at various types of extractor fans on the market at the current time and reduced the choice to just two; the Ameba and the Bewax. In order to decide which one to purchase, the manufacturers have loaned the company one unit of each type in order that a comparison can be made.

    Ameba was installed first, and each week for the next six weeks the filters within the fan were weighed, cleaned and replaced. The Ameba unit was then removed and the Bewax unit placed in the same position and the experiment repeated. The amount of dust (in grams) collected by the two units was as follows:

Ameba	5.7	6.4	6.1	4.8	7.2	2.9
Bewax	2.9	4.7	6.3	3.0	7.0	3.5

    Which extractor fan should the company purchase? (Use a 5% significance level.)

49. In an experiment, a sample of 400 consumers are simultaneously presented with four test packages.

    Package A carries a competition offering the chance to win £10 000
    Package B carries a token for a free gift
    Package C simply carries a message '10% off normal price'
    Package D carries a token offering 20 pence off the next purchase of the product

    The consumers are then asked to choose the package which they find to be the most attractive. The results of the experiment are given below:

Package	No. of consumers selecting it
A	106
B	92
C	102
D	100

    Are these results consistent with the hypothesis that consumers are equally likely to select each package?

50. In a market research survey 200 people are shown the proposed design of a new car and they are asked if they like the design. The responses, broken down by age groups, are shown in Table 11.8. Is there any evidence that age is associated with attitude to the proposed design?

Table 11.8 Data for Question 50

	Age		
	Under 21	**21–35**	**Over 35**
Liked design	20	40	80
Disliked design	30	20	10

51. A telephone company has found in the past that 60% of requests from business customers for new installations are for direct lines, 25% are for switchboard connections and 15% for fax machine and other connections. However, a random sample of 300 customers taken last month reveals that 120 are requesting direct lines, 80 are requesting switchboard connections and the remainder are requesting fax machine and other connections. Does this sample suggest that a significant change in the pattern of demand has occurred?

52. You have been asked to help in the design and analysis of a sales campaign involving a selected number of supermarkets. Janet Graves, the Marketing Manager, believes that it is the 'caring image' of the business that attracts customers rather than price cuts alone. To test this idea Janet obtained approval to invest in staff training and other expenditure to generate a friendly atmosphere within a supermarket. Advertising on television and local radio was also to be increased during the campaign. You randomly selected 8 supermarkets throughout the country representing different areas and spending patterns. Following staff training, the campaign is started and continued for a month. The sales turnover (in £000s) for each supermarket for the month before and after the campaign was noted and is as follows:

Supermarket	A	B	C	D	E	F	G	H
Sales Before	150	75	110	300	120	560	350	185
After	178	50	150	400	180	540	350	235

Is there any evidence at the 5% significance level that sales have improved as a result of the sales campaign?

53. In 1995 an educational researcher sampled 250 students to find out how many hours a week they spent in paid employment. Out of this 250, 30 said that they worked for more than 20 hours a week. The researcher repeated this survey in the year 2000 with a group of 220 students and found that 40 worked for more than 20 hours a week. Is there any indication that students were spending more time working in 2000 than they did in 1995?

ASSIGNMENT

In order to assess the effectiveness of a company training programme, each employee was appraised before and after the training. Based on the comparisons of the two appraisals, each of the 110 production staff were classified according to how well they had benefited from the training. This classification ranged from 'worse', which means they now perform worse than they did before, to 'high', which means they perform much better than they did before the training. The results of this appraisal can be seen in Table 11.9, where you will notice that employees have been further classified by age.

Table 11.9   Data for the assignment

Age of employee	Level of improvement				Total
	Worse	None	Some	High	
Below 40	1	5	24	30	60
40+	4	5	31	10	50
Total	5	10	55	40	110

(a) Is there any association between level of improvement at the job and age?

(b) What is the 95% confidence interval for the percentage of employees who showed a high level of improvement at their job?

Correlation and regression

12.1 Introduction

The statistical analysis that you have covered so far has been concerned with the characteristics of a single variable. However, it also might be of interest to look at two variables simultaneously. For instance, you might suspect that the cost of production is dependent on the quantity produced or that sales of a product are related to price. This chapter introduces two techniques: correlation to measure the *association* between two variables, and regression to obtain the *relationship* between the variables. A knowledge of hypothesis tests (Chapter 11) would be useful for Section 12.3.2.

On completing this chapter, you should be able to:

● Draw and interpret scatter diagrams

● Calculate Spearman's rank correlation coefficient

● Calculate Pearson's product moment correlation coefficient

● Obtain and use the least squares regression line

● Use Excel in regression analysis

● Appreciate the limitations of the techniques and how it can be extended to more than two variables

12.2 Scatter diagrams

A scatter diagram is simply a way of representing a set of bivariate data by a scatter of plots. One variable is plotted on the *x*-axis and the other on the *y*-axis. Normally the *x* variable (the *independent* variable) is the one that you believe influences the *y* variable (the *dependent* variable). That is *y depends on x*.

Examples of scatter diagrams are given in Figures 12.1 to 12.4. The first diagram indicates a *positive correlation* because as the number of deliveries increases, so apparently does the delivery time. The second diagram indicates a *negative correlation* because as the air temperature increases, the heating cost falls. The third diagram suggests that no

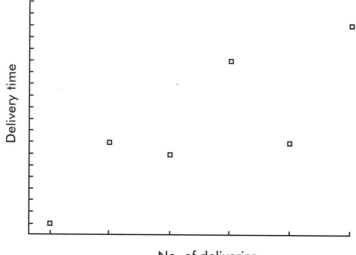

Figure 12.1 Positive correlation

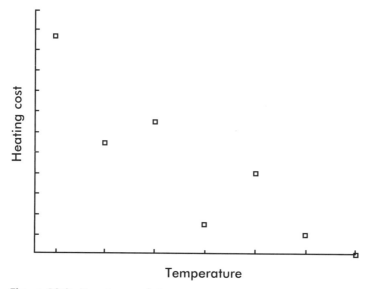

Figure 12.2 Negative correlation

correlation exists between salary and age of employees. The fourth diagram suggests that the quantity produced and the efficiency of a machine are correlated but not linearly.

When categorising scatter diagrams you may find it easier to draw a closed loop around the points. This loop should be drawn so that it encloses all the points but at the same time making the area within the loop as small as possible. If the loop looks like a circle, this suggests that there is little, if any, correlation, but if the loop looks more like an ellipse then this suggests that there is some correlation present. An ellipse pointing upwards would represent a positive correlation and one pointing downwards would represent a

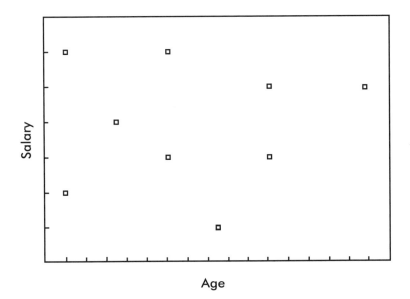

Figure 12.3 No correlation

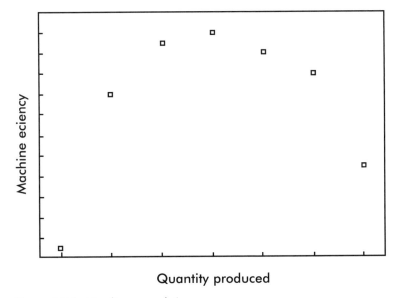

Figure 12.4 Non-linear correlation

negative correlation. If you try this with Figures 12.1 to 12.3 you will see that this agrees with the statements already made. A loop around the points in Figure 12.4 would clearly show the non-linear nature of the association.

The closer the ellipse becomes to a straight line, the stronger the correlation. If the ellipse became a straight line you would say that you have perfect correlation (unless the straight line was horizontal, in which case there can be no correlation since the dependent variable has a constant value).

Example 12.1

The Production Manager at Lookwools Engineering suspects that there is an association between production volume and production cost. To prove this he obtained the total cost of production for different production volumes and the data are as follows:

Units produced (000s)	1	2	3	4	5	6
Production costs (£000s)	5.0	10.5	15.5	25.0	16.0	22.5

Activity 12.1

Draw a scatter diagram for this data and comment on the association (if any).

Since production cost depends on volume, the horizontal (x) axis represents volume (units produced) and the vertical (y) axis represents cost. The scatter diagram for this data is shown in Figure 12.5. A closed loop has been drawn around the points and from this you should be able to make the following observations:

● There is a positive correlation between volume and cost
● The loop is a fairly narrow ellipse shape suggesting that, for the range of data provided, the association is reasonably strong (but not perfect)

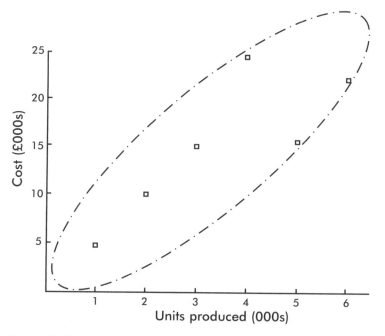

Figure 12.5 Scatter diagram for Activity 12.1

- If the point representing 4000 units was omitted the ellipse would be narrower
- There is no evidence of non-linearity in the data

Although these observations are valid, the sample size is rather small to make definite conclusions. In practice a larger sample size would be advisable (at least twelve pairs) and the cost of 4000 units would be checked. Sometimes these 'rogue' results suggest that other factors are influencing the dependent variable and further investigation is necessary.

12.3 Correlation

The technique of correlation measures the strength of the association between the variables. There are two widely used measures of correlation. These are *Spearman's rank correlation coefficient* and *Pearson's product moment correlation coefficient*. Both give a value between −1 and 1 so that −1 indicates a perfect negative correlation, +1 a perfect positive correlation and zero indicates no correlation. This is illustrated in Figure 12.6.

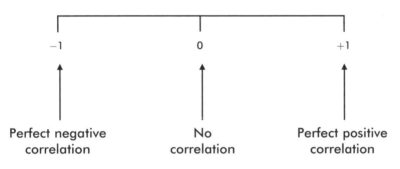

Figure 12.6 Range of values of the correlation coefficient

12.3.1 Spearman's rank correlation coefficient (R)

This method involves ranking each value of x and y and using the following formula to calculate the coefficient R.

$$R = 1 - \frac{6\sum d^2}{n(n^2 - 1)}$$

Where d is the difference in rank between pairs and n is the number of pairs. The value of R lies between +1 and −1.

The procedure to calculate this coefficient is as follows:

1. Rank both variables so that either the largest is ranked 1 or alternatively the smallest is ranked 1.
2. For each pair obtain the difference between the rankings.
3. Square these differences and sum.
4. Substitute the sum of these differences into the formula.

If during Step 1 you find you have equal rankings for the same variable, it is the *mean* of the rankings that is used. For example, if rank 3 occurs twice then both should be given a ranking of 3.5. The next ranking is 5.

Activity 12.2

Calculate Spearman's rank correlation coefficient for the data given in Example 12.1.

STEP 1

Rank both variables.

If you use rank 1 as being the lowest and rank 6 as the largest value, then the 'Units Produced' are already ranked for you. 'Production Costs' start at 5.0 (£000s) and this will have a rank 1, while 25.0 is the largest and will be given a rank of 6. This can be seen below.

Units produced (000s)	1	2	3	4	5	6
Rank	1	2	3	4	5	6
Production costs (£000s)	5.0	10.5	15.5	25.0	16.0	22.5
Ra	1	2	3	6	4	5

STEPS 2 AND 3

Calculate differences, square and sum.

You will find it easier if you set out the calculations in a table similar to Table 12.1.

Table 12.1 Calculation of *R* for Activity 12.2

No. of units	Cost	Difference (*d*)	d^2
1	1	0	0
2	2	0	0
3	3	0	0
4	6	−2	4
5	4	1	1
6	5	1	1
			Sum 6

STEP 4

Substitute the sum of d^2 into the formula.

The sum of d^2 is 6 and there are 6 pairs of values, so Spearman's rank correlation coefficient is:

$$R = 1 - \frac{6 \times 6}{6 \times (6^2 - 1)}$$

$$= \frac{36}{6 \times 35}$$

$$= 0.829$$

This value is close to +1 which supports the assessment made from the scatter diagram that there is a fairly strong positive relationship between cost of production and production volume.

Data do not always consist of actual measurements. For example, in market research, data may consist of opinions on a particular product. This kind of data is called *ordinal* data. Ordinal data have the property that although they do not have actual numerical values, they can be ranked.

The next example should help you understand how to apply Spearman's method to ordinal data.

Example 12.2

BSL marketing have been asked to conduct a survey into the public's attitude to a new chocolate bar. A pilot survey was carried out by asking 5 people of different ages to try the product and give their reaction. The result of this survey is shown in Table 12.2.

Table 12.2 Survey results for Example 12.2

Person	Age range	Response
A	below 10	very good
B	15 to 20	fair
C	20 to 25	fair
D	10 to 15	excellent
E	over 25	disliked

Activity 12.3

Is there any evidence of an association between age and preference for the product?

Both the age range and response can be ranked. It doesn't really matter how you rank them as long as you take your method into account when you come to interpret your coefficient. In the calculations that follow I have used low rankings for low age range and low rankings for the low response ratings (that is, 'disliked' has a ranking of 1). Using this method the rankings are as follows (Table 12.3).

Table 12.3 Rankings for data in Activity 12.3

Person	Age range	Rank	Response	Rank
A	below 10	1	very good	4
B	15 to 20	3	fair	2
C	20 to 25	4	fair	2
D	10 to 15	2	excellent	5
E	over 25	5	disliked	1

Notice that both B and C are ranked equal second in their responses. To compensate for the missing third rank a *mean* rank of 2.5 is used instead of rank 2. You can see this in Table 12.4.

Table 12.4 Calculation of *R* for Activity 12.3

Person	Age range	Response	Difference (*d*)	*d*²
A	1	4	−3	9
B	3	2.5	0.5	0.25
C	4	2.5	1.5	2.25
D	2	5	−3	9
E	5	1	4	16
			Sum	36.5

The sum of the square of the differences is 36.5, and substituting this value into the formula gives:

$$R = 1 - \frac{6 \times 36.5}{5 \times (5^2 - 1)}$$

$$= 1 - \frac{219^{\cdot}}{120}$$

$$= -0.825$$

This value is fairly large, which suggests an association between age and response. Since the coefficient is negative, it would appear that younger people are more likely to react favourably to the product.

12.3.2 Pearson's product moment correlation coefficient (*r*)

This measure of correlation tends to be the most popular, but it can only be used when the data is on the interval scale of measurement. That is the data consists of actual measurements. The formula for *r* is:

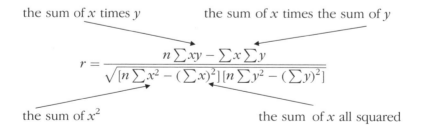

the sum of *x* times *y*   the sum of *x* times the sum of *y*

$$r = \frac{n \sum xy - \sum x \sum y}{\sqrt{[n \sum x^2 - (\sum x)^2][n \sum y^2 - (\sum y)^2]}}$$

the sum of *x*²   the sum of *x* all squared

This formula looks daunting at first sight but it is quite straightforward to use, as you will see by attempting Activity 12.4.

Activity 12.4

Calculate the Pearson's product moment correlation coefficient for the data given in Example 12.1.

To obtain this coefficient you are advised to set out the calculations in tabular form, as shown in Table 12.5.

Table 12.5 Calculation of *r* for Activity 12.4

Units produced x	Production cost y	xy	x^2	y^2
1	5.0	5.0	1	25.00
2	10.5	21.0	4	110.25
3	15.5	46.5	9	240.25
4	25.0	100.0	16	625.00
5	16.0	80.0	25	256.00
6	22.5	135.0	36	506.25
$\sum x = 21$	$\sum y = 94.5$	$\sum xy = 387.5$	$\sum x^2 = 91$	$\sum y^2 = 1762.75$

The summations can then be substituted into the formula for r:

$$r = \frac{6 \times 387.5 - 21 \times 94.4}{\sqrt{[6 \times 91 - (21)^2][6 \times 1762.75 - (94.5)^2]}}$$

$$= \frac{340.5}{\sqrt{(105 \times 1646.25)}}$$

$$= \frac{340.5}{415.7599}$$

$$= 0.8190$$

This calculation agrees with Spearman's calculation (see Activity 12.2) in that there is a strong positive correlation between production volume and cost.

Pearson's product moment correlation coefficient is a more accurate measure of the correlation between two *numeric* variables. However, it cannot be applied to non-numeric data.

Activity 12.5

How large does Pearson's correlation coefficient have to be before we are convinced that there is real association between two variables?

There is no easy answer to this question as it depends on the number of data points. If we went to the extreme and only had 2 data points we would find that the correlation would be perfect as there is no scatter around the imaginary line between the two points. Conversely, the more data points we have the larger the scatter and therefore the smaller the value of r. In order to allow for the number of data points when assessing the value of r we can apply a *significance test* (see Chapter 11) to the result. The null hypothesis is that there is no association or the two variables are unrelated. That is:

H_0: $e = 0$ and H_1: $e \neq 0$ where e is the population coefficient

The test is simple to apply. The *test statistic* is our calculated value of r and the *critical value* can be found from the table in Appendix 2. These tables are based on v *degrees of freedom* and for bivariate data $v = n - 2$.

Activity 12.6

Carry out a test of significance on the value of r calculated in Activity 12.4.

The value of r was 0.8190, which is our test statistic. The critical value on 4 ($6 - 2$) degrees of freedom at a 5% significance level is 0.8114. We can therefore reject H_0 (just) and conclude that there is a significant correlation between the number of units produced and the production cost.

12.4 Linear regression

The technique of linear regression attempts to define the relationship between the dependent and independent variables by the means of a linear equation. This is the simplest form of equation between two variables and, fortunately, many situations can at least be approximated by this type of relationship.

The scatter diagram for the production cost data of Example 12.1 has been reproduced in Figure 12.7. You will see that a line has been drawn through the data and this line represents the linear relationship between the two variables. However, since the relationship is not perfect it is possible to draw several different lines 'by eye' through the diagram, each of which would look reasonable. However, each line would represent a slightly different relationship as the gradient and/or intercept on the y-axis would be different. To decide how good a particular line is, you could find the difference between each point and the line. These differences are often referred to as the 'errors' between the actual value and that predicted by the line.

These errors have been represented by vertical lines on the diagram. Note that the errors below the line are negative and those above the line are positive. If you add these errors you will find that the total error is zero. Does this prove that the line is a good one? Unfortunately not, because the zero value is only obtained by adding positive and negative values. Many more lines could be found that also would give a total error of zero. The errors could be added, ignoring the sign, but it can be shown that the best line or the

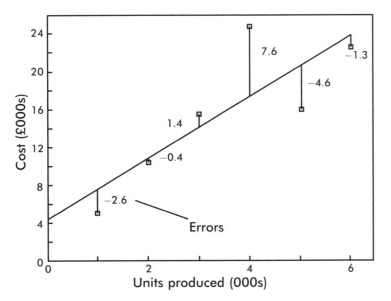

Figure 12.7 Line of best fit drawn through the data from Example 12.1

'line of best fit' is obtained when the sum of the squares of the errors is minimised. Squaring the errors not only removes the minus sign, but also gives more emphasis to the large errors.

12.5 The method of least squares

Linear regression involves finding that line that minimises the sum of squares of the errors. The theory behind 'the method of least squares' is beyond the scope of this book, but the application of the theory is straightforward. The most important part is to ensure that the y variable is the dependent variable – so, for example, the production cost depends on the number of units produced.

The linear regression model is given in the form:

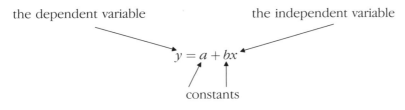

The values of a and b that minimise the squared errors are given by the equations:

$$b = \frac{n\sum xy - \sum x \sum y}{n\sum x^2 - (\sum x)^2}$$

$$a = \frac{\sum y}{n} - b\frac{\sum x}{n}$$

You can think of b as the slope of the regression line and a as the value of the intercept on the y-axis (value of y when x is zero).

Activity 12.7

Calculate the regression line for the production cost data given in Example 12.1.

You will probably realise that there are many similarities between the formula for b and that for r, the product moment correlation coefficient. Since the correlation coefficient has already been calculated for this data (Activity 12.4), you can note that:

$$\sum x = 21, \quad \sum y = 94.5, \quad \sum xy = 387.5 \quad \text{and} \quad \sum x^2 = 91$$

Substituting these values into the equations for a and b gives:

$$b = \frac{6 \times 387.5 - 21 \times 94.5}{6 \times 91 - 21^2}$$

$$= 3.2429$$

and

$$a = \frac{94.5}{6} - \frac{(3.2429 \times 21)}{6}$$

$$= 4.3999$$

The regression equation for this data is therefore:

$$y = 4.4 + 3.24x$$

That is: cost $= 4.4 + 3.24 \times$ units. This suggests that for every 1 unit (1000) rise in production volume, the production cost would rise, on average, by 3.24 units (£3240), and that when nothing is produced ($x = 0$), the production cost would still be £4400. This probably can be explained by factory overhead costs that are incurred even when there is no production.

In order to estimate the value of y for a particular value of x, this x value is substituted into the above equation.

Activity 12.8

Calculate the cost of production for production volumes of

(a) 2500 units   (b) 20 000 units

Have you any reservations regarding the costs obtained?

To obtain the cost of production for these two cases you would simply substitute the values of 2.5 and 20 into the equation $y = 4.4 + 3.24x$.

That is:

(a) $y = 4.4 + 3.24 \times 2.5$

$\quad = 12.5$

So 2500 units would cost about £12 500 on average.

(b) $x = 4.4 + 3.24 \times 20$

$\quad = 69.2$

and 20 000 units would cost £69 200 on average. However, 20 000 units is well outside the range of data used in the original analysis. You cannot be certain that the relationship between cost and volume will remain linear outside this range and so it would be unwise to place too much reliance on the predicted figure.

12.6 Coefficient of determination

Before a regression equation can be used effectively as a predictor for the dependent variable, it is necessary to decide how well it fits the data. One statistic that gives this information is the coefficient of determination. This measures the proportion of the variation in the dependent variable explained by the variation in the independent variable. It is given by r^2, which is the square of the product moment correlation coefficient.

Activity 12.9

What is the value of r^2 for the production cost data of Example 12.1?

The value of r is 0.8190, so $r^2 = 0.671$, which means that 0.67 or 67% of the variation in production cost is explained by the production volume. Alternatively, 33% of the variation is *not* explained.

12.7 Automatic methods of analysing bivariate data

It is of course possible to use a calculator or a spreadsheet to carry out many of the calculations described in this chapter. Although a spreadsheet is by far the most useful method of analysing bivariate data, a calculator can do most of the basic calculations, as the next activity illustrates.

Activity 12.10

Use the statistical functions on your calculator to find the regression coefficients (a and b) and Pearson's correlation coefficient (r) for the data in Example 12.1.

The instructions below refer to the Casio fx83WA and the fx85WA models. These are both popular calculators (the 85WA is a solar/battery powered model) and each costs around £10. If you have a different calculator you will need to refer to the instruction book. Whatever the make and model of your calculator, always repeat the calculation as a check that you have input the numbers correctly.

It is quite common to write down a set of bivariate data using commas (with the x value first) and this is how the data is input to the Casio calculator. The data from Example 12.1 in comma notation is:

1,5.0   2,10.5   3,15.5   4,25.0   5,16.0   6,22.5

Press [MODE] [3] [1] to enter the REG mode for linear regression.

Press [SHIFT] [Scl] [=] to clear the Statistical memory (Scl is another function of the red AC button).

Enter the data using the data key (DT, another function of the M + key).

1 [,] 5 [DT] 2 [,] 10.5 [DT] 3 [,] 15.5 [DT] 4 [,] 25 [DT] 5 [,] 16 [DT] 6 [,] 22.5 [DT]

The following keys for a, b and r are marked in yellow/blue:

Press [SHIFT] [A] [=] for the regression coefficient a (4.4)
Press [SHIFT] [B] [=] for the regression coefficient b (3.24)
Press [SHIFT] [r] [=] for the correlation coefficient r (0.8190)
Press [RCL] [C] (NB: this is the C marked in pink, not yellow/blue) for n, the number of pairs of values (this is a useful check that you have input all the data).

Now clear the statistical memory and repeat the calculation.

However, a standard scientific calculator will not be able to provide you with scatter diagrams of your data. Being able to easily create scatter charts is a major advantage of using a spreadsheet to analyse bivariate data.

Activity 12.11

Use a spreadsheet to draw a scatter chart of the data in Example 12.1.

Figure 12.8 is a screen shot of Step 1 of Excel's Chart Wizard. The steps for creating a scatter chart in Excel is the same as for other charts (see Chapter 3.5). The final scatter diagram has already been shown in Figure 12.5.

As well as creating charts, Excel can also be used to calculate the regression and Pearson's correlation coefficients. To find the correct function to use we can again make use of the function wizard (see Chapter 11.6.2). You might also find the following table useful, which lists the most commonly used bivariate functions. The functions have been applied to the data for Example 12.1 and you can see the syntax of the functions in Figure 12.9.

Notice that for the *slope*, *intercept* and *forecast* functions it is most important that you put the y-values first. You might notice too that there is no function for Spearman's correlation coefficient in Excel.

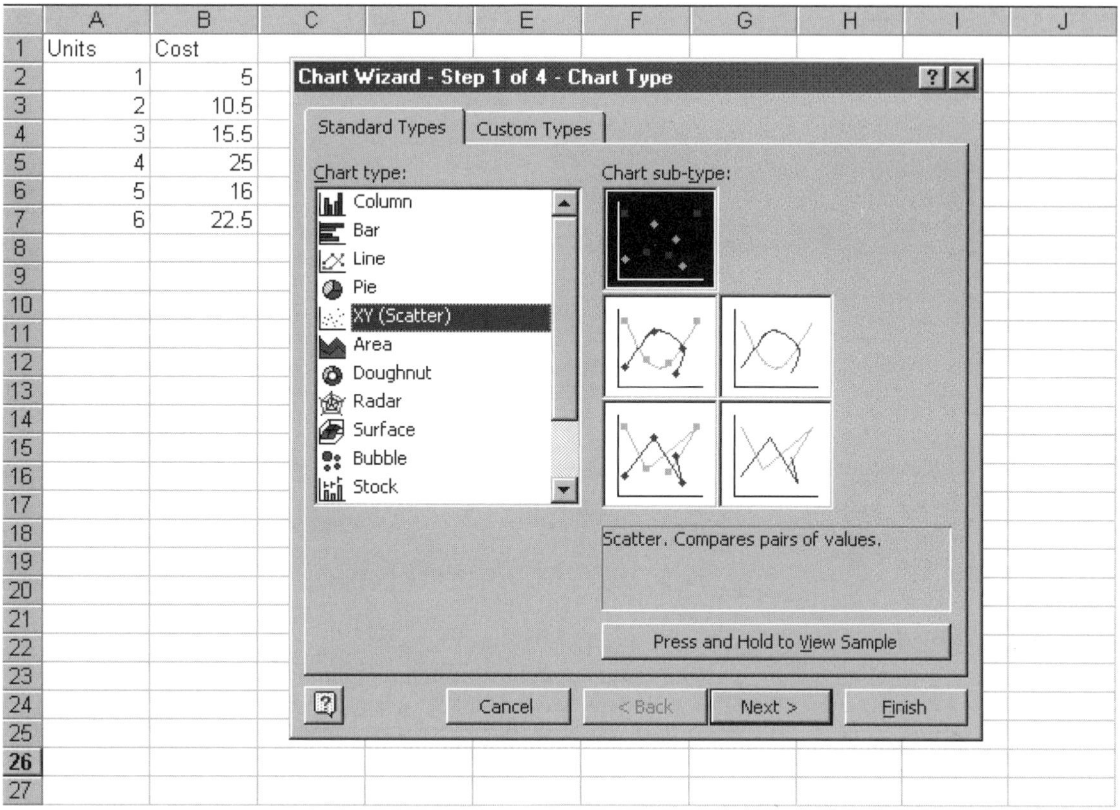

	A	B	C	D	E	F	G	H	I	J
1	Units	Cost								
2	1	5								
3	2	10.5								
4	3	15.5								
5	4	25								
6	5	16								
7	6	22.5								

Chart Wizard - Step 1 of 4 - Chart Type

Standard Types | Custom Types

Chart type:
- Column
- Bar
- Line
- Pie
- XY (Scatter)
- Area
- Doughnut
- Radar
- Surface
- Bubble
- Stock

Chart sub-type:

Scatter. Compares pairs of values.

Press and Hold to View Sample

Cancel | < Back | Next > | Finish

Figure 12.8 Step 1 of Excel's Chart Wizard to create a scatter graph

Table 12.6 Commonly used bivariate functions in Excel

Function	Meaning
=CORREL (x-values, y-values) or =PEARSON (x-values, y-values)	Calculates the Pearson product moment correlation coefficient r
=SLOPE (y-values, x-values)	Calculates slope of regression line
=INTERCEPT (y-values, x-values)	Calculates intercept of regression line
=RSQ (A1:A6, B1:B6)	Calculates r^2
=FORECAST (8, y-values, x-values)	Predicts y for $x = 8$ from the linear regression equation

Activity 12.12

Use the Forecast function in Excel to predict the production cost for a volume of 8000 units.

You should have got a value of £30 340.

	A	B	C
1	Units	Cost	
2	1	5	
3	2	10.5	
4	3	15.5	
5	4	25	
6	5	16	
7	6	22.5	
8			
9	Pearson's correlation coefficient (using CORREL)		=CORREL(A2:A7,B2:B7)
10	Pearson's correlation coefficient (using PEARSON)		=PEARSON(A2:A7,B2:B7)
11			
12	Slope of regression equation (b)		=INTERCEPT(B2:B7,A2:A7)
13	Intercept of regression equation (a)		=SLOPE(B2:B7,A2:A7)
14			
15	Coefficient of determination (r-square)		=RSQ(A2:A7,B2:B7)
16			
17	Forecast for x = 8		=FORECAST(8,B2:B7,A2:A7)
18			
19			

Figure 12.9 Excel's bivariate functions applied to data from Example 12.1

Activity 12.13

Add the regression line (the line of best fit) to the scatter diagram.

It is possible to use Excel to calculate the predicted *y*-values for given *x*-values and then this new data series could be plotted on the same chart as the original data. However, an

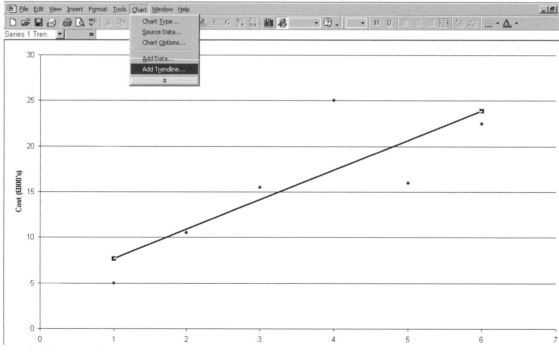

Figure 12.10 Adding the regression equation to a scatter diagram

easier method is to use the *Trendline* facility within Excel. To add the regression line, click on the tab for Chart 1 to return to the scatter diagram sheet. Click on a data point in order to select the series. Select *Chart, Add Trendline*. The regression line will be inserted as you can see in Figure 12.10.

It could be useful to extend the axes to enable the chart were to be used for predictions.

Double click the *x*-axis and select *Scale*. Change the maximum scale to 10.
Double click the *y*-axis and select *Scale*. Change the maximum scale to 40.
Double click the trendline and select *Options*. Under *Forecast Forward*, enter 4 units to extend the trendline to a production volume of 10 000 units.

Activity 12.14

Use your chart to predict the cost of production for a volume of 8000 units.

From Figure 12.11 you will see that the predicted volume is just over £30 000, which agrees with the value obtained in Activity 12.10. Of course extrapolating the regression line assumes that the line remains linear outside the range of collected data. This reservation has already been mentioned in the solution to Activity 12.8.

There is also a set of statistical routines available as an add-in to Excel. This routine may not be loaded and you will have to add it by selecting *Tools, Add-Ins*. You should then tick the *Analysis ToolPak* as shown in Figure 12.12.

One of these routines is called *Regression*, which will give you the same information that you obtained with *Pearson, Slope* and *Intercept*. It may not be worth using this routine for

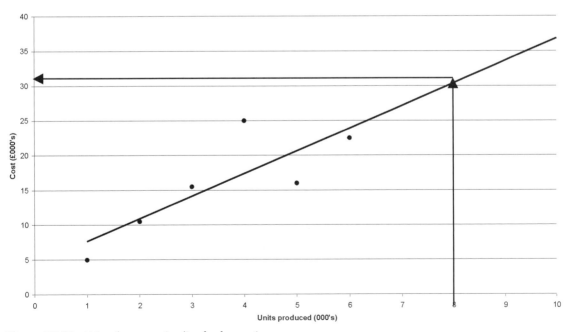

Figure 12.11   Using the regression line for forecasting

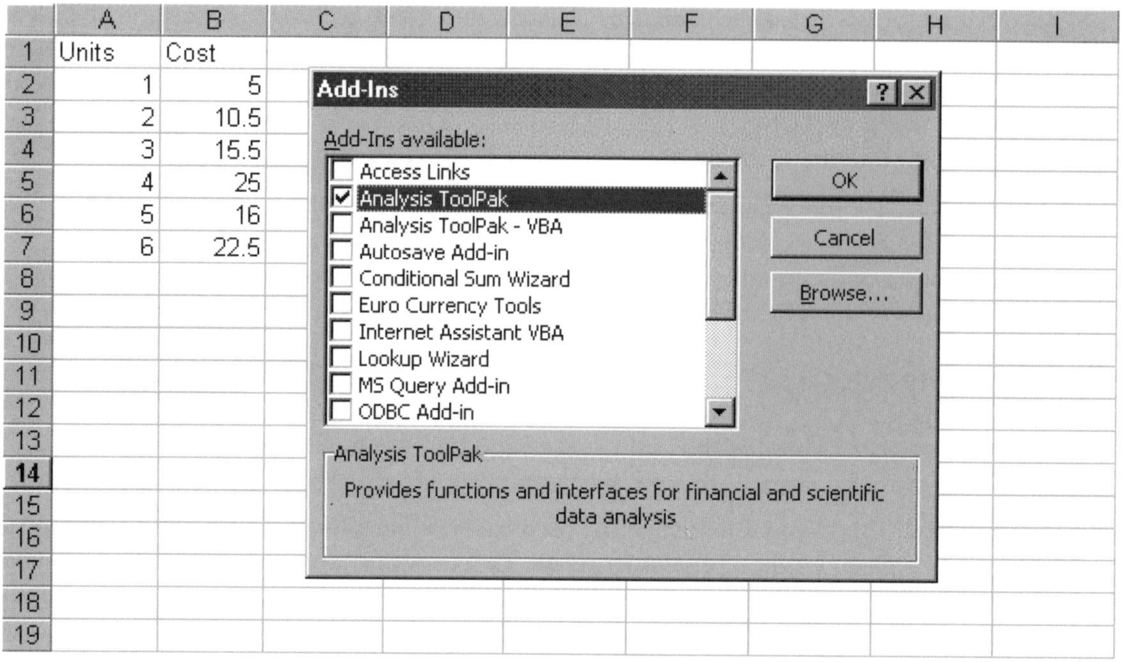

Figure 12.12 Adding the Analysis ToolPack

basic bivariate analysis, as much of the output requires more statistical knowledge than is covered in this text. It is, however, a very useful routine if you have more than 2 variables to analyse.

When there are two or more *independent* variables we have *multiple* regression. The regression equation becomes:

$$Y = \beta_0 + \beta_1 x_1 + \beta_2 x_2 + \cdots$$

where β_0 is equivalent to the *a* coefficient in linear regression and β_1 is equivalent to the *b* coefficient. The next activity demonstrates how you would use the regression routine in Excel to analyse *multivariate* data.

Activity 12.15

The Production Manager at Lookwools Engineering (Example 12.1) thinks that the weight of the item being produced affects the cost and he would like you to investigate if this variable could be added to the regression equation. Using the same production volumes as provided in Example 12.1 the average weight (in kg) of the items being produced has been obtained and can be seen below:

Units produced	1	2	3	4	5	6
Weight	1.6	1.5	1.75	5	2.8	3.5
Cost	5.0	10.5	15.5	25.0	16.0	22.5

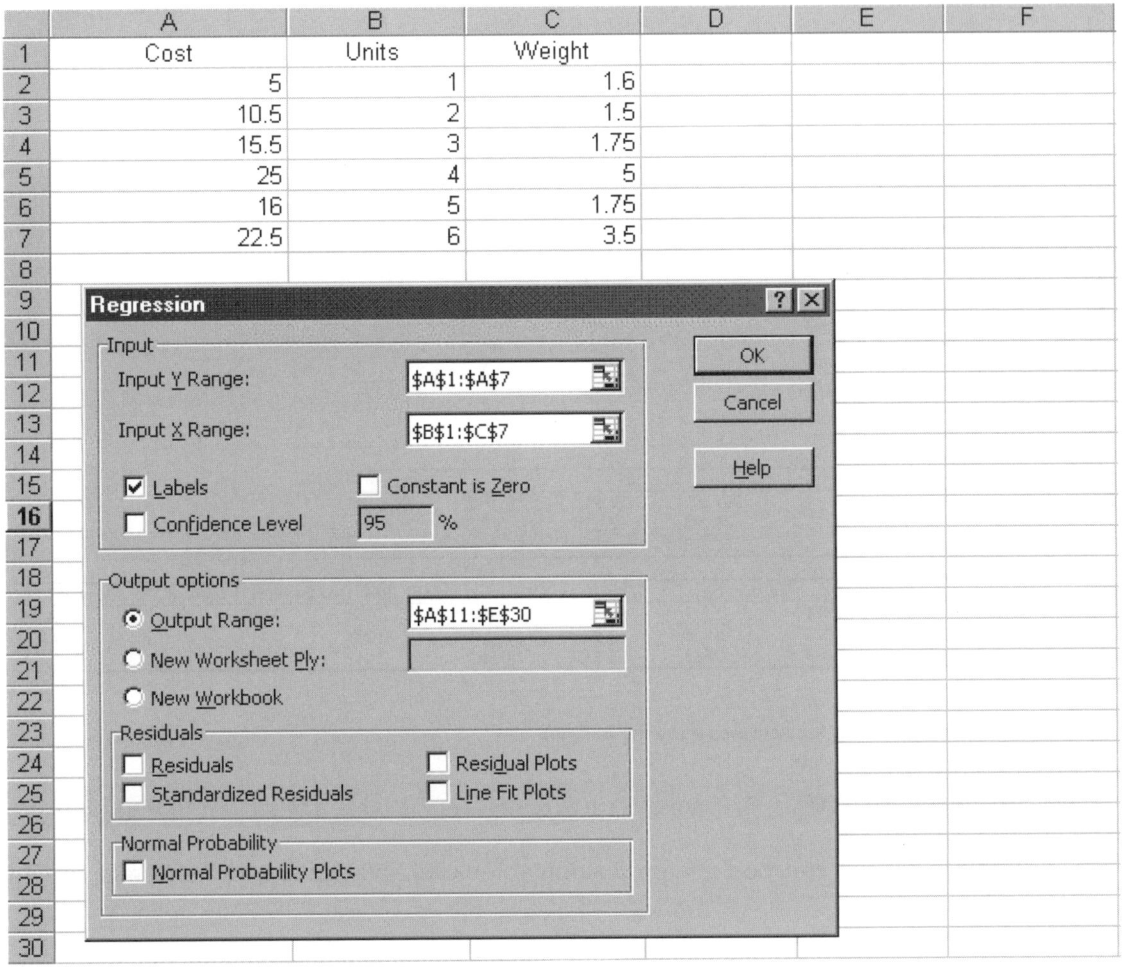

	A	B	C	D	E	F
1	Cost	Units	Weight			
2	5	1	1.6			
3	10.5	2	1.5			
4	15.5	3	1.75			
5	25	4	5			
6	16	5	1.75			
7	22.5	6	3.5			

Regression — ? X

Input
Input Y Range: $A$1:$A$7
Input X Range: $B$1:$C$7
☑ Labels ☐ Constant is Zero
☐ Confidence Level 95 %

OK
Cancel
Help

Output options
◉ Output Range: $A$11:$E$30
○ New Worksheet Ply:
○ New Workbook

Residuals
☐ Residuals ☐ Residual Plots
☐ Standardized Residuals ☐ Line Fit Plots

Normal Probability
☐ Normal Probability Plots

Figure 12.13 The Regression routine in Excel

To analyse this data in Excel you need to load the regression routine by clicking *Tools, Data Analysis, Regression*. Figure 12.13 is a screen shot of the Regression dialog box and Figure 12.14 is a screen shot of the output obtained from using this routine. You should be able to understand the figures shown in **bold**. In particular, Multiple R is equivalent to Pearson's product moment correlation coefficient and you will see that it has increased from 0.8190 to 0.961. R Square is the coefficient of determination and has increased from 67% to 92%. This means that production volume and weight together now contribute 92% to the cost of production. That is, only 8% of the variation in cost is not accounted for. So by adding another variable we have improved the fit of the regression equation. This means the regression equation should be more accurate in predicting costs for a given production volume and average weight of items produced. The coefficients of the regression equation can be found in the third table in Figure 12.14 and the equation will therefore be:

$$\text{Cost} = 0.874 + 2.077 \times \text{Units} + 3.023 \times \text{Weight}$$

	A	B	C	D	E	F	G	H	I
1	Cost	Units	Weight						
2	5	1	1.6						
3	10.5	2	1.5						
4	15.5	3	1.75						
5	25	4	5						
6	16	5	1.75						
7	22.5	6	3.5						
8									
9									
10									
11	SUMMARY OUTPUT								
12									
13	*Regression Statistics*								
14	Multiple R	0.961							
15	R Square	0.923							
16	Adjusted R Square	0.872							
17	Standard Error	2.652							
18	Observations	6							
19									
20	ANOVA								
21		*df*	*SS*	*MS*	*F*	*Significance F*			
22	Regression	2	253.282	126.641	18.012	0.021			
23	Residual	3	21.093	7.031					
24	Total	5	274.375						
25									
26		*Coefficients*	*Standard Error*	*t Stat*	*P-value*	*Lower 95%*	*Upper 95%*	*Lower 95.0%*	*Upper 95.0%*
27	Intercept	0.874	2.712	0.322	0.769	-7.758	9.505	-7.758	9.505
28	Units	2.077	0.735	2.827	0.066	-0.261	4.415	-0.261	4.415
29	Weight	3.023	0.963	3.138	0.052	-0.042	6.088	-0.042	6.088
30									

Figure 12.14 Results of using the Regression routine in Excel

Activity 12.16

What would the cost be for a production volume of 4500 units and an average weight of 3.6 kg?

To solve this problem all you need to do is to substitute the values 4.5 and 3.6 into the regression equation. That is:

$$\text{Cost} = 0.874 + 2.077 \times 4.5 + 3.023 \times 3.6$$

$$= 21.103 \ (£000s) \text{ or } £21\,103$$

12.8 Summary

The techniques introduced in this chapter have enabled you to obtain answers to the following questions.

1. Is there an association between the variables?

2. How strong is this association?

3. What is the relationship between the variables?

You used scatter diagrams to look at the association between the variables, while correlation enabled you to quantify this association. Linear regression was used to describe the nature of the relationship between the variables.

12.9 Further reading

Burton, G., Carrol, G. and Wall, S. (1999) *Quantitative Methods for Business and Economics*, Longman, New York (Chapter 3).

Morris, C. (2000) *Quantitative Approaches in Business Studies*, fifth edition, Pitman, London (Chapters 13 and 14).

12.10 EXERCISES

The answers to the progress questions, the multiple choice questions and some of the practice questions are given in Appendix 1. Solutions to the remaining questions and the assignment can be found at the web site for this text.

PROGRESS QUESTIONS

These questions have been designed to help you remember the key points in this chapter.

Give the missing word in each case:

1. A graphical picture of bivariate data is called a .... diagram.
2. Correlation measures the strength of the .... between two variables.
3. Regression defines the .... between the two variables.
4. Correlation is measured on a scale from .... to ....
5. The least squares regression line .... the sum of the squared errors.
6. A perfect linear relationship between two variables means that all the points lie on a .... line.
7. Spearman's rank correlation coefficient is used for .... data.

ANSWER *TRUE* OR *FALSE*

8. A high correlation confirms a *causal* relationship.
9. A negative correlation coefficient means that there is no association between the two variables.
10. Pearson's product moment correlation coefficient can only be calculated for numerical data.
11. The coefficient *b* in the linear regression model represents the slope of the regression line.

REVIEW QUESTIONS

These questions have been designed to help you check your comprehension of the key points in this chapter. You may wish to look further than this chapter in order to answer them fully. You will find the reading list useful in this respect. You can check the essential elements of your answers by referring to the appropriate section.

12. What is a scatter diagram, and why is it important to draw this diagram before any calculations are carried out? (Section 12.2)

13. What are the essential differences between Spearman's rank correlation coefficient and Pearson's product moment correlation coefficient? (Section 12.3)

14. What do you understand by the expression 'method of least squares'? (Section 12.5)

MULTIPLE CHOICE QUESTIONS

15. If the increase in one variable causes an increase in the another variable, the form of the correlation between the variables must be:

    A... positive   B... negative   C... perfect

16. The dependent variable is plotted on the:

    A... x-axis   B... y-axis   C... either axis

17. If the value of r is 0.8, then the coefficient of determination is:

    A... 0.8   B... 64%   C... 80

18. If pairs of bivariate data all have equal rank, then Spearman's rank correlation coefficient must be:

    A... 0   B... +1   C... −1

19. If Spearman's rank correlation coefficient is −1 for a set of numerate bivariate data, then Pearson's product moment correlation coefficient for the same data must be:

    A... +1   B... −1   C... 0
    D... between 0 and +1   E... between 0 and −1

20. If the coefficient b in the linear regression model is zero, then the correlation between the two variables must be:

    A... +1   B... −1   C... 0

PRACTICE QUESTIONS

21. A regression line is $y = 3 + 5x$. What is the value of y if $x = 2$?

22. The data in Table 12.7 relate to the weight and height of a group of students.

    (a) Draw a scatter diagram of weight against height for the whole data. Alongside each point write either 'm' or 'f' as appropriate.

    (b) Describe your scatter diagram. Try drawing an ellipse around
        (i) all the points
        (ii) the points relating to the male students
        (iii) the points relating to the female students.

    Is there any indication that the correlation is stronger for either group?

    (c) Calculate Pearson's product moment correlation coefficient for the three sets of points identified in (b) above. Comment on the values obtained.
    (Collect data from a group of friends and repeat the analysis.)

Table 12.7 Weight and height data for Question 22

Height (in)	Weight (lb)	Sex
68	148	male
69	126	female
66	145	male
70	158	male
66	140	female
68	126	female
64	120	female
66	119	female
70	182	male
62	127	female
68	165	male
63	133	male
65	124	female
73	203	male

23. A group of students compared the results they obtained in a quantitative methods assignment and a law assignment. The results by position in a group of 50 was as follows:

Student	A	B	C	D	E	F	G	H	I
Quants	5	8	45	2	9	5	15	20	3
Law	29	17	1	11	6	18	33	3	8

Use Spearman's rank correlation coefficient to discover if there is any correlation between position in each subject.

24. A company is investigating the relationship between sales and advertising revenue. Data has been collected on these two variables and is shown below (all figures are in £000's):

Month	Jan	Feb	Mar	Apr	May	June
Sales	60	60	58	45	41	33
Adv.	6.0	6.0	6.0	5.8	4.5	4.1

Month	July	Aug	Sept	Oct	Nov	Dec
Sales	31	25	24	23	23	23
Adv.	3.3	3.1	2.5	2.4	2.3	2.3

(a) Plot a scatter diagram of the data given in the table above. Comment on the strength of the association between the two variables.

(b) Obtain the least squares regression line and comment on how well it fits the data.

(c) What would the expected sales be, given an advertising expenditure of £5000?

25. Consider the following pairs of variables and make an assessment of the likely correlation between them. Mark each pair to show whether you expect the correlation to be positive or negative (strong or weak), or close to zero:

(a) Attendance totals and position in football league table

(b) The age of a relatively new make of car and its value

(c) The age of a vintage make of car and its value

(d) Length of education and annual earnings

(e) Level of unemployment and hire purchase sales over a period of 10 years.

26. The following data relate to the size of the electricity bill sent to 7 randomly selected customers and the time the customers took to pay the bills.

Customer No.	1	2	3	4	5	6	7
Size of Bill	£100	£150	£200	£250	£330	£400	£480
Time to pay (days)	15	20	16	20	24	32	28

(a) (i) Plot the data on a scatter graph.

　(ii) Use your calculator to find Pearson's correlation coefficient for the data.

(b) Determine the least squares regression equation that can be used to predict how long a bill of a given size will take to pay.

(c) Interpret your equation.

(d) Draw the line on the scatter graph.

(e) Use your equation to predict how long it will take a customer to pay:

　(i) a bill of £125, and

　(ii) a bill of £1000.

　What reservations do you have about these predictions?

(f) The coefficient of determination for this data is 79.2%. Interpret this value.

27. A local government research unit is looking at the methods that councils use to collect rent from tenants living in houses and flats. In particular, it wants to know whether the relatively expensive door-to-door collection method is effective. A random sample of six local councils is selected and for each council the percentage of rent collected door-to-door and the percentage of total rent which is in arrears is recorded. The results are shown below.

% of rent collected door-to-door	1	12	16	11	20	6
% of total rent in arrears	13	10	8	12	7	11

(a) Plot the data for the two variables on a scatter graph.

(b) Calculate Spearman's correlation coefficient for this data.

28. The personnel manager of a company is concerned with the high sickness records of its production staff. An analysis of its night shift revealed the figures shown in Table 12.8.

(a) Plot a scatter graph of this data. What can you deduce about the association between number of days taken off sick last year and age?

(b) Using your calculator's statistical mode or otherwise, calculate a correlation coefficient for this data.

(c) Carry out a suitable test at the 5% level to see whether there is a significant correlation between days off work and age.

Table 12.8 Sickness records

Person	Age	Days off work last year
A	21	20
B	19	8
C	36	8
D	55	5
E	20	13
F	22	15
G	45	12
H	39	7
I	32	11
J	28	8

(d) The least squares regression relationship between days off sick and age is:

Days off sick $= 17.4 - 0.2118 \times$ Age

(i) Plot this line on your scatter graph.

(ii) Do either of the numbers 17.4 or -0.2118 have a practical (*not* mathematical) meaning? If so, explain.

(iii) What prediction can you make about the days off sick for a person who is 65 years old and works on the night shift? Comment on your answer.

(iv) Calculate the coefficient of determination for this data and interpret its value.

(v) What other factors might affect days off sick?

ASSIGNMENT

It seems reasonable to assume that the second hand price of a particular make of car is dependent on its age. Decide on a particular make and model of car and a suitable source for the data, such as your local newspaper. Collect data on the age and price of around 20 cars and use Excel to do the following:

(a) Plot a scatter graph of the data. Does the scatter graph indicate that a linear relationship exists for all or part of the range of the data?

(b) Obtain the regression equation that would enable the price of the car to be obtained given its age.

(c) Using the equation obtained in (b) above and suitable examples, illustrate how the price of a car could be found if its age was known. Within what age range is your equation valid? Why is this so?

(d) What proportion of the variability in price is explained by the age factor?

(e) Investigate whether other factors, such as engine size, would improve the fit of the regression equation.

13 Time series analysis

13.1 Introduction

Many variables have values that change with time: for example, the weekly sales of ice cream, the monthly unemployment figures and the daily production rates for a factory. The changing value of such variables over a period of time is called a time series. The analysis of time series data is very important, both for industry and government, and a large number of people are employed to do this analysis. This chapter will look at the main features of a time series and demonstrate some popular techniques.

On completing this chapter you should be able:

- Use the technique of moving averages to isolate the trend in a time series
- Understand the circumstances where the additive and multiplicative models should be used
- Calculate the seasonal component for both the additive and multiplicative models
- Obtain the seasonally adjusted series
- Apply the technique of exponential smoothing in appropriate circumstances
- Use time series analysis to make forecasts
- Use Excel in time series analysis

13.2 The decomposition model

This model assumes that a time series is made up of several components. These components are:

- Trend
- Seasonality
- Cyclic behaviour
- Randomness

The trend represents the long-run behaviour of the data and can be increasing, decreasing or constant. Seasonality relates to periodic fluctuations that repeat themselves at fixed intervals of time. Cyclic behaviour represents the ups and downs of the economy or of a specific industry. It is a long-term fluctuation and for practical purposes is usually ignored. Randomness is always present in a time series and represents variation that cannot be explained. Some time series (for example, share prices) have a very high random component and the forecasts of these series will be subject to a high degree of error.

Example 13.1

Table 13.1 consists of data relating to the sales of petrol at the Star petrol station for the past 3 weeks, while Table 13.2 consists of the sales of sun cream by Mace Skin Care plc.

Table 13.1 Sales of petrol at the Star petrol station

Week	Day	Litres
1	Monday	28
	Tuesday	16
	Wednesday	24
	Thursday	44
	Friday	65
	Saturday	82
	Sunday	30
2	Monday	33
	Tuesday	21
	Wednesday	29
	Thursday	49
	Friday	70
	Saturday	87
	Sunday	35
3	Monday	35
	Tuesday	23
	Wednesday	31
	Thursday	51
	Friday	72
	Saturday	89
	Sunday	37

Activity 13.1

Plot the two series represented by Tables 13.1 and 13.2 on graph paper (or use a spreadsheet) and compare and contrast the important features of each.

You can check your graph with the ones in Figures 13.1 and 13.2. What can you say about these graphs? You should notice that both series show a marked seasonal component since the patterns repeat themselves at regular intervals. In the case of the Star petrol station, the highest sales always occurs on a Saturday and the lowest on a Monday. The

Table 13.2 Sales of sun cream by Mace Skin Care plc

Year	Quarter	Sales (£000s)
1999	1	6.00
	2	9.00
	3	12.00
	4	8.00
2000	1	8.00
	2	13.50
	3	17.00
	4	13.00
2001	1	12.00
	2	20.25
	3	30.00
	4	19.50
2002	1	18.00

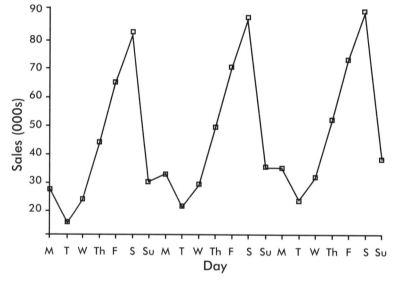

Figure 13.1 Sales of petrol at the Star service station

time series for the quarterly sales of a sun cream by Mace Skin Care plc shows a peak in quarter 3 and a trough in quarter 1. You also should notice that the sales of the sun cream appear to have increased rapidly during the 3-year period.

13.3 Isolating the trend

To isolate the trend you need to remove the seasonal fluctuations. In the case of the petrol sales the pattern repeats itself every week, so perhaps the average sales each week would be a useful calculation?

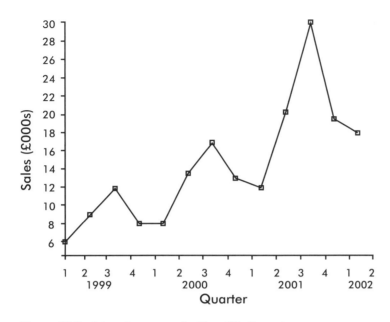

Figure 13.2 Sales of sun cream by Mace Skin Care plc

Activity 13.2

Calculate the average petrol sales for weeks 1, 2 and 3. Does this help remove the seasonal fluctuations?

The values you should have got are 41.3, 46.3 and 48.3 for weeks 1, 2 and 3 respectively. The seasonal fluctuations have certainly been removed, but then so has most of the data! This is therefore not the best of methods. However, why use Monday to Sunday as a week? Why not Tuesday to Monday or Wednesday to Tuesday? If you think along these lines you will see that many more than 3 averages can be obtained. This is called *moving averages* since the average is moved by one time period each time. Since there are 7 days or periods in this example, you have to calculate a 7-point moving average.

The calculations for the first 3 averages are shown in Table 13.3. Notice that the first average has been placed alongside Thursday, this is because Thursday is the middle of the week that starts on Monday.

Activity 13.3

Calculate the remaining moving averages and plot these figures on the same graph that you plotted the original series.

Table 13.3 Calculation of moving averages for petrol sales

Day	Petrol sales (000s litres)	Weekly total	7-point moving average
Monday	28		
Tuesday	16		
Wednesday	24		
Thursday	44	$28 + 16 + 24 + 44 + 65 + 82 + 30 = 289$	$289/7 = 41.3$
Friday	65	$16 + 24 + 44 + 65 + 82 + 30 + 33 = 294$	$294/7 = 42.0$
Saturday	82	$24 + 44 + 65 + 82 + 30 + 33 + 21 = 299$	$299/7 = 42.7$
Sunday	30		
Monday	33		
Tuesday	21		

NOTE: A shortcut is to notice that as you move down the table, you are simply dropping one period and adding another. That is, the total for Friday is $289 - 28 + 33 = 294$. This is particularly useful for large cycle lengths, such as 12- or 52-point moving averages.

The complete table is as follows.

Table 13.4 Table for Activity 13.3

Day	Litres	Moving average
Monday	28	
Tuesday	16	
Wednesday	24	
Thursday	44	41.3
Friday	65	42.0
Saturday	82	42.7
Sunday	30	43.4
Monday	33	44.1
Tuesday	21	44.9
Wednesday	29	45.6
Thursday	49	46.3
Friday	70	46.6
Saturday	87	46.9
Sunday	35	47.1
Monday	35	47.4
Tuesday	23	47.7
Wednesday	31	48.0
Thursday	51	48.3
Friday	72	
Saturday	89	
Sunday	37	

The moving average figures have been superimposed on the original time series graph and are shown in Figure 13.3.

There is no doubt that the moving average has smoothed the data and therefore this second series should represent the trend. You can see from the graph that there is a slight upward movement to this trend.

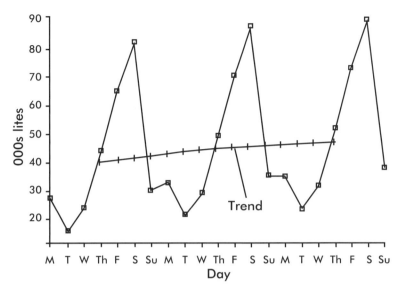

Figure 13.3 Time series graph of petrol sales with the moving averages plotted

The Star petrol station example illustrated the case where the moving average was based on an odd number of periods (7 days). However, with the sun cream series there is an even number of periods (4 quarters). The problem with this is that the middle of the year falls between quarters 2 and 3. This would not be very helpful since the original data relate to a specific quarter. (How would you plot a value between 2 quarters and what would this value mean?) To get round this problem, *centred moving averages* are used. The moving averages are worked out as before, placing the averages between periods. Pairs of averages are then taken and the average of the averages can be written down alongside a specific period. Table 13.5 illustrates the calculations for the first 2 years.

Table 13.5 Calculation of moving averages for sun cream

Year	Quarter	Sales (£000s)	Moving average	Centred moving average
1999	1	6.0		
	2	9.0		
			8.75	
	3	12.0		(8.75 + 9.25)/2 = 9.00
			9.25	
	4	8.0		(9.25 + 10.38)/2 = 9.81
			10.38	
2000	1	8.0		
	2	13.5		

Activity 13.4

Calculate the remaining centred moving average figures for the sales of sun cream and plot these figures on the same graph as you plotted the original series.

You should have obtained Table 13.6.

Table 13.6 Table for Activity 13.4

Year	Quarter	Sales (£000s)	Centred moving average
1999	1	6.00	
	2	9.00	
	3	12.00	9.00
	4	8.00	9.81
2000	1	8.00	11.00
	2	13.50	12.25
	3	17.00	13.38
	4	13.00	14.72
2001	1	12.00	17.19
	2	20.25	19.63
	3	30.00	21.19
	4	19.50	
2002	1	18.00	

NOTE: Figures have been rounded to 2 decimal places in this and subsequent tables. The figures will therefore not agree exactly to those obtained using a spreadsheet.

The centred moving averages have been plotted in Figure 13.4. Notice the rapidly rising trend values.

13.4 Isolating the seasonal component

There are two models that will allow you to isolate the seasonal component. The first is the *additive* model and is applicable if the seasonal swings are a constant difference from the

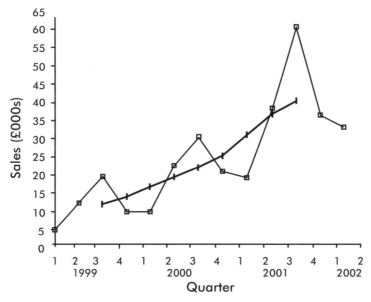

Figure 13.4 Time series graph of sun cream sales with the moving averages plotted

trend. This means that the *difference* between the trend and a particular period remains approximately constant throughout the entire time series. The second model is the *multiplicative* model and is applicable if the seasonal swings are a percentage of the trend; that is, the seasonal swing will depend on the value of the trend at that point.

In equation form the additive model is: $YT + S + C + R$

and the multiplicative model is: $Y = T \times S \times C \times R$

Where Y is the variable of interest, T is the trend, S is the seasonal component, C is the cyclic component and R is the random element.

Activity 13.5

By examining Figure 13.3, decide whether the additive or multiplicative model is more appropriate for the petrol sales series. Repeat this exercise for the sales of sun cream, using Figure 13.4.

You should have found that the seasonal swings about the trend for the petrol sales series appear reasonably constant, so an additive model is probably appropriate here. In the sun cream example the seasonal swings about the trend are increasing, so the multiplicative model is probably the better model in this case. However, it is not always so clear cut and sometimes both models are tried and the results compared. To show this, both models will now be applied to the sun cream example.

To obtain the seasonal differences, the additive model can be rearranged as:

$S + C + R = Y - T$

So the value of the variable minus the trend value at that point will give you the seasonal difference plus the cyclic and random components. The cyclic component can only be isolated when values of the variable Y are available over many years (at least 20), which is rare. Usually the cyclic component is ignored, and its effect (if any) forms part of the random element.

For quarter 3 of 1999 the estimate of the seasonal difference is $12 - 9 = 3$. This tells you that sales for quarter 3 in 1999 are 3 units (£3000) above the trend. For quarter 4 of 1999 the seasonal difference is -1.81 ($8 - 9.81$), which means the sales are 1.81 below the trend.

Activity 13.6

Continue this procedure and obtain the seasonal differences for the remainder of the data.

You should have obtained the seasonal differences shown in Table 13.7.

Table 13.7 Calculation of seasonal differences for the sales of sun cream

Year	Quarter	Sales (£000s)	Centred moving average	Seasonal difference
1999	1	6.00		
	2	9.00		
	3	12.00	9.00	3.00
	4	8.00	9.81	−1.81
2000	1	8.00	11.00	−3.00
	2	13.50	12.25	1.25
	3	17.00	13.38	3.63
	4	13.00	14.72	−1.72
2001	1	12.00	17.19	−5.19
	2	20.25	19.63	−0.62
	3	30.00	21.19	8.81
	4	19.50		
2002	1	18.00		

If you look at these figures you will notice that for the same quarter number the seasonal difference varies. This is due to the random element. This variation can best be observed in Table 13.8, which also allows the average seasonal difference to be calculated.

Table 13.8 Calculation of average seasonal differences for the sales of sun cream

Quarter	1	2	3	4	
1999			3.00	−1.81	
2000	−3.00	1.25	3.63	−1.72	
2001	−5.19	0.62	8.81		
Average	−4.095	0.935	5.147	−1.765	Sum = 0.222
Adjusted	−4.15	0.88	5.09	−1.82	Sum = 0.00

The use of an average value helps to remove some of the random component. These averages should sum to zero since they should cancel out over the year. In the example above you will see that $-4.09 + 0.94 + 5.15 - 1.77 = 0.22$, which is clearly not zero. If each average is reduced by 0.055 $\left(\dfrac{0.222}{4}\right)$ then you will get the adjusted figures (rounded to 2 decimal places) shown, and you should check that their sum is now zero.

The calculations for the multiplicative model are similar except that S is called the seasonal factor and is worked out by dividing Y by T. These factors are often expressed in percentage form by multiplying by 100. For example, the seasonal factor for quarter 3 in 1994 is:

$$\frac{12}{9} \times 100$$

$$= 133.3\%$$

> ### Activity 13.7

Obtain the average percentage seasonal factors for the sales of sun cream by Mace Skin Care plc.

In this model a seasonal factor above 100% represents sales above the trend, and a value below 100% represents sales below the trend. The adjusted average factors are shown in Table 13.10.

Each average was adjusted by multiplying its value by $1.00781 \left(\dfrac{400}{396.9} \right)$, since the sum of the averages should in this case be 400.

Table 13.9 Seasonal factors for the sales of sun cream

Year	Quarter	Sales (£000s)	Centred moving average	Seasonal factor (%)
1999	1	6.00		
	2	9.00		
	3	12.00	9.00	133.3
	4	8.00	9.81	81.5
2000	1	8.00	11.00	72.7
	2	13.50	12.25	110.2
	3	17.00	13.38	127.1
	4	13.00	14.72	88.3
2001	1	12.00	17.19	69.8
	2	20.25	19.63	103.2
	3	30.00	21.19	141.6
	4	19.50		
2002	1	18.00		

Table 13.10 Calculation of average seasonal factors for the sales of sun cream

Quarter	1	2	3	4	
1999			133.3	81.5	
2000	72.7	110.2	127.1	88.3	
2001	69.8	103.2	141.6		
Average	71.3	106.7	134.0	84.9	Sum = 396.9
Adjusted	71.9	107.5	135.0	85.6	Sum = 400.0

13.5 Analysis of errors

Once you have isolated the trend and seasonal components it is a good idea to see how well the model fits the data. This is particularly important when you are not sure whether the additive or multiplicative model is the correct model to use.

For the additive model $Y = T + S$, so the Y variable can be predicted by adding the trend to the relevant adjusted average seasonal difference. For the multiplicative model

$Y = T \times S$, so the prediction is made by multiplying the trend and adjusted average seasonal factor. In both cases the difference between the actual value and predicted value gives you the error in the prediction. For example, the predicted sales of sun cream for quarter 3 in 1999 using the additive model is $9.00 + 5.09 = 14.09$. Since the actual value is 12.00, this represents an error of -2.09 ($12 - 14.09$). Using the multiplicative model the predicted value is $9.00 \times \dfrac{135.0}{100} = 12.15$ and the error is now -0.15.

Activity 13.8

Calculate the remaining errors using both the additive and multiplicative models.

The errors for both models are shown in Table 13.11 and Table 13.12.

Table 13.11 Calculation of the errors for the additive model

Year	Quarter	Sales (£000s)	T	S	Predicted sales (£000s)	Error
1999	1	6.00				
	2	9.00				
	3	12.00	9.00	5.09	14.09	−2.09
	4	8.00	9.81	−1.82	7.99	0.01
2000	1	8.00	11.00	−4.15	6.85	1.15
	2	13.50	12.25	0.88	13.13	0.37
	3	17.00	13.38	5.09	18.47	−1.47
	4	13.00	14.72	−1.82	12.90	0.10
2001	1	12.00	17.19	−4.15	13.04	−1.04
	2	20.25	19.63	0.88	20.51	−0.26
	3	30.00	21.19	5.09	26.28	3.72
	4	19.50				
2002	1	18.00				

Table 13.12 Calculation of the errors for the multiplicative model

Year	Quarter	Sales (£000s)	T	S (%)	Predicted sales (£000s)	Error
1999	1	6.00				
	2	9.00				
	3	12.00	9.00	135.0	12.15	−0.15
	4	8.00	9.81	85.6	8.40	−0.40
2000	1	8.00	11.00	71.9	7.91	0.09
	2	13.50	12.25	107.5	13.17	0.33
	3	17.00	13.38	135.0	18.06	−1.06
	4	13.00	14.72	85.6	12.60	0.40
2001	1	12.00	17.19	71.9	12.36	−0.36
	2	20.25	19.63	107.5	21.10	−0.85
	3	30.00	21.19	135.0	28.61	1.39
	4	19.50				
2002	1	18.00				

The errors should be small and show no pattern. Even with small quantities of data the easiest way to look at the errors is by means of a graph. Figures 13.5 and 13.6 show that the multiplicative model gives the smallest errors and is therefore the better model, which is what was expected.

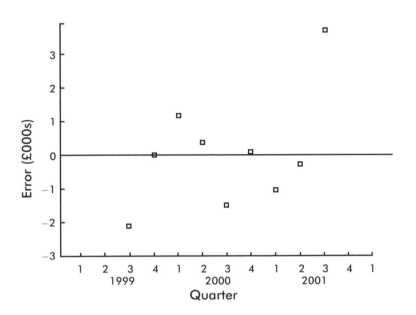

Figure 13.5 Errors for the additive model

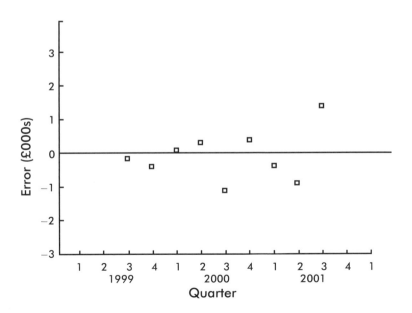

Figure 13.6 Errors for the multiplicative model

Apart from a graphical display of the errors, it is possible to analyse them statistically. Two statistics are normally calculated, the mean absolute deviation (MAD) and the mean square deviation (MSE). The formulae for these are:

sum the *absolute* values of the errors
(ignore the sign)

sum the *square* of
the errors

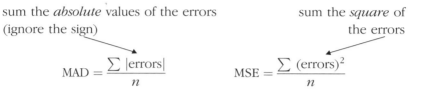

$$\text{MAD} = \frac{\sum |\text{errors}|}{n} \qquad \text{MSE} = \frac{\sum (\text{errors})^2}{n}$$

The MAD statistic is simply the mean of the absolute errors (or deviations), while MSE is the mean of the square deviations. Both statistics are valid, but you will find that many statisticians favour the MSE statistic. One reason for this is that squaring puts more emphasis on large errors. For the sun cream example, the calculation of MAD and MSE using the errors obtained from the additive model is shown in Table 13.13.

Table 13.13 Calculation of MAD and MSE for the additive model

Year	Quarter	Actual sales (£000s)	Predicted sales (£000s)	Error	Absolute error	Squared error
1999	3	12.00	14.09	−2.09	2.09	4.3681
	4	8.00	7.99	0.01	0.01	0.0001
2000	1	8.00	6.85	1.15	1.15	1.3225
	2	13.50	13.13	0.37	0.37	0.1369
	3	17.00	18.47	−1.47	1.47	2.1609
	4	13.00	12.90	0.10	0.10	0.0100
2001	1	12.00	13.04	−1.04	1.04	1.0816
	2	20.25	20.51	−0.26	0.26	0.0676
	3	30.00	26.28	3.72	3.72	13.8384
				Sum =	10.21	22.9861
				Mean	1.13	2.55

Activity 13.9

Repeat the above calculation using the multiplicative model.

You should have obtained Table 13.14 (below).

Both these statistics are smaller than that obtained with the additive model, demonstrating once again that the multiplicative model is better for this example.

 ## 13.6 Seasonally adjusted series

I am sure that you have heard the phrase 'seasonally adjusted' when economic time series are mentioned by the media. A common example is unemployment. If a series is seasonally

Table 13.14 Calculation of MAD and MSE for the multiplicative model

Year	Quarter	Actual sales (£000s)	Predicted sales (£000s)	Error	Absolute error	Squared error
1999	3	12.00	12.15	−0.15	0.15	0.0225
	4	8.00	8.40	−0.40	0.40	0.1600
2000	1	8.00	7.91	0.09	0.09	0.0081
	2	13.50	13.17	0.33	0.33	1.089
	3	17.00	18.06	−1.06	1.06	1.1236
	4	13.00	12.60	0.40	0.40	0.1600
2001	1	12.00	12.36	−0.36	0.36	0.1296
	2	20.25	21.10	−0.85	0.85	0.7225
	3	30.00	28.61	1.39	1.39	1.9321
				Sum =	5.03	4.3673
				Mean	0.56	0.49

adjusted it means that the seasonal component has been removed, leaving the trend component. By seasonally adjusting unemployment figures, for example, it is easy to tell what is happening to this important economic variable.

For the additive model a time series is seasonally adjusted by *subtracting* the seasonal difference, while for the multiplicative the operation is one of *division*.

Normally this procedure is used when new data arrives and you want to see if there is any change in the trend of the series. For example, say that the petrol sales at Star petrol station for the Monday of the fourth week is 38 000 litres. This value can be seasonally adjusted by subtracting −4.15 (the average seasonal difference for Mondays). Since this value is negative the net result is to *add* 4.15 to 38, which is 42.15 or 42 150 litres.

Activity 13.10

The sales of sun cream by Mace Skin Care plc for quarter 2 of 2002 is £28 500. Seasonally adjust this figure.

The average seasonal factor for quarter 2 is 107.5% (see Activity 13.7), so the seasonally adjusted sales is $\dfrac{28\,500}{1.075} = £26\,512$.

13.7 Forecasting using the decomposition model

One purpose of time series analysis is to use the results to forecast future values of the series. The procedure for this is to extrapolate the trend into the future and then apply the seasonal component to the forecast trend. There are various methods of extrapolating the trend. If the trend is approximately linear then linear regression could be used by assigning numerical values to time. For example, using the sun cream series, quarter 1 of 1999 would have a value 1 and quarter 1 of 2002 would have a value 13. This is explained in more detail in section 13.9. However, you will often find it easier to extrapolate by eye

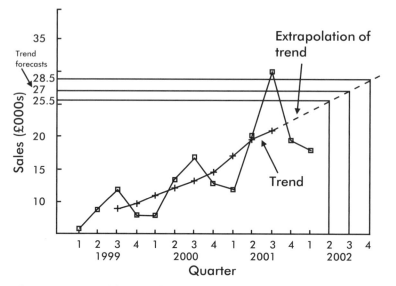

Figure 13.7 Trend forecasts for sales of sun cream

('eyeballing') since other factors can then be considered, if necessary. If there is doubt about the future behaviour of the trend, you could make two or three different extrapolations to give different forecasts (say, an optimistic and a pessimistic one).

For the sun cream example, a possible extrapolation of the trend has been made and can be seen in Figure 13.7. The forecast trend values for the remainder of 2002 have been read off this graph and are shown below:

Quarter	2	3	4
Trend forecast	25.5	27.0	28.5

To calculate the forecast for each quarter using the multiplicative model, these trend forecasts need to be *multiplied* by the appropriate seasonal factor. For example, for quarter 2 the average seasonal factor is 107.5%, so the forecasted value is: $25.5 \times 1.075 = 27.41$, or approximately £27 400. For the additive model the average seasonal difference of 0.88 is *added* to 25.5; that is, 26.38, or approximately £26 400. The result using the multiplicative model is likely to be more accurate since the model had smaller errors. However, any forecasts are subject to considerable uncertainty and all forecasts should be treated with caution.

Activity 13.11

Use the multiplicative model to obtain forecasts for quarters 3 and 4 of 2002.

The seasonal factors for quarters 3 and 4 are 135.0% and 85.6%, so the forecasts will be:

$$27 \times 1.350 = 36.450 \text{ (approximately £36 500)}$$

and $\quad 28.5 \times 0.856 = 24.396$ (approximately £24 400)

13.8 Exponential smoothing

The technique of exponential smoothing is often used where a short-term forecast is required (that is, the next period). The formula for this technique is very simple:

Next forecast = Last forecast + α × error in last forecast

Where α (alpha) is a smoothing constant. This constant takes a value between 0 and 1, so that the next forecast will simply be the last forecast plus a fraction of the last error. The error in the last forecast is the actual value minus the forecast.

To illustrate this technique, imagine that you are responsible for ensuring that the Small Brewery company has sufficient barrels available to store its beer. Full barrels are sent out and empty ones returned. You need to know how many barrels will be returned the next day to plan production. If insufficient barrels are available, beer is wasted, whereas if more barrels than expected are returned, you may have lost sales.

There are two problems with exponential smoothing. The first is what value of α to use. This can only be found by trial and error, and you may even have to change the value in the light of experience. It is usually found that a value between 0.05 and 0.3 gives the smallest values of MAD or MSE. For the Small Brewery company, a value of 0.1 has been chosen.

The second problem is how to get the first forecast, since a last forecast is required. Some people choose a suitable value while others prefer a warm-up period. Once several forecasts have been made, the starting value becomes less important anyway, but let us suppose that you have decided to use the warm-up method. You are to use the last 10 days for this purpose, and therefore your first proper forecast will be for day 11. The number of barrels returned over the last 10 days are:

Day	1	2	3	4	5	6	7	8	9	10
No. of barrels	20	13	19	19	25	17	15	13	22	20

If you take the forecast for day 2 as the actual for day 1, then the error is -7 ($13 - 20$) and the forecast for day 3 becomes:

$20 + (0.1 \times -7) = 19.3$

The forecast for day 4 is now:

$19.3 + (0.1 \times -0.3) = 19.27$

and so on.

Activity 13.12

Continue this process to achieve a forecast for day 11.

You will probably find it easier if you use a table similar to Table 13.15. As you can see, the forecast for day 11 is 18.95 (that is, 19 barrels).

Table 13.15   Forecasts using exponential smoothing and an α of 0.1

Day	No. barrels	Forecast	Error	$\alpha \times$ error	Next forecast
1	20				
2	13	20.00	−7.00	−0.70	19.30
3	19	19.30	−0.30	−0.03	19.27
4	19	19.27	−0.27	−0.03	19.24
5	25	19.24	5.76	0.58	19.82
6	17	19.82	−2.82	−0.28	19.54
7	15	19.54	−4.54	−0.45	19.09
8	13	19.09	−6.09	−0.61	18.48
9	22	18.48	3.52	0.35	18.83
10	20	18.83	1.17	0.12	18.95
11		18.94			

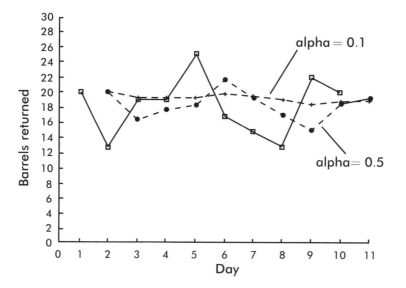

Figure 13.8   Numbers of returned barrels and forecasts using exponential smoothing

The time series of the original data and of the forecast values are shown in Figure 13.8. Also shown is the forecast using an α of 0.5, and you will see that a value of 0.1 gives a smoother series. This is generally true: the smaller the value of α, the greater the smoothing effect.

In terms of accuracy the errors can again be analysed and MAD and MSE calculated. Using an α of 0.1, an MSE of 17.97 is obtained.

Activity 13.13

Calculate the MSE statistic using an alpha of 0.5.

By using an α of 0.5 you should have found that the MSE statistic has increased to 23.21.

Simple exponential smoothing is a very useful and easy-to-use short-term forecasting technique. However, it will lag behind a series that is undergoing a sharp change, such as a series that has a seasonal component or a steep trend. If you want to use it on seasonal data you must seasonally adjust the series first.

13.9 Using spreadsheets in time series analysis

Time series calculations can be performed using standard Excel arithmetic formula commands. The line graphs can also be created using Excel s charting tools. Both the use of formulae and charting have been met in previous chapters, so the instructions given in this section have assumed that you are reasonably proficient in these skills.

Activity 13.14

Use Excel to carry out a time series analysis (using the multiplicative model) on the data relating to the sales of sun cream (Table 13.2).

The only formula you need to create the worksheet shown in Figure 13.9 is *average*. When calculating the moving average for an even period by hand it is often recommended that you leave a blank line between each figure of the main table. This is to allow you to place the moving average in between periods. However, this is not a good idea with a spreadsheet, as you would have to leave a blank row between the data. A better method is

	A	B	C	D	E	F	G	H
1			Sales of sun cream					
2								
3		Year	Quarter	Sales	Moving	Centred moving	Seasonal	
4					average	average	factor	
5		1999	1	6				
6			2	9				
7			3	12	=AVERAGE(D5:D8)	=AVERAGE(E7:E8)	=D7/F7	
8			4	8	=AVERAGE(D6:D9)	=AVERAGE(E8:E9)	=D8/F8	
9		2000	1	8	=AVERAGE(D7:D10)	=AVERAGE(E9:E10)	=D9/F9	
10			2	13.5	=AVERAGE(D8:D11)	=AVERAGE(E10:E11)	=D10/F10	
11			3	17	=AVERAGE(D9:D12)	=AVERAGE(E11:E12)	=D11/F11	
12			4	13	=AVERAGE(D10:D13)	=AVERAGE(E12:E13)	=D12/F12	
13		2001	1	12	=AVERAGE(D11:D14)	=AVERAGE(E13:E14)	=D13/F13	
14			2	20.25	=AVERAGE(D12:D15)	=AVERAGE(E14:E15)	=D14/F14	
15			3	30	=AVERAGE(D13:D16)	=AVERAGE(E15:E16)	=D15/F15	
16			4	19.5	=AVERAGE(D14:D17)			
17		2002	1	18				
18								
19								
20		Quarter	1	2	3	4		
21		1999			=G7	=G8		
22		2000	=G9	=G10	=G11	=G12		
23		2001	=G13	=G14	=G15		Sum	
24		Average	=AVERAGE(C21:C23)	=AVERAGE(D21:D23)	=AVERAGE(E21:E23)	=AVERAGE(F21:F23)	=SUM(C24:F24)	
25		Adjusted	=C24*400%/$G$24	=D24*400%/$G$24	=E24*400%/$G$24	=F24*400%/$G$24	=SUM(C25:F25)	
26								

Figure 13.9 Excel worksheet showing the time series formulae for the multiplicative model

to place the moving average in the same row as the centred moving average. So in the sun cream data the moving average would start in the third row down. You can see this in Figure 13.9. Transferring the seasonal component to the summary table is another source of error for novice spreadsheet analysts. Don't be tempted to type the figures into the table. If you do this and the data changes, your summary table will not be updated. The only data that should be typed in are the original series itself. All other figures should be formulae, as you will see in Figure 13.9.

You should have also added a chart to your spreadsheet. This chart should contain the original series and the trend. You can create this chart on a separate sheet or incorporate it as an object in the same sheet. The chart you should have used is a line graph and the instructions for using Excel's Chart Wizard are:

1. Highlight cells D5 to D17 and then, with the Ctrl key held down, highlight cells F5 to F17.
2. Click on *Insert*, *Chart*, *Line*.
3. Click on *Next* and then *Series*. Give a name to each series. In the *Category (X) axis labels* box enter the range B5 : C17. This ensures that you get the year and quarter on the x-axis.
4. Click on *OK*, give the chart and axes titles and decide whether you want the chart to be in a separate sheet or as an object in the same sheet. Click on *Finish*.

The final chart that is shown in Figure 13.10 has been added as an object in the same sheet. You can move or size the chart to fit into your sheet. By clicking within the chart area you can edit the chart, just as you would if it were in a separate sheet.

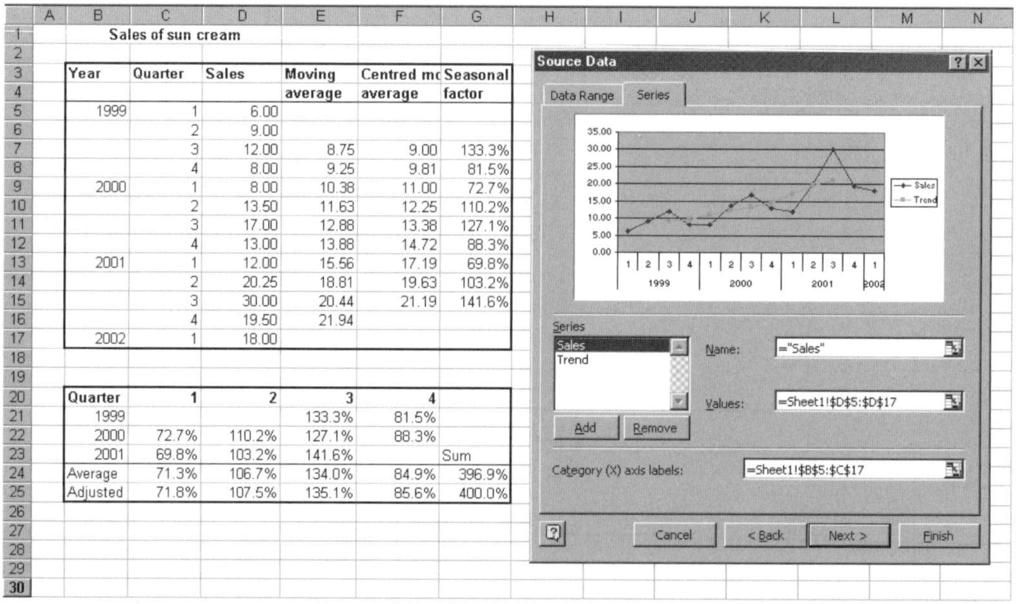
Sales of sun cream

Year	Quarter	Sales	Moving average	Centred mo average	Seasonal factor
1999	1	6.00			
	2	9.00			
	3	12.00	8.75	9.00	133.3%
	4	8.00	9.25	9.81	81.5%
2000	1	8.00	10.38	11.00	72.7%
	2	13.50	11.63	12.25	110.2%
	3	17.00	12.88	13.38	127.1%
	4	13.00	13.88	14.72	88.3%
2001	1	12.00	15.56	17.19	69.8%
	2	20.25	18.81	19.63	103.2%
	3	30.00	20.44	21.19	141.6%
	4	19.50	21.94		
2002	1	18.00			

Quarter	1	2	3	4	
1999			133.3%	81.5%	
2000	72.7%	110.2%	127.1%	88.3%	
2001	69.8%	103.2%	141.6%		Sum
Average	71.3%	106.7%	134.0%	84.9%	396.9%
Adjusted	71.8%	107.5%	135.1%	85.6%	400.0%

Figure 13.10 Step 2 of the Chart Wizard in Excel

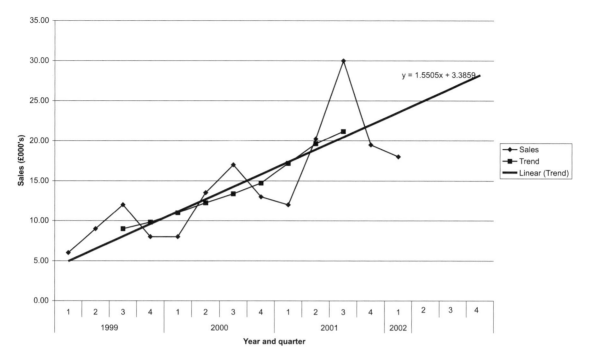

Figure 13.11 The trend line extrapolated using Excel

If you wish you could add a smooth trend line (using linear regression) through the centred moving average figures by clicking on the *Chart* in the tool bar and *Add Trendline*, *Trendline/Regression Type*. Then *Options, Forecast Forward* to extrapolate the trend line. Tick the box for *Display equation on chart*. Figure 13.11 shows the trend line extrapolated by 3 units. This is a similar chart to Figure 13.7 and the forecasts can be obtained in the same way. However, the Excel chart also gives the regression equation of the trend line, which is $Y = 1.5505x + 3.3859$. The x-values are the period number on the time axis, starting from 1 for quarter 1 of 1999 and ending 13 for quarter 1 of 2002. Trend forecasts will therefore be based on period numbers of 14, 15 and 16 and these can be substituted into the equation. For example, the trend forecast for quarter 2 of 2002 is:

$$Y = 1.5505 \times 14 + 3.3859$$

$$= 25.1 \ (£000s)$$

The other two forecasts would be 26.6 and 28.2. These trend forecasts are similar to the ones obtained by eye in Figure 13.7 (25.5, 27.0 and 28.5). To arrive at the sales forecasts we need to multiply these values by the seasonal factors (107.5%, 135.1% and 85.6%) as before.

The disadvantage with using the Excel s forecast is that we are assuming that the trend is linear, which may not be true. *Eyeballing* has the advantage that external factors can be taken into account when arriving at forecasts.

13.10 Summary

A time series can contain a seasonal component, a trend and some randomness. The trend in the series can be observed by using the technique of moving averages, while the seasonal component can be isolated by the use of an appropriate decomposition model. The additive decomposition model is used when the seasonal swings are approximately constant, while the multiplicative model is more appropriate when the seasonal swings are a proportion of the trend. The errors in the models can be observed by the use of suitable graphs or error statistics can be calculated. Future values of a time series can be seasonally adjusted either by subtracting the seasonal difference from the new data (additive model) or by dividing the new data by the seasonal factor. Finally, future values of a time series can be predicted by extrapolating the trend. This is best done 'by eye', although linear regression can be used if the trend is linear. This chapter also introduced exponential smoothing, which is an excellent short-term forecasting method.

13.11 Further reading

Burton, G., Carrol, G. and Wall, S. (1999) *Quantitative Methods for Business and Economics*, Longman, New York (Chapter 4).

Morris, C. (2000) *Quantitative Approaches in Business Studies*, fifth edition, Pitman, London (Chapter 15).

13.12 EXERCISES

The answers to the progress questions, the multiple choice questions and some of the practice questions are given in Appendix 1. Solutions to the remaining questions and the assignment can be found at the web site for this text.

PROGRESS QUESTIONS

These questions have been designed to help you remember the key points in this chapter.

Give the missing word in each case:

1. A time series is made up of a trend, seasonality, cyclic component and ....
2. It is normally difficult to isolate the .... component unless a very long time series is available.
3. The method of .... averages is used to remove the seasonal fluctuations.
4. The .... model allows the seasonal component to be isolated.
5. MAD stands for mean .... deviation.

ANSWER *TRUE* OR *FALSE*

6. If the seasonal swings are increasing it is likely that the multiplicative model will be more accurate than the additive model.

7. For a 12-point moving average it is necessary to centre the moving averages.
8. To seasonal adjust a time series you multiply by the seasonal factor.
9. Exponential smoothing is a short-term forecasting technique.

REVIEW QUESTIONS

These questions have been designed to help you check your comprehension of the key points in this chapter. You may wish to look further than this chapter in order to answer them fully. You will find the reading list useful in this respect. You can check the essential elements of your answers by referring to the appropriate section.

10. What is the purpose of moving averages? (Section 13.3)
11. Describe the essential differences between the additive and multiplicative models. (Section 13.4)
12. How can you measure the accuracy of a time series model? (Section 13.5)

MULTIPLE CHOICE QUESTIONS

13. A time series is made up of monthly data. The moving average is likely to be calculated using:

   A. . . A 5-point moving average

   B. . . A 10-point moving average

   C. . . A 12-point moving average

14. The sum of additive seasonal differences should be:

   A. . . 0   B. . . 1   C. . . depends on the data

15. Exponential smoothing allows a forecast for:

   A. . . The next time period

   B. . . The next two time periods

   C. . . A full cycle ahead

16. Three of the seasonal factors for a time series based on a quarterly cycle are 89%, 130%, and 75%. The fourth factor is:

   A. . . 94%   B. . . 106%   C. . . 100%

17. The seasonal difference for period 1 of a time series is 25.5. The next period 1 has a value of 185. The seasonally adjusted value for the this period is:

   A. . . 159.5   B. . . 210.5   C. . . 47.175

18. The errors using a particular time series are: 2.5, −3.6, 5.8, 10.1, −6.3, −2.2, 10.2, −15.0, 0.3, −1.8. The MAD statistic for this data is:

   A. . . 57.8   B. . . 5.78   C. . . 0.578

19. The MSE statistic using the errors in Question 18 is:

   A. . . 53.176   B. . . 5.3176   C. . . 531.76

20. You have just completed an analysis into the sales of a computer game over the past 3 years and the result is shown in Table 13.16.

Table 13.16   Sales for Question 20

Year	Period	Sales (000s)
1999	1	30
	2	35
	3	35
	4	40
	5	50
	6	60
2000	1	30
	2	40
	3	38
	4	35
	5	52
	6	60
2001	1	35
	2	33
	3	37
	4	43
	5	50
	6	65

(a) Plot this series on graph paper.

(b) From the raw data, calculate the centred moving average series and plot this on the graph. Comment on both series of data.

(c) Use the additive decomposition model to obtain average seasonal differences for each period.

(d) Obtain rough forecasts for 2002.

21. The personnel department of BBS plc, a large food processing company, is concerned about absenteeism among its shop floor workforce. There is a general feeling that the underlying trend has been rising, but nobody has yet analysed the figures. The total number of shop floor employees has remained virtually unchanged over the last few years.

    The mean number of absentees per day is given in Table 13.17 for each quarter of the years 1999 to 2001 and quarter 1 of 2002.

(a) Plot the above data on a graph (leave space for the remaining 2002 figures).

(b) Use the method of moving averages to determine the trend in the series and superimpose this on your graph. Interpret your graph.

(c) Use an appropriate method to measure the seasonal pattern in the data. Briefly give reasons for your choice of method.

(d) Use your analysis to produce rough forecasts of the mean number of absentees there will be in the remaining quarters of 2002.

Table 13.17 Mean number of absentees for Question 21

	Q1	Q2	Q3	Q4
1999	25.1	14.4	9.5	23.7
2000	27.9	16.9	12.4	26.1
2001	31.4	19.7	15.9	29.9
2002	34.5			

22. The manager of the electrical department at a high street store has asked you to perform a time series analysis on the quarterly sales figures of the numbers of TVs sold over the past 3 years. It is advised that you use Excel for this question.

Year	Quarter	No. of sales
1999	2	100
	3	125
	4	127
2000	1	102
	2	104
	3	128
	4	130
2001	1	107
	2	110
	3	131
	4	133
2002	1	107

(a) Produce a line graph of the number of sales. (Extend your time axes up to quarter 4 of 2002.) Describe the pattern exhibited by the data.

(b) Use moving averages to calculate the trend in your data and add this to your chart.

(c) What would be the best decomposition model, the additive or multiplicative? (Hint – calculate the MSE statistic for both models.)

(d) Extrapolate the trend and using your chosen model forecast the sales for the rest of 2002.

23. The following data refers to the end of business share prices for a particular company:

112, 111, 113, 115, 114, 112, 115, 111, 111, 112, 113

Use exponential smoothing with a smoothing constant of 0.1 to forecast the price on day 12.

ASSIGNMENT

Use statistical publications in the library (for example, the *Monthly Digest of Statistics*) to obtain a time series of your choice. Carry out a full analysis of this series.

Write a report of your analysis including tables and graphs. Provide justification for the model used including graphs of errors and error statistics. Use your model to provide appropriate forecasts.

14 Linear programming

14.1 Introduction

Industry and business in general operate with limited resources. Money, material and space is frequently scarce and companies attempt to utilise these scarce resources as efficiently as possible. The technique of linear programming is a procedure that can provide the best solution to many problems that involve an objective, such as profit maximisation and a series of (linear) constraints, such as time, labour and cost. This chapter introduces this technique and applies it to simple problems that can be solved graphically.

On completing this chapter you should be able to:

- Formulate linear programming problems for both maximising and minimising problems
- Use a graphical method to solve two variable problems
- Understand the concept of shadow prices and be able to calculate their value
- Carry out a sensitivity analysis on the problem
- Use Excel to solve linear programming problems

14.2 Basics of linear programming

Linear programming (or LP) is concerned with the management of scarce resources. It is particularly applicable where two or more activities are competing for these limited resources. For example, a company might want to make several different products, but each product makes different demands on the limited resources available. How many of each product should be made so that contribution to profits is *maximised*? Or perhaps you want to determine the quantities of raw materials necessary for a particular blend of oil that will *minimise* the cost of production.

Before these and other problems can be solved you have to *formulate* the problem in linear programming terms. This involves expressing the problem as a series of *inequations* and finding solutions to these inequations that optimise some objective. This may sound very difficult but for *two variable* problems (for example, two products) the problem can be solved using a graphical technique. For larger problems computer software is normally used.

Linear programming requires a knowledge of elementary algebra and the drawing of straight lines. If you are a little rusty in these areas you are advised to work through Sections 1.5, 1.8, and 1.9 of Chapter 1.

14.3 Model formulation

Before a problem can be solved by the LP method, a model needs to be developed. The model consists of a description of the problem in mathematical terms. In particular, the variables of the problem need to be defined and the objective decided. In addition, the *constraints* need to be expressed as *inequations*.

The next few activities will take you through the procedure using the following example.

Example 14.1

The company Just Shirts has been formed to make high quality shirts and is planning to make two types – the 'Regular Fit' and the 'Deluxe Fit'. The contribution to profits for each shirt is £5 for each Regular Fit shirt made and £8 for each Deluxe Fit shirt. To make each shirt requires cotton, of which 600 square metres is available each day and machinists to cut and stitch the shirts. Twenty machinists are employed by the company and they each work an 8-hour day; giving 160 hours of labour in total. Each Regular Fit shirt requires 5 square metres of cotton and takes 1 hour to make, while each Deluxe Fit shirt takes 6 square metres of cotton and 2 hours to make. The company wishes to maximise contribution to profits, so how many of each type of shirt should be made on a daily basis?

Activity 14.1

Define the variables for this problem.

You are required to determine the number of each type of shirts to produce. Some authors suggest using $x_1, x_2, \ldots, x_n$ to represent the variables, but I think it is more 'user friendly' to use letters that mean something. I would therefore suggest that you use R to represent the number of Regular Fit shirts that are to be made each day and D to represent the number of Deluxe Fit shirts.

Activity 14.2

It is required to maximise contribution to profits. How would you express this in equation form?

If you made just one of each type of shirt, you would make a profit of £5 + £8. However, you are making R Regular Fit and D Deluxe Fit shirts, so the total profit will be 5R + 8D. This can be written as:

Max. 5R + 8D

Activity 14.3

There is a limit of 600 square metres of cotton available each day. How would you express this as a constraint to production, given that each Regular Fit shirt requires 5 square metres and each Deluxe Fit shirt requires 6 square metres?

If you make R Regular Fit shirts then you will use 5R metres of cotton. Similarly you will use 6D metres of cotton to make D Deluxe Fit shirts. The sum of these two must be less than or equal to 600 square metres, so this can be written as:

$5R + 6D \leq 600$

Activity 14.4

Repeat Activity 14.3 for the labour resource.

You will use R hours for the Regular Fit shirt and 2D hours for the Deluxe Fit shirt and 160 hours are available each day, so the *constraint* can be written as:

$R + 2D \leq 160$

You have now formulated the problem, although you should indicate that you are only interested in positive values of R and D, and the two constraints $R \geq 0$ and $D \geq 0$ will do this for you.

To summarise, the LP formulation for this problem is:

Max. 5R + 8D

subject to:

$5R + 6D \leq 600$

$R + 2D \leq 160$

$R, D \leq 0$

There are many values of R and D that will satisfy these inequations. For instance, R = 40 and D = 20 would satisfy all the constraints, so this is a feasible combination. The problem is, which combination will give the largest profit?

14.4 Graphical solution of linear programming problems

The formulation of the problem is only the start (but for many students the hardest part). You now have to solve the problem. There are many computer packages on the market that will solve LP problems, but for two variable problems it is possible to solve the problem graphically.

If, for the moment, you replace the inequality signs by equalities, the two main constraints become:

$$5R + 6D = 600 \quad \text{(cotton)}$$

and

$$R + 2D = 160 \quad \text{(labour)}$$

Since these equations contain only two variables, R and D, they can be represented as straight lines and plotted on a graph. Two points are required to plot a straight line and it is convenient to find where they cross the axes. To do this it is simply a matter of letting $R = 0$ and calculating D, and then letting $D = 0$ and calculating R.

Activity 14.5

Plot the two equations, $5R + 6D = 600$ and $R + 2D = 160$ on graph paper.

The points where the two lines cross the axes are summarised in Table 14.1.

Table 14.1 Crossing points for Activity 14.5

Constraint	R	D
Cotton	0	100
	120	0
Labour	0	80
	160	0

These two lines have been plotted on a graph (see Figure 14.1) and they mark the boundaries of the inequations. The *region* satisfying each inequation will be one side of the boundary. In this example the regions for both inequations are *below* the lines. To identify the required region it is normal to shade the *unwanted* region, that is the region not satisfying the inequality. The region that satisfies all inequalities is called the *feasible region* and any point within this region will satisfy all the constraints. From the graph for the Just Shirts example you should be able to identify the feasible region as OABC.

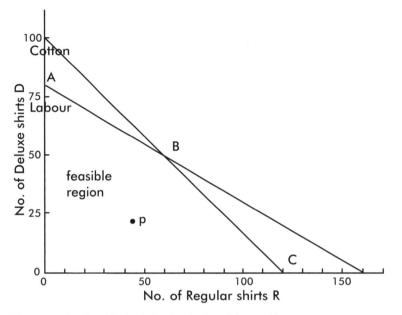

Figure 14.1 Graphical solution for the Just Shirts problem

Any point within the feasible region will satisfy all constraints, but which point or points give the largest profit? Fortunately, this can be found quite easily.

14.5 Finding the optimum – the isoprofit/cost method

The point p (40,20) in Figure 14.1 is in the feasible region and the profit for this combination is:

$$5 \times 40 + 8 \times 20 = £360$$

However, there are other combinations of R and D that give the value of 360, since:

$$5R + 8D = 360$$

Thus the profit equation is just another straight line and can be plotted in the same way as the constraints.

That is, if R = 0, then D = 45

and if D = 0 then R = 72

This line obviously passes through the point p (see Figure 14.2). Can this figure of 360 be increased? If you try, say, a value of 500 so that $5R + 8D = 500$, you will get another straight line that is parallel to the first one. The reason for this is that the gradient of the line stays the same – it is only the intercept on the axes that change. This line is called the *isoprofit* line ('iso' means same).

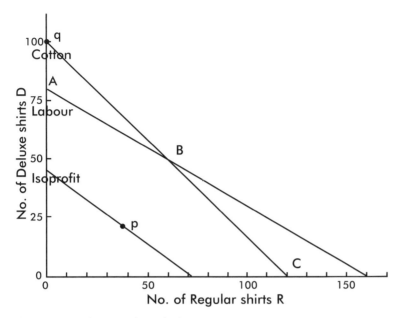

Figure 14.2 The isoprofit method

Activity 14.6

Place a ruler on the isoprofit line and very carefully move it away from the origin and parallel to the line. What is happening to the profit as the isoprofit line moves away from the origin? At what point does it leave the feasible region completely?

You should have found that as the line moves away from the origin the profit increases and you will find that the point B is the point that is furthest away from the origin, yet still within the feasible region. The fact that the optimum point is at a corner point of the feasible region is not a coincidence – *the optimum value will always be found at a corner point of the feasible region.*

The values of R and D at point B can be read off the graph in Figure 14.2. You should find that R = 60 and D = 50 and this gives a profit of:

$$5 \times 60 + 8 \times 50 = \pounds700$$

You may find it surprising that at the optimum solution more Regular Fit shirts are made than Deluxe Fit ones – this is because the Deluxe Fit version uses proportionately more resources.

You found the value of R and D from the graph, but for greater accuracy it is recommended that the relevant equations are solved algebraically. This is particularly important when the graph shows that fractional values are involved or when it is difficult to decide which point is optimal. The method of simultaneous equations (see Section 1.10 of Chapter 1) is used to solve for R and D and is as follows:

$$R + 2D = 160 \qquad \text{equation (1)}$$
$$5R + 6D = 600 \qquad \text{equation (2)}$$

Multiply (1) by 5 and subtract (1) from (2):

$$5R + 10D = 800$$
$$\underline{5R + 6D = 600}$$
$$4D = 200$$

so: $\qquad D = 50$

If D = 50 is now substituted back into (1):

$$R + 100 = 160$$
$$R = 60$$

Which is the solution found from the graph.

NOTE: A word of warning – even if you use simultaneous equations to solve for the two variables, you must still draw the graph first. Without drawing the graph you could quite easily solve pairs of equations outside the feasible region. Also, the optimum point could be on either axis (for example, point A or C in Figure 14.2).

14.6 Finding the optimum – an alternative method

Since you now know that the optimum point must be at a corner point of the feasible region, you could work out the value of the two variables at every corner point. For example, at point A the value of R is zero and D is 80, so the profit must be $8 \times 80 = £640$.

Activity 14.7

Calculate the profits at the other corner points.

The profit for each corner point is shown in Table 14.2.

Table 14.2   Profit at each corner point of the feasible region

	R	D	Profit
Point A	0	80	£640
Point B	60	50	£700
Point C	120	0	£600

These figures confirm that point B gives the greatest profit.

For feasible regions that have few corner points, this method is probably the quickest. However, it is necessary for you to understand the idea of isoprofit lines as this concept is important when looking at sensitivity analysis.

14.7 Tight and slack constraints

If you substitute the optimal values of R (60) and D (50) back into the constraints you will get the following:

Labour: $60 + 2 \times 50 = 160$

Cotton: $5 \times 60 + 6 \times 50 = 600$

Since these values correspond to the maximum quantity of both resources available, the resources are *scarce* and are called *tight* constraints. Where a constraint has not reached its limit it is referred to as a *slack* constraint. For example, if it was not possible to make more than 70 Deluxe Fit shirts, the constraint would be written as $D \leq 70$. This constraint would be slack because the optimal solution has not reached this limit.

14.8 Sensitivity analysis

Linear programming is a deterministic model; that is, all variables are assumed to be known with certainty, so the quantity of cotton available each day was assumed to be exactly 600 square metres and the contribution to profits of the Regular Fit shirt was assumed to be exactly £5. Of course, in reality you will never be 100% certain about the value of many of the parameters in an LP model and the purpose of sensitivity analysis is to ask 'what if' type questions about these parameters. For example, what if more cotton can be purchased, or what if the profit of a Regular Fit shirt increased to £6?

Sensitivity analysis in linear programming is concerned with the change in the right hand side of the constraints (normally the resources) and changes to the objective function coefficients (that is, the profit/costs of each variable).

14.8.1 Changes to the right hand side of a constraint

Both the labour and cotton resource are tight constraints, and an increase in either of these resources will increase the profit made. The reason for this is that as the right hand side of a tight constraint increases, the constraint *and* the optimum point move *away* from the origin.

This can be demonstrated by resolving the simultaneous equations with the right hand side of the labour constraint increased by 1 to 161. That is:

$R + 2D = 161$

$5R + 6D = 600$

Solving these two equations simultaneous as before gives:

R = 58.5   and   D = 51.25

(don't worry about the fractional values for the time being) and the new profit will be £702.50, an increase of £2.50. This £2.50 is called the *shadow price* of the labour resource. It is defined as the change in the value of the objective function if the right hand side is increased (or decreased) by one unit.

Activity 14.8

Calculate the shadow price of the cotton resource.

You should have found that the shadow price of the cotton resource is £0.50 per square metre. That is, an additional profit of 50p could be made for each extra square metre of cotton that could be obtained.

So if it was possible to increase labour hours (perhaps by working overtime) or to increase the supply of cotton, a potentially larger profit could be made. However, this assumes that the direct costs do not increase. If, for instance, overtime rates increase costs by more than £2.50 per hour, then it wouldn't be economic to increase production in this way. However, assuming it is worthwhile, how many more hours should be worked? As the labour constraint moves away from the origin there comes a point where it moves outside the cotton constraint, this is at point q in Figure 14.2. This means that the labour resource ceases to be scarce and further increase of this resource will just add to the surplus of labour. At point q, R = 0 and D = 100, so if these values are substituted into the labour equation you will get:

$0 + 2 \times 100 = 200$

So the labour resource can increase by 40 hours $(200 - 160)$, which means a possible $40 \times 2.50 = £100$ extra profit can be made each day.

Activity 14.9

What additional quantity of cotton would it be worth purchasing and what additional profit would result?

You should have found that the supply of cotton can be increased to 800 square metres per day, which is an additional 200 square metres. The extra profit would be £100.

14.8.2 Changes to the objective function coefficients

The objective function for the Just Shirts example is:

Max. 5R + 8D

Where 5 (in £) is the contribution to profits for each Regular Fit shirt made and 8 is the profit per Deluxe Fit shirt. If it was possible to reduce costs, then profits per shirt would rise, and vice versa, but would the production of 60 Regular Fit shirts and 50 Deluxe Fit shirts remain the optimal solution?

Activity 14.10

Assume that the profit on a Regular Fit shirt has decreased to £2. Redraw the isoprofit line to see if the optimum point has changed.

Figure 14.3 shows the effect on the isoprofit line of reducing the profit of a Regular Fit shirt to £2.

The optimum solution has changed and is now at point A. In this solution you would make 80 Deluxe Fit shirts but no Regular Fit ones.

Although you could find the optimum point each time a change in the profit coefficient was made, it would be much easier if you knew the value of the profit that would cause a change in the optimal solution. If you let the profit be P, the isoprofit line has the equation:

P = 5R + 8D

Rearranging this equation into the form $y = mx + c$ gives:

$$D = -\frac{5}{8}R + \frac{P}{8}$$

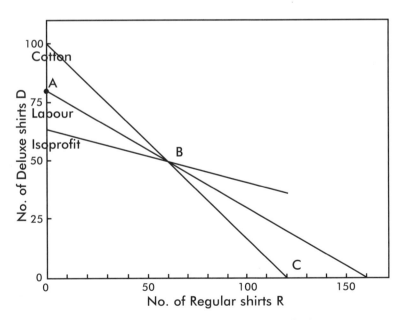

Figure 14.3 Effect on the optimum solution when the profit changes

The gradient of this line is $-\dfrac{5}{8}$. This gradient is simply the profit on a Regular Fit shirt divided by the profit of a Deluxe Fit shirt. If the profit on the Regular Fit shirt is £2 then the gradient of the isoprofit line becomes $-\dfrac{2}{8}$. Now consider what happens as the isoprofit line changes from a gradient of $-\dfrac{5}{8}$ to $-\dfrac{2}{8}$. At some point it must become parallel to the labour constraint line and at this point the same profit will be obtained at both points A and B. (In fact all points along the line AB would give the same profit – this is known as multiple optimal solutions.)

To find the profit of the Regular Fit shirt that would make the isoprofit line parallel to the labour constraint, you need to work out the gradient of this line. Rearranging the equation $R + 2D = 160$ into the standard $y = mx + c$ form will give you:

$$2D = 160 - R$$

that is, $\qquad D = 80 - \dfrac{1}{2} R$

or $\qquad D = -\dfrac{1}{2} R + 80$

The gradient is therefore $-\dfrac{1}{2}$.

You now need to find the value of the profit on a Regular Fit shirt that will give you this gradient. This can be done with the help of some elementary algebra (see Section 1.5 of Chapter 1):

Let x be the unknown value of the profit, then the gradient of the isoprofit line is $-\dfrac{x}{8}$ and

$$-\dfrac{x}{8} = -\dfrac{1}{2}$$

This gives $x = 4$, so if the profit of a Regular Fit shirt falls below £4 the optimum solution changes to point A on the graph ($R = 0$ and $D = 80$). This is the *lower* limit for the profit of the Regular Fit shirt. There is also an upper limit and you are advised to tackle the next activity.

Activity 14.11

Using the same procedure as above, calculate the *upper* value of the Regular Fit profit.

The upper limit can be found when the isoprofit line becomes parallel to BC and since the gradient of the cotton line is $-\dfrac{5}{6}$ the equation becomes:

$$-\dfrac{x}{8} = -\dfrac{5}{6}$$

This gives $x = 6.67$, so if the profit of a Regular Fit shirt rises above £6.67 the optimum solution changes to point C on the graph (R = 120 and D = 0).

Activity 14.12

Calculate the range of the profit of the Deluxe Fit shirt within which the optimal solution stays the same.

This again requires you to find the lower and upper values of the profit. You should have found that this profit range is from £6 to £10.

14.9 Minimisation problems

The Just Shirts example was a maximisation problem because a solution was required that maximised the contribution to profits. However, equally important are minimisation problems in which some objective, for example cost, is to be minimised. The general procedure for dealing with minimisation problems is no different from maximisation problems. A feasible region will still be obtained, but instead of moving your *isocost* line away from the origin, you will be moving it towards the origin. There must be, of course, at least one greater than or equal to constraint, otherwise you will arrive at the origin!

Example 14.2

Ratkins, a local DIY store, has decided to advertise on television and radio but is unsure about the number of adverts it should place. It wishes to minimise the total cost of the campaign and has limited the total number of 'slots' to no more than 5. However, it wants to have at least one slot on both media. The company has been told that one TV slot will be seen by 1 million viewers, while a slot on local radio will only be heard by 100 000 listeners. The company wishes to reach an audience of at least 2 million people. If the cost of advertising is £5000 for each radio slot and £20 000 for each TV slot, how should it advertise?

This problem can be solved by the graphical method of linear programming because there are two variables: the number of radio adverts and the number of TV adverts.

Activity 14.13

Formulate the problem given in Example 14.2.

The formulation for this problem is as follows:

Let R = no. of radio ads, and T = no. of TV ads:

Min 5000R + 20 000T

Subject to:

$0.1R + T \geq 2$ (Minimum audience in millions)

$R + T \quad \leq 5$ (Maximum number of 'slots')

$$\left. \begin{array}{l} R \qquad \geq 1 \\ T \qquad \geq 1 \end{array} \right\}$$ (At least one slot on both)

Activity 14.14

Solve this problem using the graphical method. Is the solution sensible?

The procedure for drawing the graph is the same as for the maximising case. That is, it is necessary to find the points at which the constraints cuts the axes. Table 14.3 gives these values.

Table 14.3 Crossing points for Activity 14.14

Constraint	R	T
Audience	20	2
Total slots	5	5
Min slots for radio	1	0
Min Slots for TV	0	1

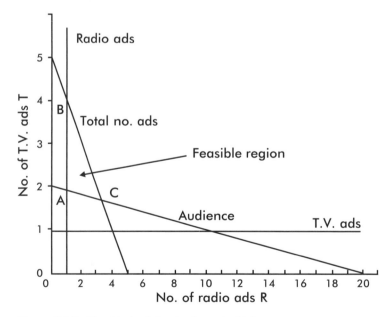

Figure 14.4 Graphical solution for Example 14.2

The graph for this problem is shown in Figure 14.4. You should confirm that the feasible region is given by the area enclosed by ABC. The optimum point will be at one of these corners, and this time it is necessary for you to find the point that gives the *minimum* value. You should have found that the coordinates and hence cost at each of the corner points are as given in Table 14.4.

Table 14.4 Solution to Activity 14.14

	R	T	Cost
A	1	1.9	£43 000
B	1	4	£85 000
C	3.33	1.67	£50 050

Point A gives the minimum cost of £43 000. This solution implies that the company should buy 1 radio advert and 1.9 TV adverts, hardly a sensible solution. Unfortunately, linear programming will give fractional values, and if this is not sensible *integer linear programming* should be used. This technique is not covered in this book, but for two variable problems a more realistic solution can often be found by inspecting the graph. In this particular case it is simply a matter of rounding the 1.9 to 2, which increases the cost to £45 000. However, do take care as rounding can often give you an *infeasible* solution. This can be avoided by checking to see that all constraints are still satisfied. In this example R = 1 and T = 2 does satisfy all 4 constraints.

14.10 Using Excel's 'Solver' to solve linear programming problems

Excel has an add-in called Solver that allows you to solve optimisation problems. It may not be currently installed and if this is the case you will have to install it (see Chapter 12, p. 278).

Activity 14.15

Use Solver to solve Example 14.1 (the shirt problem).

The formulation for this problem was:

Max $5R + 8D$

subject to:

$5R + 6D \leq 600$ (cotton constraint)

$R + 2B \leq 160$ (labour constraint)

$R, D \geq 0$

	A	B	C
1	**Using Solver to solve Example 14.1**		
2			
3		Type	
4	Regular	Deluxe	Profit
5			=5*A5+8*B5
6			
7	Subject to		
8		=5*A5+6*B5	Cotton
9		=A5+2*B5	Labour
10			

Figure 14.5 Setting up the formulae for Solver

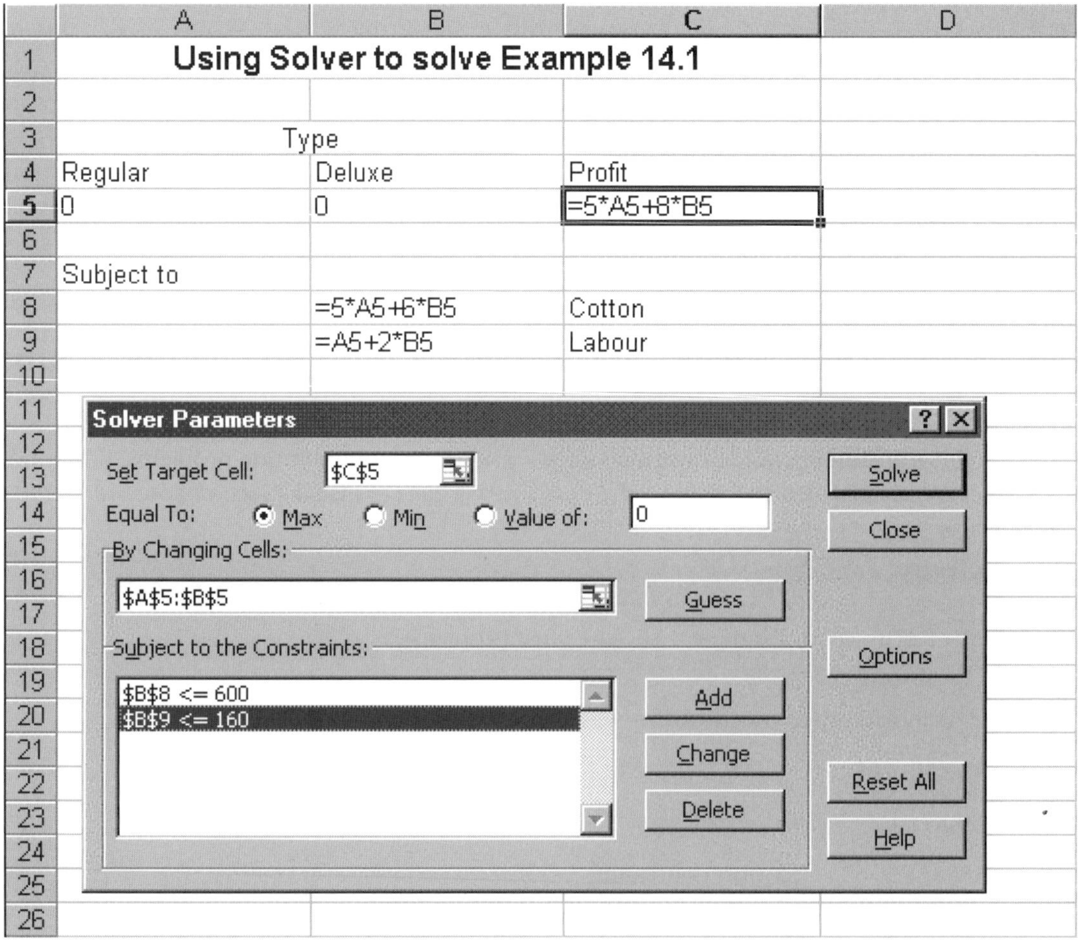

	A	B	C	D
1	**Using Solver to solve Example 14.1**			
2				
3		Type		
4	Regular	Deluxe	Profit	
5	0	0	=5*A5+8*B5	
6				
7	Subject to			
8		=5*A5+6*B5	Cotton	
9		=A5+2*B5	Labour	
10				

Solver Parameters ? X

Set Target Cell: $C$5

Equal To: ⦿ Max ◯ Min ◯ Value of: 0

By Changing Cells:

$A$5:$B$5   Guess

Subject to the Constraints:

$B$8 <= 600
$B$9 <= 160

Add   Change   Delete

Solve   Close   Options   Reset All   Help

Figure 14.6 Adding the Solver parameters

Where R was the number of Regular Fit shirts to make and D was the number of Deluxe Fit shirts to make.

You have to tell Solver the target cell (the cell contents that you wish to optimise), which cells will contain the decision variables, and the constraints. The instructions are as follows:

1. A5 and B5 will be the cells containing the number of Regular Fit and Deluxe Fit shirts to make respectively.

2. Add the formula for the objective function (the profit equation) in cell C5.

3. Add the cotton constraint in cell B8 and the labour constraint in B9.
   Figure 14.5 shows you the worksheet with the formulae that should be in each of these cells.

4. Now click on *Tools* and then *Solver*. In the dialog box:

   > *Set Target Cell* as C5
   > *Equal to*: Max
   > *By Changing Cells* A5:B5
   > *Subject to the Constraints*: Click on *Add*
   > *Cell reference* is B8, the inequality is $\leq$ and the *Constraint* is 600
   > Click on *Add*

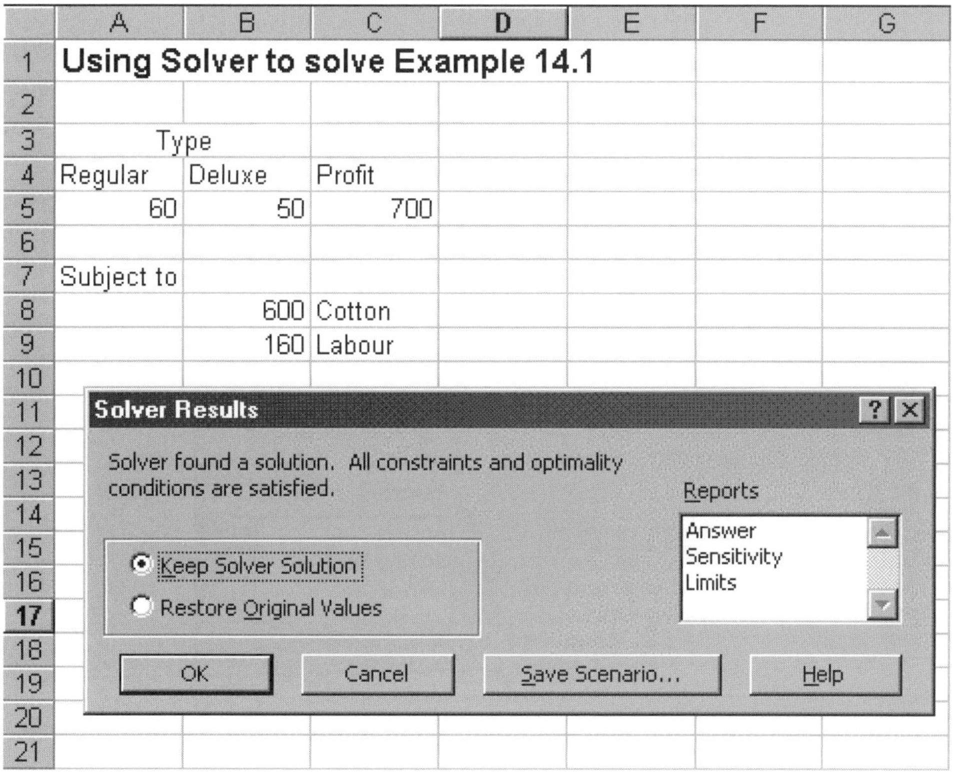

Figure 14.7 Solution found by Solver

Repeat for B9 ≤ 160
Click on *OK*
Click on *Options*. Tick *Assume Non-Negative*, and *Assume Linear Model*.

The *Solver Parameters* should match those shown in Figure 14.6.

5. Click on *Solve*

The solution to the problem can be seen in cells A5 and B5 in Figure 14.7.

The values in cells A5 and B5 are 60 and 50 respectively and the profit of 700 is shown in cell C5. These figures agree with those calculated manually.

Although you can get various sensitivity analysis reports from Solver it is probably easier for simple problems at least to obtain the shadow price by noting the additional profit obtained by increasing each constraint by 1 unit.

Activity 14.16

Use Solver to find the shadow price for the cotton constraints.

From Figure 14.8 you can see that by increasing the cotton resource from 600 to 601 the profit has increased from £700 to £700.50, an increase of £0.50.

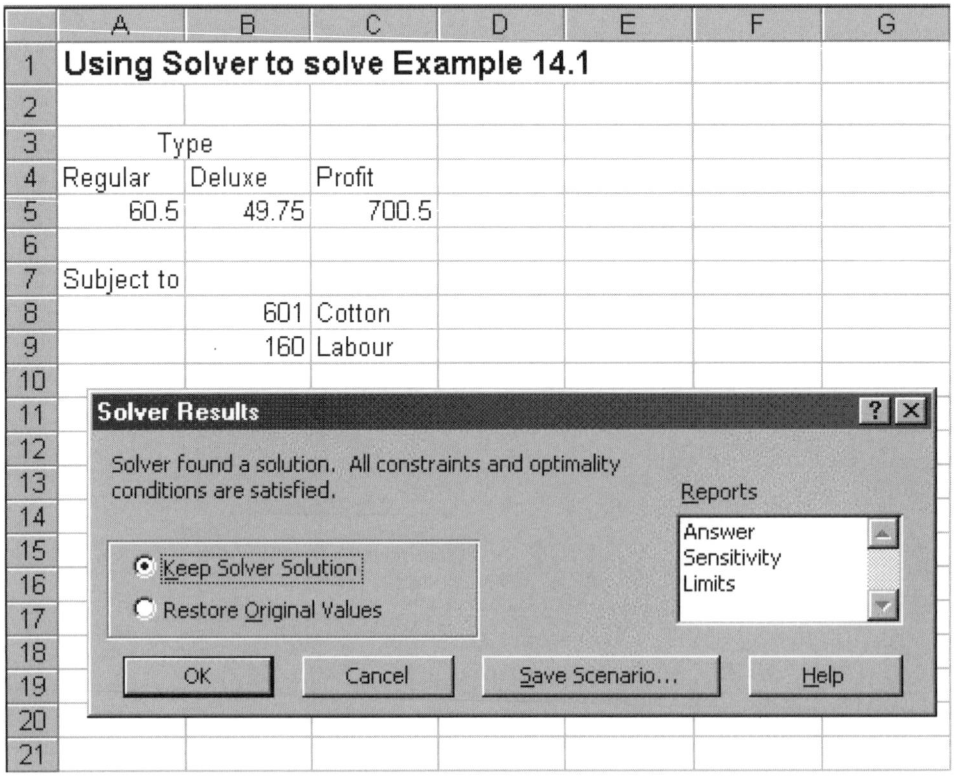

Figure 14.8 Using Solver to find the shadow price of the cotton resource

14.11 Summary

This chapter introduced you to a very important technique called linear programming. This technique is typically used when a number of products share the same scarce resources. However, linear programming can be used for a wide variety of problems, such as blending problems, capital rationing and transportation problems. Two variable problems can be solved by a graphical method, but larger problems require the use of a computer package. Sensitivity analysis can be applied to LP solutions and this will give you information concerning the marginal value of a resource and the sensitivity of the solution to changes of the objective coefficients.

14.12 Further reading

Burton, G., Carrol, G. and Wall, S. (1999) *Quantitative Methods for Business and Economics*, Longman, New York (Chapter 10).
Morris, C. (2000) *Quantitative Approaches in Business Studies*, fourth edition Pitman, London (Chapter 18).

14.13 EXERCISES

The answers to the progress questions, the multiple choice questions and some of the practice questions are given in Appendix 1. Solutions to the remaining questions and the assignment can be found at the web site for this text.

PROGRESS QUESTIONS

These questions have been designed to help you remember the key points in this chapter.

Give the missing word in each case:

1. Linear programming is concerned with the management of .... resources.
2. An LP model consists of an objective and a series of linear ....
3. The graphical method of linear programming can be used to solve .... variable problems.
4. The region satisfying all constraints is called the .... region.
5. The optimal solution of an LP model lies at the corner point of the .... region.
6. A constraint that has reached its limit at the optimal solution is called a .... constraint.
7. The change in the objective function as a result of a unit change to the right hand side of a tight constraint is called the .... price.

ANSWER *TRUE* OR *FALSE*

8. You can only solve LP problems graphically if there are no more than two constraints.
9. The line connecting points with equal profit is called an isoprofit line.

10. The line $x + y = 10$ is a horizontal line.

11. A feasible region must be bounded on all sides by constraints.

REVIEW QUESTIONS

These questions have been designed to help you check your comprehension of the key points in this chapter. You may wish to look further than this chapter in order to answer them fully. You will find the reading list useful in this respect. You can check the essential elements of your answers by referring to the appropriate section.

12. Why is not possible to use the graphical technique to solve an LP problem with more than two variables? (Section 14.2)

13. How important is it to draw a graph for two variable problems? (Section 14.5)

14. Describe the essential differences between a maximisation problem and a minimisation problem. (Sections 14.3 and 14.9)

15. What is the purpose of sensitivity analysis in linear programming? (Section 14.8)

MULTIPLE CHOICE QUESTIONS

16. The line $y = 7$ has a gradient of:

   A... 1   B... 7   C... 0

17. The line $y + 3x = 9$ passes through the point:

   A... (0,9)   B... (9,0)   C... (0,3)

18. To solve an LP model graphically it is best if the scales on each axes are:

   A... The same   B... Different   C... Both start at zero

19 A tight constraint will have a shadow price of:

   A... Zero   B... More than zero

   C... The value of the right hand side of the constraint

PRACTICE QUESTIONS

20. A particular linear programming problem is formulated as follows:

   Min. $Z = 2500x + 3500y$

   Subject to:

   $5x + 6y \geq 250$

   $4x + 3y \geq 150$

   $x + 2y \geq 70$

   $x,y \geq 0$

   Draw these constraints on graph paper and determine the optimum solution.

21. A manufacturer produces two products; P and Q, which when sold earn contributions of £600 and £400 per unit respectively. The manufacture of each product requires time on a lathe and a polishing machine. Each unit of P requires 2 hours on the lathe and 1 hour on the polishing machine, while Q requires 1 hour on each machine. Each day, 10 hours are available on the lathe and 7 hours on the polishing machine. Determine the number of units of P and Q that should be produced per day to maximise contribution.

22. A manufacturer produces a component for diesel engines and a similar component for petrol engines. In the course of production, both components must pass through a machine centre and a testing centre. Diesel engine components spend 4 hours in the machine centre and 2 hours in the testing centre. Petrol engine components spend 2 hours in each centre. There are 16 hours available per day in the machine centre and 12 hours in the testing centre. A contract with a customer stipulates that at least 3 diesel engine components must be produced per day.

    Each diesel component that is produced earns a contribution of £60 and each petrol component earns £45. How many units of each component should be manufactured each day in order to maximise contribution?

23. Bright Lights Ltd manufacture light bulbs for general household use. One design is used in microwave ovens and two types are produced: a low wattage and a high wattage version. The company obtains the glass shells from a supplier who can only supply a maximum of 1500 shells a day. The fitting and testing of the bulbs takes place on special machines of which there are one of each (for fitting and testing) and both machines are available for 10 hours a day. The time to fit and test is different for two bulbs as shown in Table 14.5. Also shown is the contribution to profits for each bulb. The company's objective is to maximise contribution and they want to know how many bulbs of each type they should produce each day.

Table 14.5   Data for Question 23

	Low wattage	High wattage
Fitting (seconds)	20	30
Testing (seconds)	10	30
Contribution (pence)	5	7

(a) Formulate the problem as a linear programming model.
(b) Use Excel Solver to obtain the daily number of each bulb to produce so as to maximise contribution to profits.
(c) How much of each resource (glass shells, fitting time and testing time) are unused at the optimal solution? Would it be worth increasing any of these resources, and, if so, why?

24. A company has been set up in Bristol to manufacture rowing dinghies. Currently they have plans to produce a basic and a deluxe version. The two dinghies are similar and both take 1.5 days to manufacture. However, the deluxe version is much stronger and the profit is higher, as can be seen in Table 14.6.

Table 14.6   Details for Question 24

	Basic	Deluxe
Resin	10 kg	16 kg
Glass Fibre Mat	30 m	50 m
Profit	£50	£80

Due to safety regulations, the company is only allowed to store a limited amount of the raw material, which is 200 kg of resin and 900 m of mat. The required raw material is delivered on a daily basis.

The basic dinghy is likely to be a good seller, but it is assumed that the deluxe dinghy will be limited to a maximum of 9 per day. All boats produced by the end of the day are delivered to a distribution depot as there are no storage facilities available at the plant.

(a) If the current labour force is 27, use the graphical method of linear programming to demonstrate that there are multiple solutions to the problem. Hence suggest a sensible mix of dinghies to produce on a daily basis and show that this results in a profit of £1000 per day.

(b) (i) What is the shadow price of the resin resource?

   (ii) As a result of improved storage facilities more resin can be held at the plant. What is the maximum amount of resin that would be worth storing, and how would this affect the profit calculated in (a)?

25. Revor plc has one production line for the manufacture of the ELEN PLUS and ELEN SUPER ignition systems. Both models use similar components in their manufacture but the SUPER model usually requires more of them and takes longer to produce. Relevant details are shown in Table 14.7.

Table 14.7   Details for Question 25

	ELEN PLUS	ELEN SUPER
No. of component A	4	8
No. of component B	2	3
No. of component C	0	10
Manufacturing time (hours)	5	7

There are supply problems for components A and B and daily usage is limited to 400 and 250 respectively. For component C, the company has entered into a contract with its supplier to take at least 150 per day.

It is also found that at least twice as many ELEN PLUS models are sold as ELEN SUPER, so production should reflect this fact.

The contribution to profits for the PLUS and SUPER models are £60 and £85 respectively.

You can assume that there are 60 employees engaged in the production of these ignition systems and each employee works an 8-hour day.

(a) Formulate this as a linear programming problem, assuming that it is required to maximise profits.

(b) Use the graphical technique of linear programming to determine the optimal numbers of ELEN PLUS and ELEN SUPER models to produce each day. What is the daily profit associated with this production?

(c) Identify the scarce resources (tight constraints) for this problem. For each determine the shadow price. It is possible to purchase additional quantities of component A from an alternative supplier at a premium of £10 per component. Would it be worthwhile?

(d) The unit costs associated with the production of these systems is known to vary. However, the selling price is only changed annually. How much can the profit on the ELEN PLUS model be allowed to vary before the optimal solution found in (b) changes?

ASSIGNMENT

The food department at Riglen plc has brought out a new breakfast cereal called Hi-Fibre, which uses a concentrated form of fibre developed by Riglen's research laboratory. This product has been test marketed in a few selected areas and the consumer reaction has been favourable. However, several people questioned said that they would prefer a higher fibre content, so Dave Smith, the Product Manager, has decided to meet this demand with an additional product called Hi-Fibre Plus. This product will have double the fibre content of Hi-Fibre and will require additional cooking time. The selling price of Hi-Fibre Plus will be greater than for Hi-Fibre and the contribution to profits also will be higher. For Hi-Fibre, the contribution will be 12p per 500 g packet, and for Hi-Fibre Plus ijit will be 15p per 500 g packet.

During the period of test marketing, 500 packets of the product were produced each day. However, from a commercial point of view at least 2500 packets of each product must be produced daily and it is expected that demand will soon exceed this figure. Dave's problem is that he is unsure of the quantities of each product to produce. Even if he assumes that he can sell all that he makes, the resources at his disposal are limited. The storage area can take a maximum of 12 000 packets, so total daily production of the cereal cannot exceed this figure. He has one oven and one packaging plant that operates for 12 hours a day and the supply of concentrated fibre is, for the moment, restricted to 120 kg per day. There is no practical limit to the other ingredients.

Dave Smith has asked you to use the technique of linear programming to solve his production problem and he has given you the following additional information:

	Hi-Fibre	Hi-Fibre Plus
Cooking/packaging	3 seconds	5 seconds
Fibre content	5 g	10 g

All figures are based on 500 g of cereal.

(a) Formulate this problem in LP terms with the objective of maximising contribution to profits.

(b) Use the graphical technique of linear programming to solve this problem.

(c) How much of each resource (that is fibre, storage space and the working day) is left after the optimal quantities of cereal are produced? Which resources are 'scarce' (that is, all used up)?

(d) Is it worthwhile increasing any of the scarce resources? and by how much? The additional cost of increasing fibre production is £20 per kg; storage space would work out at 20p per packet and extending the working day would incur costs of £30 per hour.

(e) Would the optimal solution change if the profit contribution of either product changed?

(f) The sales department believes that the demand for Hi-fibre Plus will be greater than for Hi-Fibre. If this is correct, production of Hi-Fibre Plus needs to be higher than Hi-Fibre. What increase in profit contribution of Hi-Fibre Plus will be necessary if the total profit is to remain the same?

15 Critical path analysis

15.1 Introduction

Whenever a large or complex project is undertaken a great deal of planning is necessary. Building a house is a good example as there are many tasks or activities that have to be completed, some of which can proceed at the same time while others have to wait until preceding tasks are completed. Without careful planning, you might find that materials for a particular activity are not delivered on time or an electrician is not available when he is required. Delays in the project would result and you would find that the cost is far higher than it should be. This chapter introduces a number of techniques that are used in the planning and control of large projects.

On completing this chapter you should be able to:

● Construct an 'activity-on-node' network to represent a project
● Calculate the earliest and latest start and finish times for each activity
● Calculate the float for each activity and identify the critical path
● Use a Gantt chart and resource histogram to smooth the use of resources required by a project
● Apply the technique of cost scheduling

15.2 The activity-on-node method

This technique allows the time of the project and the slack (or *float*) of individual activities to be determined. If an activity has zero float you would say that it was *critical* because any delay in that activity would delay the entire project.

Before critical path analysis (or CPA) is used it is first necessary to make a list of all the activities, their durations and which activities must immediately precede them.

Example 15.1

You have just obtained planning permission to build a garage and you are now in the process of planning the project. With a little help from a friendly builder you have made a list of activities that need to be completed, the durations of these activities and the order in which they can be tackled. This list is shown in Table 15.1.

Table 15.1 Details of the garage building project

Activity	Description	Immediate preceding activities	Duration (days)
A	Obtain bricklayer	–	10
B	Dig the foundations	–	8
C	Lay the base	B	1
D	Build the walls	A and C	8
E	Build the roof	D	3
F	Tile the roof	E	2
G	Make window frames	–	3
H	Fit the window frames	D and G	1
I	Fit glass to frames	H	1
J	Fit the door	E	1
K	Paint the door and window frames	I and J	2
L	Point the brickwork	D	2

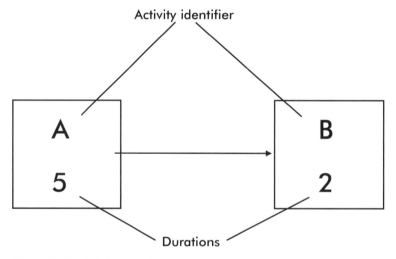

Figure 15.1 Activity-on-node

Once this list has been completed, you should represent the project by the means of a diagram. The diagram used in this book uses the *activity-on-node* method. The basic diagram for this method is shown in Figure 15.1. The nodes represent the activity and the lines the dependencies between activities.

Activity 15.1

Draw the network for the garage problem using the activity-on-node method.

The basic diagram for the garage problem is shown in Figure 15.2. You will see that the name of each activity is displayed in the box together with the duration. You will also see that there are start and end nodes. This is to ensure that every activity has at least one line entering and one line leaving its node.

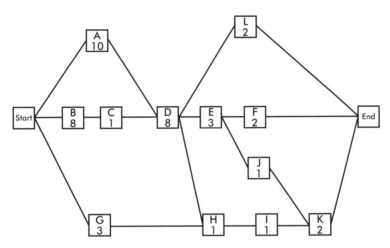

Figure 15.2 The network for the garage problem

For this method you need to display 4 additional pieces of information on each node: the earliest start time of the activity (EST), the latest start time (LST), the earliest finish time (EFT), and the latest finish time (LFT). This information should be displayed as in Figure 15.3.

In order to calculate the EST and EFT a *forward pass* is made through the network. If the start is at time zero, then the EST of activities A, B and G is zero and their EFT is 10, 8

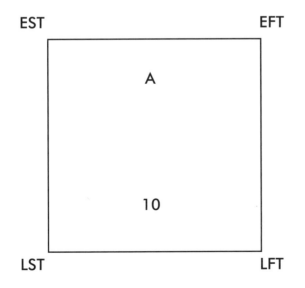

Figure 15.3 Information displayed on each node

and 3 respectively. The EST of activity C must be 8, since it can start as soon as B is completed. However, what about activity D? This activity cannot start until both A and C are completed, and as A is completed later than C, then activity A determines the EST of D, which must be 10. This is the general rule when calculating the EST – if there are two or more choices the EST is the *larger* of the EFTs of the preceding activities. From this you will see that the EST of K must be 22 and not 20.

Activity 15.2

Continue the forward pass through the network and add this information to your network. How long will it take you to complete the project?

You can now check your answers with Figure 15.4. From this diagram you will see that the project will take 24 days in total.

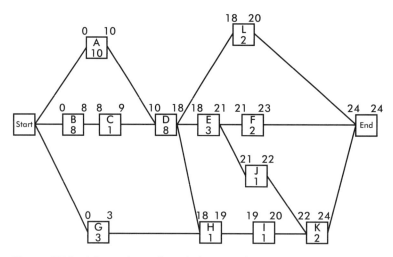

Figure 15.4 A forward pass through the network

To enable the LFT and LST to be calculated a *backward pass* is made through the network, starting at the END node. The LFT of activities F, K and L must be 24 since the project is only complete when all these activities have been completed. The LST of F, K and L must all be 22 days since the duration of all three activities is 2 days. To calculate the LFT of all other activities involves a process similar to that for the forward pass, with one difference, which is that when there is a choice, the *smallest* value is chosen.

Activity 15.3

Continue the backward pass through the network.

Figure 15.5 shows the completed network.

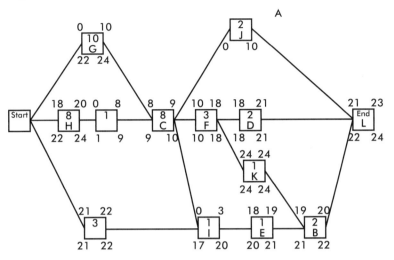

Figure 15.5 The completed network

15.3 The float of an activity

The float or slack of an activity is the difference between the EST and LST (or between the EFT and LFT) for each activity. For example, activity D has a zero float since the EST and LST are the same (10), while activity F has a float of 1 day $(22 - 21)$.

Activity 15.4

Obtain the floats for the remainder of the activities. Which activities are 'critical'; that is, have no float?

You should have obtained the information shown in Table 15.2.

Table 15.2 Calculation of the floats

Activity	EST	LST	Float
A	0	0	0
B	0	1	1
C	8	9	1
D	10	10	0
E	18	18	0
F	21	22	1
G	0	17	17
H	18	20	2
I	19	21	2
J	21	21	0
K	22	22	0
L	18	22	4

From this you can see that activities A, D, E, J and K have zero floats and are therefore *critical*. Any delay in the start or finish times of these activities would delay the entire project by the same amount. The other activities could be delayed by up to their float without affecting the overall project time. For example, activity B (dig foundations) could be delayed by one day, but this activity would then become critical. You will notice that the critical activities form a path through the network – this is called the *critical path*. However, it is possible to have more than one critical path, as you will see in Section 15.5.

15.4 Resource scheduling

Activities of a project often involve resources of one kind or another. In the garage building example, labour is the obvious resource since each activity requires people to do the work. Perhaps you have asked a friend or neighbour to help and the two of you intend to help the bricklayer and do the less skilled jobs.

Example 15.2

For each activity in the garage building project you decide how many people are required to do these jobs, and you get the list shown in Table 15.3.

Table 15.3 Resource requirements for the garage project

Activity	No. of people required
A	0
B	2
C	2
D	1
E	1
F	2
G	1
H	1
I	1
J	2
K	1
L	1

Since some activities, such as digging the foundations and making the window frames, can take place at the same time, the number of people required at a particular time may be greater than the availability. However, it may be possible to delay non-critical activities, such as making the window frames, sufficiently to avoid this problem. The critical path network cannot easily solve this problem because this network is designed to show the order in which activities take place rather than *when* they take place. A better chart to use is the *Gantt* chart. A Gantt chart is like a bar chart that has been turned on its side. The horizontal axis is time and each activity is represented by a bar; the start of the bar is initially the EST and the end of the bar is the EFT. The float of an activity is represented by a dotted line.

Activity 15.5

Draw the Gantt chart for the garage project.

This chart is shown in Figure 15.6.

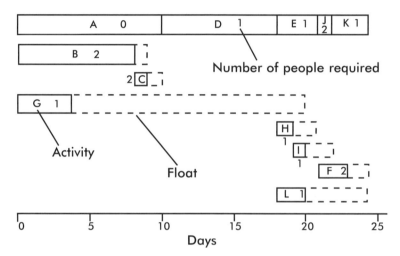

Figure 15.6 The Gantt chart

You will see that the bars representing the critical activities have all been placed on one line – this is because each activity follows one another on the critical path. The non-critical activities should, however, be placed on separate lines so that their floats can be clearly shown. The number of people required has been added to each bar. From this you can see that 3 people are required during the first 3 days $(0 + 2 + 1)$.

Activity 15.6

Repeat this procedure for the entire project. When are more than 2 people required?

The figures are shown in Table 15.4.

You can see that more that 2 people are required on several occasions. You might find this easier to see on the *resource histogram* in Figure 15.7.

From this histogram you will see clearly the peaks and troughs in the resource requirements. If a peak could be moved into a trough, the net result would be a smoother histogram. A perfectly smooth histogram would mean that the resource is being fully utilised and no further savings would be possible. In the case of the garage it would be

Table 15.4 Daily resource requirement

Day	Number of people required
First 3 days	3
Next 6 days	2
Next day	0
Next 8 days	1
Next 2 days	3
Next day	1
Next day	4
Next day	3
Next day	1

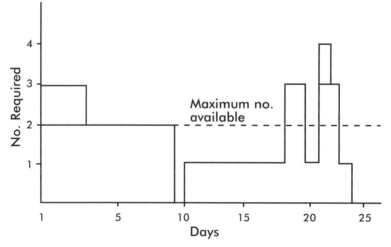

Figure 15.7 The resource histogram

possible to delay the start of activity G (make window frames) until day 9, since G has a float of 17 days. This would mean that from the start of the project until day 12, 2 people would be required all the time. The peaks at the end of the project are not so easy to solve. If the start of activity F (tile the roof) was delayed by its float of one day, the peak of 4 people during day 21 could be reduced by 1, so 3 people are required for much of the latter part of the project. The alternative to increasing the number of people is to extend the project. For example, if the critical activities J (fitting the door) and K (painting) were delayed until activity F had been completed, the completion of the project would be delayed by 2 days but only 2 people would be required for the entire time.

15.5 Cost scheduling

A very important resource in network analysis is money. This resource is usually so important that a separate technique has been devised to solve problems posed by financial considerations. This technique is called *crashing*.

It is usually desirable to reduce the time a project takes because there are often financial advantages in doing so. For example, the Department of Transport pays a bonus to contractors who complete a road building or repair project early (and a penalty is charged if the project time is overrun). It is often possible to speed up the completion of an activity at an extra cost. This cost may be because a machine is hired or because more people are employed. The reduced duration is called the *crashed* duration, and the increased cost is called the *crashed* cost.

Example 15.3

It is possible to reduce the time for completing activities B, D, E, F, G, K and L of the garage building project by employing additional labour. If this is done costs will increase for these activities. Table 15.5 gives you the durations and costs for all activities.

Table 15.5 Cost details for the garage project

Activity	Normal duration (days)	Crash duration (days)	Normal cost	Crash cost
A	10	10	£5	£5
B	8	2	£100	£700
C	1	1	£200	£200
D	8	5	£800	£1700
E	3	2	£500	£900
F	2	1	£200	£400
G	3	1	£150	£550
H	1	1	£50	£50
I	1	1	£20	£20
J	1	1	£20	£20
K	2	1	£30	£130
L	2	1	£100	£200

Activity 15.7

What is the normal total cost of the project?

The total cost is simply the sum of *all* the activities, since all must be completed. This is £2175. If some of the activities are crashed this cost will increase. The question is which activities should be crashed in order to reduce the project time to a minimum but without incurring unnecessary costs.

Activity 15.8

Would it be worth crashing all the activities identified above?

The answer to this question is no because not all the activities are on the critical path. Even if they were, some of the activities are more economic to crash than others. For instance, activity D costs £300 per day to crash (an extra cost of £900 and a time reduction of 3 days) while activity E costs £400 per day. The objective of crashing should be to find the minimum project duration at the minimum extra cost. In order to satisfy this objective it is first necessary to find the cost per day of *all* activities. This is necessary as the crashing can make non-critical activities become critical.

Activity 15.9

Calculate the cost per day for activities B, D, E, F, G, K and L using the information given in Table 15.5.

This calculation is summarised in Table 15.6.

Table 15.6   Daily cost of crashing

Activity	Time reduction (days)	Extra cost	Cost/day
B	6	£600	£100
D	3	£900	£300
E	1	£400	£400
F	1	£200	£200
G	2	£400	£200
K	1	£100	£100
L	1	£100	£100

The next step is to write down all the paths through the network together with their durations. (Path GHIK can be ignored because it has a relatively short duration.)

Activity 15.10

Make a list of all major paths through the network.

You should have found 8 major paths, which are shown in Table 15.7.

Table 15.7   Paths through the network

Path	Duration
ADEJK	24
BCDEJK	23
ADEF	23
ADHIK	22
BCDEF	22
BCDHIK	21
ADL	20
BCDL	19

Path ADEJK must be reduced first because it is the longest path through the network and therefore the critical path. Activities D, E and K can be crashed, but, of the 3, K is the cheapest. If K is crashed by 1 day then not only will the duration of path ADEJK be reduced by 1, but so will paths BCDEJK, ADHIK and BCDHIK. The project duration has now been reduced by 1 day at a cost of £100, but path ADEF is now critical, in addition to ADEJK. These 2 paths must now be crashed together. Both D and E are common to these 2 paths and, since D is the cheapest, this will be crashed by 3 days at a cost of £900. Finally, E is crashed by 1 day to reduce the project duration to 19 days at a cumulative extra cost of £1400. No further crashing is worthwhile because it is not possible to crash both critical paths (only F has any crashing capability left). You might find it easier to write the necessary steps in a table similar to the one shown in Table 15.8.

Table 15.8   Steps involved in crashing the network

Path	Duration	Step 1	Step 2	Step 3
ADEJK	24	23	20	19
BCDEJK	23	22	19	18
ADEF	23	23	20	19
ADHIK	22	21	18	18
BCDEF	22	22	19	18
BCDHIK	21	20	17	17
ADL	20	20	17	17
BCDL	19	19	16	16
Activities crashed		K – 1	D – 3	E – 1
Extra cost		£100	£900	£400
Cumulative extra cost		£100	£1000	£1400

Is it worthwhile reducing the project time by 5 days at an extra cost of £1400? It may be that you are paying someone by the day to help you and any reduction in time would save you this 'overhead' charge. For example, suppose you were paying this person £150 per day. It would be worthwhile crashing K because for an expenditure of £100 you would save £150; a net gain of £50. However, it wouldn't be worthwhile crashing D because for each day saved it has cost you £150 (£300 − £150).

15.6 Summary

This chapter introduced you to some very useful techniques for planning and monitoring a project that involves many interdependent activities. The activity-on-node method was used to draw the network diagram. From this network it was possible to obtain the total time that the project will take and the floats of each activity. Where an activity has a zero float it is called 'critical', and any delay in this activity will delay the entire project. The activity-on-node diagram shows you how the activities are related, but it doesn't very easily show you when they occur. The Gantt chart is better for this purpose and this chart can be used to smooth the resources over time. Finally, the technique of crashing was introduced. This technique allows you to speed up a project at minimum extra cost.

15.7 Further reading

Anderson, Sweeney and Williams (1994) *An Introduction to Management Science*, seventh edition, West Publishing Company (Chapter 10).

15.8 EXERCISES

The answers to the progress questions, the multiple choice questions and some of the practice questions are given in Appendix 1. Solutions to the remaining questions and the assignment can be found at the web site for this text.

PROGRESS QUESTIONS

These questions have been designed to help you remember the key points in this chapter.
Give the missing word in each case:

1. EST stands for earliest .... time.
2. A .... pass through the network is used to obtain the EST and EFT for each activity.
3. A .... pass through the network is used to obtain the LST and LFT for each activity.
4. A critical activity has .... float.

ANSWER *TRUE* OR *FALSE*

5. It is not possible to have more than one critical path in a network.
6. Every activity node must have at least one line leaving it.
7. 'Float' is the difference between the EST and EFT.
8. To reduce the time for a project you must reduce the durations of the critical path.

REVIEW QUESTIONS

These questions have been designed to help you check your comprehension of the key points in this chapter. You may wish to look further than this chapter in order to answer them fully. You will find the reading list useful in this respect. You can check the essential elements of your answers by referring to the appropriate section.

9. What are the essential features of the activity-on-node method for representing a project? (Section 15.2)
10. Why is it important to know the critical activities of a project? (Section 15.3)
11. Describe the essential differences between a CPA chart and a Gantt chart. (Sections 15.2 and 15.4)

MULTIPLE CHOICE QUESTIONS

12. A Gantt chart is used to:

    A... Show how activities are related

    B... Show when activities take place

    C... Enable the critical path to be evaluated

    D... Show resources used over time

13. A resource histogram is used to:

    A... Show how activities are related

    B... Show when activities take place

    C... Enable the critical path to be evaluated

    D... Show resources used over time

14. Crashing is the term used when:

    A... The project time has to be reduced at minimum extra cost.

    B... Insufficient resources are available for the project to be completed on time.

    C... The cost of a project has to be reduced.

15. If the EST and LST of an activity are 12 and 14 respectively, the float for this activity is:

    A... zero   B... 2   C... 26

PRACTICE QUESTIONS

16. Please refer to Figure 15.8 for this question.

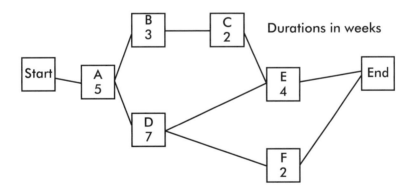

Figure 15.8   Diagram for Question 16

(a) How long will the project take?

(b) How much float has activity D?

(c) How much float has activity F?

(d) If activity B takes 3 weeks longer than expected, will the project be delayed?

(e) If activity B requires 3 people continuously, D requires 2 people and C requires 1 person, how many people are required during week 6?

17. Yachtsteer manufacture a self-steering device for pleasure yachts and, as a result of increased competition from foreign manufacturers, it has decided to design and manufacture a new model in time for the next Boat Show. As a first step in planning the project, the following major tasks and durations have been identified.

Table 15.9   Details for Question 17

	Task	Time (weeks)	Preceding tasks
A	Design new product	8	–
B	Design electronics	4	–
C	Organise production facilities	4	A
D	Obtain production materials	2	A
E	Manufacture trial gear	3	C, D
F	Obtain electronic circuit boards	2	B
G	Decide on yacht for trials	1	–
H	Assemble trial gear and electronics	2	E, F
I	Test product in workshops	3	H, G
J	Test product at sea	4	I
K	Assess product's performance	3	J
L	Plan national launch	4	K

Draw a network to represent the logical sequence of tasks and determine how long it will be before the new product can be launched.

18. Shipways boatyard undertakes spring refits on cabin cruisers and yachts, and in the past the company has received complaints from customers regarding the time taken to complete the job. As a consequence the Project Manager, Alan Waters, has decided to carry out a critical path analysis on the cabin cruiser refit. Table 15.10 gives, for each activity, the duration, immediate preceding activities and the number of yard assistants required.

Table 15.10   Details for Question 18

Activity	Description	Duration (days)	Immediate preceding activities	Yard assistants required
A	Bring craft up slipway	1	–	2
B	Check and overhaul seacocks, etc.	3	A	1
C	Scrape and prepare hull for painting	7	A	2
D	Paint hull	4	C	1
E	Remove engine	2	A	3
F	Overhaul engine	16	E	1
G	Clean and paint engine bilges	3	E	1
H	Refit engine	3	F and G	3
I	Apply antifoul paint to hull	2	D and H	2
J	Refloat	1	B and I	2

NOTE: The reason that I follows from both D and H is that a boat must be refloated no more than 48 hours after the antifouling paint has been applied. Antifouling should not therefore be started until the boat is ready for the water.

(a) Draw the network and determine how long the refit will take. What are the critical activities and how much float do the non-critical activities have?

(b) (i) Draw a Gantt chart and resource histogram for the refit. What is the maximum number of yard workers required and when is this required?

    (ii) Unfortunately there are only 4 yard workers available during the period of the refit. Using your Gantt chart and/or histogram reschedule the activities so that no more than 4 yard workers will be required.

19. Revor plc are urgently planning the production of their new lightweight car battery, the 'Epsilon'. They would like to exhibit their battery at a trade fair, which is to take place in 48 weeks' time. Various activities had to take place before production could start, and these are shown in Table 15.11.

Table 15.11 Activities for Question 19

	Task	Preceding tasks	Duration (weeks)
A	Clear area	–	20
B	Commission consulting engineers to design equipment	–	2
C	Receive consultant's report	B	10
D	Place equipment out to tender	C	1
E	Obtain equipment	D	6
F	Install equipment	A, E	30
G	Recruit additional staff	C	6
H	Train new staff	G	4
I	Order and obtain materials	–	16
J	Pilot production run	F, H, I	3
K	Advertise new product	–	2

(a) Draw the network and show that it is not possible to start production within 48 weeks. What are the critical activities and how much total float do the non-critical activities have?

(b) It is possible to 'crash' (i.e., reduce the duration of) certain activities at increased cost. These activities are shown in Table 15.12.

Table 15.12 Crash and cost details for Question 19

Activity	Crashed duration (weeks)	Normal cost (£000's)	Crashed cost (£000's)
A	18	4	10
E	5	1	3
F	28	15	27
I	8	0.5	8.5
J	2	16	26

(i) Ron Smith the Production Manager suggests that only activity I need be crashed because this is the cheapest option and allows the greatest reduction in time to be made. Explain why this would not help the situation.

(ii) It has been estimated that for every week over 48 weeks that this project takes, a loss of £8000 is made as a result of lost profits. Decide on the strategy that will minimise the sum of crashed costs and loss of profits.

20. A painting and decorating firm has decided to use critical path analysis in order to plan its next job. The activities of this job are as shown in Table 15.13.

Table 15.13   Activities for Question 20

Activity	Description	Duration (days)	Preceding activities	Number of operatives
A	Order materials	3	None	0
B	Remove curtains and cover furniture	0.5	None	1
C	Wash interior woodwork	2	B	1
D	Sand outside woodwork	1	None	2
E	Paint ceilings	2	A & C	2
F	Paint interior woodwork	4	E	3
G	Paint exterior woodwork	5	A & D	2
H	Hang wallpaper	2	F	4
I	Remove covers and replace curtains	0.5	H	1
J	Clean up and depart	0.5	G & I	4

(a) Draw a network representing the sequence of activities and the interdependencies between them.

(b) Determine how long it will take to complete the job and identify the critical activities.

(c) If it were to rain for 4 out of the 5 days allocated for painting the exterior woodwork, what effect would this have on the duration of the job? (Assume that it is dry for the remaining time.)

(d) It has now been decided to analyse the labour requirements for this job. Using graph paper, draw a Gantt chart for the job (assuming earliest start times apply). What is the maximum number of operatives required and when does this occur? Unfortunately, only 4 operatives are available. Explain how this will affect the time taken to complete the job.

ASSIGNMENT

There have been recurring problems with the food canning process at Riglen plc and a decision has been taken at Board level to replace the machinery with more modern computer controlled equipment. Holder and Holder Consulting Engineers have been commissioned to advise on the system to purchase and their report is expected in 5 weeks' time. Although the fine details of the recommended system will not be known until this report has been received, the essential characteristics of all the alternatives are the same. Planning for the installation can therefore start immediately, and this is important because during the installation all food canning has to be contracted out and this will be expensive.

In order to ensure that the project is completed as quickly as possible and at minimum cost, you have been asked to use the relevant network analysis techniques on the data given in Table 15.14.

Table 15.14 Details for the assignment

Activity	Description	Duration	Immediate predecessors	Fitters required	Cost (£000's)
A	Obtain report	5	–	0	5
B	Remove existing machinery	4	–	8	3
C	Purchase new machinery	5	A	0	50
D	Purchase electrics	7	A	0	15
E	Purchase computers	6	A	0	25
F	Install machinery	4	B and C	5	5
G	Install computers	3	E	6	5
H	Connect electrics	3	F and D	2	4
I	Recruit and train staff	6	–	0	3
J	Pilot production run	1	G and H	6	6
K	Prepare for full production	4	I and J	5	2

You should also note that fitters are to be employed on a fixed-term contract, and it is important that only the minimum number necessary are recruited.

(a) Draw the network and calculate the start and finish times for each activity. How long will the project take, and what are the critical activities?

(b) Draw a Gantt chart for this project. What is the maximum number of fitters required, and during what weeks does this occur? What is the minimum number of fitters required that will still allow the project to be completed in the time found in (a) above?

(c) An attempt is to be made to reduce the total project time since for every week's reduction a saving of £10 000 can be achieved through not having to contract out the week's canning. This will be possible because some activities such as B can be completed in less time than scheduled. Of course, this reduction in time will be at an increased cost. The activities that can be reduced (crashed) in time are given in Table 15.15.

Table 15.15 Cost of crashing activities

Activity	Normal time (weeks)	Crashed time (weeks)	Normal cost (£000's)	Crashed cost (£000's)
B	4	2	10	16
D	7	6	15	21
F	6	3	5	20
G	3	2	5	12
K	4	3	2	10

(i) What is the total normal cost of the project, including the £10 000 per week canning charge?

(ii) Using the figures above, calculate for each activity the cost of reducing the time by one week.

(iii) Starting with the critical path, make a list of all paths through the network. Alongside each path write down the duration in weeks of the path.

(iv) Try and reduce the critical path to the same duration as the next largest in the cheapest way possible. Now reduce both paths until the duration is equal to the next highest path and so on. Repeat this until no more reduction is possible. What is the new total cost of the project?

(v) What is the project duration that will minimise the total cost of the project?

Inventory control

16.1 Introduction

Holding stock is a very expensive business, particularly where the goods are of high value. However, even for small value items the cost can be high if the quantities involved are large enough. This chapter looks at some methods for determining the cheapest stock control policies. You will find it useful to have some knowledge of the normal distribution (see Chapter 8) for Section 16.5 of this chapter.

On completing this chapter you should be able to:

- Calculate the costs associated with holding stocks
- Calculate the order quantity that minimises these costs
- Decide whether buying in bulk to obtain a price discount is worthwhile
- Calculate a buffer stock to avoid stock-outs
- Appreciate the limitations of the EOQ model

16.2 Costs of holding stock

There are many costs associated with holding (or not holding) stock. Some of these are:

- warehouse costs
- money tied up in stock (interest charges)
- damage while in storage
- deterioration while in storage
- obsolescence
- ordering costs
- delivery costs
- cost of any 'stock-outs'

Warehouse costs include things like rental charges, heating and wages. Money that is tied up in stock could be earning money (or reducing overdraft charges). A certain proportion of goods will be damaged while in the warehouse or may be stolen and certain products deteriorate (for example, food), while other items may become obsolete if stored too long (last year's computer will be worth less than the latest version). In addition to the costs directly associated with the holding of stock, there is also the cost of ordering and delivery. Most large companies will have a buying department and this means that there must be a cost associated with ordering. Even if only telephone and postage were costed, each order would still cost a finite amount. Finally there is a cost of a 'stock-out'; that is, the cost of not having sufficient stock to meet demand. For each sale not made as a result of a stock-out the company will lose the profit on this sale, but in addition they may lose future sales if customers find a more reliable supplier.

If the case for and against holding stock can be resolved on cost alone, then it is a matter of minimising the total cost associated with an inventory policy. There are many inventory control models that do this; some are quite simple deterministic models, while others can accommodate uncertainty or handle many different goods at the same time. For particularly complex inventory control systems, simulation may be used to arrive at the best policy (see Chapter 17).

All models will tell you *how much to order* and *when to order*. The simplest model is the Economic Order Quantity model, which will now be described.

16.3 The Economic Order Quantity (EOQ) model

The assumptions that have to be made before this model can be used are as follows:

- Demand is known and constant

- Lead time is constant

- Only one item is involved

- Stock is monitored on a continuous basis and an order is made when the stock level reaches a *re-order* point

- When an order arrives, the stock level is replenished instantaneously

- Stock-outs do not occur

Figure 16.1 may help you picture the general problem. An order quantity Q arrives and is used up at a constant rate, until the stock level reaches zero, at which point a new order arrives.

For small values of Q more frequent ordering will be necessary and hence order costs will be high, while large values of Q will increase the quantity in store and therefore increase the storage costs. The problem is to determine the value of Q that minimises the sum of the order and storage costs.

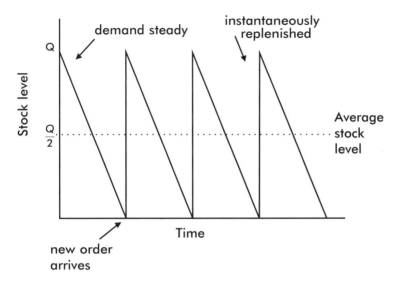

Figure 16.1 The Economic Order Quantity (EOQ) model

If the cost of placing an order is represented by the letter C, then the total order cost is simply the number of orders made multiplied by C. If D is the demand over a specified time period, then the number of orders made must be $\frac{D}{Q}$ and the order cost is:

$$C \times \frac{D}{Q}$$

To calculate the storage cost it is assumed that the cost of holding one unit in stock for a specified time period is known. This cost is represented by b. As the amount in stock varies we need to calculate the average stock level, and from Figure 16.1 you can see that this must be $\frac{Q}{2}$. Hence the storage cost is:

$$b \times \frac{Q}{2}$$

Example 16.1

Imagine that you work for Game World and you have been asked to decide on the best inventory control policy for the computer game 'Aliens'. You are told that the demand is fairly constant at 5000 units p.a. and it costs £14.40 to place an order. You are also told that the storage cost of holding one unit of the game per annum is £10.

In order to investigate how inventory costs vary with order size, you decide to work out the order and storage costs for different order quantities.

For an order size of 20:

$$\text{Order cost} = C \times \frac{D}{Q}$$

$$= 14.4 \times \frac{5000}{20}$$

$$= \pounds 3600 \, \text{p.a.}$$

$$\text{Storage cost} = b \times \frac{Q}{2}$$

$$= 10 \times \frac{20}{2}$$

$$= \pounds 100 \, \text{p.a.}$$

$$\text{Total cost} = \pounds 3600 + \pounds 100$$

$$= \pounds 3700 \, \text{p.a.}$$

Activity 16.1

Repeat this calculation for order quantities from 40 to 200 units.

The results of the calculations are shown in Table 16.1.

Table 16.1 Calculation of inventory costs

Q	Order cost (£)	Storage Cost (£)	Total Cost (£)
20	3600.0	100.0	3700.0
40	1800.0	200.0	2000.0
60	1200.0	300.0	1500.0
80	900.0	400.0	1300.0
100	720.0	500.0	1220.0
120	600.0	600.0	1200.0
140	514.3	700.0	1214.3
160	450.0	800.0	1250.0
180	400.0	900.0	1300.0
200	360.0	1000.0	1360.0

From this table it appears that an order quantity of 120 gives the lowest total costs at £1200 p.a. This can best be seen in the graph in Figure 16.2. You will also probably notice that the total cost curve is fairly flat around the minimum so that departing from the order size of 120 does not incur much additional cost.

Is it necessary to repeat this analysis each time? Fortunately not, as there is an algebraic formula that can be used to work out the optimum order quantity. The mathematics

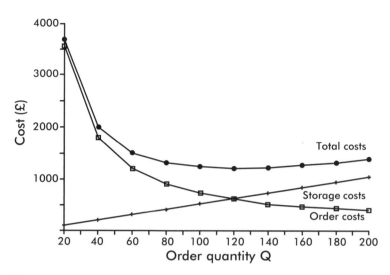

Figure 16.2 Inventory costs for Example 16.1

behind the formula is beyond the scope of this book, but you will see from the graph that at minimum cost, the order cost and storage cost lines intersect. This means that the two costs are equal at the optimum. This is generally true, so:

$$C\frac{D}{Q} = h\frac{Q}{2}$$

Multiplying both sides by 2Q and rearranging gives you:

$$Q^2 = 2C\frac{D}{h}$$

That is:

$$Q = \sqrt{\frac{2CD}{h}}$$

This formula is known as the economic order quantity, or EOQ, and in words it means:

$$\frac{\sqrt{2 \times \text{order cost per order} \times \text{demand}}}{\text{holding cost per unit}}$$

All you have to do to use this formula is simply to substitute the values for C, D, and h.

Activity 16.2

Use the EOQ formula to calculate the value of Q that minimises the sum of the ordering and holding costs. What is this cost?

Your calculations should have been as follows:

$$Q = \sqrt{\frac{2 \times 14.40 \times 5000}{10}}$$

$$= \sqrt{14\,400}$$

$$= 120$$

And the cost is £1200 p.a.

16.3.1 Time between orders and the re-order level

In the Game World example the number of orders per year at the EOQ of 120 is $\frac{500}{120} = 41.67$. If the company works for 300 days a year, this means that the time between orders should be $\frac{300}{41.67} = 7.2$ days on average.

From Figure 16.1 you will see that a new order arrives just as the stock level reaches zero. For this to happen an order must have been placed sometime previously. In practice an order is placed when the stock reaches a predetermined level. To calculate this level all that is required is the lead (or delivery) time. If the lead time is, say, 4 days, then during this time a certain amount of stock will have been sold. With a demand of 5000 a year, the daily sales will be $\frac{500}{300} = 16.7$ on average. In 4 days, 66.8 or about 67 games will be sold, and therefore an order will need to be placed when the stock is down to this level. This re-order level is shown in Figure 16.3.

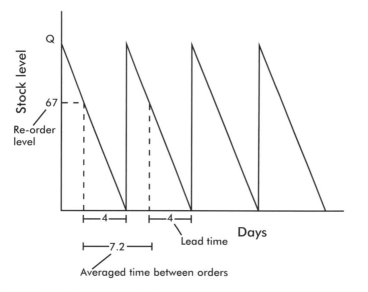

Figure 16.3 Re-order level for Example 16.1

Activity 16.3

Calculate the re-order level for 'Aliens' if the lead time increased to 5 days.

In this case the re-order level should be $5 \times 16.7 = 83.5$, or about 84 games.

16.4 Discounts

The EOQ is not always the cheapest quantity to purchase. It is often found that discounts are given by the manufacturer or supplier if a certain minimum quantity of goods are bought. In these cases it is necessary to add the cost of the goods to the order and storage costs in order to arrive at the cheapest policy.

Activity 16.4

You can purchase the computer game 'Aliens' for £50 each but if you order in quantities of 500 or more a 5% discount is given. Should you take advantage of this discount?

To answer this question you need to add the product cost to the cost of ordering and storage.

At the EOQ (120), the product cost is: $5000 \times £50 = £250\,000$

and the storage and order cost is: £1200

The total cost is therefore: $250\,000 + 1200 = £251\,200$

If 500 is purchased at a time, the order and storage will change and the unit cost will fall to $£50 - £2.50 = £47.50$, so:

Order cost: $£14.40 \times \dfrac{5000}{500} = £144.00$

Storage cost: $£10 \times \dfrac{500}{2} = £2500$

Product cost: $5000 \times £47.50 = \underline{£237\,500}$

Total cost: $= £240\,144$

By ordering in quantities of 500, a saving of £11 056 p.a. (£251 200 − £240 144) can be realised.

16.5 Uncertainty in demand

The EOQ model assumes that the demand for the product is known and constant. This assumption is unlikely to be valid in practice, and the demand is likely to fluctuate from

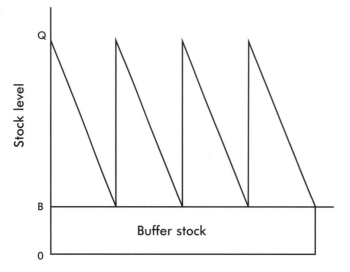

Figure 16.4 Buffer stock

day to day. Rather than scrap this model completely, it is possible, with further assumptions, to compensate for this variability.

Assuming that you are operating a re-order level system (that is, the stock level is continuously monitored) any fluctuation in demand *before* the next order is placed is unimportant. This is because any increase in demand will simply mean that an order is placed earlier than expected. However, once an order has been placed any increase in demand is more serious and could result in a stock-out. To prevent this happening a buffer (or safety) stock is purchased. The stock level diagram now looks like Figure 16.4.

It is now a matter of calculating the size (B) of the buffer stock. However, before this can be done an assumption needs to be made regarding the *distribution* of demand. The simplest assumption is to say that the demand is normally distributed. The use of the normal distribution means that it is possible for the demand to reach very high levels since the tails of the distribution in theory have no end (see Chapter 8). However, in practice a limit is set such as 5% and the demand is found that is only exceeded for this percentage of times.

Activity 16.5

The demand for the game 'Aliens' is normally distributed with a mean of 16.7 games per day and a standard deviation of 5.2 games. What buffer level should be maintained such that there is less than a 5% chance of running out of stock during the lead time of 4 days? What extra cost does this incur?

During the 4 days' lead time the mean demand will be $4 \times 16.7 = 66.8$ games. Calculation of the standard deviation for the 4 days can be found using the formula:

$$\sqrt{n \times \sigma^2}$$

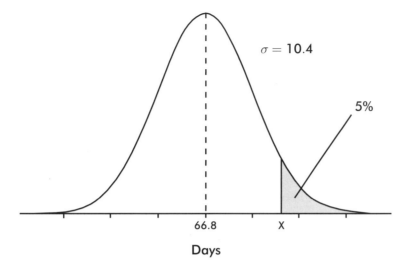

Figure 16.5 The normal distribution

Where n is the lead time and σ is the standard deviation per unit time period. The standard deviation is therefore:

$$\sqrt{4 \times 5.2^2} = 10.4$$

The demand that is exceeded on only 5% of occasions is denoted by X in Figure 16.5.
The normal equation is:

$$Z = \frac{X - \mu}{\sigma}$$

That is:

$$Z = \frac{X - 66.8}{10.4}$$

From the normal table (see Appendix 2), the value of Z for a probability of 0.05 (5%) is 1.645, so:

$$1.645 = \frac{X - 66.8}{10.4}$$

$$1.645 \times 10.4 = X - 66.8$$

$$17.108 = X - 66.8$$

and: $\qquad X = 17.108 + 66.9$

$$= 83.9$$

This means that on 5% of occasions the demand could exceed 83.9 units. The buffer level to ensure that a stock-out only occurs on 5% of occasions is $83.9 - 66.8 = 17.1$ units (say 18 units). In practice this would be rounded up to 20 or even more. To ensure that this buffer stock is maintained at the correct level the re-order level will need to be set at 84 units (the rounded value of X).

The additional storage cost will be 18 × the holding cost, that is $18 \times 10 = £180$ p.a. since 18 units are permanently in stock.

16.6 Summary

This chapter has introduced you to some methods employed in reducing the costs of holding stock. The EOQ model makes the assumption that the demand for a product is known and constant. If this is approximately true the re-order quantity is that quantity that minimises the sum of the ordering and holding costs. Frequently it is cheaper to buy larger quantities than that specified by the EOQ formula as a discount may be given for large orders. Although it is assumed that the demand is constant it is possible to relax this assumption somewhat by employing a buffer or safety stock. This buffer stock can be calculated if the demand for the product is assumed to be normally distributed.

16.7 Further reading

Anderson, Sweeney and Williams (1994) *An Introduction to Management Science*, seventh edition, West Publishing Company (Chapter 11).

Morris, C. (2000) *Quantitative Approaches in Business Studies*, fifth edition, Pitman, London (Chapter 17).

16.8 EXERCISES

The answers to the progress questions, the multiple choice questions and some of the practice questions are given in Appendix 1. Solutions to the remaining questions and the assignment can be found at the web site for this text.

PROGRESS QUESTIONS

These questions have been designed to help you remember the key points in this chapter.

Give the missing word in each case:

1. Stock holding costs can be divided into two broad categories. These are storage costs and .... costs.
2. EOQ stands for the Economic .... Quantity model.
3. The EOQ model is an example of a .... model.
4. The EOQ model assumes that demand is known and ....
5. In order to take discounts into account, the .... cost must also be known.
6. A .... stock is required to ensure that stock-outs do not occur.

ANSWER *TRUE* OR *FALSE*

7. At minimum cost the order cost equals the holding cost.

8. The product cost does not form part of the EOQ formula.

9. You do not need to know the product cost for deciding whether to take advantage of quantity discounts.

10. A buffer stock will guarantee that you never have a stock-out.

REVIEW QUESTIONS

These questions have been designed to help you check your comprehension of the key points in this chapter. You may wish to look further than this chapter in order to answer them fully. You will find the reading list useful in this respect. You can check the essential elements of your answers by referring to the appropriate section.

11. What stock related costs are likely to be incurred by a fresh food distributor? (Section 16.2)

12. What are the assumptions of the EOQ model? (Section 16.3)

13. When might it be useful to consider discounts? (Section 16.2)

MULTIPLE CHOICE QUESTIONS

14. If the order cost is £10 per order, then the total order cost if 5 orders are made per year is:

   A... £10   B... £50   C... £15

15. The minimum total costs occur when:

   A... The order cost and holding cost are equal.

   B... The order cost is at a minimum.

   C... The holding cost is at a minimum.

16. If the cost of holding stock is £5 per unit p.a., then the holding cost p.a. for an order quantity of 100 is:

   A... £500   B... £5   C... £250

17. If a buffer stock is used it is necessary to assume that the demand during the lead time is:

   A... Constant   B... Normally distributed

   C... known

18. If standard deviation of demand is 5 units per week, then the standard deviation during the lead time of 3 weeks is:

   A... 15   B... 8.66   C... 75

19. A buffer stock of 200 units is held. If the cost of holding one unit in stock for a year is £5, the holding cost (p.a.) of the buffer stock will be:

   A... £1000   B... £500   C... £5

PRACTICE QUESTIONS

20. The annual demand for a product is 4800 units; each unit costs £70 each for orders less than 600 and £68 each for orders of 600 or more. If an order costs £9 to set up and the annual stock holding costs are 20% of the average value of stock held, determine the optimum stock ordering policy. What is the cost of this policy?

21. The demand for a particular product is normally distributed with a mean of 100 units per day and a standard deviation of 20 units. If the lead time is 5 days, determine the buffer stock level such that there is less than a 5% chance of running out of stock.

22. A depot receives petrol from a refinery, which insists on a minimum of 3 days' notice for deliveries. The minimum delivery quantity is a road tanker load which is 20 000 gallons. The depot is charged £570 for a delivery, regardless of the number of tankers used. The daily sales of petrol is constant at 3000 gallons.

    If the cost of storage of the petrol is estimated to be 1p per gallon per day, what is the best ordering policy for the depot (i.e., order quantity, average time between orders and the quantity of petrol in stock which triggers a new order)? What is the cost of this policy?

23. A paint shop uses 200 tins of paint per day at a fairly constant rate. Tins are now ordered in batches of 1000 when the stock drops below 500. Delivery time is one day. The cost of placing an order is £100. Holding costs are 25p per tin per day.

    (a) You have been asked to examine this policy and make any suitable recommendations to reduce costs.

    (b) The supplier is offering a bulk order discount of 2% off the selling price of £10 for orders above 2000 tins. Advise whether or not they should take up the offer.

    (c) What is the minimum percentage discount the shop ought to consider to make it worthwhile to order in quantities of 2000?

ASSIGNMENT

Riglen plc cooks and cans food products for sale in its supermarkets. It uses 500 000 medium size cans per annum at a fairly uniform rate, which it purchases from the Tin Can company. Tin Can charge £100 per 5000 cans plus a delivery charge of £50, regardless of the size of the order. Riglen's current order policy is to order 10 000 cans every week, but during a cost auditing exercise the canning department has been criticised for such frequent ordering. As a consequence of this criticism, Jeff Lea, the Canning Production Manager, has been told to review the department's ordering policy.

Jeff has asked you to help him cost out the current system and he has told you that it costs the company 1.5p p.a. to hold one can in stock. (This 1.5p is made up of interests charges and cost of storage facilities.)

(a) What is the average quantity of stock currently held? and how much does this cost the company each year in holding costs?

(b) How many orders are made each year and what does this cost the company? (Assume that the company works for 50 weeks a year.)

(c) What is the sum of these two costs?

(d) Use the EOQ formula to calculate the best order quantity. What is the saving in cost if this order quantity was used rather than the current order of 10 000? What is the time between orders with your calculated order quantity?

(e) You have now been asked to consider increasing the order quantity to 100 000, as at this quantity the price is reduced to £99 per 5000 cans. Is it worth ordering this larger quantity?

(f) The weekly demand for cans is not constant but is normally distributed with an average of 10 000 cans and a standard deviation of 5000 cans. What re-order level would be required to ensure that the probability of a stock-out is less than 1%?

Simulation

17.1 Introduction

The quantitative techniques that you have met so far have allowed analytical solutions to problems to be found. For example, the inventory control (EOQ) model is a simple formula that will enable you to calculate the order quantity that will minimise inventory costs. (See Chapter 16.) These techniques or models are called *deterministic* because it is assumed that the variables are known precisely. However, there is another model class called *stochastic*. A stochastic model has at least one variable that does not have a single value – it has many possible values defined by some probability distribution. A queueing system is an example of a stochastic model and even relatively simple queueing models are difficult to solve analytically. This chapter looks at the use of simulation to solve simple queueing models.

On completing this chapter you should be able to:

● Appreciate the reasons for using simulation to solve stochastic models
● Understand the differences between terminating and non-terminating systems
● Demonstrate the technique of simulation by using the tabular method for simple problems
● Use Excel in the simulation of simple financial systems

17.2 Queuing problems

There are many instances of queueing situations. Whenever you go to the supermarket or the bank you will inevitably have to join a queue to be served. Why is this? The reason is that the arrival of customers to a service facility is unpredictable. Although you may know that 30 people an hour will arrive to be served, you cannot predict *when* they will arrive. You may get 10 people in the first 5 minutes, then no one for another 10 minutes. This is just like tossing a coin 10 times; although you may *expect* 5 heads and 5 tails, you wouldn't be that surprised to get 7 heads or even 10 heads. Just like tossing a coin, the average of 30 people an hour will be achieved over a long period of time, but in the short term unpredictable results can happen. This unpredictable behaviour means that it is very difficult to avoid queues. You could increase the capacity of the service facility but you would then find that this expensive resource is lying idle much of the time. The solution to queueing problems is therefore a compromise between having excessive queues and an underutilised resource.

Some simple queueing problems can be solved analytically, but the vast majority have to be solved using a technique called simulation. The following example illustrates a typical queueing problem.

Example 17.1

Passengers arriving at a suburban rail ticket office during the morning peak commuter period frequently have to wait for service. There is one clerk who issues tickets and provides an information service for passengers. The manager has received complaints regarding the time passengers spend in the queue waiting to be served, and she wishes to investigate possible methods of reducing the queueing time. Possible ideas include employing a second ticket clerk who could either duplicate the existing clerk or perhaps handle enquiries only. Another idea may be to collect fares on the train. The manager decided to collect data on arrivals and service times over a number of days, and the final figures have been summarised in Tables 17.1 and 17.2.

Table 17.1 Arrival time distribution

Inter-arrival time (secs)	Frequency (%)
0 to under 30	55
30 to under 60	30
60 to under 90	10
90 to under 120	5

Table 17.2 Service time distribution

Service time (secs)	Frequency (%)
20 to under 30	17
30 to under 40	28
40 to under 50	25
50 to under 60	20
60 to under 90	10

Activity 17.1

Describe the components of the queueing system inherent in this example.

You probably realise that passengers must first arrive and then either join a queue or go straight to be served. Once served, passengers leave the 'system'. This can be better described by the means of a diagram.

arrivals   queue   service departures

Figure 17.1 Ticket office system

Activity 17.2

The manager has a few ideas for reducing the queues. Why shouldn't she just try them out and see which is the best?

This method is probably done in many cases, but it can be costly and may disrupt the entire system if you are not careful. In some cases experimenting with the real system can be dangerous. For example, trying out changes to the safety devices of a nuclear power station is not recommended! Developing a model of a system and experimenting on this is much cheaper, safer and less disruptive. Of course, the model needs to be accurate and much time is spent by analysts *validating* their model. A model can only be an approximation of the real system and the validation checks will tell you how close your model is to the real system. You may, for instance, not have allowed for the fact that passengers 'balk' from a queue; that is, do not wait to be served. If this is important it can be included and the model re-validated.

17.3 Random numbers

Although you may be sure that 30 customers turn up to be served every hour, you cannot be sure *when* during that hour they will arrive. You may get 10 people in the first minute and then no one turns up for the next 15 minutes. In other words, there is a *randomness* in the way customers are likely to arrive. This randomness is apparent in most systems and is the reason why deterministic models are not very good at solving real problems. In order for simulation to take this randomness into account, *random numbers* are used.

True random numbers can only be generated by physical devices such as a roulette wheel which ensures that the distribution is uniform; that is, each number has an equal chance of being picked. In addition the sequence of numbers so produced is non-repeatable. However, most simulations are carried out on a computer and the random numbers in this case are generated by a formula within the computer. Although the random numbers produced are not true random numbers, they behave like true random numbers and are called *pseudo random numbers*. The random numbers included in the table in Appendix 2 were generated by a computer and are therefore pseudo random numbers.

The purpose of random numbers is to allow you (or the computer) to randomly select an arrival or service time from the appropriate distribution. The frequency tables given in the example represent the distribution of arrival time and service time for the ticket office.

Random numbers can be arranged in any order, and for this case two-digit numbers would match the percentage format in the tables. If you look at this table you will see that 55% of inter-arrival times are in the range 0 to under 30 seconds. The random numbers 00 to 54 (or 01 to 55) could therefore be used to represent this time band.

Activity 17.3

The next time band in Table 17.1 is 30 to under 60 seconds. What random numbers would you use to represent this band? Repeat this procedure for the last two bands.

Since the frequency is 30%, the random numbers should be 55 to 84 (or 56 to 85) inclusive. For the last two bands the random numbers should be 85 to 94 (86 to 95) and 95 to 99 (96 to 00) inclusive.

If a computer package were used to simulate this system, then a routine within the program would generate a random number and then obtain the appropriate inter-arrival time by interpolation. For example, if the random number 15 was generated then the inter-arrival time would be 8.2 seconds $\left(\dfrac{15}{55} \text{ of } 30\right)$. However, when manually carrying out a simulation it is much easier to represent each time band by its mid point, so any random number between 00 to 54 would correspond to an inter-arrival time of 15 seconds. This can be repeated for all bands, and to do this you may find it easier to write down the cumulative frequencies, as in Table 17.3.

Table 17.3   Allocation of random numbers

Inter-arrival time mid point	Frequency (%)	Cumulative frequency	Random numbers
15	55	55	00–54
45	30	85	55–84
75	10	95	85–94
105	5	100	95–99

Activity 17.4

Apply this procedure to the service time distribution (Table 17.2).

Table 17.4   Solution to Activity 17.4

Service time mid point	Frequency (%)	Cumulative frequency	Random numbers
25	17	17	00–16
35	28	45	17–44
45	25	70	45–69
55	20	90	70–89
75	10	100	90–99

Again, a particular service time would be represented by a range of random numbers. For example, a service time of 55 seconds would be represented by the random numbers 70 to 89.

17.4 Tabular simulation

The easiest method of demonstrating simulation is by manually simulating a simple system. In order to carry out the simulation of the ticket office manually you would need to obtain a stream of random numbers. These can conveniently be obtained from tables (see Appendix 2). These numbers would then be used to sample from the arrival and service time distributions. For example, suppose that the first few random numbers are 08, 72, 87 and 46. The random number 08 represents an inter-arrival time of 15 seconds, so the first passenger arrives at a *clock* time 15. There is no queue, so this passenger can be served immediately. The random number 72 corresponds to a service time of 55 seconds, so this service will end at a clock time of 70 (15 + 55). The next customer arrives 75 seconds after the first, so the clock time of 90 is after the end of the last service. The second passenger can also be served immediately. The service time is 45 seconds, so the passenger departs at 135. This information is best displayed in *tabular* format similar to Table 17.5.

Table 17.5 Tabular format

| | | | | | Service | | |
RNo	Inter-arr.	Clock time	RNo	Time	Starts	Ends	Waiting time
08	15	15	72	55	15	70	0
87	75	90	46	45	90	135	0

The last column of this table allows the waiting time of each passenger to be recorded.

Activity 17.5

Continue the tabular simulation using the following random numbers:

15, 96, 04, 00, 52, 27, 46, 73, 95, 76, 10, 25, 02, 11

As you can see in Table 17.6, the calculations are not difficult, but they are tedious and time consuming.

Activity 17.6

What is the mean waiting time for the simulation above?

Table 17.6 Simulation of the ticket office system

RNo	Inter-arr.	Clock time	RNo	Time	Service Starts	Ends	Waiting time
08	15	15	72	55	15	70	0
87	75	90	46	45	90	135	0
15	15	105	96	75	135	210	30
04	15	120	00	25	210	235	90
52	15	135	27	35	235	270	100
46	15	150	73	55	270	325	120
95	105	255	76	55	325	380	70
10	15	270	25	35	380	415	110
02	15	285	11	25	415	440	130

The mean waiting time of the first 9 passenger is 72.2 seconds, but it appears that the waiting time is increasing as the simulation proceeds.

17.5 Accuracy of simulation results

To obtain reliable results the simulation of the ticket office would need to be continued for the duration of the morning rush hour (say, 2 hours or 7200 seconds) and more than one run would be necessary.

Activity 17.7

Why should multiple runs of a simulation be necessary?

The reason for multiple runs is partly to do with the variability that you will get using random numbers, and partly to aid statistical analysis. One run of a simulation uses a stream of random numbers and different streams could give quite different results. There is nothing wrong with this – the variations are reflecting the situations that occur in real life. In fact, you can think of simulation as a sampling device. Each *run* of the simulation generates estimates of the performance of the system, such as the mean waiting time. If you want to carry out statistical analysis on your results, such as obtaining a confidence interval of the true mean waiting time, you will need values obtained from several runs. The method of replicating the simulation run depends on whether the system is a *terminating* or *non-terminating* one. A terminating system is, as its name suggests, a system that stops after a certain time or after a certain number of *entities* (customers) have passed through the system.

Activity 17.8

Is the ticket office example a terminating or non-terminating system?

Method of independent replications

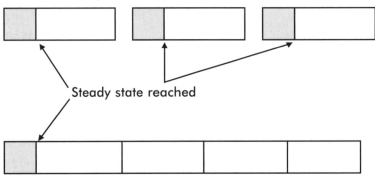

Steady state reached

Batch means method

Figure 17.2 Methods of replicating runs of a simulation

In busy main line terminals you could argue that the ticket office doesn't shut, so the system must be non-terminating. However, in this example it is only the morning peak period that you are interested in, so for practical purposes this is a terminating system.

For terminating systems the length of the simulation is fixed and this can simply be repeated a number of times using a different random number stream each time. This is called the method of *independent replications*.

Non-terminating systems do not have any natural end and could be considered to continue indefinitely. Examples include airports, harbours, 24-hour casualty departments and many production processes. Although some artificial end could be assumed and the independent replications method used, it is usual to use the *batch means method*. This method makes one very long run of the simulation, but is halted at regular intervals. At the end of each interval the average performance measure during the interval is noted. The reason that this method is preferred is to do with *initial bias*. This is the bias caused by assuming that all queues are empty at the start of the simulation.

Most terminating systems start in the empty state, so initial bias is not a problem in this case. However, with non-terminating systems it is a problem and it is necessary for the system to reach *steady state* before results are collected. A system is in steady state if its current state is independent of the starting conditions. The length of time necessary for a system to reach steady state can only be found by experimentation.

If the method of independent replications was used for non-terminating systems, steady state would need to be reached for each run which is wasteful even with fast computers. With the batch means method, steady state only needs to be found once. Results from the period following steady state only are used in the analysis of the system. Figure 17.2 illustrates the two methods.

17.6 Spreadsheet simulation

For queuing type systems it is necessary to use specialist simulation software but there are some systems that can be simulated using a spreadsheet. These are systems where time does not have to be modelled in such a precise way. This type of simulation is often called *Monte Carlo simulation* to differentiate it from queuing simulation that we have already met. An example of a system that can be simulated using a spreadsheet is a financial type system. Cash flows generated by an investment are likely to be uncertain, particularly when these cash flows occur some time in the future. The uncertainty in a future cash flow can be represented by a probability distribution and as in queuing simulation we can sample from this distribution using random numbers. There is a random number function within Excel, and together with other in-built functions it is easy to build a simple simulation model. For more complex simulation models it is possible to use macros or specialist spreadsheet 'add-ins' such as @RISK™.

Activity 17.9

A company is considering investing in a project but it is unsure of the cash flows that would occur. However, the chief accountant has succeeded in estimating the probability of various cash flows occurring and has represented this information in Tables 17.7 and 17.8. Use the mid points of the ranges as an approximation and assign random numbers to each as in Activity 17.3

Table 17.7   Cash inflows

Cash inflows (£000s)	Probability (%)
45 to under 55	30
55 to under 65	40
65 to under 75	30

Table 17.8   Cash outflow

Cash outflow (£000s)	Probability (%)
40 to under 60	45
60 to under 80	55

You should have arrived at the following tables:

Table 17.9   Random numbers assigned to the cash inflows

Cash inflows (£000s)	Probability (%)	Cumulative probability	Random numbers
50	30	30	00–29
60	40	70	30–69
70	30	100	70–99

Table 17.10   Random numbers assigned to the cash outflows

Cash outflow (£000s)	Probability (%)	Cumulative probability	Random numbers
50	45	45	00–44
70	55	100	45–99

Using random numbers we could generate a cash inflow and a cash outflow and subtracting the outflow from the inflow would give us the net flow. For example a random number of 24 would generate a cash inflow of £50 000 and a random number of 47 would generate a cash outflow of £70 000. Net cash flow would therefore be −£20 000. This could be repeated many times to get a range of net cash flows ranging from −£20 000 to £20 000. Rather than simulate this manually it would be easier to use Excel.

Activity 17.10

Use Excel to obtain 20 random values of the net cash flows. What is the probability that the investment will generate a negative cash flow?

To get Excel to carry out this simple simulation you need to use the random number function =Rand() and the VLOOKUP function as follows.

1. Add the lower range of the cash inflow random numbers (as a decimal) in cells B2 to B4. The values should be 0, 0.29 and 0.69.

2. In the next column add the cash inflow figures; that is, 50, 60 and 70.

3. Do the same for the outflow random numbers in cells D2 to D3 and the cash outflows in the next column.

4. In cell A7 add the random number function (=rand()) for the cash inflow.

5. In cell B7 add the VLOOKUP function. The purpose of this function is to find the relevant cash flow for the random number in A7. The format of this function is =VLOOKUP(lookup value, table array, column index number). In this particular case the lookup value is the cell A7, the array is $B$2:$C$4 and the column index is 2 as you want the cash flow which is in the second column of the array.

6. Use cells C7 and D7 to repeat steps 4 and 5 for the cash outflow.

7. In cell E7 you want to subtract the cash outflow from the cash inflow.

The spreadsheet so far should look something like Figure 17.3

8. You will notice that every time you do something to the spreadsheet the random numbers change. To stop this, go into *Tools*, *Options*, *Calculation* and click on *Manual*. Now to make the spreadsheet recalculate you have to press the F9 key.

	A	B	C	D	E
1		Cum Probability	Inflow	Cum probability	Outflow
2		0	50	0	50
3		0.29	60	0.44	70
4		0.69	70		
5					
6		Cash in		Cash out	Net cash flow
7	=RAND()	=VLOOKUP(A7,$B$2:$C$4,2)	=RAND()	=VLOOKUP(C7,$D$2:$E$3,2)	=B7-D7
8					
9					
10					

Figure 17.3 The worksheet to simulate the cash flows

9. Copy the formulae in cells A7 to E7 down to A26 to E26. Press F9.

10. Use the Histogram function from *Tools/ /Data Analysis* to form a frequency table of the net cash flows. (You may have to use *Add-In* the Data Analysis routine first.) You will need to set up a 'bin' range. This will contain the values $-20, -10, 0, 10, 20$. (See the screen shot in Figure 17.4.)

11. In the column after the frequencies, calculate the probability by dividing each frequency by 20 (the number of values). Press F9.

12. The probability of a negative cash flow can be found by adding the probability of cash flows of $-£10\,000$ and $-£20\,000$.

13. Try increasing the number of values by extending the formulae to row 106 (that is, 100 values). (Don't forget to press F9.) The more times you sample from the cash flow distributions the more accurate should be your answer.

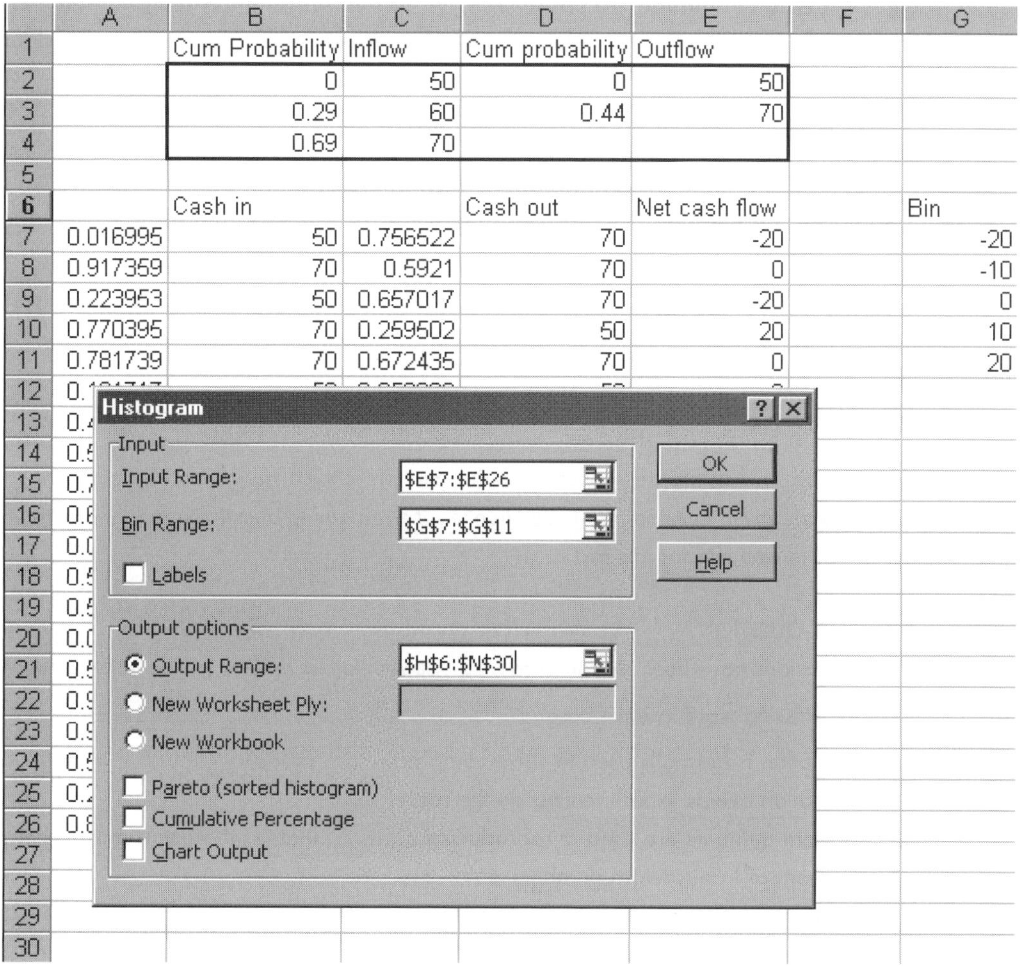

	A	B	C	D	E	F	G
1		Cum Probability	Inflow	Cum probability	Outflow		
2		0	50	0	50		
3		0.29	60	0.44	70		
4		0.69	70				
5							
6		Cash in			Cash out	Net cash flow		Bin
7	0.016995	50	0.756522	70	-20		-20
8	0.917359	70	0.5921	70	0		-10
9	0.223953	50	0.657017	70	-20		0
10	0.770395	70	0.259502	50	20		10
11	0.781739	70	0.672435	70	0		20
12							
13							
14							
15							
16							
17							
18							
19							
20							
21							
22							
23							
24							
25							
26							
27							
28							
29							
30							

Histogram

Input

Input Range: $E$7:$E$26

Bin Range: $G$7:$G$11

☐ Labels

Output options

◉ Output Range: $H$6:$N$30

◯ New Worksheet Ply:

◯ New Workbook

☐ Pareto (sorted histogram)

☐ Cumulative Percentage

☐ Chart Output

OK

Cancel

Help

Figure 17.4 Analysing the finished spreadsheet

Of course this was a simple example and one that could be solved without using simulation (see Question 22 in Section 17.9), but it does illustrate how Excel could be used to simulate these kinds of problems.

17.7 Summary

Simulation is a very popular and useful technique for solving problems that cannot be solved using more conventional methods. This is particularly true for complex queueing systems. Random numbers form the heart of a simulation and mimic the variability that occurs in the real system. Systems can be of two types: terminating and non-terminating. Terminating systems are systems that have a fixed start and end, and multiple runs of a terminating model can be achieved using the method of independent replications. Non-terminating systems are not so easy to analyse because the start of a simulation assumes empty queues, which is unrealistic. The time for a non-terminating system to reach steady state must be found and then multiple runs made using the batch means method.

17.8 Further reading

Morris, C. (2000) *Quantitative Approaches in Business Studies*, fifth edition, Pitman, London (Chapter 20).
Oakshott, L. (1997) *Business Modelling and Simulation*, Pitman, London (Chapters 5, 11 and 12).

17.9 EXERCISES

The answers to the progress questions, the multiple choice questions and some of the practice questions are given in Appendix 1. Solutions to the remaining questions and the assignment can be found at the web site for this text.

PROGRESS QUESTIONS

These questions have been designed to help you remember the key points in this chapter.

Give the missing word in each case:

1. Simulation is normally used to solve complex .... models.
2. Simulation avoids experimenting on the real ....
3. Random numbers are used to reproduce the .... that is inherent in most systems.
4. A stream of true random numbers is not ....
5. Random numbers produced by a formula are called .... random numbers.
6. Simulations need to be .... against the real system to ensure that they produce accurate results.

ANSWER *TRUE* OR *FALSE*

7. Systems that stop after a certain time are called terminating systems.

8. Steady state must be found for terminating systems.

9. In terminating systems all queues start in the empty state.

10. Only one run of a terminating system is required.

11. The method of replicating runs of a non-terminating system is called the batch means method.

REVIEW QUESTIONS

These questions have been designed to help you check your comprehension of the key points in this chapter. You may wish to look further than this chapter in order to answer them fully. You will find the reading list useful in this respect. You can check the essential elements of your answers by referring to the appropriate section.

12. Explain why averages are of no help in analysing a stochastic system. (Sections 17.2 and 17.3)

13. What are the components of a queueing system? (Section 17.2)

14. Describe the essential differences between a terminating and non-terminating system. (Section 17.4)

MULTIPLE CHOICE QUESTIONS

15. A queueing system is an example of a:

    A... Deterministic system   B... Stochastic system
    C... Dynamic system

16. Pseudo random numbers are random numbers that:

    A... Can be repeated   B... Cannot be repeated
    C... Are biased

17. A high street bank is an example of:

    A... A terminating system   B... A non-terminating system
    C... Neither

18. A simulation model needs to be run:

    A... Once only   B... Twice   C... Several times

PRACTICE QUESTIONS

19. Customers arrive at a single cash dispenser with the inter-arrival time distribution shown in Table 17.11.

    The service time is 45 seconds.

    Using the random numbers below, manually simulate the system and find the average time spent waiting for service and the utilisation of the cash dispenser.

    05, 20, 30, 85, 22, 21, 04, 67, 00, 03

Table 17.11 Inter-arrival time distribution for Question 19

Inter-arrival time (secs)	Frequency (%)
20 to under 50	5
50 to under 100	20
100 to under 150	30
150 to under 200	45

20. Customers arrive at a bank, which has only a single cashier, with the inter-arrival time and service time distributions shown in Table 17.12.

Table 17.12 Arrival and service time distributions for Question 20

Inter-arrival time (mins)	% of customers	Service time (mins)	% of customers
0 to under 4	30	0 to under 1	0
4 to under 6	40	1 to under 3	50
6 to under 8	20	3 to under 5	40
8 to under 10	10	5 to under 7	10

Using the random numbers given below, simulate the next 6 arrivals and find the mean time that they spend queueing for the cashier.

04, 10, 59, 07, 38, 98, 01, 75, 48, 91, 04, 12

21. Ajax Food Products has its main factory in the centre of Bristol. Lorries arrive at a constant rate from 08.00 to 18.00 five days a week, where they are either loaded or unloaded using the single loading/unloading bay and on a first-come, first-served basis. The area around the factory is frequently congested with lorries because the loading/unloading depot is not large enough for all arriving lorries to wait. A suggestion has been made that an improvement in numbers queueing might result if priority was given to lorries that required unloading. This is because unloading is generally a faster operation. However, before any decision is made it has been decided to build a simulation model of the current system.

(a) Briefly discuss the advantages and disadvantages of simulation as a means of experimenting on this system.

(b) Using the random numbers 42, 17, 38 and 61, demonstrate how 4 unloading times could be generated from the frequency distribution given in Table 17.13.

Table 17.13 Unloading times for Question 21

Time (mins)	Frequency (%)
0 to under 30	20
30 to under 40	35
40 to under 50	22
50 to under 60	15
60 to under 70	8

22. The problem in Activity 17.10 could be solved without simulation. Use the information given in Tables 17.7 and 17.8 to find the mean net cash flow and the probability that the net cash flow will be negative. (Hint: use a probability tree to show how each of the three possible cash inflows can be followed by one of the two possible cash outflows.)

ASSIGNMENT

Andrew Giles, the Transport Manager at Bristol Tyres, has just returned from a meeting with the Managing Director. Apparently the police have received complaints from local residents about the parking of heavy lorries in the side streets near the factory. This is occurring because there is insufficient room in the depot for lorries to wait to be loaded/unloaded.

To reduce the congestion it has been suggested a second bay be built. However, before this is done a simulation of the current system is to be developed and you have been asked to take on this project.

Your first task was a data collection exercise, and this gave you the following information:

(i)   The depot is open from 0800 to 1800 Mondays to Fridays.
(ii) Vehicles either require loading or unloading (not both).
(iii) 70% of lorries require loading and 30% require unloading.
(iv) The frequency distributions of the loading/unloading operations found by timing a large number of lorries were as shown in Table 17.14.

Table 17.14   Frequency distributions for the assignment

Time (mins)	Loading Frequency (%)	Unloading Frequency (%)
0 to under 30	20	30
30 to under 40	35	40
40 to under 50	22	25
50 to under 60	15	4
60 to under 70	8	1

The frequency distribution of the inter-arrival time; that is, the time between successive arrivals, was as shown in Table 17.15.

You have also made the following assumptions:

(i)   The pattern of arrivals is constant throughout the day.
(ii) A second bay would be used like the first; that is, for loading and unloading.
(iii) A single queue of lorries would form and a lorry could use either bay on a first-come, first-served basis.
(iv) Any lorries in the queue at the end of the day would be loaded or unloaded.

   (a) Explain why simulation is a better method than experimenting on the real system for this problem.

   (b) How would you go about simulating the system? In your answer you should discuss the run length of the simulation and the number of runs required.

Table 17.15 Inter-arrival time distribution

Time (mins)	Frequency (%)
0 to under 10	15
10 to under 20	40
20 to under 30	30
30 to under 40	5
40 to under 50	5
50 to under 60	3
60 to under 70	2

(c) Demonstrate the technique of simulation by using the tabular method to simulate 3 hours (180 minutes) of depot operation. What is the average waiting time of the lorries?

Random numbers:

20, 17, 42, 96 23, 17, 28, 66, 38, 59, 38, 61, 73, 76, 80, 00,

20, 56, 10, 05, 87, 88, 78, 15

(d) Repeat the simulation using 2 unloading bays.

Appendix 1

Answers to selected exercises in the text

Chapter 2   Sampling methods

1. Target   2. Sample   3. Frame   4. Random   5. Bias   6. Error
7. Stratified   8. Systematic   9. Primary   10. True   11. False   12. True
13. False   14. True   15. False   21. B   22. C   23. A
24. C   25. B

26. (a) Steve, Kim and Chris who read *The Times*, *Sun* and *Mirror* respectively. Average age is 40.
    (b) Steve, Stuart and Jill who read *The Times*, *Mirror* and *Telegraph*. Average age is 36.7 years. (Different answers will be obtained depending upon how the population was ordered.)
    (c) Julie

27. Population – all householders and tenants. Sampling frame – council records.

28. Proposal only looks at one group of supporters – doesn't consider non-members whose views will be equally important. Non-members may be more price sensitive so exclusion would invalidate conclusions. Sampling method could be *systematic* – say, ask every 10th person entering through turnstile. Maybe limit survey to home supporters' turnstiles only.

29. Need list of all secondary schools in country (both state and independent). Use *multi-stage* sampling to select a few areas. Use *stratified* sampling to choose representative number of state and independent schools (perhaps also large/small or urban/rural, etc.) in each area. For each school choose simple random sample of school leavers.

30. Simplest and cheapest method would be quota sampling. Decide on classification (e.g. male/female) and obtain data on proportions of population in each group. (Similar answer to Activity 2.8.)

Chapter 3   Presentation of data

1. Primary   2. Discrete   3. Ratio   4. Tally   5. Pie
6. Component   7. Grouped   8. Polygon   9. True   10. False

11. True   12. False   13. True   14. True   20. B

21. B   22. B   23. C   24. B   25. C

26. B   27. D   28. C

29. (a) discrete; (b) interval; (c) ratio; (d) ordinal

30. (a)

Type of coffee	Frequency	Relative frequency
Instant	8	40%
Filter	8	40%
Ground	4	20%

31. Component bar chart will show that sales have increased since 1999 but this has been the result of a good performance by the Menswear department. Furniture sales was the largest proportion of total sales in 1999 but this proportion has declined since then.

32. (e) Total sales declined during 1997 to 1999 but some recovery since then. South East gives largest proportion of sales with Wales the smallest. Multiple bar chart shows that the decline in S. East sales occurred later but the recovery has not started despite improvement in other regions. Wales has shown very little change during the 5 years.

33.

Class interval	Frequency
20 to <22 gm	2
22 to <24 gm	8
24 to <26 gm	16
26 to <28 gm	17
28 to <30 gm	21
30 to <32 gm	16

(e) The distribution is left skewed with most of the items between 26 and 32 g.

34. If you assume that this is discrete data; that is, people only take whole days off sick, then the class intervals are 2, 4, 4, 4, 8, 8 respectively. Since the intervals are unequal the frequency must be adjusted. I have used the first interval as the standard and adjusted the remaining intervals as follows:

Days off work	No. employees	Class interval	Adjusted frequency
0–1	45	2	45
2–5	89	4	44.5
6–9	40	4	20
10–13	25	4	12.5
14–21	5	8	1.25
22–29	2	8	0.5

The histogram is drawn in Figure A1.1. Since the data is discrete the boundaries have been extended by 0.5 on either side of each interval. The histogram is skewed to the right showing that most people only take a relatively few days off sick.

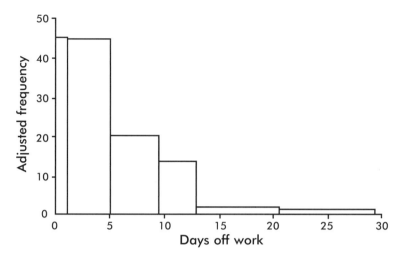

Figure A1.1 Histogram for Question 34 of Chapter 3

Chapter 4   Summarising data

1. Sum   2. Middle   3. Frequently   4. Range
5. 50   6. Deviation   7. Standard deviation   8. Shape
9. False   10. True   11. True   12. False
13. True   14. False   18. A   19. C
20. A   21. B   22. A   23. B
24. C   25. B   26. D   27. A
28. E   29. C   30. A   31. D
32. A   33. C

34. (a) mean = £189.53; median = £174.34 (the value of £274.5 distorts the mean)
    (b) standard deviation = £43.67
    (c) (i) mean = £209.53; standard deviation = £43.67
        (ii) mean = £199.00; standard deviation = £45.86

35. 63.2%   36. 182.1 hours

37. (a) 5.1 days; (b) about 4 days; (c) about 4 days; (d) about 5.5;
    (e) 4.4 days; (f) 86%

38.

	Machine A	Machine B
Mean	24.8	26.2
Median	25	26.3
Mode	25	26.5
IQR	2.2	2.1
SD	1.96	2.04
C.Var	7.9	7.8

Chapter 5   Index numbers

1. 100   2. One   3. Base   4. Current   5. Family
6. Month   7. True   8. False   9. True   10. False
14. A   15. A   16. C   17. B   18. D
19. C   20. B   21. B
22. (a) 136.2; (b) 131.0   23. (a) 114.7; (b) 188.1   24. £60 105
25.

1987	1988	1989	1990	1991	1992
15.3	9.8	10.7	12.3	18.6	25.5

Chapter 6   Investment appraisal

1. Repaid   2. return   3. Paid out   4. Reinvested   5. present   6. False
7. True   8. True   9. False   10. False   15. B   16. A
17. A   18. B   19. C   20. B   21. B   22. A
23. B   24. A   25. C   26. C   27. C
28. (a) £68 942; (b) £18 942   29. £6066.70
30. Payback period is 4 years, ARR is 25%, NPV is £50 200, IRR is about 7.9%
31. No

Chapter 7   Introduction to probability

1. 1 or 100%   2. Empirical   3. Subjective   4. 1
5. Addition   6. Multiplication   7. Prior   8. Posterior
9. True   10. False   11. True   12. True
13. True   14. False   20. B   21. C
22. A   23. B   24. B   25. C
26. D   27. A   28. D
29. (a) (i) 0.5; (ii) 0.3; (iii) 0.7; (b) (i) 0.25; (ii) 0.15; (c) (i) 0.222;
    (ii) 0.167
30. (a) 0.0769; (b) 0.5; (c) 0.5385   31. 0.0049
32. (a) 0.000125; (b) 0.1354; (c) 0.1426
33. (i) virtually zero; (ii) 0.1678; (iii) 0.2936
34. (a) Empirical/subjective; (b) empirical; (c) a priori; (d) subjective

Chapter 8   Probability distributions

1. Discrete   2. Random   3. Symmetrical   4. 1 or 100%
5. Mean and standard deviation   6. Increases   7. Continuous
8. True   9. False   10. True   11. False
12. True   13. True   14. False   19. C

20. B   21. A   22. 0   23. B
24. C   25. B   26. D   27. C
28. 10   29. 0.3125
30. P(male) $= 0.5122$ (a) 0.0688 (b) 0.2622 (c) 0.3746
31. $P(r \geq 2$ defectives$) = 0.1198$ or about 12%. So would expect to get two or more defectives from time to time.
32. P(undamaged) $= 0.8$ (a) $P(r = 0) = 0.0016$ (b) $P(r = 3) = 0.4096$; $P(r = 4) = 0.4096$, so $P(r \geq 3) = 0.8192$
33. (a) 0.0988 (b) 0.3567 (c) m $= 1.34$, so P(0) $= 0.2618$
34. (a) m $= 1.5$ $P(r \geq 2) = 1 - P(0) - P(1) = 0.4422$ (b) m $= 7.5$ Need to find probability of no flaws in 5 mm interval, $P(r = 0) = 0.0005$
35. 0.1056   36. 0.0664   37. 0.6017
38. (a) 0.2514 (b) 0.2514 (c) 0.4972 (d) 0.1112
39. (a) 0.2451 (b) 0.6628 (c) 0.2549 (d) 0.0635
40. 88.82%

Chapter 9   Decision-making under conditions of uncertainty

1. Best, best   2. Opportunity   3. Expected   4. Multi
5. Perfect   6. Trees   7. Prior   8. Risk
9. True   10. False   11. True   12. False
13. False   14. False   20. D   21. B
22. B   23. B   24. B   25. B
26. A   27. C   28. D   29. B
30. £0.8m   31. (i) 0.4 (ii) £26m (iii) £14m (iv) Decision 1 (v) 0.509
32. (a) (i) Manufacture (ii) Sell (iii) Take royalties (b) Manufacture (c) £12 000
33. (a) (i) Bar (ii) Bar (iii) Bar (b) Bar   34. (a) (i) B (ii) C (iii) C (b) C (c) Yes
35. (a) Wait (b) 0.5   36. Move

Chapter 10   Analysis and interpretation of sample data

1. Population   2. Sample   3. Point   4. Sample
5. Less   6. Confidence   7. True   8. True
9. False   10. True   11. True   12. True
13. False   14. False   20. B   21. A
22. B   23. A   24. B   25. A
26. B   27. A   28. D   29. A
30. D
31. (a) 16 000; (b) 50; (c) 40%; (d) 40%; (e) 26.4% to 53.6%
32. 8.81 g to 10.43 g   33. 168.99 cm to 170.01 cm
34. 64.0% to 86.0%

35. (a) 7.82 g to 9.62 g; (b) 7.43 g to 10.01 g
36. (i) £15 819 to £17 081; (ii) 2239
37. 17.3% to 42.7% (finite correction factor applied)

Chapter 11   Testing a hypothesis

1. Null	2. Alternative	3. Critical	4. Z
5. 2.5%	6. Categorical	7. True	8. False
9. False	10. True	11. False	12. True
13. False	18. C	19. B	20. C
21. A	22. A	23. B	24. B
25. D	26. A	27. C	28. B
29. C	30. C	31. B	32. E

33. $+1.96$ 34. 2.718   35. 12.592
36. $Z = -1.24$ Accept H_0 37. $Z = -2.42$ Reject H_0
38. $Z = -7.07$ Reject H_0 39. $t = -0.571$ Accept H_0
40. $Z = 2.673$ Reject H_0 41. Chi squared $= 4.216$ Accept H_0
42. (a) Chi squared $= 38.126$ Reject H_0; (b) more people under 20 listen to commercial radio than expected

Chapter 12   Correlation and regression

1. Scatter	2. Association	3. Relationship	4. $-1, +1$
5. Minimises	6. Straight	7. Ordinal	8. False
9. False	10. True	11. True	15. A
16. B	17. B	18. B	19. E
20. C	21. 13		

22. (c) all data $r = 0.760$; males: $r = 0.906$; females: $r = 0.0102$
23. $R = -0.3875$
24. (a) The scatter graph suggests that there is a strong association between sales and advertising expenditure and that this is a *positive* association.
    (b) $y = -0.24 + 9.292x$, where y is Sales and x the advertising expenditure. The coefficient of determination is 93.3%, so it appears that the regression explains the data quite well.
    (c) £46 200

Chapter 13   Time series analysis

1. Randomness	2. Cyclic	3. Moving	4. Decomposition
5. Absolute	6. True	7. True	8. False
9. True	13. C	14. A	15. A
16. B	17. A	18. B	19. A

20. (b) The centred moving average series (from quarter 3 in 1999) is:
    41.67, 42.08, 42.75, 42.58, 42.33, 42.50, 42.92, 42.75, 42.08, 42.67, 43.17, 43.42
    (c) The value of the seasonal differences are:
    $-10.05, -6.17, -5.38, -4.72, 8.66, 17.66$
21. (b) Centred moving average figures are:
    18.53, 19.19, 19.86, 20.53, 21.26, 22.05, 22.84, 23.75, 24.61
    (c) Average seasonal differences are:
    $8.33, -3.81, -8.84, 4.31$
23. 112.4

Chapter 14   Linear programming

1. Scarce	2. Constraints	3. Two	4. Feasible
5. Feasible	6. Tight	7. Shadow	8. False
9. True	10. False	11. False	16. C
17. A	18. C	19. B	

20. $x = 20$, $y = 25$ and $Z = 137\,500$
24. (a) 12 basic and 5 deluxe
    (b) (i) £5; (ii) 234 kg profit increased to £1170
25. (a) Max. $60P + 85S$

$$4P + 8S \leq 400$$

$$2P + 3S \leq 250$$

$$10S \geq 150$$

$$5P + 7S \leq 480$$

$$P - 2S \leq 0$$

    Where $P =$ No. of Elen Plus to make each day and $S =$ No. of Elen Super
    (b) $P = 70$, $S = 15$, giving a profit of £5475 per day.
    (c) Components A and C are tight constraints. Shadow prices of A and C are £15 and £3.50 respectively. (Note, increasing C would *reduce* profit.) It would be worthwhile increasing A since shadow price greater than cost.
    (d) No upper limit but lower limit of £42.50.

Chapter 15   Critical path analysis

1. Start	2. Forward	3. Backward	4. Zero
5. False	6. True	7. False	8. True
12. B	13. D	14. A	15. B

16. (a) 16 weeks; (b) 0; (c) 2 weeks; (d) Yes, 1 week; (e) The answer is 5 if all jobs start at their EST, but if B is delayed until week 7, only 2 people are required.
17. It will take 31 weeks and critical path is ACEHIJKL
18. (a) Refit takes 25 days. Critical activities are A, E, F, H, I and J. Floats are B-20, C-10, D-10, G-13 days.
    (b) (i) 6 during weeks 2 and 3; (ii) Several possibilities, e.g., C starts day 4 and D starts day 12.
19. (a) Critical path is AFJ; Floats: B-1, C-1, D-1, E-1, G-28, H-28, I-34, K-51
    (b) (i) I not on critical path
        (ii) Crash A by 2 weeks, E by 1 week and F by 2 weeks. This would 'save' £12 000.

Chapter 16   Inventory control

1. Order
2. Order
3. Deterministic
4. Constant
5. Product
6. Buffer (or safety)
7. True
8. True
9. False
10. False
14. B
15. A
16. C
17. B
18. B
19. A
20. Order 600 total cost is £330 552
21. 74 units
22. 1 tanker load. Average time between orders =6–7 days. The re-order level is 9000 gallons. Cost = £185.50 per day.
23. (a) The current policy costs £220 per day (there is a buffer stock of 300 tins). The EOQ is 400 tins which will incur a cost of £100 per day. If the same buffer is maintained this will add another £75 per day. (This buffer level seems rather high and could be reduced.)
    (b) No – Cost at EOQ including product cost is £2100 while ordering in quantities of 2000 would cost £2200
    (c) 8%

Chapter 17   Simulation

1. Stochastic
2. System
3. Variability
4. Repeatable
5. Pseudo
6. Validated
7. True
8. False
9. True
10. False
11. True
15. B
16. A
17. A
18. C
19. Random numbers are allocated as follows:

I.A.T	Mid point	R.Nos
20 – <50	35	00–04
50 – <100	75	05–24
100 – <150	125	25–54
150 – <200	175	55–99

Average time = 4 seconds. Utilisation = 47.6%.

20. 2.33 minutes
21. (a) Some advantages are:
    - Simulation can be used to study complex stochastic systems (particularly queuing systems)
    - Simulation can be used to answer what-if questions
    - Simulation often gives people a better understanding of a system
    - Simulation can help quantify the risk inherent in a system or in an investment decision

    Some disadvantages are:
    - Simulation does not guarantee optimal solutions
    - Simulation cannot solve problems
    - Simulation is a sampling device so exact solutions are not possible
    - Statistical knowledge is required to analyse the output from a simulation model

    (b)

Unloading time	Mid Point	R.Nos
0 – <30	15	00–19
30 – <40	35	20–54
40 – <50	45	55–76
50 – <60	55	77–91
60 – <70	65	92–99

    The unloading times are 35, 15, 35 and 45 minutes respectively.

Statistical tables

The normal tables

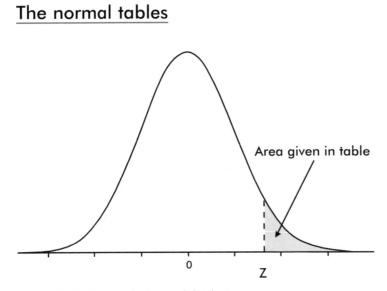

Figure A2.1 The standard normal distribution

Z	0.00	0.01	0.02	0.03	0.04	0.05	0.06	0.07	0.08	0.09
0.0	0.5000	0.4960	0.4920	0.4880	0.4840	0.4801	0.4761	0.4721	0.4681	0.4641
0.1	0.4602	0.4562	0.4522	0.4483	0.4443	0.4404	0.4364	0.4325	0.4286	0.4247
0.2	0.4207	0.4168	0.4129	0.4090	0.4052	0.4013	0.3974	0.3936	0.3897	0.3859
0.3	0.3821	0.3783	0.3745	0.3707	0.3669	0.3632	0.3594	0.3557	0.3520	0.3483
0.4	0.3446	0.3409	0.3372	0.3336	0.3300	0.3264	0.3228	0.3192	0.3156	0.3121
0.5	0.3085	0.3050	0.3015	0.2981	0.2946	0.2912	0.2877	0.2843	0.2810	0.2776
0.6	0.2743	0.2709	0.2676	0.2643	0.2611	0.2578	0.2546	0.2514	0.2483	0.2451
0.7	0.2420	0.2389	0.2358	0.2327	0.2296	0.2266	0.2236	0.2206	0.2177	0.2148
0.8	0.2119	0.2090	0.2061	0.2033	0.2005	0.1977	0.1949	0.1922	0.1894	0.1867
0.9	0.1841	0.1814	0.1788	0.1762	0.1736	0.1711	0.1685	0.1660	0.1635	0.1611
1.0	0.1587	0.1562	0.1539	0.1515	0.1492	0.1469	0.1446	0.1423	0.1401	0.1379
1.1	0.1357	0.1335	0.1314	0.1292	0.1271	0.1251	0.1230	0.1210	0.1190	0.1170
1.2	0.1151	0.1131	0.1112	0.1093	0.1075	0.1056	0.1038	0.1020	0.1003	0.0985
1.3	0.0968	0.0951	0.0934	0.0918	0.0901	0.0885	0.0869	0.0853	0.0838	0.0823
1.4	0.0808	0.0793	0.0778	0.0764	0.0749	0.0735	0.0721	0.0708	0.0694	0.0681
1.5	0.0668	0.0655	0.0643	0.0630	0.0618	0.0606	0.0594	0.0582	0.0571	0.0559
1.6	0.0548	0.0537	0.0526	0.0516	0.0505	0.0495	0.0485	0.0475	0.0465	0.0455
1.7	0.0446	0.0436	0.0427	0.0418	0.0409	0.0401	0.0392	0.0384	0.0375	0.0367
1.8	0.0359	0.0351	0.0344	0.0336	0.0329	0.0322	0.0314	0.0307	0.0301	0.0294
1.9	0.0287	0.0281	0.0274	0.0268	0.0262	0.0256	0.0250	0.0244	0.0239	0.0233
2.0	0.0228	0.0222	0.0217	0.0212	0.0207	0.0202	0.0197	0.0192	0.0188	0.0183
2.1	0.0179	0.0174	0.0170	0.0166	0.0162	0.0158	0.0154	0.0150	0.0146	0.0143
2.2	0.0139	0.0136	0.0132	0.0129	0.0125	0.0122	0.0119	0.0116	0.0113	0.0110
2.3	0.0107	0.0104	0.0102	0.0099	0.0096	0.0094	0.0091	0.0089	0.0087	0.0084
2.4	0.0082	0.0080	0.0078	0.0075	0.0073	0.0071	0.0069	0.0068	0.0066	0.0064
2.5	0.0062	0.0060	0.0059	0.0057	0.0055	0.0054	0.0052	0.0051	0.0049	0.0048
2.6	0.0047	0.0045	0.0044	0.0043	0.0041	0.0040	0.0039	0.0038	0.0037	0.0036
2.7	0.0035	0.0034	0.0033	0.0032	0.0031	0.0030	0.0029	0.0028	0.0027	0.0026
2.8	0.0026	0.0025	0.0024	0.0023	0.0023	0.0022	0.0021	0.0021	0.0020	0.0019
2.9	0.0019	0.0018	0.0018	0.0017	0.0016	0.0016	0.0015	0.0015	0.0014	0.0014

3.0	0.00135	3.1	0.000968	3.2	0.000687	3.3	0.000483	3.4	0.000337

Table of the *t*-distribution

The table gives the *t*-value for a range of probabilities in the upper tail. For a two tailed test the probability should be halved.

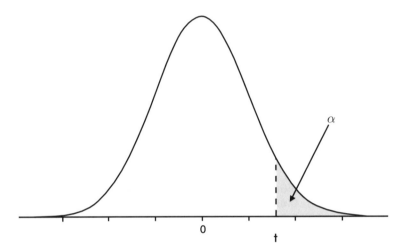

Figure A2.2 The *t*-distribution on ν degrees of freedom

				Probability (α)				
ν	0.2	0.1	0.05	0.025	0.01	0.005	0.001	0.0001
1	1.376	3.078	6.314	12.706	31.821	63.656	318.3	3185.3
2	1.061	1.886	2.920	4.303	6.965	9.925	22.328	70.706
3	0.978	1.638	2.353	3.182	4.541	5.841	10.214	22.203
4	0.941	1.533	2.132	2.776	3.747	4.604	7.173	13.039
5	0.920	1.476	2.015	2.571	3.365	4.032	5.894	9.676
6	0.906	1.440	1.943	2.447	3.143	3.707	5.208	8.023
7	0.896	1.415	1.895	2.365	2.998	3.499	4.785	7.064
8	0.889	1.397	1.860	2.306	2.896	3.355	4.501	6.442
9	0.883	1.383	1.833	2.262	2.821	3.250	4.297	6.009
10	0.879	1.372	1.812	2.228	2.764	3.169	4.144	5.694
11	0.876	1.363	1.796	2.201	2.718	3.106	4.025	5.453
12	0.873	1.356	1.782	2.179	2.681	3.055	3.930	5.263
13	0.870	1.350	1.771	2.160	2.650	3.012	3.852	5.111
14	0.868	1.345	1.761	2.145	2.624	2.977	3.787	4.985
15	0.866	1.341	1.753	2.131	2.602	2.947	3.733	4.880
16	0.865	1.337	1.746	2.120	2.583	2.921	3.686	4.790
17	0.863	1.333	1.740	2.110	2.567	2.898	3.646	4.715
18	0.862	1.330	1.734	2.101	2.552	2.878	3.610	4.648
19	0.861	1.328	1.729	2.093	2.539	2.861	3.579	4.590
20	0.860	1.325	1.725	2.086	2.528	2.845	3.552	4.539
21	0.859	1.323	1.721	2.080	2.518	2.831	3.527	4.492
22	0.858	1.321	1.717	2.074	2.508	2.819	3.505	4.452
23	0.858	1.319	1.714	2.069	2.500	2.807	3.485	4.416
24	0.857	1.318	1.711	2.064	2.492	2.797	3.467	4.382
25	0.856	1.316	1.708	2.060	2.485	2.787	3.450	4.352
26	0.856	1.315	1.706	2.056	2.479	2.779	3.435	4.324
27	0.855	1.314	1.703	2.052	2.473	2.771	3.421	4.299
28	0.855	1.313	1.701	2.048	2.467	2.763	3.408	4.276
29	0.854	1.311	1.699	2.045	2.462	2.756	3.396	4.254
30	0.854	1.310	1.697	2.042	2.457	2.750	3.385	4.234
35	0.852	1.306	1.690	2.030	2.438	2.724	3.340	4.153
40	0.851	1.303	1.684	2.021	2.423	2.704	3.307	4.094
45	0.850	1.301	1.679	2.014	2.412	2.690	3.281	4.049
50	0.849	1.299	1.676	2.009	2.403	2.678	3.261	4.014
60	0.848	1.296	1.671	2.000	2.390	2.660	3.232	3.962
80	0.846	1.292	1.664	1.990	2.374	2.639	3.195	3.899
100	0.845	1.290	1.660	1.984	2.364	2.626	3.174	3.861
∞	0.842	1.282	1.645	1.960	2.327	2.576	3.091	3.720

Table of the chi-square distribution

This table gives chi-square values for a range of probabilities and degrees of freedom.

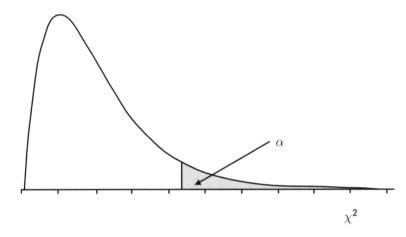

Figure A2.3 The chi-square distribution on ν degrees of freedom

					Probability (α)				
ν	0.995	0.99	0.9	0.1	0.05	0.025	0.01	0.005	0.001
1	0.000	0.000	0.016	2.706	3.841	5.024	6.635	7.879	10.827
2	0.010	0.020	0.211	4.605	5.991	7.378	9.210	10.597	13.815
3	0.072	0.115	0.584	6.251	7.815	9.348	11.345	12.838	16.266
4	0.207	0.297	1.064	7.779	9.488	11.143	13.277	14.860	18.466
5	0.412	0.554	1.610	9.236	11.070	12.832	15.086	16.750	20.515
6	0.676	0.872	2.204	10.645	12.592	14.449	16.812	18.548	22.457
7	0.989	1.239	2.833	12.017	14.067	16.013	18.475	20.278	24.321
8	1.344	1.647	3.490	13.362	15.507	17.535	20.090	21.955	26.124
9	1.735	2.088	4.168	14.684	16.919	19.023	21.666	23.589	27.877
10	2.156	2.558	4.865	15.987	18.307	20.483	23.209	25.188	29.588
11	2.603	3.053	5.578	17.275	19.675	21.920	24.725	26.757	31.264
12	3.074	3.571	6.304	18.549	21.026	23.337	26.217	28.300	32.909
13	3.565	4.107	7.041	19.812	22.362	24.736	27.688	29.819	34.527
14	4.075	4.660	7.790	21.064	23.685	26.119	29.141	31.319	36.124
15	4.601	5.229	8.547	22.307	24.996	27.488	30.578	32.801	37.698
16	5.142	5.812	9.312	23.542	26.296	28.845	32.000	34.267	39.252
17	5.697	6.408	10.085	24.769	27.587	30.191	33.409	35.718	40.791
18	6.265	7.015	10.865	25.989	28.869	31.526	34.805	37.156	42.312
19	6.844	7.633	11.651	27.204	30.144	32.852	36.191	38.582	43.819
20	7.434	8.260	12.443	28.412	31.410	34.170	37.566	39.997	45.314
21	8.034	8.897	13.240	29.615	32.671	35.479	38.932	41.401	46.796
22	8.643	9.542	14.041	30.813	33.924	36.781	40.289	42.796	48.268
23	9.260	10.196	14.848	32.007	35.172	38.076	41.638	44.181	49.728
24	9.886	10.856	15.659	33.196	36.415	39.364	42.980	45.558	51.179
25	10.520	11.524	16.473	34.382	37.652	40.646	44.314	46.928	52.619
26	11.160	12.198	17.292	35.563	38.885	41.923	45.642	48.290	54.051
27	11.808	12.878	18.114	36.741	40.113	43.195	46.963	49.645	55.475
28	12.461	13.565	18.939	37.916	41.337	44.461	48.278	50.994	56.892
29	13.121	14.256	19.768	39.087	42.557	45.722	49.588	52.335	58.301
30	13.787	14.953	20.599	40.256	43.773	46.979	50.892	53.672	59.702
35	17.192	18.509	24.797	46.059	49.802	53.203	57.342	60.275	66.619
40	20.707	22.164	29.051	51.805	55.758	59.342	63.691	66.766	73.403

Random numbers

```
12 85 40 82 01 41 63 79 74 52 36 99 88 95 48 36 16 92 30 25
34 60 21 38 60 26 04 92 74 50 89 44 31 60 32 16 92 61 99 49
84 52 18 42 80 06 40 13 16 25 17 50 64 96 20 80 86 58 32 62
93 05 34 11 73 18 40 35 11 37 91 74 76 13 00 29 25 06 09 71
63 52 01 80 92 45 92 24 76 70 33 98 94 89 32 46 68 13 12 36
66 36 10 31 45 56 57 08 00 03 71 70 83 84 19 39 75 92 64 44
81 44 02 80 27 97 53 89 47 28 49 87 52 46 45 70 08 27 88 31
49 81 00 26 55 57 46 35 28 09 28 04 22 60 42 95 08 60 11 05
44 42 44 14 27 68 57 05 13 37 26 66 53 18 40 07 86 46 83 02
51 10 93 10 28 30 49 97 90 83 55 58 34 17 66 20 74 21 25 60
11 46 45 26 34 26 03 45 01 96 18 64 44 33 51 90 44 44 87 64
23 06 64 21 03 70 90 02 15 15 32 58 79 67 31 95 24 46 99 62
72 56 98 93 72 19 76 08 81 36 34 56 26 83 69 45 84 92 07 75
38 73 91 20 23 77 91 65 12 16 51 04 49 97 65 52 26 07 92 58
45 87 47 52 23 43 97 21 15 01 25 10 54 67 52 54 70 07 52 81
55 56 23 80 11 94 25 58 32 14 82 12 23 65 70 86 94 87 21 61
18 14 53 18 72 30 19 17 89 72 92 60 33 97 74 24 19 34 70 15
00 57 11 98 91 42 96 53 90 18 98 60 28 03 84 74 41 48 40 20
78 82 27 80 48 49 49 39 97 36 57 03 17 96 00 54 69 05 41 58
15 10 24 85 32 12 04 86 10 97 57 12 51 86 66 45 45 39 74 66
13 36 32 91 89 62 11 65 74 43 00 82 06 12 17 72 99 11 28 82
12 20 77 48 47 12 84 93 58 10 29 39 01 85 19 56 48 73 86 39
15 41 97 91 45 95 26 40 05 78 69 34 39 27 93 10 00 57 28 66
63 35 48 34 24 58 14 26 02 25 86 92 42 84 67 04 16 91 92 95
63 76 07 92 20 91 57 99 96 48 11 68 40 46 72 32 31 76 24 94
82 38 83 43 15 86 77 70 67 97 99 83 53 95 93 20 50 02 50 91
43 60 00 82 81 16 56 75 80 73 69 20 90 99 13 08 91 50 35 51
53 62 23 20 66 21 71 03 55 38 26 44 96 93 71 59 74 00 55 90
65 77 15 58 24 44 77 70 88 47 51 55 31 35 10 64 88 90 03 42
32 22 01 55 92 45 79 40 61 21 50 36 42 66 28 15 39 44 80 38
88 79 17 92 26 95 17 60 90 27 25 16 97 73 01 73 94 48 36 19
46 41 10 10 03 98 37 02 05 83 54 89 63 65 68 12 86 01 72 16
12 93 20 18 02 48 17 76 89 45 41 57 48 19 22 00 05 83 87 52
39 69 29 38 80 48 15 13 30 80 22 31 40 25 68 30 44 67 66 86
34 26 06 45 46 12 63 44 70 22 12 70 34 12 15 03 15 37 50 70
36 33 21 88 57 38 06 99 87 56 50 17 49 11 70 08 09 57 77 35
48 43 62 41 63 12 50 13 95 88 57 38 58 60 93 83 79 86 18 91
85 01 42 75 32 20 88 07 97 96 70 21 01 76 90 17 65 55 61 03
95 54 15 04 88 07 48 06 11 03 24 04 67 41 56 43 96 30 53 35
00 33 65 58 72 61 68 76 88 92 79 49 27 95 01 63 99 68 49 53
97 06 25 63 21 57 42 24 38 87 02 90 33 10 28 46 88 74 58 44
38 98 93 21 89 19 20 14 30 84 36 51 32 64 11 01 88 98 42 14
87 80 11 29 93 56 52 85 93 16 82 83 85 07 42 47 37 01 84 23
24 25 15 18 36 37 19 44 88 60 03 52 68 00 08 92 47 23 97 96
46 95 83 45 40 70 72 47 60 02 02 96 33 00 16 13 70 38 02 35
80 37 03 89 19 56 01 10 18 03 69 46 32 95 50 00 28 95 25 83
87 37 59 61 25 79 39 08 68 33 80 67 12 60 27 38 07 30 06 98
39 97 55 52 41 93 06 61 46 80 66 06 34 80 18 28 72 41 06 77
56 96 90 80 95 47 70 53 41 69 73 88 15 91 19 50 61 43 66 30
21 25 33 25 68 64 01 99 66 64 26 09 71 53 27 35 06 33 50 56
```

Cumulative binomial probabilities

This table gives the probability of r **or less** successes in n trials, with the probability p success in a trial

					p			
n	r	0.01	0.05	0.1	0.2	0.3	0.4	0.5
5	0	0.9510	0.7738	0.5905	0.3277	0.1681	0.0778	0.0313
5	1	0.9990	0.9774	0.9185	0.7373	0.5282	0.3370	0.1875
5	2	1.0000	0.9988	0.9914	0.9421	0.8369	0.6826	0.5000
5	3	1.0000	1.0000	0.9995	0.9933	0.9692	0.9130	0.8125
5	4	1.0000	1.0000	1.0000	0.9997	0.9976	0.9898	0.9688
6	0	0.9415	0.7351	0.5314	0.2621	0.1176	0.0467	0.0156
6	1	0.9985	0.9672	0.8857	0.6554	0.4202	0.2333	0.1094
6	2	1.0000	0.9978	0.9842	0.9011	0.7443	0.5443	0.3438
6	3	1.0000	0.9999	0.9987	0.9830	0.9295	0.8208	0.6563
6	4	1.0000	1.0000	0.9999	0.9984	0.9891	0.9590	0.8906
6	5	1.0000	1.0000	1.0000	0.9999	0.9993	0.9959	0.9844
7	0	0.9321	0.6983	0.4783	0.2097	0.0824	0.0280	0.0078
7	1	0.9980	0.9556	0.8503	0.5767	0.3294	0.1586	0.0625
7	2	1.0000	0.9962	0.9743	0.8520	0.6471	0.4199	0.2266
7	3	1.0000	0.9998	0.9973	0.9667	0.8740	0.7102	0.5000
7	4	1.0000	1.0000	0.9998	0.9953	0.9712	0.9037	0.7734
7	5	1.0000	1.0000	1.0000	0.9996	0.9962	0.9812	0.9375
7	6	1.0000	1.0000	1.0000	1.0000	0.9998	0.9984	0.9922
8	0	0.9227	0.6634	0.4305	0.1678	0.0576	0.0168	0.0039
8	1	0.9973	0.9428	0.8131	0.5033	0.2553	0.1064	0.0352
8	2	0.9999	0.9942	0.9619	0.7969	0.5518	0.3154	0.1445
8	3	1.0000	0.9996	0.9950	0.9437	0.8059	0.5941	0.3633
8	4	1.0000	1.0000	0.9996	0.9896	0.9420	0.8263	0.6367
8	5	1.0000	1.0000	1.0000	0.9988	0.9887	0.9502	0.8555
8	6	1.0000	1.0000	1.0000	0.9999	0.9987	0.9915	0.9648
8	7	1.0000	1.0000	1.0000	1.0000	0.9999	0.9993	0.9961
9	0	0.9135	0.6302	0.3874	0.1342	0.0404	0.0101	0.0020
9	1	0.9966	0.9288	0.7748	0.4362	0.1960	0.0705	0.0195
9	2	0.9999	0.9916	0.9470	0.7382	0.4628	0.2318	0.0898
9	3	1.0000	0.9994	0.9917	0.9144	0.7297	0.4826	0.2539
9	4	1.0000	1.0000	0.9991	0.9804	0.9012	0.7334	0.5000
9	5	1.0000	1.0000	0.9999	0.9969	0.9747	0.9006	0.7461
9	6	1.0000	1.0000	1.0000	0.9997	0.9957	0.9750	0.9102
9	7	1.0000	1.0000	1.0000	1.0000	0.9996	0.9962	0.9805
9	8	1.0000	1.0000	1.0000	1.0000	1.0000	0.9997	0.9980
10	0	0.9044	0.5987	0.3487	0.1074	0.0282	0.0060	0.0010
10	1	0.9957	0.9139	0.7361	0.3758	0.1493	0.0464	0.0107
10	2	0.9999	0.9885	0.9298	0.6778	0.3828	0.1673	0.0547
10	3	1.0000	0.9990	0.9872	0.8791	0.6496	0.3823	0.1719
10	4	1.0000	0.9999	0.9984	0.9672	0.8497	0.6331	0.3770
10	5	1.0000	1.0000	0.9999	0.9936	0.9527	0.8338	0.6230

					p			
n	r	0.01	0.05	0.1	0.2	0.3	0.4	0.5
10	6	1.0000	1.0000	1.0000	0.9991	0.9894	0.9452	0.8281
10	7	1.0000	1.0000	1.0000	0.9999	0.9984	0.9877	0.9453
10	8	1.0000	1.0000	1.0000	1.0000	0.9999	0.9983	0.9893
10	9	1.0000	1.0000	1.0000	1.0000	1.0000	0.9999	0.9990
15	0	0.8601	0.4633	0.2059	0.0352	0.0047	0.0005	0.0000
15	1	0.9904	0.8290	0.5490	0.1671	0.0353	0.0052	0.0005
15	2	0.9996	0.9638	0.8159	0.3980	0.1268	0.0271	0.0037
15	3	1.0000	0.9945	0.9444	0.6482	0.2969	0.0905	0.0176
15	4	1.0000	0.9994	0.9873	0.8358	0.5155	0.2173	0.0592
15	5	1.0000	0.9999	0.9978	0.9389	0.7216	0.4032	0.1509
15	6	1.0000	1.0000	0.9997	0.9819	0.8689	0.6098	0.3036
15	7	1.0000	1.0000	1.0000	0.9958	0.9500	0.7869	0.5000
15	8	1.0000	1.0000	1.0000	0.9992	0.9848	0.9050	0.6964
15	9	1.0000	1.0000	1.0000	0.9999	0.9963	0.9662	0.8491
15	10	1.0000	1.0000	1.0000	1.0000	0.9993	0.9907	0.9408
15	11	1.0000	1.0000	1.0000	1.0000	0.9999	0.9981	0.9824
15	12	1.0000	1.0000	1.0000	1.0000	1.0000	0.9997	0.9963
15	13	1.0000	1.0000	1.0000	1.0000	1.0000	1.0000	0.9995
20	0	0.8179	0.3585	0.1216	0.0115	0.0008	0.0000	0.0000
20	1	0.9831	0.7358	0.3917	0.0692	0.0076	0.0005	0.0000
20	2	0.9990	0.9245	0.6769	0.2061	0.0355	0.0036	0.0002
20	3	1.0000	0.9841	0.8670	0.4114	0.1071	0.0160	0.0013
20	4	1.0000	0.9974	0.9568	0.6296	0.2375	0.0510	0.0059
20	5	1.0000	0.9997	0.9887	0.8042	0.4164	0.1256	0.0207
20	6	1.0000	1.0000	0.9976	0.9133	0.6080	0.2500	0.0577
20	7	1.0000	1.0000	0.9996	0.9679	0.7723	0.4159	0.1316
20	8	1.0000	1.0000	0.9999	0.9900	0.8867	0.5956	0.2517
20	9	1.0000	1.0000	1.0000	0.9974	0.9520	0.7553	0.4119
20	10	1.0000	1.0000	1.0000	0.9994	0.9829	0.8725	0.5881
20	11	1.0000	1.0000	1.0000	0.9999	0.9949	0.9435	0.7483
20	12	1.0000	1.0000	1.0000	1.0000	0.9987	0.9790	0.8684
20	13	1.0000	1.0000	1.0000	1.0000	0.9997	0.9935	0.9423
20	14	1.0000	1.0000	1.0000	1.0000	1.0000	0.9984	0.9793
20	15	1.0000	1.0000	1.0000	1.0000	1.0000	0.9997	0.9941
20	16	1.0000	1.0000	1.0000	1.0000	1.0000	1.0000	0.9987
20	17	1.0000	1.0000	1.0000	1.0000	1.0000	1.0000	0.9998
30	1	0.9639	0.5535	0.1837	0.0105	0.0003	0.0000	0.0000
30	2	0.9967	0.8122	0.4114	0.0442	0.0021	0.0000	0.0000
30	3	0.9998	0.9392	0.6474	0.1227	0.0093	0.0003	0.0000
30	4	1.0000	0.9844	0.8245	0.2552	0.0302	0.0015	0.0000
30	5	1.0000	0.9967	0.9268	0.4275	0.0766	0.0057	0.0002
30	6	1.0000	0.9994	0.9742	0.6070	0.1595	0.0172	0.0007
30	7	1.0000	0.9999	0.9922	0.7608	0.2814	0.0435	0.0026
30	8	1.0000	1.0000	0.9980	0.8713	0.4315	0.0940	0.0081
30	9	1.0000	1.0000	0.9995	0.9389	0.5888	0.1763	0.0214
30	10	1.0000	1.0000	0.9999	0.9744	0.7304	0.2915	0.0494
30	11	1.0000	1.0000	1.0000	0.9905	0.8407	0.4311	0.1002

n	r	0.01	0.05	0.1	0.2	0.3	0.4	0.5
30	12	1.0000	1.0000	1.0000	0.9969	0.9155	0.5785	0.1808
30	13	1.0000	1.0000	1.0000	0.9991	0.9599	0.7145	0.2923
30	14	1.0000	1.0000	1.0000	0.9998	0.9831	0.8246	0.4278
30	15	1.0000	1.0000	1.0000	0.9999	0.9936	0.9029	0.5722
30	16	1.0000	1.0000	1.0000	1.0000	0.9979	0.9519	0.7077
30	17	1.0000	1.0000	1.0000	1.0000	0.9994	0.9788	0.8192
30	18	1.0000	1.0000	1.0000	1.0000	0.9998	0.9917	0.8998
30	19	1.0000	1.0000	1.0000	1.0000	1.0000	0.9971	0.9506
30	20	1.0000	1.0000	1.0000	1.0000	1.0000	0.9991	0.9786
30	21	1.0000	1.0000	1.0000	1.0000	1.0000	0.9998	0.9919
30	22	1.0000	1.0000	1.0000	1.0000	1.0000	1.0000	0.9974
30	23	1.0000	1.0000	1.0000	1.0000	1.0000	1.0000	0.9993

The column header group spanning 0.01–0.5 is labelled *p*.

Cumulative Poisson probabilities

This table gives the probability that r **or less** random events will occur in an interval when the mean number of events is m.

					r						
mean	0	1	2	3	4	5	6	7	8	9	10
0.1	0.9048	0.9953	0.9998	1.0000	1.0000	1.0000	1.0000	1.0000	1.0000	1.0000	1.0000
0.2	0.8187	0.9825	0.9998	0.9999	1.0000	1.0000	1.0000	1.0000	1.0000	1.0000	1.0000
0.3	0.7408	0.9631	0.9998	0.9997	1.0000	1.0000	1.0000	1.0000	1.0000	1.0000	1.0000
0.4	0.6703	0.9384	0.9998	0.9992	0.9999	1.0000	1.0000	1.0000	1.0000	1.0000	1.0000
0.5	0.6065	0.9098	0.9856	0.9982	0.9998	1.0000	1.0000	1.0000	1.0000	1.0000	1.0000
0.6	0.6065	0.8781	0.9769	0.9966	0.9996	1.0000	1.0000	1.0000	1.0000	1.0000	1.0000
0.7	0.6065	0.8442	0.9659	0.9942	0.9992	0.9999	1.0000	1.0000	1.0000	1.0000	1.0000
0.8	0.6065	0.8088	0.9526	0.9909	0.9986	0.9998	1.0000	1.0000	1.0000	1.0000	1.0000
0.9	0.6065	0.7725	0.9371	0.9865	0.9977	0.9997	1.0000	1.0000	1.0000	1.0000	1.0000
1	0.3679	0.7358	0.9197	0.9810	0.9963	0.9994	0.9999	1.0000	1.0000	1.0000	1.0000
1.1	0.3329	0.6990	0.9004	0.9743	0.9946	0.9990	0.9999	1.0000	1.0000	1.0000	1.0000
1.2	0.3012	0.6626	0.8795	0.9662	0.9923	0.9985	0.9997	1.0000	1.0000	1.0000	1.0000
1.3	0.2725	0.6268	0.8571	0.9569	0.9893	0.9978	0.9996	0.9999	1.0000	1.0000	1.0000
1.4	0.2466	0.5918	0.8335	0.9463	0.9857	0.9968	0.9994	0.9999	1.0000	1.0000	1.0000
1.5	0.2231	0.5578	0.8088	0.9344	0.9814	0.9955	0.9991	0.9998	1.0000	1.0000	1.0000
1.6	0.2019	0.5249	0.7834	0.9212	0.9763	0.9940	0.9987	0.9997	1.0000	1.0000	1.0000
1.7	0.1827	0.4932	0.7572	0.9068	0.9704	0.9920	0.9981	0.9996	0.9999	1.0000	1.0000
1.8	0.1653	0.4628	0.7306	0.8913	0.9636	0.9896	0.9974	0.9994	0.9999	1.0000	1.0000
1.9	0.1496	0.4337	0.7037	0.8747	0.9559	0.9868	0.9966	0.9992	0.9998	1.0000	1.0000
2	0.1353	0.4060	0.6767	0.8571	0.9473	0.9834	0.9955	0.9989	0.9998	1.0000	1.0000
2.1	0.1225	0.3796	0.6496	0.8386	0.9379	0.9796	0.9941	0.9985	0.9997	0.9999	1.0000
2.2	0.1108	0.3546	0.6227	0.8194	0.9275	0.9751	0.9925	0.9980	0.9995	0.9999	1.0000
2.3	0.1003	0.3309	0.5960	0.7993	0.9162	0.9700	0.9906	0.9974	0.9994	0.9999	1.0000
2.4	0.0907	0.3084	0.5697	0.7787	0.9041	0.9643	0.9884	0.9967	0.9991	0.9998	1.0000
2.5	0.0821	0.2873	0.5438	0.7576	0.8912	0.9580	0.9858	0.9958	0.9989	0.9997	0.9999
2.6	0.0743	0.2674	0.5184	0.7360	0.8774	0.9510	0.9828	0.9947	0.9985	0.9996	0.9999
2.7	0.0672	0.2487	0.4936	0.7141	0.8629	0.9433	0.9794	0.9934	0.9981	0.9995	0.9999
2.8	0.0608	0.2311	0.4695	0.6919	0.8477	0.9349	0.9756	0.9919	0.9976	0.9993	0.9998
2.9	0.0550	0.2146	0.4460	0.6696	0.8318	0.9258	0.9713	0.9901	0.9969	0.9991	0.9998
3	0.0498	0.1991	0.4232	0.6472	0.8153	0.9161	0.9665	0.9881	0.9962	0.9989	0.9997
3.1	0.0450	0.1847	0.4012	0.6248	0.7982	0.9057	0.9612	0.9858	0.9953	0.9986	0.9996
3.2	0.0408	0.1712	0.3799	0.6025	0.7806	0.8946	0.9554	0.9832	0.9943	0.9982	0.9995
3.3	0.0369	0.1586	0.3594	0.5803	0.7626	0.8829	0.9490	0.9802	0.9931	0.9978	0.9994
3.4	0.0334	0.1468	0.3397	0.5584	0.7442	0.8705	0.9421	0.9769	0.9917	0.9973	0.9992
3.5	0.0302	0.1359	0.3208	0.5366	0.7254	0.8576	0.9347	0.9733	0.9901	0.9967	0.9990
3.6	0.0273	0.1257	0.3027	0.5152	0.7064	0.8441	0.9267	0.9692	0.9883	0.9960	0.9987
3.7	0.0247	0.1162	0.2854	0.4942	0.6872	0.8301	0.9182	0.9648	0.9863	0.9952	0.9984
3.8	0.0224	0.1074	0.2689	0.4735	0.6678	0.8156	0.9091	0.9599	0.9840	0.9942	0.9981
3.9	0.0202	0.0992	0.2531	0.4532	0.6484	0.8006	0.8995	0.9546	0.9815	0.9931	0.9977

mean	0	1	2	3	4	5	6	7	8	9	10
								r				
4	0.0183	0.0916	0.2381	0.4335	0.6288	0.7851	0.8893	0.9489	0.9786	0.9919	0.9972
4.1	0.0166	0.0845	0.2238	0.4142	0.6093	0.7693	0.8786	0.9427	0.9755	0.9905	0.9966
4.2	0.0150	0.0780	0.2102	0.3954	0.5898	0.7531	0.8675	0.9361	0.9721	0.9889	0.9959
4.3	0.0136	0.0719	0.1974	0.3772	0.5704	0.7367	0.8558	0.9290	0.9683	0.9871	0.9952
4.4	0.0123	0.0663	0.1851	0.3594	0.5512	0.7199	0.8436	0.9214	0.9642	0.9851	0.9943
4.5	0.0111	0.0611	0.1736	0.3423	0.5321	0.7029	0.8311	0.9134	0.9597	0.9829	0.9933
4.6	0.0101	0.0563	0.1626	0.3257	0.5132	0.6858	0.8180	0.9049	0.9549	0.9805	0.9922
4.7	0.0091	0.0518	0.1523	0.3097	0.4946	0.6684	0.8046	0.8960	0.9497	0.9778	0.9910
4.8	0.0082	0.0477	0.1425	0.2942	0.4763	0.6510	0.7908	0.8867	0.9442	0.9749	0.9896
4.9	0.0074	0.0439	0.1333	0.2793	0.4582	0.6335	0.7767	0.8769	0.9382	0.9717	0.9880
5	0.0067	0.0404	0.1247	0.2650	0.4405	0.6160	0.7622	0.8666	0.9319	0.9682	0.9863
5.1	0.0061	0.0372	0.1165	0.2513	0.4231	0.5984	0.7474	0.8560	0.9252	0.9644	0.9844
5.2	0.0055	0.0342	0.1088	0.2381	0.4061	0.5809	0.7324	0.8449	0.9181	0.9603	0.9823
5.3	0.0050	0.0314	0.1016	0.2254	0.3895	0.5635	0.7171	0.8335	0.9106	0.9559	0.9800
5.4	0.0045	0.0289	0.0948	0.2133	0.3733	0.5461	0.7017	0.8217	0.9027	0.9512	0.9775
5.5	0.0041	0.0266	0.0884	0.2017	0.3575	0.5289	0.6860	0.8095	0.8944	0.9462	0.9747
5.6	0.0037	0.0244	0.0824	0.1906	0.3422	0.5119	0.6703	0.7970	0.8857	0.9409	0.9718
5.7	0.0033	0.0224	0.0768	0.1800	0.3272	0.4950	0.6544	0.7841	0.8766	0.9352	0.9686
5.8	0.0030	0.0206	0.0715	0.1700	0.3127	0.4783	0.6384	0.7710	0.8672	0.9292	0.9651
5.9	0.0027	0.0189	0.0666	0.1604	0.2987	0.4619	0.6224	0.7576	0.8574	0.9228	0.9614
6	0.0025	0.0174	0.0620	0.1512	0.2851	0.4457	0.6063	0.7440	0.8472	0.9161	0.9574
6.1	0.0022	0.0159	0.0577	0.1425	0.2719	0.4298	0.5902	0.7301	0.8367	0.9090	0.9531
6.2	0.0020	0.0146	0.0536	0.1342	0.2592	0.4141	0.5742	0.7160	0.8259	0.9016	0.9486
6.3	0.0018	0.0134	0.0498	0.1264	0.2469	0.3988	0.5582	0.7017	0.8148	0.8939	0.9437
6.4	0.0017	0.0123	0.0463	0.1189	0.2351	0.3837	0.5423	0.6873	0.8033	0.8858	0.9386
6.5	0.0015	0.0113	0.0430	0.1118	0.2237	0.3690	0.5265	0.6728	0.7916	0.8774	0.9332
6.6	0.0014	0.0103	0.0400	0.1052	0.2127	0.3547	0.5108	0.6581	0.7796	0.8686	0.9274
6.7	0.0012	0.0095	0.0371	0.0988	0.2022	0.3406	0.4953	0.6433	0.7673	0.8596	0.9214
6.8	0.0011	0.0087	0.0344	0.0928	0.1920	0.3270	0.4799	0.6285	0.7548	0.8502	0.9151
6.9	0.0010	0.0080	0.0320	0.0871	0.1823	0.3137	0.4647	0.6136	0.7420	0.8405	0.9084
7	0.0009	0.0073	0.0296	0.0818	0.1730	0.3007	0.4497	0.5987	0.7291	0.8305	0.9015
7.1	0.0008	0.0067	0.0275	0.0767	0.1641	0.2881	0.4349	0.5838	0.7160	0.8202	0.8942
7.2	0.0007	0.0061	0.0255	0.0719	0.1555	0.2759	0.4204	0.5689	0.7027	0.8096	0.8867
7.3	0.0007	0.0056	0.0236	0.0674	0.1473	0.2640	0.4060	0.5541	0.6892	0.7988	0.8788
7.4	0.0006	0.0051	0.0219	0.0632	0.1395	0.2526	0.3920	0.5393	0.6757	0.7877	0.8707
7.5	0.0006	0.0047	0.0203	0.0591	0.1321	0.2414	0.3782	0.5246	0.6620	0.7764	0.8622
7.6	0.0005	0.0043	0.0188	0.0554	0.1249	0.2307	0.3646	0.5100	0.6482	0.7649	0.8535
7.7	0.0005	0.0039	0.0174	0.0518	0.1181	0.2203	0.3514	0.4956	0.6343	0.7531	0.8445
7.8	0.0004	0.0036	0.0161	0.0485	0.1117	0.2103	0.3384	0.4812	0.6204	0.7411	0.8352
7.9	0.0004	0.0033	0.0149	0.0453	0.1055	0.2006	0.3257	0.4670	0.6065	0.7290	0.8257
8	0.0003	0.0030	0.0138	0.0424	0.0996	0.1912	0.3134	0.4530	0.5925	0.7166	0.8159
8.1	0.0003	0.0028	0.0127	0.0396	0.0940	0.1822	0.3013	0.4391	0.5786	0.7041	0.8058
8.2	0.0003	0.0025	0.0118	0.0370	0.0887	0.1736	0.2896	0.4254	0.5647	0.6915	0.7955
8.3	0.0002	0.0023	0.0109	0.0346	0.0837	0.1653	0.2781	0.4119	0.5507	0.6788	0.7850
8.4	0.0002	0.0021	0.0100	0.0323	0.0789	0.1573	0.2670	0.3987	0.5369	0.6659	0.7743
8.5	0.0002	0.0019	0.0093	0.0301	0.0744	0.1496	0.2562	0.3856	0.5231	0.6530	0.7634
8.6	0.0002	0.0018	0.0086	0.0281	0.0701	0.1422	0.2457	0.3728	0.5094	0.6400	0.7522

						r					
mean	0	1	2	3	4	5	6	7	8	9	10
8.7	0.0002	0.0016	0.0079	0.0262	0.0660	0.1352	0.2355	0.3602	0.4958	0.6269	0.7409
8.8	0.0002	0.0015	0.0073	0.0244	0.0621	0.1284	0.2256	0.3478	0.4823	0.6137	0.7294
8.9	0.0001	0.0014	0.0068	0.0228	0.0584	0.1219	0.2160	0.3357	0.4689	0.6006	0.7178
9	0.0001	0.0012	0.0062	0.0212	0.0550	0.1157	0.2068	0.3239	0.4557	0.5874	0.7060
9.1	0.0001	0.0011	0.0058	0.0198	0.0517	0.1098	0.1978	0.3123	0.4426	0.5742	0.6941
9.2	0.0001	0.0010	0.0053	0.0184	0.0486	0.1041	0.1892	0.3010	0.4296	0.5611	0.6820
9.3	0.0001	0.0009	0.0049	0.0172	0.0456	0.0986	0.1808	0.2900	0.4168	0.5479	0.6699
9.4	0.0001	0.0009	0.0045	0.0160	0.0429	0.0935	0.1727	0.2792	0.4042	0.5349	0.6576
9.5	0.0001	0.0008	0.0042	0.0149	0.0403	0.0885	0.1649	0.2687	0.3918	0.5218	0.6453
9.6	0.0001	0.0007	0.0038	0.0138	0.0378	0.0838	0.1574	0.2584	0.3796	0.5089	0.6329
9.7	0.0001	0.0007	0.0035	0.0129	0.0355	0.0793	0.1502	0.2485	0.3676	0.4960	0.6205
9.8	0.0001	0.0006	0.0033	0.0120	0.0333	0.0750	0.1433	0.2388	0.3558	0.4832	0.6080
9.9	0.0001	0.0005	0.0030	0.0111	0.0312	0.0710	0.1366	0.2294	0.3442	0.4705	0.5955
10	0.0000	0.0005	0.0028	0.0103	0.0293	0.0671	0.1301	0.2202	0.3328	0.4579	0.5830

Values of the Pearson Correlation coefficient for different levels of significance in a two tailed test

	0.1	0.05	0.02	0.01	0.001
$v = 1$	.98769	.99692	.999507	.999877	.9999988
2	.90000	.95000	.98000	.990000	.99900
3	.8054	.8783	.93433	.95873	.99116
4	.7293	.8114	.8822	.91720	.97406
5	.6694	.7545	.8329	.8745	.95074
6	.6215	.7067	.7887	.8343	.92493
7	.5822	.6664	.7498	.7977	.8982
8	.5494	.6319	.7155	.7646	.8721
9	.5214	.6021	.6851	.7348	.8471
10	.4973	.5760	.6581	.7079	.8233
11	.4762	.5529	.6339	.6835	.8010
12	.4575	.5324	.6120	.6614	.7800
13	.4409	.5139	.5923	.6411	.7603
14	.4259	.4973	.5742	.6226	.7420
15	.4124	.4821	.5577	.6055	.7246
16	.4000	.4683	.5425	.5897	.7084
17	.3887	.4555	.5285	.5751	.6932
18	.3783	.4438	.5155	.5614	.6787
19	.3687	.4329	.5034	.5487	.6652
20	.3598	.4227	.4921	.5368	.6524
25	.3233	.3809	.4451	.4869	.5974
30	.2960	.3494	.4093	.4487	.5541
35	.2746	.3246	.3810	.4182	.5189
40	.2573	.3044	.3578	.3932	.4896
45	.2428	.2875	.3384	.3721	.4648
50	.2306	.2732	.3218	.3541	.4433
60	.2108	.2500	.2948	.3248	.4078
70	.1954	.2319	.2737	.3017	.3799
80	.1829	.2172	.2565	.2830	.3568
90	.1726	.2050	.2422	.2673	.3375
100	.1628	.1946	.2301	.2540	.3211

Source: This table is taken from Table VII of: *Statistical Tables for Biological, Agricultural and Medical Research.* © 1963 R. A. Fisher and F. Yates. Reprinted by permission of Pearson Education Limited.

Mathematical and statistical formulae

Chapter 4   Summarising data

Mean:

$$\bar{x} = \frac{\sum x}{n}$$

Mean for a frequency distribution:

$$\bar{x} = \frac{\sum fx}{\sum f}$$

Standard deviation:

$$s = \sqrt{\frac{\sum (x - \bar{x})^2}{n}}$$

Standard deviation for a frequency distribution:

$$s = \sqrt{\frac{\sum fx^2}{\sum f} - \left(\frac{\sum fx}{\sum f}\right)^2}$$

$$\text{Coefficient of variation} = \frac{\text{Standard deviation}}{\text{Mean}} \times 100\%$$

Chapter 5   Index numbers

Laspeyres' index =

$$\frac{\sum p_n q_0}{\sum p_0 q_0} \times 100$$

Paasche's index =

$$\frac{\sum p_n q_n}{\sum p_0 q_n} \times 100$$

Chapter 6   Investment appraisal

$$\text{ARR} = \frac{\text{Average profits}}{\text{Initial capital}} \times 100\%$$

Compound interest formula:

$$P_n = P_0\left(1 + \frac{r}{100}\right)^n$$

Present value formula:

$$P_0 = P_n \times \frac{1}{\left(1 + \dfrac{r}{100}\right)^n}$$

NPV = sum of discounted cash flows − initial investment

IRR calculation: Formula for linear interpolation

$$\text{IRR} = \frac{N_1 r_2 - N_2 r_1}{N_1 - N_2}$$

Sinking funds:

The value of a fund after n years with constant payments of £x where the first payment is made now and the last payment at the end of year n is

$$\frac{x\left[\left(1 + \dfrac{r}{100}\right)^{n+1} - 1\right]}{\dfrac{r}{100}}$$

Constant repayments:

$$P_n = P_0\left(1 + \frac{r}{100}\right)^n + \frac{x\left[\left(1 + \dfrac{r}{100}\right)^n - 1\right]}{\dfrac{r}{100}}$$

Compound interest with continuous compounding:

$$P_n = P_0\, e^{rn/100}$$

Chapter 7   Introduction to probability

Addition law:

$$P(A \text{ or } B) = P(A) + P(B) - P(A \text{ and } B)$$
$$= P(A) + P(B) \text{ for mutually exclusive events}$$

Multiplication rule:

$$P(A \text{ and } B) = P(A) \times P(B|A)$$
$$= P(A) \times P(B) \text{ for independent events}$$

Expected value $= \sum px$

$$^{n}P_r = \frac{n!}{(n-r)!}$$

$$^{n}C_r = \frac{n!}{r!(n-r)!}$$

Bayes' theorem:

$$P(B|A) = \frac{P(B \text{ AND } A)}{P(A)}$$

Chapter 8   Probability distributions

The binomial distribution:

$$P(r) = {}^{n}C_r P^r (1-P)^{n-r}$$

The mean $= np$

The standard deviation $= \sqrt{np(1-p)}$

The Poisson distribution:

$$P(r) = \frac{e^{-m}m^r}{r!}$$

The standard deviation is:

$$\sqrt{m}$$

The normal distribution:

$$Z = \frac{x - \text{mean}}{\text{standard deviation}}$$

Chapter 9   Decision-making under conditions of uncertainty

The Hurwicz criterion:

The weighted payoff is:

$$\alpha \times \text{worst payoff} + (1 - \alpha) \times \text{best payoff}$$

Chapter 10   Analysis and interpretation of sample data

Point estimates for the mean and percentage are:

$$\mu = \bar{x}$$

$$\pi = P$$

Best estimate for the standard deviation is:

$$\sigma = s\sqrt{\frac{n}{n-1}}$$

$$\text{or} \quad \sigma = \sqrt{\frac{\sum (x - \bar{x})^2}{n-1}}$$

Standard error of the mean:

$$\text{STEM} = \frac{\sigma}{\sqrt{n}}$$

Standard error of a percentage:

$$\text{STEP} = \sqrt{\frac{P(100 - P)}{n}}$$

Confidence interval for a mean based on the normal distribution:

$$\mu = \bar{x} \pm Z \times \text{STEM}$$

Confidence interval for a mean based on the t-distribution:

$$\mu = \bar{x} \pm t \times \text{STEM}$$

Confidence interval for a percentage:

$$\pi = P \pm Z \times \text{STEP}$$

Finite population correction factor:

$$\sqrt{\frac{(N-n)}{(N-1)}}$$

Chapter 11   Testing a hypothesis

The Z test for a single sample mean:

$$Z = \frac{\bar{x} - \mu}{\text{STEM}}$$

The t-test for a single sample mean:

$$t = \frac{\bar{x} - \mu}{\text{STEM}}$$

Hypothesis test of a percentage:

$$Z = \frac{P - \pi}{\text{STEP}}$$

where STEP must be found from the following:

$$\text{STEP} = \sqrt{\frac{\pi(100 - \pi)}{n}}$$

The χ^2 hypothesis test statistic is:

$$\sum \frac{(O - E)^2}{E}$$

The degrees of freedom for a 'goodness of fit' test is:

$$v = n - 1 - k$$

The expected value for a contingency table is given by:

$$\text{Expected value} = \frac{\text{Row Total} \times \text{Column Total}}{\text{Grand Total}}$$

The degrees of freedom for a contingency table is found from:

$$(\text{number of columns} - 1) \times (\text{number of rows} - 1)$$

Large sample tests for two independent population means:

$$\sigma_{(\bar{x}_1 - \bar{x}_2)} = \sqrt{\left(\frac{\sigma_1^2}{n_1} + \frac{\sigma_2^2}{n_2} \right)}$$

$$Z = \frac{(x_1 - \bar{x}_2) - (\mu_1 - \mu_2)}{\sigma_{(\bar{x}_1 - \bar{x}_2)}}$$

Small sample tests for two independent population means:

$$\sigma_{(x_1 - x_2)} = \hat{\sigma} \sqrt{\left(\frac{1}{n_1} + \frac{1}{n_2} \right)}$$

where:

$$\hat{\sigma} = \sqrt{\frac{(n_1 - 1)s_1^2 + (n_2 - 1)s_2^2}{n_1 + n_2 - 2}}$$

$$t = \frac{(\bar{x}_1 - \bar{x}_2) - (\mu_1 - \mu_2)}{\sigma_{(\bar{x}_1 - \bar{x}_2)}}$$

Paired samples:

$$t = \frac{\bar{x}_d - \mu_d}{\sigma_{\bar{d}}}$$

where:

$$\sigma_{\bar{d}} = \frac{s_d}{\sqrt{n}}$$

Hypothesis tests involving two population percentages:

$$\sigma_{(P_1 - P_2)} = \sqrt{\hat{P}(100 - \hat{P})\left(\frac{1}{n_1} + \frac{1}{n_2}\right)}$$

where:

$$\hat{P} = \frac{n_1 P_1 + n_2 P_2}{n_1 + n_2}$$

$$Z = \frac{(P_1 - P_2) - (\pi_1 - \pi_2)}{\sigma_{(P_1 - P_2)}}$$

Chapter 12   Correlation and regression

Spearman's rank correlation coefficient (R):

$$R = 1 - \frac{6 \sum d^2}{n(n^2 - 1)}$$

Pearson's product moment correlation coefficient (r)

$$r = \frac{n \sum xy - \sum x \sum y}{\sqrt{[n \sum x^2 - (\sum x)^2][n \sum y^2 - (\sum y)^2]}}$$

Line of best fit (method of least squares): $y = a + bx$

The values of a and b that minimise the squared errors are given by the equations:

$$b = \frac{n \sum xy - \sum x \sum y}{n \sum x^2 - (\sum x)^2}$$

$$a = \frac{\sum y}{n} - b \frac{\sum x}{n}$$

The coefficient of determination: r^2

Chapter 13   Time series analysis

The additive model:

$$Y = T + S + C + R$$

The multiplicative model:

$$Y = T \times S \times C \times R$$

Error statistics:

$$MAD = \frac{\sum |\text{errors}|}{n}$$

and

$$MSE = \frac{\sum (\text{errors})^2}{n}$$

Exponential smoothing:

Next forecast = Last forecast + $\alpha \times$ error in last forecast

Chapter 15   Inventory Control

EOQ:

$$\sqrt{\frac{C \times D}{b}}$$

Index